*Routledge Revivals*

# Introduction to Economics

# Introduction to Economics

by
**John Roscoe Turner**

Routledge
Taylor & Francis Group

First published in 1919 by Charles Scribner's Sons

This edition first published in 2019 by Routledge
2 Park Square, Milton Park, Abingdon, Oxon, OX14 4RN
and by Routledge
52 Vanderbilt Avenue, New York, NY 10017, USA

*Routledge is an imprint of the Taylor & Francis Group, an informa business*

© 1919 by Taylor and Francis

**Publisher's Note**
The publisher has gone to great lengths to ensure the quality of this reprint but points out that some imperfections in the original copies may be apparent.

**Disclaimer**
The publisher has made every effort to trace copyright holders and welcomes correspondence from those they have been unable to contact.
A Library of Congress record exists under ISBN:

ISBN 13: 978-0-367-24619-8 (hbk)
ISBN 13: 978-0-367-24620-4 (pbk)
ISBN 13: 978-0-429-28352-9 (ebk)

ISBN: 9781313126007


Published by:
HardPress Publishing
8345 NW 66TH ST #2561
MIAMI FL 33166-2626

Email: info@hardpress.net
Web: http://www.hardpress.net

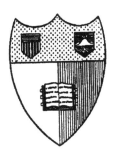

# INTRODUCTION TO ECONOMICS

BY

## JOHN ROSCOE TURNER, Ph.D.

PROFESSOR OF ECONOMICS AND DEAN OF WASHINGTON SQUARE COLLEGE
NEW YORK UNIVERSITY

CHARLES SCRIBNER'S SONS

NEW YORK          CHICAGO          BOSTON

A

# PREFACE

This book is an outgrowth of classroom discussions. It contains in substance the talks on economics which have been made, for the past eleven years, to my classes in Cornell and New York Universities.

No apology is offered for the fact that this volume is limited to a discussion of principles. Even the concluding chapters on corporations are designed to exemplify principles. The time has long since passed when a single volume can treat exhaustively the whole field of economics. I shall be more than content if this work justifies the scope indicated for it in the title—Introduction to Economics.

Designed as an introduction, this book will serve as a means to the end of a more intelligent study of economic questions. It does not dispense with the necessity of reading the many excellent treatises devoted to the different phases of economics; rather it distinctly calls for such readings. It merely prepares the mind of the student for the thought contained in the more advanced and specialized works on the subject and the practical applications they reveal.

At the end of each chapter are appended exercises in the form of questions, problems, and fallacies, the object being to stimulate independent thinking as well as to develop the power of applying what the student has learned. In so far as may be, the problems are stated in the form in which they appear in practical affairs.

The effort has been made to avoid obscure reasoning,

loose generalities, and controversial entanglements. There are text-books in economics which set forth the subject soundly but in a manner too obscure to be well adapted for the beginner. The author of a book for beginners must hold the needs of the student constantly in mind. Some writers apparently are so obsessed by fear of the critic as quite to forget the needs of the student. Other authors, though they write fearlessly, load the evidence in favor of this contention or that, thus failing to secure the balance and proportion becoming to a science. Still others skim the principles in haste, wishing to introduce the beginner forthwith to a discussion of the great practical problems. These authors are unmindful of the fact that without a substantial grounding in fundamentals the student's thought must go astray when attacking the great social problems, involving, as they do, burning issues replete with "isms." These superficial writings are productive of harm and deserve to be frowned upon. There was never a greater need for sound thinking in economics than in these unsettled times following the war. But to sound thinking there is only one true guide—the knowledge of fundamentals. How far I have succeeded in the attempt to serve this end must be left for others to decide.

I have made persistent effort to keep the dynamic distinct in thought from the static theory, but the separation has been in thought rather than in space. The student must proceed with both in mind if he would at once conceive principles and appreciate their practical importance in a world of change and progress. The laws of economics, like the rules of arithmetic, are true, but you undertake the impossible in attempting to hold the student's attention to subject-matter so dry apart from the practical aid of illustration. To put actual changes out of sight is to deaden the student's interest in the subject.

I have avoided the introduction of terms for which there is not sufficient precedent; have followed the tendency to abandon the artificial classification of productive factors into land, labor, and capital; have preferred to use the term desirability rather than utility in the value problem. Too much juggling with the term utility has left it with no distinct meaning. And, moreover, the word desirability (for the use of which there is sufficient precedent) excellently expresses the idea of the fitness or quality of an object to excite a wish to possess. The word utility finds use in the problem of social production.

I have been anxious to avoid the novel, but this has not prevented some departures here and there from the current statements of theories.

The first four chapters were written in the belief that economic institutions can be adequately comprehended only in the light of their historical development. The student will have deeper regard for the institutions under which he lives when he contemplates that they are the outgrowth of progressive changes through many centuries; he will have only contempt for the constitution meddlers who would remodel our economic life over a week's end. He will know that these institutions form no barrier to progress when they are subject to modification as needs require. Following the study of essential institutions, the problems of value and price are presented. The remainder of the book is devoted to the following topics in the order here given: Money and banking; production and rent; labor and wages; capital and interest; corporations, monopoly, and trust legislation.

I wish to acknowledge with gratitude the valuable suggestions received during the preparation of this book from my colleagues—Willard Fisher, Major B. Foster, David Friday, Charles W. Gerstenberg, Joseph French Johnson, and, particularly, Arthur L. Faubel who has read the proof searchingly, constructively. Acknowledgment is also made to my friend and former teacher, Frank A. Fetter, of Princeton, for his careful reading and criticism of three chapters. No formal acknowledgment is sufficient to express my deep obligation to Herbert J. Davenport, of Cornell, who went over the entire first draft of the work in a rigorously critical and constructive manner.

J. R. T.

NEW YORK UNIVERSITY,
    May 1, 1919.

# CONTENTS

## CHAPTER I

## CHAPTER II

## CHAPTER IX

## CHAPTER X

## CHAPTER XI

## CHAPTER XV

## CHAPTER XVI

## CHAPTER XVII

## CHAPTER XVIII

## CHAPTER XIX

## CHAPTER XX

*Contents*

## CHAPTER XXI

PAGE

## CHAPTER XXII

## CHAPTER XXIII

## CHAPTER XXVII

# INTRODUCTION TO ECONOMICS

# INTRODUCTION TO ECONOMICS

## CHAPTER I

### INTRODUCTION: THE BEGINNING OF ECONOMIC INSTITUTIONS

**1. The Science of Economics.**—Science originates in man's endeavor to answer the eternal question "why." In answer to this question, thinkers are ever on the alert to detect agreements and differences among things. The untutored see a million phenomena, but these in chaotic mass. The scholar sees the same phenomena, but subjects these to law and order. He ties things with like qualities into a bundle by themselves, and this bundle is the subject-matter of a science.

Why are there panics in the business world? Why does the cost of living continue to rise? Why does a movie actor get more for a single performance than a

1

common laborer gets for a year's work? Why is there mutual profit in trading? Why do we have monopolies? and why are some monopoly prices high and others low?

Problems of this sort are legion, but when exposed to examination they are found to exist in causal relationship. They may be tied into one bundle, and they form the subject-matter of one science—the science of Economics.

2. **Requirements of the Economist.**—This group of related thought is subject to scientific classification and inquiry. But the ability to make such classification implies a grasp of the principles which underlie the science. New specimens of animals must remain stray individual curiosities to him who is ignorant of the eight great sub-kingdoms of animals. Likewise, no rigorous classification of the varied business phenomena is possible apart from the fundamental economic laws which these phenomena obey.

The student incapable of comprehending beyond his five senses is advised to let economics alone, for the characteristic feature of this science is the interdependence of its subject-matter. A sixth sense is required, that of the detection of hidden relations. In addition to this sense, the mental equipment of a first-rate economist comprises, first of all, greatness of mind, then breadth of scholarship, and finally the knowledge of application which converts dead facts into quick thought.

3. **Mistakes in Early Specialization.**—The surest road to failure as an economist is for the student to begin with a special branch of the subject and pursue it to the exclusion of other studies. Specialization there must be, but this does not imply ignorance of all excepting one's chosen field. Each separate field of inquiry furnishes its own par-

ticular type of training, method of thought, and point of view. The mere specialist, who cannot bring to his aid the assistance of liberal training, can grasp facts but not situations, can solve isolated problems, but cannot deal with them in the broad aspect of their relationships with current economic activities. Like the perverted eye specialist who would prescribe for his patient with a sour stomach a new pair of spectacles, there are narrow specialists in labor, or money, or trusts, who would treat all economic ills from their one limited point of view.

**4. Principles First, then Specialization.**—An economic fact is never an isolated datum; it is always the result of a combination of forces. To think through an economic problem requires mental power sufficient to marshal forces to a common end, and sufficient mental balance to see forces in their proper state of poise, for if any force is not given its due weight, the conclusion will be either only partially correct or wholly wrong. Two separate forces guide the earth around the sun: overemphasis upon the one leads to the conclusion that the earth must fly away into empty space; the direful conclusion from overemphasizing the other must be that the earth will fall into the sun and be consumed in fire. If one treats lightly the power of volitional control and overemphasizes procreation, he must conclude that the growth of population will outstrip the means of subsistence, resulting thus in actual starvation and premature death from disease. If one would approach his specialty in economics with a proper mental poise, he must first put himself in command of the general principles of the science.

**5. From Objective to Subjective Control.**—In his primitive state man, like the animals about him, lived from the gratuitous fruits of nature. He produced no article of food, drink, or clothing, but hunted things and appropriated them. Every step of his progress from savagism to the highest-attained civilization has been marked by improved instrumentalities. Back of all physical developments, however, were his developments in knowledge. In power of body and swiftness of foot, in keenness of scent, taste, hearing, and sight, man is an inferior in the animal world. His power of supremacy is in his power of mind, and as this power is weaker he is more nearly an animal, and thus more dependent upon the free gifts of nature. As this power is stronger, however, he more and more controls the animals about him, and so directs the laws of nature that they do his bidding.

6. **Knowledge is Power.**—For time out of mind men have seriously debated as to which controls, nature or man. The contenders, pro and con, would have ceased their vain parleys long since, had they paused to define the word "control," for, indeed, the whole contention has been a play upon this one word. Whether man levels obstacles or goes around them is of no consequence; it is enough to know that he is not compelled to suffer them. One argues that man deceives himself in the "magnanimous claim that he conquers nature, for man's part is that of adapting himself to natural forces which he can neither create nor annihilate." The implication is that to conquer is to annihilate. These terms have little in common; the pugilist who lands the knock-out blow conquers, but does not annihilate his adversary. Call it conquer, adaptation, or what not, the issue of importance in man's economic development is this: His knowledge of natural forces is cumulative, and this knowledge is the power which

enables him to levy tribute upon nature for the necessities, comforts, and luxuries of life. The peculiarity of a natural law is that it obeys only as it is obeyed. Learning this peculiarity, man in obedience to nature's law, directs her forces to the end of gratifying his desires. In the direction of natural forces, truly "knowledge is power."

7. **From Physical to Mental.**—The knowledge of these forces gives rise to inventions which harness and set them to work. As the artist exhibits his thought on canvas or chisels it in marble, so the scientist exhibits his thought in the form of ingenious devices calculated to make easier the labor of man, and to allot to natural forces a larger share in production. In order of supremacy nature was first, and then man—first the supremacy of objective laws and finally that of subjective laws.

The development of sciences has, with few exceptions, taken precisely the same order—first the objective or physical sciences and then the moral or mental sciences.

During the seventeenth and eighteenth centuries the laws of physical science engrossed the attention of scholars. Thinkers followed a method and point of view which was in strict keeping with the order of thought prevailing in the physical sciences. At this time economics had its beginning, and what could be more natural than that the physical elements of this science should have been vitalized? The mental aspects of the subject were neglected almost as if they were beyond scientific statement, and so vividly were the objective laws painted by the old masters that they came to obsess the economists, and this holds true for many devotees of the subject even in our own time.

As we progress through the following pages, we shall see

how mental laws step by step take predominance over physical force, how they motivate all economic activity and direct the operations of all economic forces.

**8. Three Stages of Progress.**—The history of economic progress bears witness to the truth of the above observations. Even prior to authentic history, conjectural study permits this classification of economic progress:

> The hunter stage.
> The pastoral stage.
> The agricultural stage.

**9. The hunter stage** sees man, devoid of industrial equipment and ignorant of natural laws, living, as the brute beasts about him, upon such wild fruits, nuts, and animal flesh as he could find and appropriate. He was subject to nature's lottery of weather, be it fair or foul, and enjoyed abundance or suffered want as the seasons varied. From hand to mouth, and from feast to famine, he neither took forethought nor made provision for the morrow. Having no fixed abode, such private property as may have been his was of a movable type, and formed an integral part of his own personality. He had brain for thought but no ideas upon which to build. His single handicap was his want of scientific knowledge, for, had he this, he could have given shape to tools and form to new industries that would have lifted him from the level of the brute beast to the higher plane of human supremacy. Wholly subservient to nature and without vision for the future, he contributes no lesson to the modern science of economics.

**10. The Pastoral Stage.**—Different conjectures have been made as to how or why man came to domesticate animals. The "pet theory" seems to prevail; namely, that some of the savages who caught young animals would prefer to amuse themselves by playing with the captives rather than destroying them for food. This contact between savage and pet enabled the former to learn the value of the latter, enabled him to make selection among animals, retaining the more serviceable, and killing or driving away the objectionable ones. Domestication has long since, even long before the beginning of authentic history, been accomplished. "It is worthy of remark," says Professor Carver, "that our branch of the human race has not reduced a single new animal to domestication since the beginning of recorded history."

**11. Domestication and Indirect Production.**—It little matters how animals came to be domesticated—this much is certain, a long step was made toward civilization when man learned to secure indirectly the means of subsistence through the agency of animals. The shepherd, although a wanderer in search of pasture, had a more abundant and certain food-supply than did the hunter in the previous stage. We cannot overstate the importance to civilization of the art of conserving and distributing products through time. Were crops consumed and destroyed as produced, we could not survive the winter or non-producing seasons; without saving there could be no cumulative wealth, no durable agencies of production, no provision for sickness or old age. Values would fluctuate panic-like from one season to another, and no settled state of economic life could exist. The utilization of animals made a great contribution to the stability of economic life by way of furnishing milk, eggs, and meat in recurring order.

**12. Conflicting Interests.**—But these, like most economic blessings, gave rise to conflicts of interests. There are men to-day who reason that, because land is a free gift of nature, each and all should have a free and equal license to the use of it. And so the shepherds reasoned in the days of old. Tribal property in herds, however, proved contrary to the idea of equal rights for all tribes to the same land. It seemed a monstrous idea, contrary to justice, that the herd of one tribe should occupy a favored pasture to the exclusion of other herds. As the population grew and herds multiplied, contests, even tribal warfare, arose over the occupancy of the better pastures. The plan of Abraham and Lot proved best when they agreed that property in herds made necessary also property in land. They agreed to separate and each restrict his pasturing within fixed bounds, for the land was limited and the herds were multiplying, thus giving rise to frequent quarrels.

13. **Pressure and Progress.**—The ancient herdsmen have taught us yet another lesson, namely, that the pressure of numbers is a cause of progress. The sequence of more people, more herds, and less land for each herd, forced the tribes to invent means for a more intensive use of land. This led them to classify plants in order that they might proceed to destroy the unfit and to multiply the more useful. Thus economic pressure gave birth to agriculture.

14. **Tribal Property.**—Still another lesson we inherit from the experience of the ancient shepherd. A tribe is a group of related persons who claim descent from a common male ancestor. One was admitted to membership in the tribe only when he stood the test of blood-relationship; the fact that he might live in the same geographic area furnished no reason why he should be admitted to the tribe, although it might furnish decisive reason why he should be decapitated. Thus the tribe was a large family

with one family religion, government, and a common ownership of property. What we call private property to-day is, for the most part, the ownership of wealth by the family, which wealth is directed by the head of the family.

**15. Variety and Trade.**—But the property of that day was too similar in nature to give rise to extensive trading among tribes. Extensive trade implies variety in production, and the possession of unlike things by the several traders. It is when production is subdivided into many parts that there is need for considerable trading. The reason for little trading among tribes is that all followed the same occupation.

**16. Self-Sufficiency.**—Where there is no trading the consumer must depend upon his own production for support. Where a person, family, community, or tribe—without the intervention of trade—supplies its own provisionings, it lives in a "state of self-sufficiency."

We shall find that self-sufficiency also characterizes the agricultural stage of economic progress.

**17. The Agricultural Stage.**—We have seen how a growth of population led to economic pressure, and this, in turn, to a higher stage of production—the agricultural stage. We shall see that a further growth of population gave rise to an extension of man's knowledge, that he was forced to devise improved arts of husbandry, and to extend further the principle of ownership or property.

A problem to be solved sets the mind to work in search of a solution. This truth has many bearings: human ailments gave rise to the science of medicine; injustice among men called into being the science of law in order that justice might be had; maladjustments in nature made need for the science of engineering; and the pressure of a growing population upon the earth for subsistence made demand for the science of agriculture.

18. **What the Agriculturist Must Know.**—Much knowledge is required in order that man may make wise selection among plants as to the fittest types for cultivation, in order that he may adjust the different types of plants to the proper qualities of soil, in order that he may know when and how to plant, to cultivate, and to reap. The further demand for necessities must needs increase this fund of scientific knowledge in order that the land may produce more. Soil must be utilized more intensively, and the area of cultivation extended to include new lands. Swamps must be drained and arid lands irrigated. Fertilizers must be manufactured and these adopted in right proportions to the different qualities of soil.

Human history records no more worthy examples of the growth in knowledge than these: development of systems in the rotation of crops to prevent soil exhaustion; increasing discoveries regarding the effect of different kinds of crops upon the chemical qualities in soil; extension in the art of grafting and in the selection of seeds. Additional to these, and not less remarkable in development, comes the breeding and improvement of animals. The knowledge here indicated is of later date than in the stage of progress under consideration; it is high credit to that remote age that it began this development which we now so fully enjoy.

19. **Three Essentials of Thrift.**—Such is the nature of agriculture that, even in its first stages, it becomes socially necessary for men to acquire these three essentials of thrift, namely, foresight, abstinence, and a higher respect for private property. Land must be cleared and improvements

made for their future yield. Likewise, foresight is required in making necessary improvements, in the preservation of flocks, or in planting now in order to reap at a later date. Foresight gives rise to abstinence. The former points out foreseen opportunities or future difficulties, and calls upon abstinence to be sparing now in order to save for the future need. Abstinence in its turn requires a high respect for property rights, for one can save only that which he owns. One could not save his garden-vegetables, neither would he labor to produce them, apart from the institution of property, for then all who enjoy vegetables would be permitted to help themselves.

20. **A Settled Life.**—Not least, probably greatest, among the influences of agriculture upon civilization is the fact that men were forced to cease wandering and settle down. The old shepherds could drive their flocks from one grazing-place to another, but the farmer's property, being immovable, required him to maintain a fixed abode. This gave origin to home life, to more durable social relations among men, and to the beginning of social institutions. As for building, it is safe to say that men on the march had no need for durable structures, but among the first demands made by a fixed abode is that of structures more or less durable. Lands and houses, moreover, created a further extension of private property in the form of household goods and chattels.

21. **Production and Civilization.**—Civilization does not imply a static situation or fixed state of accomplishment; it signifies a progressive interaction between the inner man and his environment. There is no separating the history of production from the history of civilization; the one may almost be defined in terms of the other. The production

of the press gave wings to knowledge and enlightened mankind. The production of gunpowder, which made foot-soldiers superior to armored knights, robbed the feudal caste of its strength, and worked to the equalization of man. The production of trade facilities introduced into each community the different kinds of goods, the variety in consumption, the different methods and ideas known to every other section. The advanced civilization of ancient times in the Mediterranean basin, in some respects unequalled even in our own time, took its origin and found its development in the art of trade.

Whether it be the spread of religion, education, or liberty; whether it be the power to bridge rivers, tunnel mountains, or sail the seas; whether it be improvement in the quality and variety of food, clothing, or shelter—whatever the blessing, even to life itself, it must go back for its explanation to the one word: production. But rapid progress depends upon variety in production. Agriculture made possible a large yield of food upon a limited area to support a large and settled population. It enabled a portion of the population to produce enough farm-produce for all, thus liberating a portion of the people who turned their efforts to new lines of industry. Manufacturing and commercial cities came into being, and with them the beginnings of a division of labor and varied production.

In early times cities sprang up in the valleys, and by overland routes were enabled to trade with distant places. City-dwellers devoted their time to hand-work of all sorts. In the Tigris, Nile, and Euphrates valleys, in particular, there are records of flourishing trade between country and city people.

**22. Slavery.**—A noteworthy phase of the extension of private property during this stage was the captivity and enslavement of human beings. Is slavery to be justified? Yes and no. During the early stages in human development the introduction of slavery is a step forward. Tribes and races of people never enslave their own members; the slaves of a tribe or race are the captives from another tribe or race. Previous to the time when it became profitable to enslave the captives, they were killed by their conquerors. Slavery is justified when the issue becomes either the loss of liberty or the loss of life.

In the second place, the primitive man preferred to plunder rather than to work; it was with difficulty that he could be induced to work at all. Prejudice aside, our better judgment would welcome slave-labor as a vast improvement over the free idleness of savage plunderers.

But the economics of slavery goes deeper. The time under review was prior to the introduction of improved tools and labor-saving machinery. Labor was performed by hand with the aid of a few crude instrumentalities. Superior workmanship upon the land, requiring specialized knowledge, had not yet made its appearance. Only muscular labor for heavy, coarse work was needed. Such labor may be performed by slaves. But this must be added: the slave has no more interest in the quality of the good he produces or in the price for which it will sell than the horse has in the load that it pulls. It follows that, without incentive for improvement, the products of his labor must remain of a crude and rough type.

While cultivation was in the beginning stages, land was so plentiful and cheap that it figured but little in the expenses of production, and tools were a negligible factor.

Under these conditions men thought of the cost of production almost wholly in terms of muscular labor. Put differently, labor was the limiting factor of production and, therefore, the expensive factor. This fact, coupled with the coarse type of production then required, made slave-labor very profitable.

Slave-labor, however, is not a free good. Prior to captivity those destined to become slaves are valueless, but so also are the fur-bearing animals of Siberia while still in their native haunts. Subject these to human control, however, and value and price are forthwith attached. He who sells furs will not hesitate to attach a price because the product was once a free good. Here we have learned a first principle in the value problem; namely, the thing valued must be subject to control. Moreover, if slaves are reared from infancy, the process is both time-consuming and expensive. The matter comes to this: slaves are expensive to rear and maintain; they represent invested capital; they are sold at prices corresponding with their productive capacity. Whether one will hire free labor or buy slaves is very like the problem whether it is better to buy a home or rent. The two problems differ in this— one can buy a superior house, but he cannot buy superior slave-labor.

23. **The conclusion** to which we are brought is in strict keeping with the history of the case. As industries develop and are broken up into specialized parts, the producers require skilled labor and labor that is readily adjustable to the varying demands of a changing market. Machinery comes into use, thus making a demand for mechanical skill. Then, too, the varying needs of the market require the business man to have on hand a large

labor force at one time, whereas in slack periods few workmen are needed. Thus the free-wage system in an open labor market fills the requirements of modern conditions better, and in a manner far more economical, than could slave-labor.

**24. From Primitive to Manoral Times.**—Between the primitive economy we have so hastily reviewed and the manoral economy now to be studied there was a long lapse of time. Nor was this time without its interesting lessons for the economist. During this period economic changes brought about the decay of certain institutions and gave rise to others of a new and higher form. I say economic changes, not the plans of a great leader or group of influential men, forced the remodelling of institutions so that they conform in time and step with the march of human progress.

**25. Feudalism.**—As stated by the Yale historian, Professor B. G. Adams, "It is almost impossible even with the most discriminating care to give a brief account of completed feudalism and convey no wrong impression." And he quotes De Quincey thus: "It is a natural resource that whatsoever we find it difficult to investigate as a result, we endeavor to follow as a growth. Failing analytically to probe its nature, historically we seek relief to our perplexities by tracing its origin. . . . Thus, for instance, when any feudal institution eludes our deciphering faculty from the imperfect records of its use and operation, then we endeavor conjecturally to amend our knowledge by watching the circumstances in which that institution arose."[1]

The circumstances under which feudalism arose were

[1] Ency. Brit., eleventh ed., vol. 10, p. 300.

two: (*a*) For centuries, particularly in Greece and Rome, men had developed their industries and arts until civilization had reached a high level. But in the fourth, fifth, and sixth centuries the migrations of barbarian hordes from the north worked havoc with the political and economic environment of the people and laid this splendid civilization in ruins. (*b*) Existing social institutions had to be transformed to meet new requirements.

The new situation is difficult of explanation because of the confusion which prevailed. Nor was the situation everywhere the same. But this much was true then as it is to-day: the object of organized tyranny takes the form of murder, loot, pillage, and destruction. This brought the peaceful arts into neglect, the superb Roman roads into disuse, commerce into abandonment, and the power of sovereign governments into a state of disintegration.

Everywhere a cry arose for protection—protection against the sudden attacks of invading tribes, against oppressive neighbors, against exacting government officers, and against unwarranted taxes of the governments themselves. In almost every relation of life and on every side the weak freeman and small landholder were attacked, yet the decaying empires were incapable of extending relief. Protection, which normally it is the business of the government to furnish, had to be sought elsewhere, and at whatever price might be demanded for it.

The safest guarantee of the helpless against the formidable invaders was, in many cases, to group in small communities and put themselves under the protection of a powerful leader or expert fighter. But the protection of this chief personage was not free from charge; he held the land and granted protection in return for payments and services. And this was the origin of the manoral system.

**26. The Manoral System in England.**—It would not serve our purpose to trace the peculiarities of the origin of this system in England. It is enough to say that in their conquest of 1066 the Normans found the system in operation and took advantage of it as a convenient basis for reorganizing the kingdom. To the victor belonged the spoils, and William the Conqueror, with generous hand, granted the existing manors to his followers. Not content with this, the Doomsday Survey, the most complete survey of agricultural resources ever made, was carried out, and the entire kingdom was divided among favored landlords.

**27. Ashley's Picture of the Eleventh-Century Manor.[1]** "Let us picture to ourselves an eleventh-century manor in Middle or Southern England. There was a village street, and along each side of it the houses of the cultivators of the soil, with little yards around them: as yet there were no scattered farmhouses, such as were to appear later. Stretching away from the village was the arable land, divided usually into three fields, sown one with wheat or rye, one with oats or barley, while one was left fallow. The fields were again subdivided into what were usually called 'furlongs'; and each furlong into acre or half-acre strips, separated, not by hedges, but by 'balks' of unploughed turf; and these strips were distributed among the cultivators in such a way that each man's holding was made up of strips scattered up and down the three fields, and no man held two adjoining pieces. Each individual holder was bound to cultivate his strips in accordance with the rotation of crops observed by his neighbors. Besides the arable fields, there were also meadows, enclosed for hay-harvest, and divided into portions by lot or rota-

[1]Ashley's Introduction to English Economic History and Theory, book I, pp. 6–7.

tion or custom, and after hay-harvest thrown open again for the cattle to pasture upon. In most cases there was also some permanent pasture or wood, into which the cattle were turned, either 'without stint' or in numbers proportioned to the extent of each man's holding."

**28. Tenants.**—Those who lived under the direction of the manor were under compulsion to render some form of assistance in the cultivation of the lord's land. The villagers may be classified as free tenants, villeins, handicraftsmen, and slaves. Free tenants made their payments to the lord in money or in kind. When one pays in kind he tenders a portion of what he produces; thus payment in kind might consist of eggs, poultry, vegetables, or grain. This class of tenants were socially superior to the next or villein class, who rendered their pay in manual labor. Handicraftsmen were little more than common slaves who performèd various functions upon the estates and in the household. The Normans found that slaves constituted about nine per cent of the population of England. Slavery formed no integral part of manoral life. Absolute slavery disappeared within a century after the conquest (1066.) Slaves became customary holders of small plots, but under onerous conditions.

**29. Self-Sufficiency on Manors.**—Each manor was a community existing apart from others. Such would-be roads as might connect these communities were too dangerous for commerce because the traveller was subject to outlawry. The records indicate that almost the whole of what the manors purchased from the outside were these essentials: millstones, salt, and iron for the making of tools. Each manor developed its own customs, and provided its own court, church, and mill. It provided food, clothing, and the other necessities for its own needs. The manor system furnishes an excellent example of the economy of self-sufficiency.

30. **The Relation of Property to Government.**—We have seen how among primitive peoples the institution of property took its beginning and extended its growth. We now see the relationship of this institution to government. Property implies power, the power to control. In a well-established government the social power is organized in the sovereignty of the state. The state may delegate to persons or corporations, full, partial, or no property rights, as it wills. Moreover, the power to delegate a property right implies the power to take it away. If the expression of the sovereign power, in the form of votes, should declare against private property, that moment the institution would die. When the old governments began to decay, power passed from the states to the expert fighters, and with this transfer went the transfer of the power that is property. But the fighter has a self-interest which the state has not, and he will not, therefore, be so generous in his grants of property as would be the state.

Self-interest implies a personal greed that would make levy upon the wealth, even upon the person, of others. And the motive of self-interest predominates the rule of a person, be he the lord of a manor or the ruler of a great people. Should Cuba, for instance, come under the complete domination of a single great ruler, her people would be levied upon for contribution, and their holdings be modified to conform to the self-interest of that ruler.

The characteristics of a democratic government, on the contrary, are unselfishness and the rule of common sense. Guizot was right when he said: "Common sense is the characteristic of humanity." A democratic government is the organized form of the will of humanity. These facts teach us in the United States not to take alarm because of the great and growing accumulations of private wealth. Nor need we fear the opposite extreme of unbridled socialism. Social institutions are always on trial, open to inspection, to inquiry, and under experiment. The common sense of the people outweighs that of the would-be reformer, and these people are free to vote institutions in or out. They may move too slowly for the impatient, but in the end the institutions which are good and fit will survive, while the bad and unfit will be eliminated.

Under the lord of the manor there could be no individual liberty, in the sense in which we understand it, and, in consequence, no private property. Men were forbidden to sell any product without the lord's permission; they were bound to the soil as much as the trees upon it; their services were at the disposal of the lord; their position was little superior to that of slaves.

**31. Exercises.**—1. How does a science originate, and what is the essential condition that any discipline may become a science?

2. Shall a piece of coal be studied in geology, botany, physics, chemistry, or economics? (Fetter.)

3. Write a description of one of the three stages of progress mentioned in paragraph 8.

4. Why was the domestication of animals of great economic importance? "Invention and machinery is but furthering the progress which had its beginning in the domestication of animals." Justify this statement.

5. "Economic pressure gave birth to agriculture" (paragraph 13) and to property rights. Tell why this statement is true.

6. How did agriculture bring about foresight, abstinence, a higher respect for private property, and a settled life?

7. Are there any conditions under which slavery is justifiable? If so, what are they?

8. Apart from political and moral considerations, could slavery exist in an advanced stage of industrial development? Defend your answer.

9. What were the circumstances under which feudalism arose?

10. Write a description of the eleventh-century manor in England.

11. What does the word property mean? How is it related to government?

# CHAPTER II

## ENGLISH GUILDS AND THE DECLINE OF LOCAL RESTRICTIONS

1. Man as user of tools. 2. The interdependence of industries in a civilized state. 3. The old and new in England's development. 4. Development of great wealth. 5. Isolation and local unity. 6. The alliance against lords of manors. 7. Guilds. 8. The Guild is an economic institution. 9. Merchant guilds. 10. In France. 11. The craft guilds. 12. The Hundred Years' War between England and France. 13. Changes during the war: in religion; in language; knighthood; the Black Death; the Peasants' Revolt of 1381; enclosures. 14. Exercises.

**1. Man as User of Tools.**—Man differs from the lower animals in two respects: first, he is provided with reason that enables him to make things, and, secondly, he is not provided, as are the lower animals, with the means of protection, or with provision for bodily comfort, and such is his digestion that he requires a superior quality of food. His mental capacity gives him the power and his natural shortcomings give him the motive, or furnish the necessity, for him to invent things. The making, or, if a longer word is preferred, the manufacturing, of things must have been practised from the earliest times, otherwise the race could not have survived. Even in the hunting stage there must have been at least some crude instruments.

**2. The Interdependence of Industries in a Civilized State.**—When man raised himself above the level of animals and began a civilized life he found that tools were not less needed than the land itself. The resources of nature and the tools of production are to each other as the mouth is to the stomach, for neither could support man in a degree of comfort without the co-operation of the other.

We have said that agriculture requires a settled state of living; it should be added that the tilling of the soil also requires the population to be scattered. On the contrary, manufacturing or the source of tools, particularly in a civilized state, calls for congregated labor and for the exchange of goods. Manufacture and trade find most facilities and must, for the most part, exist in towns or cities. Whether cities attract manufactories or are built up around them is not a question debatable; they each react upon the other and grow together.

Within a well-organized society agriculture is supplied with tools and finished products from the city, and the city is supplied with raw materials from the farm. They are interdependent; towns feed from the surplus of agriculture, and the tillers of the soil draw their finished products from the workshops of the town. This interdependence or mutual benefit is effected through the agency of commerce.

If agriculture should decline, the towns will decay and commerce must diminish. So mutually dependent are these three parts of industry that the weakness of one means the infirmity of all. How they develop together as one large movement is well exemplified in the industrial development of England.

**3. The Old and New in England's Development.**—English commerce now covers every sea, and there is not a port the world over unfrequented by her ships of trade. So commanding is her position in trade that all peoples of the earth quote their international exchanges in terms of her finance. Her giant institutions of finance are the

models of excellence for the rest of mankind. Her manufacturing cities and productive agriculture, her harbors
and rivers, her beds of iron and coal, are so bound together
by a network of railways as to make of the whole a veritable
workshop. The opportunities before her people are great,
but not as great as are the people who made them. Her
capitalists, enterprisers, and laborers are of the highest
order, and worthy of their great attainments.

The area of England, including Wales, is but a little
over one-fifth of the area of Texas. It is smaller than
Missouri by 11,080 square miles, yet it supports in a high
state of comfort nearly 40,000,000 of souls.

Contrast the England of to-day with the England that
the Normans found in 1066. The total population recorded in the Doomsday numbered but 283,242. Certain
omissions were made in that great survey, and Ashley estimates the total numbers at 1,500,000, although he says:
"This estimate is probably too high." It is safe to say
that in the eleventh century all England supported an
impoverished population which numbered fewer by a
quarter of a million than does the city of Philadelphia.

So striking a contrast in the industrial orders of the two
periods suggests an educational contrast, because indigence
and poverty keep the company of ignorance, while a high
state of well-being is inseparable from education. To
quote from Green's Short History: "Instead of long fronts
of venerable colleges, of stately walks beneath immemorial
elms, history plunges us into the mean and filthy lanes of
a mediæval town. Thousands of boys, huddled in bare
lodging-houses, clustering around teachers as poor as themselves in church porch and 'house porch—drinking, quarrel-
ling, dicing, begging at the corners of the streets—take

the place of the brightly-colored train of Doctors and Heads—Mayor and Chancellor struggle in vain to enforce order or peace on this seething mass of turbulent life."

4. **Development of Great Wealth.**—The land is not more now than then, nor has nature added to its fertility. Whence this change from a sparse population, barely able to eke out a living, to a large population living in a state of abundance? The Normans injected into England new blood, new ideas, and money-lending which gave rise to a new form of industrial evolution. This evolution was the work of forces in society itself, operating upon their material environment. In our own country not more than 500,000 American Indians could maintain a meagre existence where now dwell 60,000,000 or more of the most prosperous people of which there is record. The powers of knowledge are the seeds of development, and these, united with a rich environment, are the cause of great wealth wherever it is found.

But the development in knowledge and power of application is, as we have said, coincident with variety in production, and such variety is impossible apart from the production of a surplus in agriculture. This surplus was small on the English manors, and so the small towns, or manufacturing villages, numbered not more than eighty at the time of the Conquest.

5. **Isolation and Local Unity.**—The population dwelt either upon manors or in towns, and was, therefore, divided into small isolated groups. For want of good roads and safe travel the different groups had little in common, but there was close personal association within groups. Personal contact, together with a oneness of interest, produced a strong sense of unity that enabled the group to act as a

corporate body. In the absence of a strong protecting government self-preservation was imposed upon the group, thus making more desirable the power to act as a corporate body.

**6. The Alliance Against Lords of Manors.**—While the towns and manors were similar in some respects, they differed in others. The citizens of the town were free; they had many rights of self-government, among others the right to levy taxes, regulate trade, and administer justice. This freedom caused serfs to flee from the oppression of the feudal lords, and go to the towns, where they were accepted and made freemen. The lords of the manors resented this, for it threatened their power, and rivalries arose between the lords of the manors and the manufacturing cities.

The government did not hesitate to favor the cities, because the power of some lords, who were jealous of the King himself, was so great as to threaten the safety of the state. The self-interests of both the King and the townspeople made an alliance for mutual benefit inevitable. The dwellers in cities received from the King special privileges in the form of royal charters, and they repaid the King with contributions to the royal exchequer and a promise of unswerving loyalty in time of emergency.

Being a centre of manufacture and trade, it is but natural that the first request of a town would be for the special privilege of monopoly in its line of trade. This brings us to the formation of guilds—a new type of economic institution.

**7. Guilds.**—As the manor was limited to agriculture, so the guild was limited to manufacture and trade. Some historians reason that guilds have grown out of the spirit of brotherhood in Christianity; others see them as a continuation of the old Roman fraternities; others advance the theory that guilds are derived from the early Scandinavian banquets. These unlike theories have this in common—guilds are the outgrowth of a pre-existing institution. The economist could have little confidence in such theories. The ancient and noisy revels of the Scandinavians had neither unity nor durability of association, and these were prime characteristics of the guild. The Roman fraternities had no continuity, as did the guild. Nor does the guild suggest the spirit of Christianity and brotherly love. It was designed, on the one hand, to form a monopoly of trade by keeping others out, and, on the other hand, to cheat in trade.

**8. The Guild Is an Economic Institution,** and for the explanation of such institutions we must look into the facts of human nature. Economic changes modify man's behavior and give new direction to his plans. An institution is no more than a device for the execution of a plan, and must, therefore, change with the change of plan. It is a part of man's nature to form associations, whether for the support of the body or the salvation of the soul. Social animals enjoy association, and where there is a motive in common among men we have the explanation for an organized association or institution to carry out the motive.

As between the present form of corporation with monopoly power and the guild of mediæval England and Europe there are many points of difference, but back of the form the motive for forming and the real essence of the institutions is the same—that of securing advantage in trade through the possession of monopoly power.

**9. Merchant Guilds.**—An organization which embodies many interests is weaker and less durable than one with a single interest and purpose. The merchant guild was comprehensive in scope, covering all those who had occasion to buy or sell anything beyond provisions for daily use. Whether limited, as some, to trade within the town of its location, or permitted, as others, to extend their command of trade throughout the kingdom, they had monopoly power over many lines of trade.

There was no free competition where the guild ruled. It bought and paid for its rights in trade as truly as it did the commodities in which it dealt. And these purchased privileges took the form of oppressive regulations even to the minutest details. When and where might goods be sold? in what quantities? at what prices? by whom and to whom? These and other questions too numerous for mention were subjects for definite regulation by the guilds, and for enforcement by the wardens of the guild. To break one of these precious rules furnished an occasion for public censure and fine, or else imprisonment and expulsion from the guild.

Note the spirit of oppressive regulation which characterized that backward age. Whether in the city guilds or the country manors and whether in England or upon the continent, regulation was the rule.

10. In France.—Prior to 1798 in France the King systematically obtained the choice bits of scandal by opening private letters which passed through the post; not fewer than 168 censors passed upon publications; instead of a single code of law, there was a legal variety of 300 different laws, which were enforced by fines, tortures, and mutilations. The King was wont to garner riches through the sale of monopoly rights.

Thus arose a grievous hindrance to trade. Internal commerce was harassed by frequent tolls and customs duties on goods passing from province to province. A vessel descending the Saône and Rhône Rivers had to stop and pay charges as many as thirty times, the whole amounting to from 25 to 30 per cent of the value of the cargo. Hardly a trade or industry escaped the oppressive regulation of the guild. "Each week for a number of years," said an inspector of manufactures, "I have seen burned at Rouen 80 to 100 pieces of goods because some regulation concerning the weaving or dyeing had not been observed at every point."[1]

11. **The Craft Guild.**—The merchant guild, with its many interests, gradually gave way to the craft guild, which was stronger in organization because of its oneness of interest. It was an organization of artisans engaged in the same particular handicraft or trade. Its rules were not less rigorous nor less strictly enforced than in the merchant guild. Some of its regulations were commendable, and similar rules are to-day insisted upon by governments and trades-unions. They provided for honest work, fraternal improvements, correct weights and measures, and against night work in some cases, and against the adulteration of products in all cases.

Within recent years in the United States we have witnessed the gradual decay of the Knights of Labor, embracing all trades and classes of workers, and the rise of trades-unions which include only men who work at the same trade and who, therefore, have a unity of interest. Very like this change from the general to the particular in unions was the development in the guilds. And so with progress in general; it is from the general to the particular.

12. **The Hundred Years' War** between England and

---

[1] Harding's Essentials in Mediæval and Modern History, p. 346.

France came to an inglorious end for England in 1453. Its ultimate effect upon both nations was the overthrow of the oppressive local institutions, among them guilds and manors. The French were victorious and took England's continental possessions, excepting Calais. A strong national sentiment was born, and the prestige of the French King elevated him above his rivals and into the position of an almost absolute monarch. But not so with the Lancastrian Kings of England—in that country Parliament increased its powers, even to the control of the purse. A national spirit arose, but it was organized in Parliament rather than in the King.

13. **Changes During the War.**—Social and economic movements during this war stimulated the people by ushering in new lines of thought and by breaking down industrial barriers.

(*a*) Religion: The church had a monopoly of religion, and had accumulated vast estates which were free from taxation. John Wyclif (1324–1384) accused the clergy of irreligion due to the close connection between church and state. Believing it Christ's will that the clergy remain poor, he urged that the church be disestablished and its property confiscated for state use. He denied the supremacy of the Pope, and disavowed important dogmas of the Roman Catholic Church. Translating the Bible into English, he openly revealed the teachings of the Scriptures to all readers. Missionary priests were trained by him, who went all over England teaching the people that they were losing the true gospel instruction necessary to save their souls, and that the great wealth of the church, so needed by the poor, was wasted. His followers (Lollards) multiplied rapidly, and twice it was seriously proposed in Parliament to confiscate the temporalities of the church. This proved to be a most significant educational movement.

(*b*) The Language: After 1066 the Norman-French tongue enriched the Anglo-Saxon and gave rise to the modern English language. Chaucer, in his Canterbury Tales, established the English language—"the King's English"—and portrayed, in matchless style, the state of English society in the middle of the fourteenth century.

(*c*) Knighthood, originally concerned with landed possessions and military service on horseback, came to concern itself with standards of honor, courtesy, and duty. Its members were pledged to aid the oppressed, to honor women, and to maintain the right.

(*d*) *The Black Death* is italicized for its significant economic bearings. A sweeping transformation of social institutions was caused by this singular calamity known as the Black Death. It first ravaged Europe and finally reached England in 1348. It was a violent typhus fever, accompanied by eruptions and black blotches on the skin. Half of the rural population died within a year, and the death-rate among the clergy was particularly high because their duties took them to the bedside of the sick. Twenty-four thousand Franciscan friars died. London, then only a small city, set aside a cemetery thirteen acres in extent, and this was crowded with the bodies of fifty thousand victims of the malady. Business came to a standstill, so much so that grass grew in the market-place of Bristol. In short, the Black Death found England with a population of four millions, and left that stricken land with but two millions.

This was the laborer's opportunity, and he hastened to take advantage of it. Despite its serious aspects, this malady may be called a blessing in disguise; probably no war has done more for the liberation of mankind. Labor was suddenly cut short, with the result that employers in England and on the Continent were set to bidding against each other for such labor as was available. Wages advanced rapidly and villeins, disregarding the protests of their masters, declared their independence of the manors. They offered their services as freemen to the highest bidder for a money wage.

Another significant lesson: The hard-pressed employers persuaded Parliament to enact the "Statute of Laborers," which forbade higher wages, and a later law provided severe punishment for runaway villeins. Here we have economic law and legal law in conflict: The former favors higher wages due to the law of supply and demand; the latter favors low wages and would arbitrarily enforce them. As if once was not enough, the statute was re-enacted thirteen times, but all to no avail. Labor will sell for its worth—not less and not more—in a competitive market. Minimum wage advocates would do well to contemplate more upon this fact.

(e) The Peasants' Revolt of 1381 is both an evidence of the new independence felt by labor and an effective demand for the betterment of labor. This Statute of Laborers proved oppressive to the villeins and they, with the townspeople, resented the tolls which added to their cost of living. All were burdened with a heavy tax to support "a useless foreign war." Their long brooding over these troubles prepared the way for John Ball, whose speeches to the lower classes might easily be mistaken for the language of a modern single-taxer. In behalf of abolishing class distinctions and private property in land, he said: "Are we not descended from the same parents, Adam and Eve? And what can they [the upper classes] show, or what reasons give, why they should be more the masters than ourselves? . . . They are clothed in velvets and rich stuffs ornamented with ermine and other furs, while we are forced to wear poor cloth; they have wines, spices, and fine bread, when we have only rye and the refuse of the straw, and if we drink, it must be water; . . . but it is from our labor they have wherewith to support their pomp!"

Literally thousands were ready for revolt when, in 1381, the poll-tax collector came along and insulted Wat Tyler's daughter, only to be struck dead by her father. The fight was on. Tyler's friends in misery arose to plunder and murder the tax-collectors, and they did no discriminating, in this particular, against other government officers. Much property was destroyed in their search for the manor copy-rolls, which they desired to burn. Congregating in London, they demanded the abolition of villeinage. Soon Tyler was killed, and the King outwitted the mob by assuming the leadership of the insurgents and promising redress of grievances. Thirty clerks were put to it to draw up new charters, then the insurgents dispersed.

Consequences: The lords of the manors ceased to be dictators, and had to bargain on equal terms with labor. Wages were so high that the landlords, for the most part, found more profit in leasing their estates and stock in small lots to tenants. Thus arose the modern type of small farmer who paid rent to the owner of the land, and he paid wages to other laborers.

(*f*) Enclosures: The enclosing of land was the influence to complete the downfall of the manorial system and to usher in a money economy. High wages caused the old form of agriculture, grain-raising, to decline; meanwhile sheep-raising was becoming very profitable. England had a good export market for her wool, and during the fourteenth century a number of woollen-factories were introduced into the country, thus adding to the demand and increasing the price of the raw wool.

High wages were no obstacle to sheep-raising, because a shepherd and his dog could care for a large drove of sheep. The lords of the manors found it profitable to convert their lands into sheep-ranches. Moreover, large boundaries of common land were fenced in for the same purpose. Many persons owned as many as 24,000 sheep, consequently the land had to be enclosed into very large pasture-fields. This process of enclosing or fencing in land is known as "enclosing," and upon certain conditions the state gave the encloser property in the land.

The tenants, with few exceptions, were forced to surrender their holdings when the land was taken up in this manner. Many of those who enclosed land were non-residents, and due to the fact that but little labor was needed to care for the sheep, the tenants received little consideration and were forced to seek employment elsewhere.

Wealthy merchants and professional men, desiring to become landlords, bought and enclosed lands. Thus for the first time lands became marketable, and with this change rents rose ten and even twentyfold. This brought the poor to the verge of starvation, and the whole realm was overrun with beggars and thieves. Bishop Latimer, a noted clergyman of that day, declared that if every farmer should raise two acres of hemp there would not be enough to hang the thieves. He preached against the change, but to no avail. "Let the preacher preach," he said, "till his tongue is worn to the stumps; nothing is amended."

Public resentment grew strong, riots broke out and the government legislated against the change. Between the years 1488 and 1624 act after act was passed against enclosures, but all such legislation was ineffective. Despite severe hardships and opposing legislation, industrial conditions forced a change to private property in land. A considerable portion of the tillable and pasture land of England was enclosed at that time.

**14. Exercises. 1.** What is meant by the interdependence of industries? What is the connection between the development of industries and the growth of cities?

2. Contrast the numbers and prosperity of the English people to-day with the numbers and prosperity in 1066. Make a brief summary of the causes of this development.

3. Account for the rise of guilds. What was the difference between merchant guilds and craft guilds? What was the chief characteristic of a guild?

4. Has economics anything to do with religion? With the development of a language? With knighthood?

5. Following the Black Death, the Statutes of Laborers were passed in 1351, and subsequent years. They had very little practical effect. Account for their failure.

6. Summarize the chief economic changes which followed the Peasants' Revolt of 1381.

7. Why did sheep-raising become so important and extensive in England during the fourteenth and fifteenth centuries?

8. Write a report of one page (not over 300 words) which will contrast the economic life of the English people before the changes described in this chapter with the economic life after the changes.

# CHAPTER III

## NATIONAL CONTROL AND THE INDUSTRIAL REVOLUTION

**1. The National System.**—The religious, educational, and industrial movements, which were outlined in the last chapter, enabled the common people to sense their power. The inevitable result was the breakdown of local restriction and the rise of movements national in scope. National sentiment became solidified under the rule of the strong and popular line of Tudors.

It was in a period of internal dissension, when the public mind was prepared to welcome a ruler with power to restore unity and peace, that Henry VII took the throne. He interpreted well the spirit of the time, and enlisted the people's confidence by a selection of able advisers. This was the beginning of a series of statesmen chosen from the ranks of the people. He found England in dissension, but transmitted it to his very capable son, Henry VIII, a strong and well-organized government. After twenty-five years of rule, "Henry, head of the state, became also head of the church or, briefly, the English pope." Soon afterward came the "Virgin Queen," Elizabeth, who was a curious compound of qualities masculine and feminine. She was the most novel statesman known to history. The ablest statesmen of England were chosen her ministers, yet she was clearer-brained and farther-sighted than any of them. Coquetry was her diplomatic weapon, and with it the winsome queen had her own way.

2. **Monopolies.**—Queen Elizabeth (1558–1603) appraised the power of granting patents of monopoly to her favorites as "the fairest flower of her garden." She granted exclusive rights to private parties to deal in certain articles of common use. Competition was thereby destroyed and prices fixed by the privileged few. Such necessities as salt, iron, calfskins, vinegar, lead, and paper were controlled by patentees. Prices became exorbitant and the abuses of the monopolists intolerable.

In 1601 the House of Commons brought pressure to bear on the Queen and she promised reform. The memorable Act of Parliament of 1624 made null and void all monopolies which controlled the buying, selling, and making of goods and manufactures. "This act effectually secured the freedom of industry in England; and in the opinion of excellent authorities has done more to excite the spirit of invention and industry and to accelerate the progress of riches in that country than any other in the statute-book." The historian Gibbon says: "The spirit of monopolists is narrow, lazy, and oppressive. Their work is more costly and less productive than that of independent artists, and the new improvements, so eagerly grasped by the competition of freedom, are admitted by them with slow and sullen reluctance." Restrictions and special privileges extended beyond internal affairs and applied to foreign trade as well. These industrial changes were accompanied by changes in economic thought.

**3. Mercantilism or Colbertism.**—Colbert, the famous finance minister of Louis XIV of France, had an idea that money is the greatest index of national wealth. To his mind great wealth and an abundance of money were synonymous terms. His anxiety to enrich France led him to advocate tariff restrictions such as would cause that country to export more goods than she imported, and to collect "the favorable balance of trade" in money. Many statesmen throughout Europe and England held similar views— these statesmen, not economists, are called Mercantilists.

It was an age of nation-building and of international jealousies. The argument that great sums of money were required to maintain foreign fleets and armies was a forceful one. Moreover, money was considered the most important form of wealth, because of its durability and its exchangeability. It was pointed out that if the merchant does not convert his stock into money he fails, and from this it was argued that the nation should sell its goods for money. A result of such teachings was that Spain, Portugal, Scotland, France, and England forbade the exportation of gold. We cannot emphasize too strongly that Mercantilism was a national policy rather than a local policy. Furthermore, the purpose of the policy was to create a strong national state. It was broader than money-making; it was state-making under severe restrictions and regulations. These restrictions covered trade, manufacturing, agriculture, and labor—in fact, they covered all of the industrial relationships of society. The false doctrine was then current that when a trade is made one party must get cheated. Accordingly, it would be good statesmanship to devise a system that would cheat foreigners in trade, and make collection of the favorable balance in money.

**4. Restrictions.** To this point we have found that the history of industrial England was characterized by restrictions—restrictions in manor life, then in guild life, then in all trade between provinces; and, finally, the breakdown of local restrictions and the rise of national restrictions.

**5. National Ideals.**—I have neglected mention of important events which profoundly influenced the economic life of England. Nothing has been said of the awakened enterprise following the discovery of the New World. No reference has been given to the religious wars of Europe, which drove so many skilled artisans to England. Nor has mention been made of international commercial treaties, which made foreign trade safe, large, and profitable. Not least of the omitted items was the formation of trading companies, such as the famous East India Company, which carried English commerce into every port, and introduced that nation's customs and flag to all the world.

Our purpose has been not to detail items, however interesting, except as they might show how economic influences give form to new ideas, and how these react, giving form to new lines of enterprise. The futility of attempting to study economic progress apart from national ideals may be seen in these words from Professor Kimball:[1] "It is to be especially noted that national ideals, popular opinion, or some similar influence has always greatly influenced industrial organization. Thus, in India the caste

[1] Principles of Industrial Organization, p. 4.

system for countless years prohibited all forms of factories and all production was by simple handicraft, definite kinds of work being assigned to particular classes of people. Under the Roman system the armorers or *fabri* were a class of artisans set apart for this sole purpose, and they could not change their calling. It was a form of state-supported and regulated slavery. History abounds with similar instances of the effect of public opinion or national necessity upon the method by which the nation was provided with the necessities of life. While, therefore, the essential features of our modern system will probably continue indefinitely, it need not be a matter of surprise or alarm that many changes and regulations have been made and will be made in deference to public opinion or national necessity."

**6. The Domestic System.**—Between the decay of the feudal system and the beginning of the industrial revolution stands the domestic system. Domestic is defined as belonging to the house or home, and, in keeping with this, the simple industries of that time were not housed in factory buildings, but were carried on around the family firesides. This system began at a time when farming was the primary interest of the householder. But he, with his family, devoted his spare time to some simple handicraft—particularly spinning and weaving. The spinning-wheel, now a fit antique for exhibition in a museum, was found in all well-to-do homes. In time these domestic arts took on more importance.

A master workman, employing a few helpers who lived with him, carried out in his own home all the processes of spinning, weaving, and dyeing cloth. The food for the workers would be produced upon their own land, that is, they did farming as well as weaving. Perhaps a farmer's wife and children would utilize spare time in weaving cloth from the wool of their own sheep. What trade there was moved in a very limited circle because of the poor roads. Goods were produced for immediate consumption, the worker knew his market and regulated his output accordingly. There was a close personal relation between maker and consumer, and between master and workman.

7. **The Industrial Revolution.**—There was virtue, intelligence, and a certain charm in the simple life and dignity of manners in primitive England. The customs of life and the household appointments of that people were almost exactly duplicated in many sections of our South prior to a generation ago. In many an isolated community of the South to-day the manipulation of the hand-cards, spinning-wheel, and the old-fashioned loom is far from being a lost art. There is an economic independence and rude comfort which these people get from direct contact with the freshness and richness of the virgin soil.

The Industrial Revolution found the English people a brave and hardy stock who loved independence. But their primitive methods had lingered century after century, with scarcely any evidence of private thrift. The resulting poverty and stagnation of life are best described as a condition of arrested social development. Then came the marvellous industrial transformation. The change was like the brightness and hope of day, following the darkness and dread of night.

This change,—we call it the Industrial Revolution,—was a change from the home to the factory, from hand-work to machine-work, from rural to city life, from local to world markets, from a simple to a complex division of labor. But greater than these changes and the cause of them was a change in the point of view.

**8. Commerce and Need for Machinery.**—Prior to the fall of Napoleon (1815) England had acquired naval supremacy and a monopoly of commerce on the sea. This occasioned an extensive demand for the manufactured products of England, especially for her textiles. Textiles were produced by hand-cards, the spinning-wheel, and the old-fashioned loom. The pieces of goods were collected from the hamlets into the towns, from where they were hauled over all but impassible roads to the port for shipment.

The growing demand increased the pressure on old processes and called for new manufacturing processes. One weaver could use the product of six spinners, but the invention of Kay's drop-box (1783) enabled one weaver to keep ahead of ten or twelve spinners. Spinning was thus the greatest obstacle to progress, and the Royal Society offered a prize for an invention to improve spinning. Improvements followed in quick succession, and large machinery succeeded the simple tools of the domestic system.

**9. The Beginning of Industrial Classes.**—The operating of large machinery called for separate buildings in which power could be used. Furthermore, these new processes involved too great an expense for the small master to incur, so we find the capitalist buying machines and employing labor. The consequence was an employing class, separated from the workers and having no share in the actual labor, but furnishing the means of production and paying men to use these means. Naturally these new machines were installed where power was available, and the population concentrated in factory districts along the swiftly running streams of northern England.

When James Watt perfected the steam-engine, the power of steam was applied and factories multiplied still more rapidly. Improved methods of smelting iron by the use of coal were discovered and the mining industries grew. Canals and roads were improved, then railroads were built, so that within two generations England was transformed into a region of thickly populated factory towns closely connected by railroads.

**10. Scientific Farming.**—To hasten still more the changes a revolution in agricultural methods occurred at the same time. Scientific farming was introduced and farmers began to employ new methods of tilling the soil and new means of fertilizing. Such systems could be used only by the prosperous and the small farmer was forced out. He either drifted to the city to join the ranks of the factory-workers, or sank to the level of an agricultural day-laborer.

**11. Control of Natural Forces.**—Prior to the use of large machinery the output of industry was limited by the fund of human muscle and nervous energy. Then came the large machine—a device by means of which human intelligence takes control over natural forces. The limit to the output of industry was no longer fixed by the fund of muscular power; it was determined by the fund of knowledge. Knowledge gives form to machinery which, in turn, renders natural forces subservient to human will. Expressed differently: the limit to the output of an industry based upon machinery is the available power of nature.

To labor-saving machinery two meanings are attached: it substitutes for labor, and does the work formerly done by hand; it does heavy work of which human muscle is incapable. The substitution of machine-power for hand-work had its beginning at the middle of the eighteenth century.

The beginning of the great inventions is a date singled out for distinct emphasis in the history of human progress, but greater than these inventions was the change in the course of ideas which called them into existence. We must not confuse cause and effect: great inventions did not cause the Industrial Revolution, but it was the Revolution that caused the great inventions.

**12. The Long Delay.**—In our day long-distance conversation by wire, the cabling of news back and forth across the seas, the wireless telegraph, swiftly sailing steamers, skyscrapers and subways, great manufactories covering acres of ground and utilizing powerful machinery and employing thousands of men—these have become commonplace. This is a period of restless search for the novel and new. The captain of industry, even though a millionaire, sleeps upon a most restless pillow; he is thinking, concocting, scheming, and devising how to add to his wherewithal. Progress is contagious and comes to affect the whole people. It is with nations as with individuals, the more they progress the more restless they become.

From this progressive age we look back with amazement and wonder upon the non-progressive and poor yet contented peoples of the domestic system. How could mankind have dwelt upon the earth in a civilized state so long and yet have made such a very small advance in industrial methods? As H. C. Adams puts it: "Penelope, who worked at her loom while awaiting the return of Ulysses, would have found nothing very strange in the art of weaving, could she have made a visit to the home of a textile worker in the beginning of the reign of George III." Truly, the greatest wonder regarding the Industrial Revolution was its long delay.

13. **Changed Point of View.**—The significant change in ideas was simply this: The idea that machinery would substitute for muscular strain and multiply the output of industry did not appeal to the imagination of man before the Revolution; then an economic new birth came about because of the large European demand for English textiles. Hand-methods could not exploit the new opportunities; machinery must be had. England awoke; she offered prizes of £50 and £25 (large prizes for that time), respectively, for the first and next best improved method of spinning. The incentive was great and following it were the "Four Great Inventions" (Hargreaves's spinning-jenny, 1770; Arkwright's water-frame, 1781; Crompton's mule, 1779; Cartwright's power-loom, 1785). By the end of the first quarter of the last century the old idea had completely given way to the new. There was full appreciation of inventions and inventive genius was generously encouraged. The industrial greatness of to-day owes its being to this change in the idea regarding the use of machinery.

14. **Social Changes.**—One of the greatest effects of this sudden Industrial Revolution was the degeneration of the old skilled laborers and the employment of a new class— women and children. Manufacturers found that the new machines performed the work of skilled labor, and that in many cases a woman or a child could operate them effectively. Women and children were ruthlessly exploited, laboring fourteen and sixteen hours a day for a mere subsistence. Factories and factory towns sprang up quickly and were built with little regard for the health or morals of laborers.

Previous to the Industrial Revolution the country as a

whole was poor; yet the wealth was fairly well distributed, thus securing general comfort. The new forms of industry were highly productive, but they brought about extreme poverty in the midst of abundance. From 1760 to 1818 the population had increased 70 per cent, and the cost of poor relief had increased 530 per cent. The degeneration of labor, the alienation of classes, the increase of wealth and the multiplication of paupers were characteristic of this period.

Fierce competition in these new industries caused manufacturers to disregard the protection of morals, health, and even the lives of workers. The goal was high profits, and every effort on the part of public-spirited people for reform was met with opposition. The prevailing spirit of individual liberty which characterized that period made it very difficult to enact much-needed legislation to remedy the wretched conditions of workers. This new theory is so different from the Mercantile doctrine previously mentioned that a brief explanation of it is necessary.

**15. The Physiocrats.**—It will be recalled that in the seventeenth century the governments of Europe had imposed severe restrictive systems upon trade and other industrial activities. Such severity produced reaction, which was first expressed in France in the early eighteenth century by a school of economists known as the "Physiocrats." They believed in a system of "natural liberty," *i. e.*, that the right to work is the property of every man, and that he should be permitted to sell this property to the best possible advantage, with no regulation from his government except the necessary protection. The thought was that individuals are by nature endowed with different capacities, and that each can produce the greatest abundance if he follow the course for which his particular type of natural strength capacitates him. Moreover, nature furnishes him the inclination to follow his particular bent or talent. The Physiocrats urged, therefore, the removal of restriction in order that nature might take her course. Each will employ his talent most effectively and thereby produce most for himself. They concluded that because society is composed of individuals the system which is best for individuals must be best for all. When the production of each is greatest, the total for all must be largest.

16. **The Freedom of Trade and Agriculture.**—Naturally the Physiocrats were advocates of the freedom of trade. They fought against the restrictions upon imports and exports that had been placed by the Mercantilists.

They rendered another service to economic policy in discouraging the overemphasis placed upon gold and silver by the mercantilists. Agriculture was believed by them to be the only real productive industry, and they wished to foster it. To their way of thinking, the freedom of trade would make for the greatest encouragement to agriculture. Were trade free, different sections of country could be given up to those products for which nature had most highly capacitated them. While it is far from being true that agriculture is the only real productive occupation, yet this doctrine served an excellent purpose because it enabled statesmen to see that a mere accumulation of money is not the secret of national strength.

17. **Political Effects.**—Our chief interest in the Physiocrats, however, is in the political effects of their teachings. If governments followed their *laissez-faire* (let-us-alone) policy, there would be no regulations upon conditions of labor. Naturally the manufacturers wished to be left free

to reap all possible benefits from the new industrial conditions, so they championed ardently this theory. The publication of Adam Smith's Wealth of Nations in 1776 expressed for Englishmen a modified version of some of these physiocratic views. Public men became imbued with this theory of natural liberty. So closely was this doctrine of *laissez-faire* associated with the manufacturers of England that the policy is sometimes termed the "Manchester Doctrine," after the manufacturing city of that name. In keeping with these theories, the moral and physical conditions of mine and factory workers became intolerable. Public sympathy was aroused and Parliament after a deplorable delay was forced to pass laws, if only to protect human life. Then it was that "social legislation" began. Governments entered upon a new policy of regulation of industry for the interest of the public—a policy that has grown steadily since.

18. **Beginning of Social Legislation.**—The workingmen themselves were forced to combine for protection, and their trades-unions began to be felt as a political factor. As a result of the movement of the population from the country to the city, a reapportionment of the representatives in Parliament had taken place, and this new laboring class was given a voice in legislation. As they became stronger they forced new measures through, until to-day England has "Labor" members in the cabinet, laws regulating workingmen's compensation for accidents, compulsory insurance measures, old-age pensions, restrictions upon the work of women and children, and a whole mass of similar "social legislation."

19. **A Summary of Changes Which Affected Wage-Earners.**—Prior to the introduction of machinery, we have

seen that the hired man worked in the home of the employer. The simple and inexpensive tools were owned oftentimes by the laborer himself. There was no sharp distinction between capitalist and laborer. But the immediate result of large machinery was the distinct separation of one class from the other.

Much capital was required to install the new machinery, which was large and expensive. The ownership of the means of production became concentrated in the hands of capitalists. Separate buildings were required to house the machinery—thus distinct factories arose.

To operate these factories many laborers were required —thus arose congregated labor. Large machinery had the effect of a wedge driven into the side of industrial society. It separated capitalists from laborers, and this cleavage brought about two groups with unlike interests.

Losing the sympathy that comes from personal contact with hired men, employers bought labor as a mere ware. The friendly relations and mutual understanding between worker and employer came to an end. Stockholders intrusted the direction of their factories to a paid manager whose sole interest was to make a good showing in dividends for his employers. He forced the lowest wage that was possible, believing that every penny subtracted from wages was a penny added to dividends. Employers were few in number and could easily form an understanding to suppress competition on their side. This organized oppression of the capitalist class caused a reaction and the formation of unions among the laborers.

20. **The Formation of Labor-Unions.**—The separation of laborers from capitalists gave rise to misunderstandings,

and each class looked upon the other as an opportunity to be exploited. Laborers had a common purpose in opposing capitalists and a common interest in the betterment of their own conditions. This oneness of purpose and interest made the formation of labor-unions inevitable. The purpose of unions was to improve laborers, to improve their wages, and to improve their environment.

Wages they would improve either by getting more per day, or by getting the same for a shorter day. Wages are raised when the pay for an eight-hour day is increased from $2 to $3. So also are wages improved if the pay remains $2 per day, while the working hours are shortened from eight to six; the increase is from 25 to 33½ cents an hour.

So long as laborers were unorganized, however, there was little opportunity to improve wages. The individual laborer whose daily bread was from his daily labor could not bargain upon equal terms with the combined forces of capital. Collective bargaining means that labor is banded together in agreement to bargain for wages in a body. Throughout the history of labor-unions, collective bargaining has been the chief weapon to enforce their demands for a higher wage. The extent to which unions may increase wages will be a topic for special consideration later on.

An object of unions has been, and will continue to be, to improve the environment of labor. Sanitary conditions, pure drinking-water, proper light, heat, and ventilation, rest-rooms, etc., are topics which unions discuss, bring to public attention, and upon which they have enforced and will continue to enforce action. Unions, moreover, provide different forms of insurance and pensions for their members. The rise of labor-unions and their later development into trades-unions form one of the most far-reaching results of the Industrial Revolution.

**21. Exercises.**—1. What movement in England made it possible for Queen Elizabeth to grant monopolies which were national in scope? How did the method of obtaining a monopoly in her time differ from the obtaining of one to-day?

2. What was the domestic system?

3. Was labor unionized during the domestic system? Give the reason for your answer.

4. Why do the accounts of the beginning of the industrial Revolution make so much mention of the textiles?

5. J. D. Forrest says: "The industrial revolution was not the result of the great mechanical inventions: rather the inventions were the result of the revolution." C. J. Bullock says: "Between 1760 and 1840 English industries were revolutionized. The cause of this was a remarkable series of inventions which affected the cotton and woollen industries first." With which of these statements is the present chapter in accord? Write a brief argument to substantiate one of these statements and to disprove the other.

6. What was the central idea in the teaching of the Physiocrats?

7. Define *laissez-faire*. What effect did the application of this doctrine have upon the conditions of the laboring population in England?

8. Is the tendency toward a greater or less application of the *laissez-faire* doctrine? In answer to this question make mention of important laws which have been enacted regarding the tariff, pure food and drugs, the working conditions of women and children, railroad rates, and safety-appliance for machinery.

9. What conditions brought about the formation of labor-unions?

10. Summarize the chief objects which unions would accomplish.

11. *Criticisms of Mercantilism.*—These criticisms were offered by writers contemporary with the Mercantilists. It will be a helpful exercise if the student will give arguments in defense of, or against them.

(*a*) If raw materials are wanting, the factory must stop; if food is wanting the people must starve; if gold is wanting, there may be substituted barter or credit or paper money, therefore money is secondary in importance.

(*b*) Money runs after goods, but goods do not always run after money. Goods serve many purposes besides buying money, but money serves no other purpose than to buy goods. Other things may do the work of money, but money does not do the work of other things. Therefore, money is not real wealth.

(*c*) We exchange durable iron for wine in France. Why not keep iron and thus multiply durable pots and pans? Because we would soon have more than is needed. This, it is evident, would be wasteful. (This is intended to show that it is absurd for a nation to accumulate more gold than necessary simply because it is durable.)

(*d*) Foreign armies may be maintained by sending manufactured goods or raw materials, as well as by sending money, so money is not necessary for foreign wars.

(*e*) The benefit of foreign trade consists, not in a money balance, but in trading surplus products for needed goods.

(*f*) Every seller must be a purchaser and every purchaser a seller, therefore England must accept goods in exchange if she continues to trade.

(*g*) When two parties trade, one does not necessarily get cheated. Exchange profits both parties: the interest is one of man with man, of state with state in the same realm, of nation with nation.

(*h*) To nature and not to man belongs the police of the economic order; therefore all restrictions on trade should be removed.

(*i*) The nation which places a tariff against foreign Powers will be retaliated against by those Powers.

(*j*) A merchant may grow rich by accumulating money

because he can exchange his money for the products of others; the case is different with a nation, for in the long run a nation must depend upon itself for its necessities of life.

(*k*) A nation cannot accumulate money at the expense of others, because prices increase in the nation with a large amount of money and decrease in the countries where money is scarce. This causes a flow of money away from the country which has a large store of gold, thus equalizing the money supply as between nations.

# CHAPTER IV

## THE PRESENT ECONOMIC ORDER

**1. Introduction.**—The preceding chapters offer a brief survey of essential movements preceding the present economic order. The purpose of this chapter is to review some of the characteristic institutions under which economic laws are now operating.

· In a narrow sense economics is the science of which business is the art. Business as here used signifies any occupation, employment, or investment for the sake of income. A science teaches us to know, an art to do; a science logically precedes the creation of a corresponding useful art. The science of anatomy precedes the art of surgery; the science of astronomy precedes the art of navigation; the science of economics precedes the art of business. Economic science is the only true guide of industrial procedure; it contains the premises of reasoning on business affairs.

**2. Economic laws** are statements of the order or relationship of business phenomena. They affirm that if certain causes exist, certain effects follow. The true order or causal relationship of things exists long before it is ascertained. Newton did not make the fact of gravitation; he found it, and his formulation of this fact is a law. Little more than a century ago the economists stumbled upon the law of diminishing returns. From earliest times the forces which limit production had been in operation, had scattered people over the earth, and had limited their supplies for the necessities of life, but only in recent times have these forces been formulated into a law. As the nugget is not converted into gold because we find it, so an economic relationship is not transformed into a law because we discover it; we are not permitted to speak of a statement as a law until patient testing proves it worthy of that title. This science is constantly being enlarged through the discovery of relationships and the formulation of new laws and by increasing our knowledge of their scope.

An economic law states that certain causes produce certain effects only under certain conditions. Reasoning goes astray when counteracting influences are not considered along with positive influences. The law of gravitation does not teach that a stone does fall toward the centre of the earth; it teaches that a stone would so fall were counteracting influences removed. It is a law of population that the number of people tend to increase more rapidly than does the supply of food. The authors of a century ago were extremely pessimistic because, in their judgment, starvation, disease, and death were the dismal results deduced from this law. The error in their reasoning is that they too lightly regarded the counteracting forces or checks to population.

Economic laws are either of coexistence or of sequence.

It is a law of coexistence that like goods in the same market at the same time sell at the same price.   It is a law of sequence that by adding unit after unit to a supply of like goods in a market, the price, other things equal, is lowered.

3. **Theory.**—It is a commonplace though erroneous remark that something is well enough in theory, but that it will not work in practice.   It is an error to contrast theory and practice as the impractical versus the practical.   A theory is a provisional or tentative formulation of a law.   That which is true in theory must be true in practice.   It takes investigation and sound reasoning to formulate a true theory because it must fit the facts.   Theory and science cannot be divorced, for theory explains phenomena.   Theory and practice hold the relationship of explanation and execution.

4. **The present economic order** embraces the conditions under which economic laws are formulated.   Significant institutions of this order now to be discussed are: Private property, division of labor, exchange, competition, economic classes, and contracts.

5. **Private property** is the fundamental institution in the present economic order.   It has been defended upon the following bases:

(*a*) Private property has been justified on the ground of occupancy.   It would be accurate to speak of occupancy as the cause, in many cases, of private property. But occupancy can never with accuracy be given as a justification of the institution.

(*b*) Private property has been justified by the so-called natural-rights theory.   It is argued that property is necessary for the full self-realization of the individual.   But, in fact, is this not a condemnation of private property? The institution of private property leaves the many all but propertyless, whereas common ownership would distribute among all the means of self-development. Again, what things redound to our fullest self-realization? Our answer to this is not the same as it was a century ago; ideas continually change as to what is right. Socrates defended slavery on the basis of natural rights. We cannot justify private property as a natural right or as a means to the end of the most complete self-realization until we know precisely what such means are.

(*c*) Private property has been justified by the labor theory, namely that what a person creates by his muscle or brain is his. A person has a right to himself, hence the right to the use of his body and mind to acquire the means of self-preservation. This implies the right to own and enjoy the products of his labor. But this does not justify the private ownership of land and other resources which are not the products of labor. It cannot, therefore, be given as a justification or basis for the institution of private property. It is upon this ground largely that the great single-tax advocate, Henry George, denied the right of private property in land.

(*d*) Private property has been justified by the *legal theory*. This, however, is a truism and not a theory. Whatever the law recognizes as private property is such. The law simply states that this or that may be privately owned and there the matter ends.

**6. Social Expediency.**—The theories above mentioned fail to justify private property. The acquisition of private property in early times was by methods which would not meet with public sanction in our day. The standards of business ethics and the problems of ancient times differed from those we now know. Private property to-day rests upon the one ground of social expediency. If it works best, if it insures the greatest good to the greatest number, it is justified. It is a human institution which is always undergoing modification and change. Under it some suffer misery while others enjoy the comforts of the idle rich. Its workings are imperfect, as are those of all human institutions. Despite inequalities, however, it seems to stand the test of the greatest good. Another example from the industrial history of England will illuminate this point.

7. **The Revival of Enclosures.**—During the years from 1760 to 1819 as many as 6,331,800 acres of land were enclosed in England. England had formerly secured large supplies of raw materials from Europe, but during the Napoleonic Wars this market was cut off, so she had to depend upon her own soil. This change was burdensome because the tillable soil was limited and there was a dense population. In the preceding chapter we mentioned a large export demand for English products; add to this a large home demand and it is at once evident that prices for the products of the land must rise. The high prices of products caused a rise in the price of land and its rent. High land prices in turn excited a wish on the part of individuals to enclose and possess land. The government looked with favor upon the move, because the cultivation of the commons had been both wasteful and crude. It was thought that the incentive of private property would largely augment production, and that under private ownership capital would be invested in agriculture and land would be improved.

One keeps no grudging account of capital and exertion which he spends upon his own soil. He is early in the field; for each extra seed planted and every additional waste avoided means more wealth which he and his family may enjoy. One comes to personify and to love his own land, shrubs, trees, and cattle. Arthur Young, a writer on agricultural topics, now over a century ago, said: "Give a man secure possession of a bleak rock and he will convert it into a garden." To this statement the great American economist F. A. Walker added: "The vineyards of the Rhine, built up in many cases of earth brought in baskets up the sides of the mountains, are speaking witnesses to the truth of this statement; while many of the richest fields of Holland and Belgium, once drifting wastes, illustrate the other saying of the eminent traveller: 'The magic of property turns sand into gold.'" Private property, so far as we know, is the greatest incentive to thrift.

No spirited activity had attended labor on the commons; on the contrary, sloth and indolence, land-butchery and small crops were always apparent. None the less, enclosures were unpopular with the poor, who would pasture their stock and husband a meagre subsistence upon the commons. A popular piece of doggerel declared that:

> "The law locks up the man or woman
> Who steals the goose from off the common;
> But leaves the greater villain loose
> Who steals the common from the goose."

It is the testimony of Jeremiah Bentham (1748–1832), an eminent thinker and writer of that time, that, after the enclosures, "in passing through the lands which have undergone that happy change, we are enchanted as by the sight of a new colony. Harvests, flocks, smiling habitations, have succeeded to the dull sterility of a desert. Happy conquests of peaceful industry." The evidence which one gains from the literature of that time goes to show that, in spite of the apparent hardships worked by converting public lands into private property, the greater social good was served because the land was made more productive. It was upon the ground of social expediency that enclosures were defended, and it is upon that ground that we justify private property to-day.

The extent and limitations of private property will be considered in a later chapter. Enough has been said to indicate that this institution has been of slow growth, that it is subject to change with varying social needs, and that it is the foundation-stone of the present economic order.

**8. Transportation.**—The economic order of to-day is new to the world. A chief factor in determining the industrial life of our time is that of transportation facilities.

Picture a family in a self-sufficing community. It must practise a slow, wasteful, and chaotic means of getting a living. Poverty, indigence, and ignorance invariably attend such conditions. The cause of self-sufficiency is a want of transportation facilities or of means of contact with the outside world.

Given transportation, however, the products of different communities may be exchanged for one another. Transportation makes this exchange possible. When it becomes easy for localities to trade with one another, it becomes wise for the different communities to turn their productive effort to the output of goods for which they have comparative advantages in production. If nature favors community A for the growing of tobacco, and B for the manufacturing of shoes, and C for the growing of oysters, it will follow that each locality can outcompete all the others in a certain line, and those industries will localize with respect to the maximum gain.

This localization of industries in turn leads to concentration of capital. Capital in the different industries will tend to combine and to concentrate at the point of maximum advantage.

9. **The industrial development** of this country has followed the course indicated in the preceding paragraph. Prior to the Civil War transportation was inefficient; factories were small local concerns, being suited to the communities where they existed. At the middle of the century 87.5 per cent of the population was rural. The average farm family lived a life of self-sufficiency. The farmer produced his own fuel, grain, meat, leather, vegetables, milk, butter, poultry, wool, flax, and cotton. In the home were rather crude means of converting many of these raw materials into finished products.

There was a limited amount of trading, of course, but the nature of the commodities produced for trade differed with respect to the distance from the market. In western Pennsylvania grain was converted into spirits, and other communities distant from the market produced light goods of little bulk and large value. Many farmers, especially west of the Alleghanies, turned to raising swine, cattle, and horses, which could be driven to the market.

But the war taught the lesson of doing things on a large scale. By the end of the century we had the enormous total of 194,262 miles of railway. Add to this network of railways the means of instantaneous connection by wire and an excellent postal system, and we have the chief explanation of the localization and concentration of industries.

10. **The growth of cities** has been in keeping with these industrial changes. Large-scale production implies the use of large mechanical equipment. Machine production is more effective in manufacturing than in agriculture. This fact gives the urban centres the advantage over rural communities. Other reasons attract manufacturers to the large centres of population. A large factory finds it necessary to be in the midst of a large and varied supply of labor. The advantages of marketing and of transportation facilities are found in the city. An item of no little significance is that of proximity to other manufacturers. Factories depend on each other for special parts and assistance in many ways. Nearness to professional men who can provide medical aid, or give legal advice, or render expert opinions on divers questions, is very necessary.

11. **An example from statistics** will make clear the tendency toward concentration. The statistics of the manufacturing of agricultural implements is given in the following table. These will be found characteristic of most

## AGRICULTURAL IMPLEMENTS

| Year | Product (in millions) | Capital (in millions) | Wage-earners | No. of establishments |
|------|------|------|------|------|
| 1850 | $6.8 | $3.6 | 7,220 | 1,333 |
| 1860 | 20.8 | 13.9 | 17,093 | 2,116 |
| 1870 | 52.1 | 34.8 | 25,249 | 2,076 |
| 1880 | 68.6 | 62.1 | 39,580 | 1,943 |
| 1890 | 81.3 | 145.3 | 38,827 | 910 |
| 1900 | 101.2 | 157.7 | 46,582 | 715 |
| 1905 | 112.0 | 196.7 | 47,394 | 648 |

lines of industry. These figures show that in manufacturing capital increases more rapidly than labor. While capital was increasing from $3,600,000 to $196,700,000, the increase in the number of laborers was from 7,220 to 47,394. It is especially noteworthy that while the product increased from $6,800,000 to the enormous sum of $112,000,000 there was a decrease in the number of plants from 1,333 to 648.

This tendency may be shown with respect to the tendency of labor to congregate. The following table shows what percentage of the total persons employed in Germany at certain dates were engaged in manufacturing establishments of different size.

| | 1882 | 1895 | 1907 |
|---|---|---|---|
| Per cent of persons doing work alone.......... | 25.2 | 16.4 | 10.1 |
| Per cent of persons in establishments employing 2 to 5 persons........................... | 29.9 | 23.5 | 19.4 |
| Per cent of persons in establishments employing 6 to 10 persons........................... | 6.0 | 7.2 | 6.6 |
| Per cent of persons in establishments employing 11 to 50 persons........................... | 12.6 | 16.6 | 18.4 |
| Per cent of persons in establishments employing 51 to 200 persons........................... | 11.9 | 17.0 | 20.1 |
| Per cent of persons in establishments employing 201 to 1,000 persons........................... | 10.9 | 13.9 | 17.3 |
| Per cent of persons in establishments employing over 1,000 persons........................... | 3.5 | 5.4 | 8.1 |

(Table taken from Taussig's Principles of Economics, vol. I, p. 52.)

The reasons for the rapid growth of large-scale production will be considered in a later chapter. Enough has been said to show that in the present economic order the vast size and complexity of modern industrial establishments present a striking contrast to conditions of a century ago, and especially to conditions prior to the Industrial Revolution.

12. **The geographic division of labor** refers to the localization of industries, according to the principle of maximum returns. With transportation facilities and markets well developed, an industry tends to localize: (1) Where there is a supply of skilled labor in that particular industry, or in some cases where labor is cheap. Certain industries make extensive use of woman and child labor, while others, as the steel industry, use only the labor of men. In a city where steel is the important industry the slight demand for the services of women and children causes such labor to be cheap. This situation is, other things equal, an attractive centre for a cotton-mill. (2) Where soil and climate are most suitable for the products of the industry, *e. g.*, we find orange-growing in Florida, apple-growing in Washington, and tobacco-raising in Kentucky. (3) Where fuel, raw materials or water-power necessary for the industry are at hand or easily obtainable. (4) Where large markets for the output are of easy access.

One will rarely find a single district embodying all of these advantages. Not infrequently localized industries exist apart from any of these advantages. The reason for this is that industries requiring large fixed capital are difficult to move with changing conditions. They start under favorable conditions and become firmly rooted, their place of business becomes known, their good-will and business prestige are associated with their place of being. Such reasons account for the persistence of extensive metal works in New England, despite the fact that iron ore is no longer smelted there.

An enterpriser is at liberty to invest where the returns are most promising, and quite naturally he will invest his energy and capital where nature promises most co-operation. Each enterpriser acts on the principle of maximum returns for his own efforts. This, however, does not mean the maximum returns per acre or per machine. Suppose it takes the same labor and capital to cultivate five acres of tobacco at a net profit of $500 per acre as it would to cultivate forty acres of potatoes at a net profit of $100 per acre, one will plant potatoes. The geographic division of labor follows the principle of greatest net-profit return.

We have thus far studied a division of labor with respect to the different localities where industries are located. We may now turn to a study of the division of labor in the same locality and within the same plant.

**13. The Division of Labor and Mutual Dependence in the Factory System.**—The handicraft stage of production was essentially individualistic, whereas the factory system is characterized by large capital and congregated labor. The tendency of large capital is to specialize. Not many years ago the same shop produced many and varied lines of goods. More recently competition has forced the shop to concentrate on fewer lines of goods. Representative shops have now abandoned the practice of making even their own small tools and appliances. They buy such supplies cheaper than they can manufacture them. In manufacturing the matter is reduced to this: a factory which concentrates on a few products can reduce the cost per unit of its output to a minimum. It can undersell its less specialized competitor. The consequence is that factories are no longer independent; they are mutually dependent. They are dependent upon each other for their own tools and appliances as they are upon the extractive industries for raw materials.

The force of competition has so narrowed the productive process along certain lines that little flexibility is left. Each tool and machine is designed to fit its specific function, and no other. The worker has his task narrowed and limited by the same conditions. The jack of all trades finds no place in the modern factory system. As man develops, his desires call for a greater variety and a superior quality of goods, but in the field of production he tends from a varied to a concentrated production. A report of the United States Bureau of Labor states that there are eighty-four distinct processes in the manufacture of a common pair of brogan shoes. One hundred pairs of these are now turned out in ninety-eight minutes, whereas to sew them by hand would take ninety-eight hours. Moreover, a workman may be skilled in one of these processes and ignorant of the other eighty-three.

It is a complex division of labor when a process of production is thus subdivided into many parts. A simple division of labor is found when a workman carries through the whole of one of the stages of production. There was no division of labor in the self-sufficing community where the same laborer would raise cattle, tan the hides, and convert the leather into shoes for his family. It came to be a simple division of labor when one raised cattle, another tanned hides and yet another made shoes. And it developed into a complex division of labor when each of these stages of production was subdivided into fractional parts.

14. **Differentiation.**—Development takes the form of differentiation in social life as well as in animal life. Through a process of evolution animals acquire more and more specific organs for the performance of specific functions. Instead of one organ to serve for the functions of heart, lungs, stomach, etc., mutually dependent organs are

gradually developed. Similarly, in social life and in industries there is a gradual development of mutually dependent agencies to perform various functions. At one time the same person would convert the raw material into cloth, finance his own efforts, bear his own risk, pack and carry his products from place to place in search of a buyer. This work has been differentiated into manufacturing, banking, insurance, commission men, transportation, and merchandising.

15. **Trading** or exchanging arises out of differentiation. It is most obvious that when men are differentiated and specialized with respect to specific lines of employment they must be mutually dependent. If one gives his entire time and attention to the production of matches he will soon have a surplus of matches and a want for other things. Every form of specialization results in the production of a surplus. Each producer depends upon the surplus of others. Without the hatter the farmer would go bareheaded, and without the farmer the hatter would starve. Specialization and mutual dependence necessitate trade and the surpluses are the things exchanged for each other. Exchange is the grand medium through which proportion and balance are maintained among the various parts of the present economic order.

16. **Competition** is an institution in which men selfishly and independently contest for the uses of wealth. Men compete to outdo each other in the market. One merchant would take trade from another, one railroad strives to excel its competitor, and so on throughout all the lines of business. There are different kinds of competition: jockeys compete for the blue ribbon, wooers compete for the prettiest girl, politicians for office, and actresses for

notoriety. But economic competition is a contest for the uses of wealth. There is no competition for free goods. Were all goods as abundant as air, competition would not exist. Competition is for the ownership of scarce things. Thus competition is tied up with the idea of scarcity and private property.

We have seen that scarcity does not refer to the amount of goods but to the strength of the desire for goods. There may be an abundance of corn, yet if there are many consumers and the desires intense, we may say that corn is scarce. On the other hand, there may be few bumble-bees and no one would speak of them as scarce. If resources are limited they may increase in scarcity and the competition for them grow keen. Such is the case with a growing density of population. When numbers multiply with respect to resources competition sets in for the control of food and the services rendered by these resources.

Also competition may grow, irrespective of the increase of population, because of increasing desires for goods. Desires increase as they are fed, thus extending the reach of social ambition. To give one a million seems to whet his appetite for more rather than to satisfy him. The increase of population reinforced by the growth of desires causes competition to become constantly keener. The two causes mentioned—growing numbers and desires relative to resources—are primary though not the only motives that inspire economic competition.

17. **The Extent of Competition.**—Competition is found in every stage of production, from the raw material to the finished product in the hands of the consumer. "The manufacturer of cotton goods chooses between competing places for his factory; the makers of his machinery are

vying with each other to produce most economically the engines, looms, etc., that are best adapted to his work; raw products he buys from sellers competing in the open market; labor he hires from among men who bid against each other for his work; transportation companies compete with one another in cheaply transferring his goods to market; and in the market, seller is struggling with seller for the privilege of a sale with profit; buyer and seller bargain together, to agree on a price. The present century has seen barrier after barrier swept away, till the whole world enters more or less freely into the one struggle; family and social distinctions are being obliterated in the industrial world; customs and laws in restraint of trade have been set aside."[1]

18. **Self-interest**, in a narrow sense, would seek private gain at the expense of others. The farmer may wish for the grubworm and boll-weevil to take the cotton crop, sparing his own, in order that prices for his product might be high. The doctor of medicine may wish for his neighbors to be sick and for his competitors to fail in order that his practice may be increased. But if the neighbors are sick their production is cut short and little is left with which to pay the doctor. Or if his competitors fail others will spring up to take their places. Despite these counteracting arguments it often happens that one is interested, and with good reason, in the failure of other producers within his own particular field of employment.

There is no exception to the principle that it is to one's self-interest that his neighbors in other fields of employment succeed. The carpenter reasons that if his neighbor is favored with a large crop, grain will be abundant and cheap. His wages will go further when the production of

[1] Fairbanks's Introduction to Sociology, New York, 1905, p. 270.

food, clothing, and necessities are so abundant as to cause low prices. The real fact of exchange is obscured by the use of money. Money is but a medium of exchange; the real exchange consists of a transfer of goods or services for other goods or services. We produce for the market and largely buy what we consume from the market. Every commodity produced is a demand for another commodity. It is to one's self-interest to have large purchasing power. Large purchasing power consists both in large production for one's self, thereby augmenting one's command over the products of others, and in a large production on the part of others in order that the market prices which he pays will be low.

10. **Economic Classes.**—In a highly organized competitive society there are different classes to perform the different economic functions of such a society. We ordinarily distinguish three classes: laborers, capitalists, and *entrepreneurs*. In a simpler state of society where man provided his own food, wore clothes woven and made at home, built his own home and fashioned the tools he used, the means of production were simple and owned, for the most part, by the laborer. This condition prevailed prior to the Industrial Revolution, and there was no sharp distinction as between laborers and capitalists. But with the introduction of large machinery too expensive to be owned by workmen, separate classes arose. The one bought machines, constructed plants, and financed concerns, while the other worked for a wage. Again, we find those who own wealth who are in no position to use it themselves. A child may inherit a fortune, a widow may acquire her husband's estate, or a wealthy business man may retire from active service—such are capitalists in the true sense of

the word. Now, if the owner of wealth (the capitalist) be incapacitated to employ his means, and if the laborer, as such, be empty-handed, what becomes of production? Labor alone or wealth alone can produce nothing. A third party, the *entrepreneur*, is necessary. And who is the *entrepreneur*? He is the man who places labor and wealth in productive combination. The function of the *entrepreneur* is to plan a business, to borrow the wealth, hire the labor, and co-ordinate these into a going concern. The *entrepreneur* undergoes the responsibility, bears the risk, and suffers the loss or takes the net gain, as the case may be.

These three functions—performed by labor, capital, enterprise—are distinct, although the same man may perform two or all three of them. The same man may at the same time hold the offices of trustee of a school, county sheriff, and presidency of his secret order. These functions are different, although cared for by the same man. Labor, capital, and enterprise hold distinct functions and people are roughly classified with respect to them. The next institution within the present economic order to be discussed is the contract.

20. **Contracts.**—To-day business is complex and world-wide in its scope. Our producers are constructing large plants, investing enormous sums of wealth, employing large forces of labor, and making agreements months or even years ahead for the fulfilling of future contracts and for supplies of raw materials. They are producing for distant as well as for domestic markets. Our importers are contracting with oriental countries long in advance for the future delivery of laces, silks, and tapestries. Railroads are contracting ahead with the steel corporation for the

future delivery of rails, which as yet are not in existence. Industries are forced to depend upon each other. This is an age of credit. The larger portion of business is done on a credit basis. Credit is an implied or an expressed contract to pay in the future. Were men not free to make contracts or could these contracts be broken with impunity, our industrial structure could not exist for a fortnight.

21. **The Automatic Regulation of Industry.**—The primary characteristic of our economic order is the interdependence of men in society. We are, in reality, organized on the basis of co-operation. There is a grand adjustment of man to man, of industry to industry, which is maintained automatically by means of exchanging in the market. The complex of industries (mining, farming, manufacturing, transportation, etc.) are adjusted to each other, as are the tiny parts of delicate machinery, and this adjustment is maintained by a price régime. If too many mine coal and too few work in the textile trade, coal will be abundant and cheap, textiles scarce and dear. Labor and wealth will receive small returns in the one and large returns in the other. A shift of productive energy will slowly take place from the less to the more remunerative employment. The result of this shift will be that less coal is mined, its price will be higher, and the returns to labor and capital increased. The reverse of these movements will be felt in the textile trade. And the result of these movements will be an equilibrium. The self-interest of each and all to secure the largest ·returns so operates, through exchanges on the market, as to tend always to maintain an equilibrium in the present competitive order. The truth of this statement is evidenced throughout the

whole field of industry. It is the language of ignorance which says that we are living in a chaotic and unregulated economic order.

**22. Exercises.—1.** Does an economic law state a command or does it state merely an observed relation? Can it state both of these? Are economic laws subject to exceptions. Is it correct to say that "the numerous exceptions to the law of wages make it impossible to predict the outcome"? Can we "violate" a law of chemistry or an economic law?

2. Can one properly use the words **theory** and **law** interchangeably? One frequently encounters these expressions, "the theory of wages" and "the law of wages." Do they have the same meaning?

3. Define private property. Are all of the following examples of private property: one's hat, the Lincoln Highway, the Chesapeake and Ohio Railroad, a jitney bus? Name four things which may be either public or private property.

4. What is the connection between paragraphs 6 and 7 in this chapter?

5. State the causal sequence existing between the following: industrial development, growth of cities, extension of transportation, trade between localities, the geographic division of labor.

6. Could there be large-scale production without extensive transportation?

7. What is a technical division of labor? and what conditions make it possible?

8. "All other organs, therefore, jointly and individually, compete for blood with each organ, so that, though the welfare of each is indirectly bound up with that of the rest, yet, directly, each is antagonistic to the rest." "Evidently this process (of enlargement of an industry or development of a district whose products are in unusual demand) in each social organ, as in each individual organ, results

from the tendency of the units to absorb all they can from the common stock of materials for sustentation; and evidently the resulting competition, not between units simply, but between organs, causes in a society, as in a living body, high nutrition and growth of parts called into greatest activity by the requirements of the rest."

Explain the doctrine of the first sentence and show how it applies to society. What light is here thrown on competition as a mode of growth, and on the general laws of life of which competition is one phase? (Quotation taken from Spencer's Principles of Sociology, by Sumner.)

9. What is the relationship between the "doctrine of self-interest" and competition?

10. Briefly summarize the chief institutions in the present economic order.

# CHAPTER V

## THE SUBJECT–MATTER OF ECONOMICS

1. **The Subject-Matter of Economics.**—The problems which concern the economist have their origin in man's struggle for the necessities, comforts, and conveniences of life. To gratify these desires is the motive of all the economic activities of man. Whether in the sweat-shop or in the counting-house, human endeavor is guided by the one motive of gratifying desires. Necessities and conveniences, such as food, clothing, and luxuries which directly gratify desires, are termed current supplies. Life depends on current supplies, yet, without a constant source of replenishment, the present amount of these would be exhausted within a few months. This constant source of replenishment—which we shall term productive capacity is the basis of the science of economics. Its paramount significance demands for it thorough comprehension.

Productive capacity is conditioned by natural resources, and the industrial arts, together with the enterprise and knowledge which utilize them. Productive capacity, resulting, as it does, from the co-operation of man with nature, is the source from which necessities, comforts, and conveniences flow to gratify desires. In our study of productive capacity we must realize that any one factor by itself is meagrely productive. Brick and mortar cannot build a wall, nor can the plough turn a furrow without the co-operation of labor. Productive capacity necessitates a combination of agents, and the better the apportionment of these agents, the more effective is the combination. The functioning of this productive capacity and the distribution of its yield among consumers constitute the subject-matter of economics.

2. **Productive Capacity and Current Supplies.**—The distinction between productive capacity and current supplies is frequently exemplified in cases of recovery after loss. The commonest cases of loss or destruction are in connection with current supplies. Our productive capacity in the form of climate, lands, harbors, and the fund of knowledge accumulated and passed on to us from former generations, is little impaired by the devastating effects of fires, floods, earthquakes, and wars. These agencies of destruction, however, may play havoc with such current supplies as ships, homes, live stock, and crops, but full restoration is soon accomplished. Soon after the earthquake and fire San Francisco had advanced to a state of unprecedented excellence. After the Chicago and Baltimore fires the cities were not only quickly rebuilt but were noticeably improved. Narrow, crooked streets and dilapidated buildings were supplanted by broad pavements and permanent structures of brick and stone. Such experiences give us the expression, "It takes a fire to make a city." Floods

may devastate the valleys of the Ohio and the Mississippi, but after a brief interval the damages are fully repaired. The direct losses of our Civil War were beyond comprehension, yet within a few years we were more prosperous than ever. Merely temporary impoverishment is occasioned by the destruction of current supplies, if only the source of such supplies remains intact. When there is no dread of recurring calamity to paralyze incentive, and when natural resources, together with knowledge and scientific equipment, remain undiminished, there is a rapid reproduction of current supplies. They differ from productive capacity as the apple differs from the tree, or the crop from the farm. The latter is the source; the former is the usufruct.

3. **Destruction Often a Real Gain.**—An enemy may lay waste a country by fire and sword; he may carry off movable wealth, trample crops, burn factories and homes, yet there is no essential difference between these wastes and the wastes in time of peace. It is no more wasteful to burn a bridge, than not to utilize the agencies to build it.

These periods of destruction, moreover, often teach valuable lessons of construction. The Civil War taught us to concentrate the efforts of a multitude of men. Under tremendous necessity we were forced to produce munitions, food, and naval supplies on an unprecedented scale. In peaceful times the hampering effect of customs, class spirit, and industrial evils tends to deepen rather than to vanish. The breakdown of these is a wholesome effect of war. The weakening of special privilege and the liberation of new ideas prepare the way for a new dynamic progress. For instance, our Civil War gave impulse to the invention and use of labor-saving machinery. "From 4,363 patents in

1860—the high-water mark up to that time—the number rapidly grew to 8,874 in 1866. In 1869 the number of patents issued reached 12,957."

That which appears most destructive often embodies the elements of greatest progression. The lessons of war are the lessons of enforced saving, of austere living, of large organization and operation, of large production where greatest efficiency is enforced by military and financial necessity. When applied to the industries of peace these lessons had the effect of an economic new birth. In the South a new growth took place after the war that would have been impossible in a land of slaves, poor whites, and contented plantation-owners. Thus it is seen that productive capacity may be increased fully as well by the more effective utilization of old forces as by the harnessing of new.

4. **The dissemination of education** increases productive capacity. Ignorant tribes perish where natural resources are richest. There is evidence that Indian tribes wasted away in the fertile valleys of the Missouri and Mississippi Rivers. The gains of civilization are measured not by things produced but by the knowledge of how to produce them. As our fund of knowledge increases, our control over nature becomes more effective. Through education, this knowledge and the means of applying it become common property. The productive capacity of the country is increased by the dissemination of knowledge precisely as though the soil were made more fertile or the mines richer. Science, invention, education, industrial organization, development in transportation, new banking facilities, steadily enlarge this productive capacity. In this process of enlargement our industrial equipment may be scrapped, to

be replaced by the newer and more efficient; but productive capacity is increased.

5. **Social wealth** includes productive capacity and current supplies. It is the direct and indirect means of gratifying our desires for the necessities, comforts, and luxuries of life. We cannot define social wealth by an enumeration. We no more define social wealth by enumerating the things which compose it than we define the word house by making a tabulation of brick, stone, nails, and cement. We may say, in truth, that wealth embodies usable natural resources, such as land, harbors, and minerals; the knowledge of science and organization; facilitating agencies, as money and technological equipment, and all consumable goods. But we cannot get a full concept of wealth by enumerating the things which combine to make wealth. A battalion is stronger in battle as a unit than as many men acting as individuals, and a battalion under a good commander is more effective than one under a poor commander. A thousand men in a well-ordered factory, where there is a minute division of labor, are far more productive than the same thousand men acting as individual units. There is no greater element in productive capacity than the power of organization. You cannot determine the productive capacity of a factory by an enumeration of engines, tools, buildings, land, raw materials, and the like. The physical equipment of two railroads may be precisely the same—in rails, ties, rolling-stocks, stations, etc., yet they may have vastly different capacities. This might be due to unlikeness in management, or to unlike situations with respect to other industries which railroads serve. There is no definite measure of social wealth. And there is no practical need of such measure. President Hadley is suf-

ficiently correct: "The nation's wealth is to be found in the enjoyments of its members."

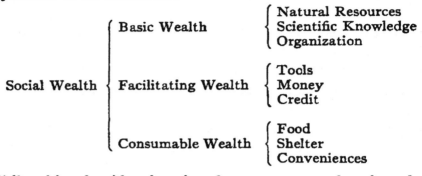

Social Wealth

Basic Wealth
 Natural Resources
 Scientific Knowledge
 Organization

Facilitating Wealth
 Tools
 Money
 Credit

Consumable Wealth
 Food
 Shelter
 Conveniences

While this classification involves some overlapping, it serves to make clear the concept of social wealth.

6. **Many writers of a century ago** limited wealth almost wholly to capacity. Lord Lauderdale (an English economist of the last century) furnished us with the noteworthy example of a privately owned supply of water. Water was so scarce and so valuable that a good well was a private fortune. Improvements were made which furnished such a supply of good water as to make the privately owned well valueless. There the creation of social wealth was the destruction of private wealth. The American economists—Daniel Raymond, A. H. Everett, Willard Phillips and less noteworthy writers of a century ago —defined wealth as "national capacity." They would not limit wealth to objects of private property which are bought, sold, and exchanged. They taught that national productive capacity (wealth) must include the free as well as the slave, a salubrious atmosphere, and a navigable river without tolls as well as a canal with tolls. They agreed with the English economists, Lord Lauderdale and David Ricardo, who reasoned that if water should become scarce and high-priced, the individual owners of it would

be richer, but society as a whole would be poorer. They would have argued that a deeper channel for the Mississippi River would be as truly an object of wealth as is an artificial levee costing many millions of dollars. They would have argued that had Providence constructed a broad-flowing and navigable river from Colon to Panama it would have been an object of wealth as truly as is a man-made canal costing upwards of three hundred and fifty millions.

Economic writings fall largely into two groups: One emphasizes social wealth in the broad sense of productive capacity; the other emphasizes wealth in the restricted sense of things owned. The early American economists emphasized the former, while the majority of recent American economists emphasize the latter. The present work recognizes the twofold aspect of wealth. Neither aspect must be overlooked, nor must they be confused.

7. **Wealth Not a Comparative Concept.**—Another misconception to be avoided is to consider wealth as a comparative term. The word *wealth* is derived from the word *weal* (from the same root as *well*), which means a prosperous state of being. Later usage caused wealth to be applied to the things which produce a prosperous state. In this sense it was used comparatively to indicate "that abundance of worldly estate which exceeds the estate of the greater part of the community." We now use the adjective *rich* in this sense. It is proper to use the word *rich* in a comparative sense; it is proper to say that the rich man has more wealth than others or that he has more purchasing power than others. The word *rich* may refer either to the possession of wealth or to the possession of value. Wealth must not be used in this comparative sense. The meagre equipment of the cobbler and the plant of the

Bethlehem Steel Company are alike wealth. It would be a gross error to say that a thing is not wealth because it does "not make any one rich in this comparative sense." Public highways, parks, schools, and a salubrious climate benefit all alike, but they are nevertheless wealth.

**8. Private Wealth and Public Wealth.**—For many purposes we sacrifice strict accuracy and speak of wealth in the terms of the things composing it. The practice of buying and selling makes it necessary to think of wealth in terms of specific things and units. Common usage gives us the notion of *private wealth*, by which is meant the *things* owned by individuals. Private wealth includes such things as houses, land, live stock, necessities, and comforts of all kinds. Further, private wealth includes those things owned by a corporation (legal person), such as railroads, water-works, factory-buildings, and machinery.

*Public wealth*, like private wealth, refers to the *appropriated things*. It is a broader term than private wealth, including everything that is owned by private persons and by governments. It includes public buildings, parks, highways, public schools, state universities. The term as commonly used does not include free goods, such as climate or large bodies of water.

Social wealth embodies both public and private wealth. This may be indicated as follows:

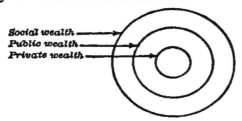

*Social wealth* ——
*Public wealth* ——
*Private wealth* ——

In the following pages the word wealth, when used without a modifying term, will signify social wealth.

9. **Per Capita Wealth and National Wealth.**—Per capita wealth means the average wealth of the citizens of a nation. National wealth is so used as to mean the aggregate of the wealth in a nation. A nation may be comparatively wealthy and its per capita wealth small. Conversely, a nation may be poor and its per capita wealth large. In the former case the aggregate wealth would be divided among a large population, while in the latter case the aggregate wealth would be divided among a small population. Aggregate wealth remaining the same, per capita wealth decreases as the population increases, or it increases as the population decreases.

10. **Increasing Aggregate Wealth and Diminishing per Capita Wealth.**—We have seen that it takes a combination of different agents to produce a commodity; seed-corn, land, labor, and tools must work together to produce a bushel of corn. Productive capacity is increased by a better apportionment of these factors. Prior to our Civil War we had a small population in comparison with our land and natural resources. Every increase in population was a blessing collectively and individually, because it made possible greater individual earnings. After a proper adjustment between the population and resources is reached, a further increase of population tends to increase aggregate wealth and to diminish per capita wealth.

11. **View-Points in Autocratic and Democratic Countries.**—In a democracy, where the people control, individual welfare and per capita wealth are emphasized. In an autocracy, where a potentate controls, national strength and national wealth are emphasized. In an autocracy economic interest would centre in theories of prosperity

or in problems of production, while in a democracy the prevailing emphasis falls on the problem of distribution. The one would say: "We must produce before we distribute; there must be something to divide before we proceed to a division; produce in abundance and distribution will automatically take care of itself." The other would say: "The greatest incentive to produce is found where there is a proper distribution; great production without adequate distribution would mean the wealth of a few and the misery of a multitude; wisely distribute, and adequate production will be properly fostered and directed."

The above statements show that for the sake of clearness the word wealth should always be modified by one of the following: Per capita, national, public, private, social.

**12. Wealth and Property.**—It is necessary at this point to distinguish between property and wealth. The neglect of this distinction has caused great confusion, especially in problems of taxation and in statistical tabulations of our national wealth. Property is a legal concept; it is a title to wealth. A house is an object of wealth; the title to a house is property. A railroad is wealth; there may be a thousand property rights to this one piece of wealth. Wealth remains the same 'whether property rights are increased, decreased, or destroyed. Should the state take away the title of individuals to land, our land wealth would remain the same. Property, and not wealth, was created when Russian peasants were made subject to purchase and sale.

We must not speak of legal instruments—deeds, franchises, stock-certificates, mortgages, and other evidences of ownership—as wealth. If we speak of a farm as wealth and also speak of the title to it as wealth, we are counting twice. If the city imposes a tax on a street-railway and in addition imposes a tax on the stock or ownership of the railway it is double taxation.

Inventions, discoveries, and new scientific methods have made additions to wealth wholly out of proportion to the gains of individuals in the form of property. The effect of improvements is to enable a given amount of goods to be produced at a lower cost, or to enable more goods to be produced at a given cost. Should an improvement enable a business to double its output without additional cost the community would enjoy greater abundance and lower prices. If an improvement should double the supply of steel and cut the price in two, there would be no perceptible increase in property of steel-owners, but a great addition to wealth.

Property enables individuals to live from the products of others. Current supplies are perishable, therefore each season must yield its crop if society be spared from want. Society must continually produce these necessities. What is true of society in this regard is not true of the individual. The individual may have property in permanent assets, and, as necessity arises, exchange these for current necessities. Private ownership or property enables the individual to depend on others. Thus private property makes possible a leisure class (called "idle rich" and "parasites").

13. **Capital and Wealth.**—Wealth consists, as we have seen, of productive capacity and of the incomes which provide the necessities, comforts, and conveniences of life. Capital, on the contrary, is acquisitive in nature. One's capital expresses his purchasing power with respect to the

products of others. It is thus a privately owned valuable right. There is much capital that is not wealth at all. When Queen Elizabeth empowered one with the legal privilege of monopolizing trade in cards, that right was not wealth, although it became a great means of private acquisition or capital. Capital may take the form of legal advantage, monopoly power, a franchise, or mere good-will.

Generally speaking, however, capital is the value of a property right to an item of wealth. A horse is an item of wealth. If horses are plentiful and cheap, the owner of a horse has a small capital or value right. When the European war creates a large demand for horses, thus making them scarce and high-priced, the owner finds that his capital is increased. Capital and scarcity are inseparably connected. The capital of certain individuals may increase while social and also per capita wealth decrease. Between 1900 and 1915 there was but little increase in the number of improved acres in farms, but the demand for land products was greatly increased, due to the vast increase of population. There was a decrease in the acreage of land per capita, and at the same time an increase in the capital in land.

14. **The Money Expression of Wealth.**—It is now evident that a sum of capital values may be misleading as an index of well-being or as an expression of national or per capita wealth. The estimate of our national wealth is made in dollars. This is faulty for two reasons: first, should we assume no change whatsoever in the amount of national wealth, yet it would be expressed as larger or smaller should the purchasing power of the dollar go down or up; second, there is much wealth which is not expressed in terms of money. The purchasing power of a dollar is

less to-day than it has been at any time in many years. Should we assume that the per capita wealth remains constant, yet a decline in the exchange power of money will show a great increase in the money worth of the per capita wealth.

The money expression of our wealth gives no adequate picture of well-being. It expresses nothing as to free goods. Much of our public property has no money estimate; our rivers and harbors are exemplary of this.

15. Economics is concerned with the utilization of wealth and labor to the end of gratifying desires. This makes of it a *human* science, and as such its subject-matter is the basis of much controversy. It is closely related to political, ethical, and historical considerations. Both for the purposes of illustration and for the application of principles the economist frequently takes excursions into these kindred fields of thought. The more strictly, however, kindred branches are separated, the better it will be for each and all. "The easiest and surest way to increase our knowledge of any subject is to isolate it, and investigate it to the strict exclusion for the time of all other subjects."

Some of the laws of economics are applicable to all forms of social organization. They apply alike to the isolated individual like Crusoe, to the cave-dweller, to the tribe of savage huntsmen, to the self-sufficing family, to the great and prosperous nation. They apply in backward communities, where trade is by barter (barter being a trade of goods or services for other goods or services, *i. e.*, trading without the use of money). They apply with equal force in a capitalistic community with an intricate system of currency.

In treating of the acquisition and utilization of wealth economics must study nefarious practices, by which unscrupulous individuals acquire wealth. It must include a consideration of such predatory agencies as the outfit of the robber or the roulette-wheel of the gamester. Economics also studies the most noble and edifying activities of men so far as these are related to the production, maintenance, and utilization of wealth. This science inquires into the cause and effect of different kinds of wealth and of different lines of business. It serves to work into the understanding of men a body of sound principles from which may be deduced practical rules and precepts for the safe guidance of human conduct to the end of social and individual well-being.

At the expense of repetition, let it be added that economics is a human science, and it is broad enough to include all the wealth-getting and wealth-using activities of man in whatever state of organization he may be found. The student must be on his guard once for all against such definitions of this science as would artificially narrow the thought to money price transactions. Buying and selling, and legal or contractual obligations which are effected by the use of money (price transactions) form an essential part. but not the whole of economics.

16. **Economic Laws and Social Institutions.**—We must distinguish natural economic laws from man-made institutions. Scientific principles may determine legislation, but legislation cannot determine scientific principles. Institutions are man-made; they may be created, modified, or destroyed by a majority vote. Institutions may be formed in accord with economic principles that promote well-being, and as such serve to the greatest social good. On

the other hand, they may be in accord with economic laws and work positive harm. A law only states what will happen under certain conditions; it is not a part of the law to state whether the consequence will be good or bad. The competitive system, which embodies private property and exchange, is an institution. The majority think that it is based on such economic principles as will direct the workings of this institution to the end of the greatest good; the minority think differently. Who is right? To answer this involves an economic problem which calls for a clear conception of the nature and workings of economic laws. The answer to this question requires investigation into social history and an analysis of social experience in order that we may learn the truth regarding the laws upon which the competitive system is based. To define economic laws in terms of the competitive system is to beg the question. Or to define economics as the science of wealth, and then define wealth in terms of the competitive system is in the beginning to beg the question. Such a procedure prepares the way not for a study of economic laws but for a mere elaboration on the competitive system.

17. **The goal of public policy** is human welfare. The word policy implies the recognition of some end to be accomplished and the definite shaping of our course toward that end. The old truism, "We can command laws only by obeying them," teaches us that we must shape our course in strict obedience to economic laws if we attain the goal of our economic policy. We must comprehend law before we can shape our course in obedience to law; the shaping of a course takes the form of an institution, therefore the study of economic law is antecedent to a sound conclusion regarding the merits of institutions.

**18. Changes in Economics.**—Economics is to be sharply distinguished from economy or economic life. Economic life refers to the nature of the customs, institutions, and activities of a people in getting a living. We say, for instance, that the Civil War brought about a great change in the economic life of the South. Formerly the plantation-owner used slave-labor in the production of things largely for his own use. Clothing, shoes, and farm-utensils were produced in small shops on the plantation. To-day he pays wages for labor, sells his products to large domestic or foreign markets and acquires his clothing, shoes, and farm-utensils indirectly from a giant corporation. This describes a change in economic life. Economic life may change while economic laws remain the same. As a government may change from one form to another, although the principles of government remain the same, so economics may change while economic laws remain the same. Economics is designed to explain economic life, and as economic life changes, the science which explains it must change in content and emphasis.

**19. Economics and Political Reform.**—Abundant natural resources in the form of timber, iron, coal, and harbors, together with a hardy people are no guarantee against poverty. Science must unite with labor in order that resources may yield their benefits. Poverty is found in the midst of potential abundance as well as in the midst of scanty resources. In either case poverty is due to maladjustment—there are too many mouths to be fed in proportion to the available supply of food, or there may be enough food, but it may be owned by the few to the exclusion of the many. In any such cases of maladjustment, social conflict gives rise to problems for the lawmaker.

What law is depends largely upon existing economic conditions. Social relations are constantly growing more complex. Factories are selling their wares for delivery a year hence even before they are produced; and in turn these factories are contracting for the future delivery of raw materials with which to make the same wares. Should there be default of contract anywhere along the line, future sales would be rendered impossible. The credit basis upon which modern business is financed makes it imperative that men meet their obligations. Instances might be multiplied to demonstrate the need of legal enforcement of contracts.

The growth of transportation facilities and the concentration of industries tend to destroy community isolation and to unite the interests of the people, hence there is need of uniform legislation. Although this unity of interests demands unity in legislation, our political organization is such as to cause a diversity in law. As each State has been added to the Union it has added a legislature and a court of last resort to the oversupply of such bodies. States, as well as individuals, have conflicting interests, and they vie with one another for advantages. Each State is anxious to attract business, and so is reluctant to pass compensation acts, child-labor laws or other remedial legislation, lest capital seek the State with fewer restrictions. One State, for instance, by legalizing concentration and restraints of trade, has attracted large corporations. "That State profits to the extent of over $3,000,000 per annum because of its pioneer position in passing liberal corporation laws." Other States, seeing these advantages, are forced to similar measures and so interstate competition only too frequently takes the form of lax legislation.

The statesman acquainted with the principles of economics knows that one state does not succeed by impoverishing another. They are not economists who wish to extend American trade by limiting or crippling the trade of England. To-day every industry is producing for the market. Every good so produced is from the moment of its existence a demand for another product. Cripple a nation or an industry and you limit the market for your product. If only for selfish reasons, we should assist other states or nations, and if our legislators were better trained in economic principles, such unwise methods of competing would not exist.

In addition, the moral level of competition is usually set by the competitor of lowest standing. The manufacturer who pays low wages, maintains poor conditions and exacts long hours, can force other employers to the same level of conduct. His lower costs would enable him to reduce his prices and take the market. Other manufacturers must conform to his low standard, or the state must maintain a higher one. Statutes dealing with conditions of factories, the employment of women and children, the maintenance of safety-appliances are all instances of laws attempting to overcome the evils of competition. In fact, legislation, for the most part, is on strictly economic subjects, such as the tariff, banking, labor troubles, and methods of competition.[1] True statesmanship would seek to

[1] An enumeration of the essential laws of the last pre-war administration lend emphasis to this statement. The chief acts passed during that administration were:

    (a)   The Federal Reserve Law.
    (b)   The Eight-Hour Law.
    (c)   The Rural Credits Law.
    (d)   The Child Labor Law.
    (e)   The Workmen's Compensation Law.

preserve the benefits of competition and to destroy its evils; it would raise the plane of competition without restricting it. Therefore lawmakers are in duty bound to have a grasp of economic principles. Voters cannot be neutral on questions of economic conduct; to vote in the negative is as positive in result as to vote affirmatively. The college graduate who has neglected the principles upon which legislation is based exercises the ballot no more intelligently than the illiterate. Since legislation is based so largely upon these principles, it is clear that intelligent voting requires some knowledge of economics.[1]

20. **Economics and Business.**—In a narrow sense economics is the science of which business is the art. Economics is therefore important for the business man to the extent that a practitioner should understand the principles of which he is making constant application. The study of economics imparts, moreover, a habit of thought and a familiarity with concepts invaluable to the man in big business, who to be successful must have a deep comprehension of principles involving a network of mutually dependent phenomena. The great generals of industry are such, for the most part, because their deep insight into mutually dependent phenomena gives them foresight and

(*f*)  A Law Creating a Tariff Commission.
(*g*)  The Good Roads Law.
(*h*)  The Income Tax Law and the Inheritance Tax Law.
(*i*)  The Agricultural Extension Law.
(*j*)  The Alaskan Railway Law.
(*k*)  The Federal Trade Commission Law.
(*l*)  The Grain Anti-Gambling Law.
(*m*)  The Safety-at-Sea Law.
(*n*)  The Cotton Futures Law.
(*o*)  The Clayton Anti-Trust Law.

[1] See H. C. Adams's Relation of States to Industrial Activity, pp. 39–47.

thereby enables them to grasp developing opportunities. The greatest principle in economics is that of proportionality—the principle of the adjustment and the interaction of mutually dependent phenomena. As the market is extending and businesses are concentrating into large units, complex and far-reaching problems cannot but develop. The solution of these requires a profound knowledge of economic principles. Some of the most notable advertising campaigns in recent years have been carried through on strictly economic grounds. Some of the most careful students of economics are men in the field of merchandising. So-called middle-men must conform their conduct to the principles of economics. Directors of large businesses and small are constantly applying these principles and should understand them.

But to say that economics is important for the business man does not say that it teaches him how to become rich. Some of the most ridiculous economic theories are adhered to by prominent financiers. These men are masters of detail within a limited field. There are successful men in phases of banking who know nothing of the principles of money and who have never read the Federal Reserve Act. One might have years of training and successful experience in particular phases of banking, and yet be as incapable as a teamster of devising a monetary policy for the Philippines. But as the economy of self-sufficiency is giving way to the economy of interdependence, even the specialist is compelled to view his task in its broader economic aspects. A treatise on economics presents principles in their relationship to each other. The problems of the business man differ with respect to time and place; with respect to changes in related businesses; with respect to different proportions of ingredients in the different problems. The business man finds no prescriptions in economics for each case, but from economics he learns how to trace causes to their effects in the mutually dependent phenomena of industry.

21. **Exercises.**—1. What is the difference between current supplies and productive capacity?

2. How may destruction be a real benefit to society? Cite three examples of this.

3. Define: social wealth, private wealth, public wealth, per capita wealth.

4. Are wealth and property co-extensive? Give two examples to illustrate your answer.

5. Wealth is any material good which satisfies a desire of man, and which is not gratuitous. It is used as a collective term, for the general conception of such goods, and, when it describes the subject or aim of political economy, it carries with it the notion of abundance. Criticise and correct this definition. Do you include in your definition the following: Honesty, health, skill, "the moral, intellectual, and physical natures" of the people, a patent right, a copyright, a bill of exchange, the voice of a singer, a good harbor, climate, and sunlight? (Sumner.)

6. If a census were taken of the wealth of the country, ought the owners of land to return it at its market value? Is the land a part of the national wealth? Ought the owners of government bonds to include them in the return? If they did so, and if the returns were added up, the national debt would be counted into the sum of the national wealth. Would that be right?

If A sells to B a bale of cotton for $500 and B gives a promissory note for it, ought B to return the cotton and A the note? If A has a certificate of stock in a railroad, ought the railroad officers to return the railroad, and ought A to return the stock? (Sumner.)

7. Are the following to be included in wealth: (1) the

original powers of the laborer; (2) his acquired powers; (3) the original properties of the soil; (4) improvements on land; (5) credit?

8. What is meant by the term "economic policy"? What bearing may questions of economic policy have on the institution of private property?

9. Why is it necessary to distinguish between economic laws and economic conduct? In what way does economics change?

10. How does a knowledge of economics assist the legislator? the business man?

11. Criticise: "A good climate is not wealth because all are equal in the enjoyment of it." Does this agree with President's Hadley's statement, "The true basis for an estimate of a nation's wealth is to be found in the enjoyments of its members"? (Economics, p. 4.) Does this statement conform to private, public, or social wealth?

12. Criticise: F. A. Walker said: "The Proclamation of Emancipation, in the United States and Russia, annihilated a vast mass of wealth."

Do you agree with David Ricardo? He said: "It is through confounding the ideas of value and wealth, or riches, that it has been asserted, that by diminishing the quantity of commodities, that is to say, of the necessities, conveniences, and enjoyments of human life, riches may be increased."

13. We associate efficiency with wealth and drunkenness with poverty. Should we classify whiskey, the means of drunkenness, as wealth?

14. Frost is not wealth but a destroyer of wealth, yet it would be wealth if privately appropriated, because one could add to the value of his own wealth by nipping his neighbor's crop in the bud. Point out the error, if there be any, in this statement.

15. The waters near our coasts are great sources of food. They are not, for the most part, privately owned, yet they

are more important to the nation than a large part of the land area. Are they wealth? If so, what kind?

16. Should you deny the concept of social wealth, could you account for the economic power of ancient Egypt, or of the United States?

# CHAPTER VI

## DESIRE, DESIRABILITY

**1. Desires as Motives.**—The movement of the blood in the body, of the ocean tides, of the winds, and of the planets sets the scientist the task of accounting for these movements. Likewise the efforts of man in the shop, store, market-place, on the farm, or in transportation, set the economist the task of accounting for these activities. Search where he may, he will find but one motive for all economic endeavor, and that is, human desires for the necessities, comforts, luxuries, and conveniences of life. Desire, then, is the starting-point in economic investigation.

The simplest form of desire, like that of the savage, child, or animal, is for food and the other elemental requirements. The craving for food stirs men up to the effort to secure it. That is the primary cause of productive labor. As the individual's intelligence broadens, he comes to attribute value not only to the immediate objects of

98

consumption, but also to the indirect means of producing these. The individual's order of thought in attributing value to things is from finished goods ready for consumption back to the direct agencies of producing these and on back to the more remote and indirect agencies. Because we recognize the utility of the apple, reason teaches us to prize the desirability of the tree which produced it, and further to attribute value to the land, labor, and other agencies back of the tree.

2. **Desires Are Recurring.**—Gratification at best is only temporary. We do to-day's reading, eating, and exercising to-day. But to-day's eating will not gratify to-morrow's desire for food. In order that one may get the greatest enjoyment through time, what is more, in order that one may live, goods of present, direct use and services must be meted out through time. These goods of direct use and services are to be thought of, not as a fund or accumulation, but as a flow. The dwelling-house is one thing and the shelter (service) it affords through time is another. The shelter of the house, the ride which the automobile affords, the protection which clothing insures, the thousand and one benefits from other productive agents, constitute a flow.

3. **Intelligence, Desire, Effort.**—Desires show progress in intelligence. Desires imply a knowledge of the thing desired. If one says, "I desire," the question which naturally follows is: "What? Do you desire a hat, a suit of clothes, a pencil, a glass of orangeade?" You have no desire for a glass of orangeade unless you know what orangeade is. Benjamin Franklin was never imbued with a desire for a Ford automobile. When there is no knowledge there is no desire and desires increase as knowledge

widens. Knowledge gives birth to desire and desire points out a path for will. Why will one risk his life further to save a drowning child than to save a drowning dog, or why will one work harder for a thousand dollars than for ten dollars? Strong desires and great effort, and weak desires and weak effort go together.

4. **Desires for Near and Remote Possession.**—It is a general rule that the *near* occasions a stronger desire than the *remote*. The child prefers one box of candy to-day to two boxes a year hence. The normal person desires more intensively the present possession of wealth or the present direct uses of goods than the future possession or the future uses of goods. The majority of the economists place emphasis on the desire for present consumption over future consumption. I wish to emphasize that the desire for present possession of wealth over future possession of wealth is far more significant. This point will occupy us at length when we come to consider the theory of interest. It is enough to say that the greater part of large credit transactions, of durable investments and of permanent improvements concern most deeply the direction of social wealth.

But while desire is stronger for present consumption or for present possession, it is common knowledge that as intelligence broadens our present desire becomes stronger for future goods. The ignorant man is not provident; he does not save for the future. The intelligent person, however, cannot but realize the need of providing for the future. This fact causes him to desire durative goods, that is, durable agents which will yield the means of gratifying desires in the future. If there were no desire for future incomes, man would not ascribe importance to durable productive agents. While the desire for consumption is back of the motive for possession, yet the determination to possess is the force which shapes industry.

5. **Standards of Consumption.**—Increasing intelligence causes desires for goods and services that are superior in quality, and the consumption of such goods and services still further increases the standard of desire. A Tennessee mountaineer told the writer that a summer's stay in New York City had changed his desire for yarn socks, hoe-cake, and moonshine. The wealthy who suffer a sudden reverse of fortune find it hard to readjust their standards. Increasing intelligence, furthermore, develops a desire for a great variety of goods. Thus increasing desires call for improvement in the quality and variety of goods. They call for better clothing in a greater variety, for better food adapted to a wider range of taste, and for superior amusements in a more liberal assortment.

6. **Harmony in Consumption.**—Then, too, increasing intelligence gives rise to the desire for harmony in the means of consumption. Harmony in dress, in the different items of the dinner, in house decoration, is demanded by the more intelligent. A thoughtful husband will not purchase his gifted wife an expensive hat unless he is prepared to foot the bill for the other articles of apparel to harmonize with it. The possession of one thing stimulates the desire for other things, thereby extending the motive for further effort. Man is by nature a social being; as such most of his economic desires are the outgrowth of his social life. In the language of W. E. Hearn, "Man is imitative, and so seeks to have what his neighbor enjoys; he is vain, and so desires to display himself and his possessions with advantage before his fellows; he loves superiority, and so

seeks to show something that others have not; he dreads inferiority, and so seeks to possess what others also possess."

**7. Desires and Productive Capacity.**—Desires as motives may be in accord with or out of accord with productive capacity. As above pointed out, the motive for production is desire. We produce what we want; we expend energy on the production of nothing else. If you wish the clew to the economic production of the people, you have but to determine what the people want. Industry is shaped around and conformed to the desires of the people. Desires create demand for goods and that which the people demand is what the factories, farms, and other industries must produce. Do the people desire articles that are rare, choice wines or scarce materials—things that nature has little capacity for producing? If so, little can be produced and nature can support but a small population. Conversely, if a cheap and nutritive food, like rice or potatoes, is desired, abundance can be produced and a large population can be supported with plenty.

The desire for a variety of goods and services causes a varied production in society. What is more, a varied production creates a larger abundance of goods. When few goods are produced many productive agencies lie idle. If we produce only cereals, garden-fruits, and vegetables, the cranberry-swamps are not utilized. The same crop will not grow on all kinds of land. Land good for wheat may not be good for oranges. A variety of crops must be grown if the great variety of soils be utilized. Furthermore, it is unwise to plant the same field to one crop year after year. The scientific rotation of crops keeps the land fertile. Thus we must have a variety of crops in order to utilize the different qualities of land, and a rotation of crops on the same field in order to secure the proper utilization of the soil.

The different agencies of our productive capacity must be utilized in order that we may employ a variety of labor and managerial talent. When industry affords opportunities to the different varieties of productive labor and talent, the better it is for each and all. It is waste to have a part of the productive energy idle. A varied production, moreover, educates the people with respect to the cooperative advantages of numerous industries working together. It shows the mutual benefits to be derived from the interrelationship of industries, from a division of labor and specialization. A varied production is conducive to the development of inventive genius, thus furthering productive capacity through new industrial processes and a higher utilization of human skill and resources. Because varied desires cause variety in production, we are furnished with the secret of the complexity of modern productive processes.

8. **" The Cost of High Living."**—The cost of high living is a coined phrase which expresses the theory that the present high level of prices is due to the fact that we come to desire those goods for which we have little productive capacity. If desires are largely directed by the love of ostentation; if our energies are turned from the cheap and abundant to the rare and exclusive, fewer necessities are produced and prices are raised. There is much truth in this theory in a society where wealth rather than brains set the style. The love of ostentation finds gratification in the consumption of only those goods which are beyond the means of the average person. It takes much wealth to buy diamonds and other objects of exclusiveness. The

rich too often refuse to associate with those who are not properly trade-marked with the required symbols. But the possessors of wealth are highly regarded and the poor desire their association. To enjoy this association the poor must buy jewels when they should buy bread, and automobiles when they should buy work-animals. To the extent that production is given to luxuries it is denied to necessities. This causes necessities to be scarce and high-priced.

9. **Desires and Ultimate Wealth.**—The kind of goods desired largely bespeaks the ultimate wealth of a society or individual in yet another way. Is one's desire for beer or music, for a big dinner or a good book, for tobacco or a painting, for the temporary means of present gratification or for the durable means of permanent gratification? The glass of beer can be enjoyed by only one and the music by many; the big dinner is consumed once for all, but the book can be read in turn by any number; the tobacco goes up in smoke, while the painting remains a source of gratification for the lovers of art. The same productive energy back of the temporary means of gratification would, in the end, yield far more enjoyment if turned to the more durable means of gratification.

Again, do we desire to use the music, the book, and the painting in private, or are we willing to share the use of these with others? The private use of these is denied to the many, but a thousand may enjoy the same open-air concert, or the same book in the public library, or the same painting in the public art collection. This suggests certain difficulties not in the present order of discussion. However, under existing conditions we do share many of these goods in common. Of course, art galleries, libraries, and the like are examples of this; these are in the nature of unearned increments for every one who utilizes them.

10. **Desires and Association of Ideas.**—As a social being man's desires are influenced by the association of ideas. This is exemplified in the change of fashions. The classes of society tend to go in groups and to follow the leaders. Those things which the leaders wear, eat, or otherwise enjoy, the followers strive to obtain.

When a style of dress becomes "common," and is worn by the lower classes, it is discarded by the fashionable people. Fashions that are absolutely repulsive at first will often be adopted if they are introduced by popular or noted persons. From his excesses Henry VIII became a bloated figure in the latter part of his life, and the aristocracy stuffed their clothing to imitate his size. Queen Elizabeth had auburn hair, and the ladies of fashion sought for a dye that would turn their hair to the aristocratic shade.

To use an example from Halleck's Psychology: When, negligee hats first made their appearance, a shrewd hatter sent for a very popular and well-dressed collegian and offered him his choice of the best hats in the store, if he would wear a negligee hat for three days. He objected to making such an exhibition of himself, until he was flattered by the hatter's wager that the hats could in this way be made the fashion for the entire town. When the collegian first put in his appearance on the campus with the hat he was guyed for its oddity. Later in the afternoon some of his friends concluded that the hat looked so well that they would invest. On the following day large numbers reached the same conclusion. For some time after this the hatter found difficulty in keeping a sufficient supply in stock. Had an unpopular or poorly dressed man appeared first on the campus with that hat, the result would have been the reverse. The hat would have been the same, but the association of ideas would have differed.

A knowledge of the power of the association of ideas is of the utmost importance in business. One man has his store so planned that all its associations are pleasing, from the manners of the clerks to the fixtures and drapery. Another store brings up unpleasant associations. A business man was about to employ a young man for an important position, when one day the elder chanced to catch sight of him in questionable company. The law of contiguity henceforth brought up this company whenever the young man was thought of, and he failed to secure the position.

11. **Altruistic desires** have a profound influence on the economic conduct of men. This is especially true in an advanced stage of civilization. There are broader traits of character than a selfish desire for wealth. We strive for personal economic advantage, but we are guided by a feeling of duty, and if we disobey this feeling our own conscience condemns us. We fear contempt and desire personal honor, also we obey the inward command to be right. We are social beings with imagination and sympathy. We think, remember, observe, and are troubled by the distress of others. It is in our nature to have altruistic desires and to spend our substance and labor to gratify them. Orphan asylums, one hundred and fifty millions for the Red Cross, homes for the aged, societies for the protection of children and of animals represent economic activity of the altruistic type. Desire and striving to improve the economic order of the world are con-

stantly increasing in scope and depth. The teachings of those who would limit economics to the selfish getting and using of wealth are fruitless, because their concept is one of unreal simplicity.

Economic desires are also altruistic with respect to succeeding generations. We follow an economic policy, indefinite and crude, perhaps, toward sounder economic conduct and greater well-being for the future. We desire to transmit a richer world than the one we have inherited from the past. Desires of this kind largely guide legislation of an economic nature, such as vast public expenditures for social and industrial improvement. Selfish desires for private acquisition and desires for a fuller productive capacity are both encompassed in the science of economics.

**12. Desires and Wants.**—"Two pounds of tea," says Hearn, "were presented to Charles II as a present worthy of a king. A century afterward the steady perseverance of the Americans in abstaining from their unjustly taxed tea was rightly regarded as the most remarkable case of self-denial that history records." And Bastiat says: "It is a phenomenon well worthy of remark, how quickly, by continuous satisfaction, what was at first only a vague desire quickly becomes a taste, and what was only a taste is transformed into a want, and even a want of the most imperious kind." A desire to see the World Series, however, cannot be termed a want. We want for things necessary to our state of being. If the educated or the wealthy are suddenly reduced by misfortune, they want for things which the ignorant and the poor would regard as luxuries. Habits of life determine wants; changing habits transform mere desires into wants. Habits are confirmed and wants are created by the continuous gratification of desires.

Painful desires or wants arise when the requirements of habits are denied. We desire for both luxuries and necessities but we never want, in the true sense of that word, for luxuries.

**13. Necessities.**—Luxuries are economic goods or services which are not necessities, whereas necessities are those goods the lack of which would occasion wants or painful desires. We may classify necessities as absolute, acquired, and conventional. Absolute necessities include warmth, shelter, and food, which are necessary to the maintenance of life. Acquired necessities include items like tobacco. In estimating the necessary outlays of the laborer who uses tobacco, it would be an error not to take account of his expenditures for tobacco, because he would deny himself other and much needed goods rather than be deprived of it. Conventional necessities include goods of a quality and style which are in keeping with one's social ranking. The minister is not expected to appear in the coarse clothing of the day-laborer. The doctor or dentist is socially ostracized whose instruments and office equipment are below a certain grade of elegance. Those goods are necessities which accord with one's station in life. Acquired and conventional necessities must form a part of the expenditures of the class concerned. The more one is forced to spend for these the less he will have to spend for other goods. Instructors are hard put to it at times because they are compelled to dress and maintain quarters which would be in keeping with a larger income.

**14. Repressibility of Desires.**—Our most irrepressible appetites are for the common necessities of life. These we will have, whether our income be large or small. Desires for the primary necessities, however, are most quickly satisfied. It is all but impossible to repress the craving for food, yet the desire for food is quickly gratified. On the contrary, our most repressible desires are our most insatiable desires. There is no end to our desires for comforts of the higher form, yet if forced to economize we cut down on the consumption of these first.

15. **The standard of life** is but a level of consumption. The habits and requirements which prevail in society call for a rather definite standard of consumption. These habits and requirements undergo gradual change, because they result from natural and social influences which are slowly modified through long periods of time. The quantity and variety of food, clothing, and shelter, the standard of public utilities required, the provision for sanitation, recreation, education, and protection, roughly measure the economic standard of life. Man's consumption is limited by his income, but his level of consumption is his standard of life, therefore, his income determines his standard of life. The forces operating on income, then, are the forces which fix this standard. The forces operating on income are two; man and his surroundings. These forces adjusted to each other constitute productive capacity. Land may be fertile and resources abundant, yet if the man element is weak or poorly adjusted to its surroundings, a low income, consequently a low standard of life, must prevail. Conversely the man element may be skilful, strong, and of superb moral character, yet, if resources are wanting, a low standard must prevail. Low production and a low standard, and high production and a high standard always accompany each other.

We have seen that desire is the motivating force of production, but another fact of primary importance is that production or income is limited by productive capacity. Furthermore, while desire stimulates production it invariably outruns production; we always desire more than we produce. Then, desire causes the standard to be as high as it is and the limits of productive capacity cause it to be as low as it is. In other words, the standard of life is determined by two forces; desire and productive capacity. This illustrates the interaction of economic phenomena. A given state of being is the result of a tendency or prevailing direction of motion of a number of forces which, individually, would operate in different directions.

Do higher desires cause a large production of income, or does the consumption of a larger income give rise to higher desires? The answer, in keeping with the above reasoning, is that these phenomena interact; both are required for economic advance. Although limited capacity holds the income in check, it must not be overlooked that desire is fundamental to production.

16. **The Notion of Scarcity.**—In the economic sense there is no such thing as scarcity apart from either a desire or a need. Fewness and scarcity are not synonyms. There are few mud-holes in dry weather, but they are not scarce in the economic sense, there being neither desire nor need of them. If there are few blacksnakes, they are not scarce. Any economic good, on the contrary, is scarce, for if it were not scarce it would be a free good and not an economic good. Goods are said to be scarce so long as our desires or needs are not fully gratified with respect to them. Should we add loaf after loaf to the supply of bread until bread became as common as leaves on the ground, then there would be no scarcity of bread. But bread is scarce so long as desires and needs are not

fully gratified. Then we cannot determine the scarcity of a thing by the amount of it; rather scarcity is measured in subjective terms. Regardless of the amount, if there be a desire or need for a particular commodity it is scarce. There are degrees of scarcity (scarce, scarcer, scarcest), corresponding to the strength of the desire or need.

17. **Desirability** is the quality of goods or services which is calculated or fitted to excite a wish to possess. Many economists employ the word utility in the sense which I have defined for the word desirability. Desirability is preferred in this book for two reasons: it expresses accurately the meaning intended, whereas utility is burdened with so many definitions as to have no one distinct meaning. Goods having desirability may be positively harmful, may detract from the well-being of the user. Goods having this quality may or may not serve our needs, but they always serve our desires. Desirability changes with respect to persons, occasions, times, and the condition of supply. The painting has desirability for the lover of art, but it can excite no wish to possess in the mind of the savage; the desirability of formal attire is greater on formal occasions; present goods have, with few exceptions, a higher desirability than future goods; and bread has a higher desirability when scarce than when abundant. In any case the desirability of a good is determined by two things —the strength of the desire to be met and the fitness of the good to meet the desire.

18. **Utility** must not be confused with desirability. These concepts may be used interchangeably at times without harm, but under other conditions they are antonyms. Utility is a social rather than an individualistic concept; it is an objective quality of goods or services.

Utility is that quality or fitness of things to promote and serve well-being. There are blessings in disguise; our needs are administered to and our well-being promoted by things which we neither desire nor understand, even by things which we would avoid as distasteful to us. Æsop said: "We would often be sorry if our wishes were gratified." It is not utility but desirability, the fitness to excite a wish to possess, which directly introduces the value problem.

19. **Diminishing desirability** expresses the elementary principle that if the quantity of shoes, tea, or any other commodity increases, its total desirability increases at a diminishing rate. An example will make this clear: Let us suppose that a caravan travelling through a desert has one pint of water. With great saving and extreme economy the traveller can perhaps survive upon this limited amount. What is its desirability for him? Being indispensable to life, its desirability is immeasurable. Add a second pint to the supply and it will have great desirability, although it is not absolutely essential for the preservation of life. If there be added a third, fourth, and on down to the twentieth pint, he will have, let us assume, a sufficiency. The undesirability of carrying another pint would be near the equivalent of its desirability. Thus we see that by adding to the amount the total desirability increases at a diminishing rate.

20. **The Equal Desirabilities of Units.**—Then, considered as a whole, all desires are insatiable but any one desire, as the desire for water, may be fully satisfied and cease to exist. Another observation is that each like unit which is added to a supply causes the desirability of each other unit in the supply to be lowered. For instance, the trav-

eller through the desert may start with two pints of water, and if to these he adds a third, fourth, and fifth pint he will not appraise the two pints so highly as if the supply had not been increased. Suppose that the five units in his possession are alike in all respects, no one of them could be more desirable than any other. Each of the units in his supply has a desirability equal to that of any other. Put as a general proposition: Like units in the same supply at the same time are of the same desirability.

Crusoe had four guns, and assume that these were exactly alike. Can we say that any one of these had more desirability for him than any other? Certainly not. To provide himself with animal food and to keep off the beasts of prey, it was absolutely essential that he have a gun, but it was not imperative that he have more than one or two. It would have been fortunate for him could he have exchanged a gun for food or clothing. This example teaches us: (1) that the like units of a supply are of equal desirability, (2) that the larger the number of units in a supply, the less is the desirability of any one of the units, (3) that we can measure the desirability of any one unit, as when we wish to exchange it for another good. But it must be clear that we cannot reason relative to the total desirability of a supply in the same way that we reason relative to one or more units in the total supply. Crusoe might well have sold a gun for the price of one bushel of grain, but it does not follow that it would be wise for him to exchange the four guns for four bushels. In the former case he would profit by the trade; in the latter he would be without the means of protecting his life.

21. **Total Desirability.**—Suppose that our caravaner would be willing to sell any one of his pints of water for

ten cents, does it follow that he would be willing to sell the twenty pints for two dollars? On first thought one would say that since the different pints are of the same desirability it would follow that if one pint is worth ten cents, twenty pints must be worth twenty times ten cents, or two dollars. This is good arithmetic but poor economics. Should the caravaner dispose of his total supply, he would die for want of water. Needless to say, he would not sell it at any price. This makes it clear that the desirability of a unit of the supply multiplied by the number of units in the supply does not give the total desirability of the supply. Then, how may we calculate the total desirability of a supply? It is evident that if the first pint be subtracted from the supply the remaining nineteen will each have a higher desirability, and, further, that the desirability of the remaining pints would be increased by the subtraction of the second, third, etc. In order to attain the total desirability of a supply we may assume that one unit at a time is subtracted in succession, and that the desirabilities of each unit are added.

**22. Graphic illustration of the equal desirabilities of different units at a given time in a total supply.**

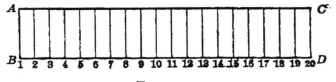

FIGURE I

The parallelogram $A$, $B$, $C$, $D$ pictures the situation of twenty units at a given time in a homogeneous supply. The perpendicular lines are of equal length and each represents the desirability of a unit.

Since each unit in the supply has the same desirability

as any other unit, the length of the lines representing these must be equal to one another. This figure, however, does not picture the total desirability of the supply.

As above pointed out, the total desirability is obtained by a succession of subtractions, each of which increases the desirabilities of the remaining units.

23. Graphic illustration of the desirabilities of units at different times, showing how they increase as the supply is diminished.

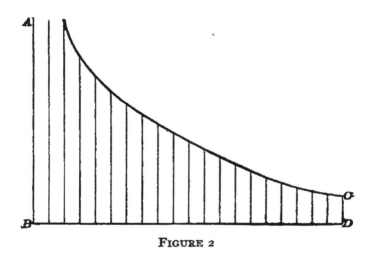

FIGURE 2

In the case above assumed (paragraph 21), it would be found, as shown in Fig. 2, that by subtracting unit after unit from *D, C* toward *A, B*, the desirabilities increase until they become immeasurable. In this case the total desirability would be immeasurable. Of course, we are assuming an extreme case, but oftentimes a principle is better grasped when presented in its extreme form.

24. Marginal desirability is the desirability of the last added portion of a supply. But the last added portion has the same desirability as any other like portion, there-

fore the marginal desirability is the desirability of a portion or unit of the supply. In case of freely reproducible goods, and these are most characteristic of the market, marginal desirability is equal to the benefits which must be foregone in acquiring them. Assume that a housewife is making out an order to Sears, Roebuck & Co. for a supply of soap which is priced at five cents a cake. How much will she order? She would probably give a dollar for a cake rather than be denied the use of soap. It goes without saying that the desirability of a cake of soap is so much stronger than the desirability of retaining the five cents for buying something else that she decides to make the purchase. A second, third, fourth, and on down to the nineteenth cake, let us assume, have each a higher desirability for her than has the alternative use of the five cents. Whether to buy the twentieth cake gives her concern. She will buy the twentieth cake if its desirability be but a small fraction above that of five cents. The twentieth cake reaches the marginal point where the cost or undesirability comes to equal the desirability.

**25. The Tendency to Equality of Marginal Desirabilities.**—Marginal desirability is an individual matter, varying from person to person, and the tendency of desirabilities of different supplies for any one person is toward equality. The housewife did not stop with a supply of twenty cakes because she desired no more soap, for had the price been four cents, she would probably have bought twenty-five cakes. Nor did she so limit her supply because she wished to save the five cents. She ceased to buy soap because she could gratify a more intense desire by spending the five cents for something else. It is a part of human nature so to spend means as to gratify the most intense desire. Rather than buy more soap, a housewife will buy fruit, buttons, sugar, or coffee. How much of each of these goods will she buy? She cannot buy all the things which have desirability for her; she must draw the line somewhere. She will so distribute her expenditures among the several goods as, in her judgment, to secure the maximum desirability. The more she buys of some goods, the less she can buy of others. Her expenditures in the several lines are limited by a boundary-line drawn through the different points of marginal desirability. Her expenditure for sugar limits the amount she can spend for coffee or any other good. Her different desires are supplied by a transfer of money from other lines of expenditure. She ceases to spend money on any good the moment that she can secure a higher desirability by transferring her purchasing power to some other class of goods. Her transfer of money from one class of goods to another, in her attempt to secure the greatest total desirability, tends to equalize the marginal desirabilities of different classes of goods.

**26. Graphic Illustration.**—Let *A*, *B*, *C*, *D*, and *E*, in Figure 3, represent five classes of goods. Let the Arabic figures represent the desirability of different units. Let *S*, *T* represent the line of satiety, and *M*, *N* the line drawn through the different points of marginal desirability. It is seen that the housewife's desire is to transfer her expenditure so as to secure the maximum desirability, and that by so doing she has brought about an equality with respect to the marginal desirabilities of the several lines of supply. The *tendency* is always to secure this

| | A | B | C | D | E | |
|---|---|---|---|---|---|---|
| | | | | | 11 | |
| | 10 | | | 10 | 10 | |
| | 9 | | 9 | 9 | 9 | |
| | 8 | 8 | 8 | 8 | 8 | |
| | 7 | 7 | 7 | 7 | 7 | |
| | 6 | 6 | 6 | 6 | 6 | |
| M | 5 | 5 | 5 | 5 | 5 | N |
| S | | | | | | T |

FIGURE 3.

equality, although it is rarely attained, in fact never attained among the poor. Now, should we assume that she desires to buy some other goods, say *F, G,* and *H,* it is at once evident that, other things equal, she will have less to spend on *A, B, C, D,* and *E.* Her supply of each of these will be less, or, what is the same, their marginal desirabilities will be raised. Thus we see that each line of goods limits the supply and increases the marginal desirability of every other class of goods. If we did not have to buy bread we could buy more clothing, and if houses were free goods we could spend more for automobiles; every line of goods is competing, in a sense, with every other line of goods. We shall see later on how a proportion and balance of all classes of productive industries are worked out in keeping with the relative market prices.

**27. Examples of Marginal Desirability.**—The purpose of this paragraph is to answer some questions which, throughout my teaching experience, I have found bothersome to beginners. Goods have marginal desirabilities, to be sure, whether they are for keep or for sale. But the comparison of marginal desirabilities of goods which one has to offer with that of the goods which he may purchase, is primary to an exchange. Marginal desirability is truly a basic concept in exchange.

(*a*) I have been asked a number of times how to dispose of the marginal desirability of free goods in our exchange economy. The answer is that a free good exists in such abundance that its marginal desirability is zero. In fact, it has no marginal desirability. Only scarce goods have marginal desirability and only such goods enter into an exchange economy.

(*b*) It was my privilege recently to converse with Mr.

N. G. Kidd, a pioneer of western Ohio, who was within three months of the marvellous age of one hundred years. His vivid memory of happenings in youth gave deep interest to his reminiscences. He remarked that while on his way from Virginia to his new abode he had travelled some days with horse and drag-sled, when it became necessary to use his axe. He was keenly disappointed to find that it had been left behind. Leaving his young sister with the horse and load, he journeyed back four days to get the axe. The desirability of the axe to the frontiersman is all but immeasurable. Did this axe, the only unit of the supply, have marginal desirability for him? The student's answer is generally in the negative. But most assuredly it did have marginal desirability, and that, too, in the highest degree. It is only for the purpose of illustration that economists speak of unit after unit being added to a supply. The one unit of a supply has marginal desirability. This marginal desirability is equal to the strength of the desire which would be defeated were the article lost or otherwise removed.

(*c*) A student put this question in class: "In case one has fifteen tons of coal in the cellar or a hundred bushels of apples in storage, does any one unit hold a marginal place in the supply?" He was answered in the negative. "Then," he continued, "if there is no marginal item there can be no marginal desirability." In reply one may say that in a homogeneous supply any unit may be considered marginal in the sense that the desire defeated by the loss of it is precisely the same as that occasioned by the loss of any other unit of the supply.

All scarce goods have marginal desirability; it makes no difference whether we consider a succession of units added one after another, or a stock of goods on hand, or a supply consisting of a single unit.

(*d*) Another and difficult query: Does a dollar serve as a common measure of marginal desirability? The answer is most emphatically in the negative. Marginal desirability is an individual matter. There may be as many marginal desirabilities as there are buyers and sellers. A dollar has a different significance to the rich and to the poor, to the spendthrift and to the miser. Assume that two men, one rich and the other poor, are in the market for a horse. The circumstances of the poor man may be such that a horse would have double the desirability for him as for the rich man, yet the latter may be willing to pay $200 whereas the former would pay not more than $100. The pressing need for alternative goods may forbid the poor man offering more, whereas the wealthy purchaser could expend $200 without denying himself any felt necessity. To these men the marginal desirability of a dollar is vastly different. To take a different supposition: The marginal desirability of a dollar may be ten times as great for the poor boy as for the rich man's son, yet both may be marginal buyers, that is, barely willing to pay a dollar, say, for a ticket to a ball-game. How account for the fact that these boys, one estimating a piece of money ten times as high as the other, are both marginal buyers of the same thing at the same price? Neither, in this assumption, would pay a penny more than a dollar for the ticket—both are strictly marginal buyers at the price of a dollar. The explanation, and the only one, is found in this: the marginal desirability of the game is ten times as great for the poor as for the rich boy. If the dollar and the game have each one unit of desirability for the rich boy, they must each have ten units for the poor boy. The equality of ratios between the alternative good to be bought with the dollar and the game is the only sense in which the marginal desirabilities of these boys are comparable. Throughout the market the marginal desirabilities of different classes of purchasers are comparable only in the sense of the equality of ratios. It is in the sense of the equality of ratios that different classes are brought together as marginal buyers in the same market at the same price.

**28. Exercises.**—1. What is the connection between intelligence, desire, and effort?

2. What reasons can you give for the fact that, as a rule, one's desire for the present possession of a good is stronger than the desire for the future possession of it?

3. What is meant by the principle of harmony in consumption? Give an example of how the purchase of one thing calls for the purchase of other things in each of the following: buying a rug, a gun, a pen, an engine, a horse.

What other industries have benefited by the great demand for automobiles within recent years?

4. Would the "simple life," causing a desire for only a few simple goods, bring about a larger or a smaller production of goods than we now enjoy? (Review paragraphs 7 and 8 before answering this.)

5. Give two examples—the one to show how a business house has been prospered, and the other to show how a business house has been injured through the association of ideas.

6. Give two examples of large expenditures during the World War to gratify the altruistic desires of the people.

7. What is meant by the standard of life? By what forces is it determined?

8. "Fewness and scarcity are not synonyms." (Paragraph 16.) Tell why.

9. Desirability and utility are not synonyms. (Paragraphs 17 and 18.) Define each of these terms in your own words.

10. By adding ton after ton to my supply of coal, the total desirability increases at a diminishing rate. What principle is involved in this statement? Show the relationship between this principle and that of the equal desirability of units in a supply of like goods.

11. Define marginal desirability.

By means of the principle of marginal desirability, explain the following:

(a) The housewife, in the above example (paragraph 24) stopped with the purchase of the twentieth cake of soap, although she desired many more. If the price had been reduced from five to four cents a cake, she would have purchased twenty-five cakes.

(b) One enjoys the maximum desirability by maintaining an equality, so far as he can, of the marginal desirabilities of the different goods he buys.

(c) An essential, such as bread, is worth less than a luxury, such as a diamond.

(d) One ordinarily attributes no value to air.

(e) A part may be worth more than the whole; for by destroying a portion the remainder goes up in price.

(f) In a fair trade, both parties are benefited.

# CHAPTER VII

## MARKET AND PRICE

**1. What Is a Market?**—In common parlance we have "the world market," "the American market," "the New York market," "the New Orleans market," etc. These expressions signify place as essential to the definition of a market. Again we have "the wheat market," "the money market," "the cotton market." These expressions centre around the idea of a particular commodity. We debate the advisability of establishing a "central city market" to which farmers may bring their various products and dispose of them direct to the consumers. Here the word market signifies the coming together of buyers and sellers with respect to a number of different commodities. The word market is abused by such a variety of uses that we spare space to give it precise definition.

The word market does not signify any particular place nor does it refer to a group of commodities indiscriminately. It means an agreement within a group of exchangers as to the price of a ·particular species of commodity. It will be seen that there is no such concept as a demand for or a supply of a group of unlike commodities. Supply and demand refer to one species of commodity, cotton, for instance, at a uniform price. The adjustment of supply and demand takes place in a market, therefore one market embodies one species of commodity and one group of exchangers. In one market are found all of the influences of supply and demand which converge toward a uniform price. Due allowance in price must be made in all cases for costs of transit which are occasioned by differences in the physical location of the goods marketed.

It is a matter of no consequence whether the buyers and sellers of a species of commodity live in the same village or in different continents, they belong to the same market by virtue of the fact that they buy from and sell to each other. In the market goods may be sold by actual exhibit, or by sample, or by mere description. The traders in a market may meet face to face or be on opposite sides of the water. They may make their offers and bids by word of mouth, by symbol, by wire, or by any other means. It has no bearing on the definition of a market whether a commodity be controlled by an absolute monopoly or subject to unrestricted competition. Many writers deny that there is a market where competition is restricted. But if a monopoly product like anthracite coal is not sold on the market, then where is it sold?

**2. Examples of a Market.**—There are as many markets as there are groups of exchangers. A manufacturer sells one hundred dozen hats of the same grade to a wholesaler. The wholesaler resells to twenty jobbers; the jobbers resell to two hundred retailers; the retailers resell to a thousand consumers. This is an example, not of one but of four markets.

There are as many markets as there are differences of

price after allowing for costs of transportation, freights, deterioration, insurance, and the like. One market implies uniformity in the grade offered for sale. It is obvious that if a vender offers different portions of his supply at different prices the purchasers will buy at the lower price. There would be no demand at the higher asking price and a keen demand at the lower, the effect of which would, of course, result in a common uniform price. Suppose, now, that the manufacturer sells fifty dozen hats to a wholesaler in Winnipeg at one price, and that he makes a similar sale to a wholesaler in Memphis at a different price; each of these sells to twenty jobbers (both sell to forty jobbers), charging each jobber a different price from all the others. Each jobber sells to ten retailers, charging no two the same price (all jobbers thus sell to four hundred retailers). How many markets are here indicated? In this example we have two prices as between the manufacturer and the wholesalers, which means two groups of exchangers and two markets; as between the wholesalers and jobbers there are forty markets, and four hundred markets between the jobbers and the retailers. This totals four hundred and forty-two markets.

Another example is needed: The manufacturer of "Mrs. Blank's Face-Cream" maintains a restricted price policy. He widely advertises the retail price of his article at 50 cents. He sells without discrimination, large lots and small, to fifty wholesalers at 30 cents; he requires the wholesalers to sell to retailers at a fixed price of 40 cents and a thousand sales are made to retailers; the retailers sell at a maintained price of 50 cents to ten thousand consumers. Here we have three and only three markets.

Briefly stated: A market means an agreement between

buyers and sellers with reference to the exchange of a species of commodities at a uniform price, with allowance for costs of transit. Like goods in a given market at the same time sell at the same price.

**3. Transportation Extends the Market.**—If there were no transportation facilities each producer would be compelled to dispose of his wares in the immediate vicinity of their production. Transportation extends the boundaries of a market, without respect to political boundaries. Extended markets permit the individuals of each community to enjoy a variety of goods coming from the different climates, soils, and deposits of resources. Trade is a means of adjusting our goods to our desires, and the broader the market the more perfect becomes the adjustment of our means to the meeting of our desires.

**4. Wheat is Sold in a Broad Market.**—The wheat-crop of 1914–15 was the largest crop in the history of this country. One would reason that the price of wheat would be correspondingly low. But, in fact, the price became so high as to alarm the public and make a demand to stop its exportation. How explain this fact?

Wheat is subject to definite classification according to grade or quality. All traders know exactly what is meant when any particular grade is mentioned, therefore they may intelligently buy and sell wheat, which may be located in any part of the world, or which, in fact, may not be harvested at the time a trade is made. Moreover, wheat is durable, thus making it capable of being transported to any part of the world. Some countries produce a surplus and export wheat, while other countries cannot supply their needs, thus becoming importers. The following tables show these facts:

## AVERAGE ANNUAL EXPORTS (1909–1913) OF WHEAT OF SIX PRINCIPAL EXPORTING COUNTRIES

| Country | Bushels | Country | Bushels |
|---|---|---|---|
| Russia | 148,262,700 | United States | 53,024,700 |
| Argentina | 96,858,600 | India | 40,711,100 |
| Canada | 65,064,500 | Australia | 36,670,700 |

## AVERAGE ANNUAL IMPORTS (1909–1913) OF WHEAT OF SIX PRINCIPAL IMPORTING COUNTRIES

| Country | Bushels | Country | Bushels |
|---|---|---|---|
| Great Britain and Ireland | 191,693,300 | Netherlands | 63,355,100 |
| Germany | 87,357,000 | Italy | 56,302,900 |
| Belgium | 73,422,800 | France | 34,169,500 |

(These tables and the remarks on the wheat market are based on chapter XII of Professor L. H. D. Weld's excellent book, The Marketing of Farm Products.)

These figures show that the large importers are confined to a small place in western Europe. Liverpool is the trade centre of this consumption area. The exporting countries are in both the northern and southern hemispheres; their crops mature in different seasons. The following table shows the sources of the Liverpool market wheat receipts throughout the year:

| To Liverpool in | January | from Australia. |
| " " " | February | " Australia, Argentina. |
| " " " | March | " Australia, Argentina. |
| " " " | April | " Argentina. |
| " " " | May | " ———. |
| " " " | June | " India. |
| " " " | July | " India. |
| " " " | August | " India, United States. |
| " " " | September | " United States, Russia. |
| " " " | October | " United States, Russia, Canada. |
| " " " | November | " Russia, Canada. |
| " " " | December | " Canada. |

Wheat may be bought and sold prior to its production, may be transported any distance, may be stored through time, matures at different times throughout the year, and from exporting countries it diverges toward a common centre at Liverpool. What is more natural than that a highly organized wheat market should grow out of these conditions? The Liverpool market may better be termed a world market because in it the influences of supply and demand are international in scope and operate toward a uniform price.

**5. Transporting Costs Taken into Account.**—The Chicago or Minneapolis price of wheat is approximately that of the Liverpool price, minus, of course, the cost of insurance, freight, handling, etc. Were the Chicago price approximately as high as the Liverpool price no American would export his wheat. But we produce a surplus beyond our needs and the competition of sellers pushes down the price, making it profitable to export to Liverpool. We are each year on an "export basis"; that is to say, we find it profitable to export, because we have a surplus.

**6. The Demand at Liverpool.**—The Liverpool demand is an aggregate of the offers of consumers who buy directly or indirectly through that market. One's demand is intense in proportion to his desire, coupled with his ability and willingness to pay. The market demand for wheat is somewhat elastic, for if the price is too high, rye, barley, and other substitutes would be used; small variations in price would occasion large variations in the volume of sales. The demand for foreign wheat would diminish if the importing countries were blessed with a large crop. Or in case these nations are impoverished by war, the demand will diminish, because the people will have but little purchasing power. A shortage of crop in Russia and Canada will operate to increase the price of wheat from other parts of the world, because prices must be forced high enough to induce a larger shipment from other countries. Liverpool can get wheat in any case only by outcompeting the potential buyers in the exporting countries. In 1914–15 the United States and Argentina had a large surplus of wheat. Russia's surplus could not get through the Dardanelles; Canada and India had small crops, and Australia's crop was a failure. There was an international play of forces which brought high prices to the American farmer.

The suppliers and demanders throughout the countries above mentioned compose a single group of exchangers within which agreements are reached as to the price of a particular commodity. This fulfils all the requirements of a market. The expression, a world market for wheat, is justified.

7. **The Communication of Information.**—We have mentioned transportation or the movement of commodities as essential to a broad market. But it must be kept in mind that a market implies intimate business relations, a meeting of the minds of buyers and sellers with respect to the price of commodities dealt in. The submarine cable brings Liverpool and the Chicago wheat-pit together, and it unites Liverpool and New Orleans with respect to cotton. Conditions of transportation and the communication of information are essential to the idea of a market. These conditions are essential to the converging of influences toward a market price. Without these conditions each community would have its own independent market, but with the perfection and extension of the agencies of com-

munication the market broadens. Local markets lose their independence with the broadening and uniting of the community of interests.

Frequent publications of statistical and other information bearing upon both the present supply and the probable future supply are of great aid to a group of exchangers. To the extent that such information is complete, man may reason rather than guess on turns in price. The tendency toward gambling is repressed, and we have the wholesome effect of an approximation toward uniform prices through time.

**8. Market Ratios and Price.**—The market ratios of exchange taken as a whole can, of course, neither rise nor fall. If to-day one ox will exchange for twenty sheep, whereas yesterday one ox exchanged for twenty-five sheep, we must say that relative to the sheep the ox has gone down, or relative to the ox the sheep have gone up. Thus we know, both cannot rise or fall at the same time in relation to each other; and what is true of the ox and sheep holds for all commodities. All commodities cannot simultaneously rise or fall in relation to each other, yet they may rise or fall in relation to any one among the number. If cattle be the species of commodity selected, commodities in general may rise or fall in relation to cattle. The exchange ratios of other commodities to one selected commodity are their *prices*. Prices are generally expressed in terms of money, "yet," says F. A. Walker, "it is equally correct to say that the price of a horse is seventy-five bushels of wheat, as to say that it is $100." And we may add that while seventy-five bushels of wheat is the price of the horse, the horse is the price of seventy-five bushels of wheat. In every exchange there are two prices; if one exchanges his dog for a fighting-cock, the price of the fighting-cock is the dog, and the price of the dog is the fighting-cock.

Despite the fact that price is the amount of one commodity given in exchange for another, we usually think of price in terms of money. The money price of a thing is nothing more or less than the amount of money given in exchange for that thing. From childhood we are accustomed to the use of money, we think in terms of it, adjust our dealings to it, evaluate commodities in terms of it. We all speak a common language, or know precisely what is meant when talking in terms of money. Money is the one form of wealth generally acceptable in exchange. Its common use and general exchangeability as between all classes in the community make it practical and necessary to speak of prices in terms of money.

9. **The market price** is the equating-point between market supply and market demand in a market. This market price tends to bring all individual prices in conformity with itself. If one could market his corn at $1 a bushel he would not sell to his neighbor at 90 cents, and his neighbor would refuse to pay $1.10 could he buy in the market at $1.

10. **The problem of price** is to explain the price movements which cause goods to be cheap or dear. Business men become expert in forecasting the prices of certain commodities. The cotton-speculator has an office equipped with every device for obtaining information which may affect the price of cotton. As a specialist on cotton his judgment regarding movements in the price of steel may be worth little or nothing. But he has at his finger's end a knowledge of the influences behind the supply of and the

demand for cotton. He knows, for instance, of the probable need of cotton for explosives, of changes in fashions, of the use of substitutes for cotton; if there has been a storm in India, or a flood in Brazil, or a boll-weevil pest in Texas, or a shortage of cars, or an attempt to corner the market, or a strike at the cotton-mills, or a blockade around the Liverpool market, he knows both the fact and its probable influence on the price. The business man is interested primarily in one or two commodities and can forecast the prices with surprising accuracy.

The economist's task goes deeper; he must explain the ultimate forces back of price movements in general. The task of the business man is easier because he searches into the narrow range of facts bearing directly upon his special field of interest. Moreover, he assumes in the beginning fundamental propositions which the economist must prove. The economist approaches this problem through an analysis of the ultimate forces behind supply and demand. Also he is compelled to explain movements in the purchasing power of money because the prices of goods are expressed in money, and must therefore vary with the purchasing power of money.

11. **The price level,** or general average of the prices of commodities, if accurately kept through a period of years, is a basis for determining the movements in the general purchasing power of a dollar. But the formulation of price levels through a series of years is in no sense a study of price movements. The prices averaged to obtain a price level simply register the results of former price movements. What caused these prices to be as they are? This question puts the problem; it sets the task of a search into the nature and causes of the movements back of

price. There are many careful students who diligently collect price statistics over a period of years and by means of index numbers formulate these data into price levels. This is excellent and needed work. But they delude themselves by terming it an account or study of price movements when, in fact, it is but an accumulation of the effects of price movements.

12. **Price-Making.**—In the market demands are made and goods are offered for sale. One observes that trade takes place at prices agreed on in the process. He observes further that higher prices attract more sellers and that lower prices attract more buyers. He sees that when prices are high keen competition among the sellers pushes the price down, and that when prices are low keen competition among buyers pushes the price up. What he does not see are the subtle and real but unexpressed marginal desirabilities limiting or fixing the lowest figure below which the sellers will not part with their goods, and the upper limit to the bids of the buyers. Whatever the hidden facts may be, however, the bald fact stands out that the expressed supply and demand, the actual and disclosed figures of the buyer and seller fix the market price. The market price, as above noted, is the point at which market supply and market demand are equated.

13. **Conditions of Price-Making.**—We may briefly outline the usual conditions under which prices are made.[1]

    I.  One seller without a limit below which he will not sell:
        (1) One seller, one non-reproducible good, one buyer.
        (2) One seller, one non-reproducible good, several buyers (one-sided competition).

[1] Monopoly prices will be discussed in another connection.

(3) One seller, a number of non-reproducible goods, several buyers (one-sided competition).

II.   One seller with a limit below which he will not sell:

(1) One seller, one non-reproducible good, one buyer.

(2) One seller, one non-reproducible good, several buyers (one-sided competition).

(3) One seller, a number of non-reproducible goods, several buyers (one-sided competition).

(4) One seller, a number of reproducible goods, a number of buyers (one-sided competition).

III.   A number of sellers with a limit below which they will not sell:

(1) A number of sellers, a number of reproducible goods, one buyer (one-sided competition).

IV.   Two-sided competition:

(1) A number of sellers, a number of reproducible goods, a number of buyers.

I. *One seller without a limit below which he will not sell.* (1) If in a forced sale there be one non-reproducible good, such as a rare antique, it is evident that if but one buyer presents himself the price may be made at a very low figure. Something must be allowed for bluff, for a pretense of hidden facts on the part of the seller, and for skill at bargaining.

(2) But the case will be very different with respect to price if a number of buyers present themselves in competition for the rare antique. Figure 1 is designed to represent the buyers by the symbols $B^1, B^2, B^3$. Their maximum subjective offers of $4, $3, $2 are given for the corresponding symbols. The seller has no limit below which he will not sell, but, of course, he is anxious to obtain the largest figure he can. The three bidders may start with

low offers, each bidding above
the others until the $2 is reached.
Beyond this point B³ refuses to.
go, leaving the competition to.
B¹ and B². These continue the
contest, neither knowing the other's maximum subject offer, until B²'s maximum limit of $3 is
reached. The price will fall at

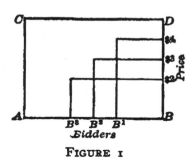

FIGURE 1

the point of B¹'s last bid, which will be somewhere between $3 and $4.

(3) In case one seller is forced to sell, for anything they
will bring, a collection of antiques (which are approximately
the same in all respects) to a number of buyers, a very different situation arises. The seller may adopt either of
two policies: he may conceal his supply, offering for sale
but one unit at a time, or he may offer the total supply at
one time. In the former case each transaction will be
carried through as indicated in Figure 1. But suppose
there are five units, five meteoric stones approximately
equal in all respects, of-
fered at one time to six
competitors. If we con-
struct a figure (Figure
2) on a similar plan to
that of Figure 1, B⁶ will
be first to drop out in the
bidding. Now, if we as-
sume that one buyer will
take one unit there will
be left five buyers for the
five units. Since all are

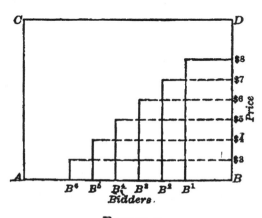

FIGURE 2

to be sold the price cannot go above $4, because B$^5$ would drop out, leaving only four purchasers. The price will be fixed at $4, or between $3 and $4. All of the units would sell at the same price, because at any one time similar units are not treated differently in the market. Like portions of a supply in the same market at the same time sell at the same price, regardless of the degree of desirability which may accompany each such portion. If one unit is held for a lower price the competition of bidders will raise its price; if one unit is held for a higher price the want of competition among bidders will lower its price. Free competition means uniformity of price under uniform conditions.

*II. One seller with a limit below which he will not sell.* (1) If the seller of a non-reproducible good, for instance the original production of an old artist, refuses to part with his good for less than $2,000, a sale is conditioned on the payment of that sum or more. Should one buyer with a maximum subjective offer of $3,000 present himself a sale will be made. The price will be fixed at $2,000 or $3,000, or more than likely between these limits. Skill at bargaining will have much to do with the fixing of the price.

Figure 3 is designed to represent the buyer by the symbol B' and the seller by the symbol S. The limit below which S will not sell and the maximum offer of B' are given for the corresponding symbols. The figure, I take it, is self-explanatory, indicating as it does that if skill at bargaining be approximately equal as between S and B, the price will fall at or near $2,500.

(2) Suppose, however, that S has widely advertised his rare production and that a number of buyers present

themselves in competition for it. We are now presented with a situation of common occurrence, where a seller with a reserve price parts with his good under the condition of one-sided competition. Again we may resort to the aid of a figure which will visualize the transaction. Figure 4 is con-

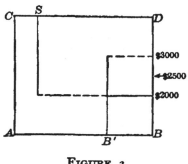

FIGURE 3

structed according to the plan of Figure 3. We have here represented one seller with a reservation price of $2,000, and six buyers whose maximum offers range from $1,000 to $6,000. A sale will be made because there are buyers willing to pay more than S holds as a reserve price. But where will the price be fixed? Competition between buyers must answer this question. Competitive bidding will first eliminate B⁶, and as it progresses B⁵, B⁴, B³ will successively drop out. B² and B¹, neither knowing what the other may have "up his sleeve," remain in the contest. B², however, drops out the moment that the maximum

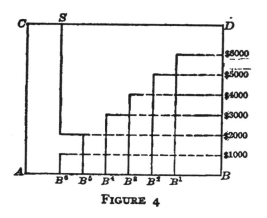

FIGURE 4

which he would pay ($5,000) is passed. This leaves the price to be fixed at any bid which B¹ may make above $5,000.

(3) A seller may have a number of non-reproducible goods, alike in all respects, which he would not sell below a

certain figure. Assume that he has a reserve price of $2,000 on each of five such goods, and that six bidders enter into competition for them. As in paragraph 3, under the heading, "One seller without a limit below which he will not sell," this seller may have either of two selling policies; he may conceal the supply and offer for sale but one unit at a time, or he may offer the whole supply at one and the same time. Assuming that each buyer will take but a single unit in any case, we may proceed to explain by aid of the accompanying Figure 5. If we assume a policy of selling one unit at a time the above description accompanying Figure 4 will show that the price of the first unit sold will be above $5,000, with $6,000 as a maximum. The second

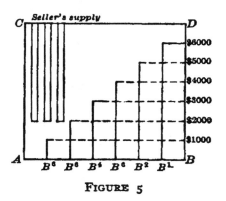

FIGURE 5

unit will be above $4,000, with $5,000 as a maximum; the third $3,000 to $4,000; the fourth $2,000 to $3,000, and the fifth will be exactly $2,000.

If all are thrown on the market at one time they must sell, as we have seen, at one uniform price. (See paragraph accompanying Figure 2 above.) This price could not be below the seller's reserve price of $2,000, nor could it be higher than $2,000, because there would be only four buyers willing to pay more than $2,000.

(4) The case of one seller of a number of reproducible goods to a number of buyers presents the case of a selling monopoly. Monopoly price holds such a conspicuous place in economics that it is thought best to re-

# Market and Price 139

III. *A number of sellers with a limit below which they will not sell.* (1) A number of sellers may actively compete in the selling of a number of commodities similar in all respects. They may or may not have a limit below which they will not sell. It is termed a buying monopoly when they have to sell to a single purchaser. This point must await its turn for consideration. It is called two-sided competition when they compete in selling to a number of competing buyers.

IV. *Two-sided competition.* (1) The selling of a number of like commodities by a group of competing sellers to a group of competing buyers is, as above stated, two-sided competition. This represents the usual manner of buying and selling on the market. We have seen that as the price is lowered the number of sales is increased in two ways: (*a*) More buyers come into the market, (*b*) each buyer may take a larger number of goods. The reverse of this is true in case the price is raised. The sellers, in turn, will throw a larger supply on the market with a rise in price, and *vice versa.* This may be indicated as follows:

| *Demand scale for bushels of wheat* | Bushels | *Supply scale of bushels of wheat* | Bushels |
|---|---|---|---|
| At $0.80 buyers will purchase | 20,000 | At $0.80 sellers will supply | 2,000 |
| " .81 " " " | 19,000 | " .81 " " " | 5,000 |
| " .82 " " " | 17,500 | " .82 " " " | 7,500 |
| " .83 " " " | 16,000 | " .83 " " " | 9,000 |
| " .84 " " " | 14,000 | " .84 " " " | 11,000 |
| " .85 " " " | 12,500 | " .85 " " " | 12,500 |
| " .86 " " " | 11,000 | " .86 " " " | 14,000 |
| " .87 " " " | 9,000 | " .87 " " " | 16,000 |
| " .88 " " " | 7,500 | " .88 " " " | 17,500 |
| " .89 " " " | 5,000 | " .89 " " " | 19,000 |
| " .90 " " " | 2,000 | " .90 " " " | 20,000 |

(2) The above supply and demand scales may be graphically represented by superimposing one curve upon the other (Figure 6). The distance from the point of intersection of the supply and demand curves, *X*, to the base

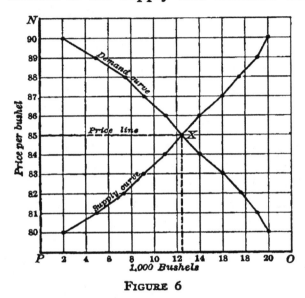

line *PO* is equal to the price, 85 cents, which free competition establishes; the length of the price line represents the number of bushels sold at the competitive price. The intersection of these curves marks the equating-point of market supply and demand. The market tends to be permanent; the market price of uniform goods at any one time is the same price (like goods in the same market at the same time sell at the same price), but there is no continuous price. Each trade represents a distinct and separate price. Price curves are drawn to show movements of the prices of particular articles through time. Such curves, however, must not be interpreted as picturing continuous prices; they show but a succession of individual prices.

Market price refers to one species of commodity. Market demand equals the amount of one species of commodity that will be purchased at the market price, and market supply equals the amount that will be sold at that price. That is to say, market supply and market demand are equal (the amount sold is equal to the amount bought) and that market price is the equating-point between them. Should the price be arbitrarily marked up to 86 cents (see Figure 6) there will be fewer who are anxious to buy and more who are anxious to sell, or if marked down to 84 cents then more would be anxious to buy and fewer anxious to sell. Such would destroy the equilibrium between supply and demand.

Under free competition the price would automatically revert to the point of equality between market supply and market demand. The market price is, under active competition, precisely at a point or margin of both market supply and market demand. The same point (market price) marks the margin for both sides of the market equation. At this point of 85 cents in a nicely adjusted market there are indifferent buyers and sellers; sellers who will withdraw if the price drops a fraction, buyers who will withdraw if the price rises a fraction. These least eager buyers and sellers are strictly marginal buyers and sellers. These have been inaptly termed *the marginal pair* (the least eager buyer and seller), as if there could be but one such person on either side of the market. There may be any number on either side of the market barely willing to exchange at this point.

A buyer and seller in the market trade at one market price. This allows a *margin of advantage* for the sellers who would take less and for buyers who would pay more. At a market price of 85 cents there is a margin of advantage of 5 cents for those buyers who would pay 90 cents, also there is a margin of advantage of 5 cents for those sellers whose reservation price is 80 cents. The buyer's margin of advantage is equal to the difference between what he does pay and the maximum which he would pay rather than forego the good, whereas the seller's margin of advantage is the difference between the market price of the good and his reservation price. The surplus desirability thus acquired is the gain or product of trading.

14. **Exercises.**—1. Does a large congregation of people among whom goods are exchanged by barter constitute a market?

2. Assume that a local merchant contracts with a farmer to take his total supply of cotton at the end of the season, paying for it the market price prevailing at the time the cotton is marketed, and that he allows the farmer to take goods from his store prior to the maturity of the crop, and that he agrees to pay the farmer the residue in money after the crop is gathered. Is this purchase made in a market? If so, is the market any particular place? If not, what is the market?

3. Assume that the cotton mentioned in the above question is sold by the local merchant to a New Orleans merchant, and resold by the latter in a cotton exchange. Do these different exchanges take place in the same market?

4. Is Montgomery Ward & Co. a market or many markets? If a market, or markets, what is the location? Is the wheat market located at Minneapolis, or Chicago, or Liverpool, or does it have a location? What is meant by a "world market for wheat?"

5. Tell what is meant by the italicised phrases in the following: All produce *for the market;* he has gone *to the market;* government control spoiled *the market* for this product; advertising created *a market* for Pears' soap; the money *market* is dull; a *central city market* tends to lower prices.

6. Define the word market, and show its function, as you have defined it, in the industrial world.

7. What is a market price? Are all prices market prices?

8. Is the problem of price the same as finding the price level?

9. Summarize the conditions, as mentioned in the latter part of this chapter, under which prices are made.

10. What would be the market price of wheat under the following conditions of supply and demand:

| *Demand scale for bushels of wheat* | | | | Bushels | *Supply scale of bushels of wheat* | | | | Bushels |
|---|---|---|---|---|---|---|---|---|---|
| At $0.40 buyers will purchase | | | | 10,000 | At $0.40 sellers will supply | | | | 1,000 |
| " | .41 | " | " | " | 9,500 | " | .41 | " | " | " | 2,500 |
| " | .42 | " | " | " | 8,750 | " | .42 | " | " | " | 3,750 |
| " | .43 | " | " | " | 8,000 | " | .43 | " | " | " | 4,500 |
| " | .44 | " | " | " | 7,000 | " | .44 | " | " | " | 5,500 |
| " | .45 | " | " | " | 6,250 | " | .45 | " | " | " | 6,250 |
| " | .46 | " | " | " | 5,500 | " | .46 | " | " | " | 7,000 |
| " | .47 | " | " | " | 4,500 | " | .47 | " | " | " | 8,000 |
| " | .48 | " | " | " | 3,750 | " | .48 | " | " | " | 8,750 |
| " | .49 | " | " | " | 2,500 | " | .49 | " | " | " | 9,500 |
| " | .50 | " | " | " | 1,000 | " | .50 | " | " | " | 10,000 |

# CHAPTER VIII

## VALUE AND DEMAND

**1. Price, a Restatement.**—The preceding chapter had to do with the making of exchanges in a market, and showed that in every exchange a price emerges. It should now be clear that there is no such thing as price, apart from an exchange of one thing for another. Shoes are exhibited for sale and marked $8, $10, and $15 a pair. Are these figures prices? They are not, although we so speak of them in common parlance; they are no more than the exhibited offers of the merchant. In the column of stock quotations one sees a certain stock offered at 115, and sees that the maximum bid for it is perhaps only 100. Does a sale take place? There is no meeting of minds as between buyers and sellers; there can be no exchange, and, in consequence, no price.

What is price? The definitions of price from the year 1771 to the present have, with great diligence, been brought together and classified by Professor F. A. Fetter.[1]

[1] The " Definitions of Price," *American Economic Review*, vol. XI, no. 4, pp. 783–813.

The conclusion of this very able contribution, together with the weight of authority upon the subject, gives us this definition: "Price is the quantity of goods given or received in exchange for another good." F. A. Walker gives a clear expression of this idea: "Price is purchasing power expressed in terms of some one article; power-in-exchange-for-that-article, be the same wheat, or beef, or wool, or gold, or silver. In common speech the word price brings up the idea of money-value, the purchasing power of an article expressed in terms of money. Yet it is equally correct to say that the price is 75 bushels of wheat, as to say it is $100."

Price implies a quantitative exchange, so many units of one thing given in trade for another. If you trade $1 for a cap, you give 23.22 grains of fine gold, or its equivalent, for the cap. You may give a unit of gold, or wheat, or iron for the cap, but in any case trade implies an exchange of quantities, and price is the quantity of one thing given in exchange for another.

In most cases price, as stated in the preceding chapter, signifies the quantity of money paid for a good or service, but there are numerous exceptions to this. Country stores usually ask two prices for their goods—the money-price and the produce-price. Coffee may be quoted at 25 cents in money, or at a slightly higher price in butter and eggs. In all barter transactions prices emerge, although no money is handled. International trade is, for the most part, barter, for comparatively little gold is involved in these transactions.

Price is not what would be given if circumstances were different, nor is it what should be given. There are no "ifs" or "shoulds" about it; it is the amount (quantity) of one thing which, in the process of exchange, is given for another thing.

The preceding chapter showed a price to be at the point of equilibrium between market supply and market demand. Price can no more be attributed to supply than to demand, or *vice versa*. Demand stationary, price changes with variations in supply. Or with supply fixed, price changes with variations in demand. A full account of price, therefore, can be reached only through a study of supply and demand. Demand, now to be considered, is based directly upon value and valuations. But what is value?

2. **Value.** The word value is burdened with a variety of meanings. It is used in the household and market-place, in senses technical and non-technical, in works on natural science and social science and in the writings of popular fiction. We hear these expressions: the value of heat units, the value of a word or phrase, valuable man, valuable idea or suggestion. In economic writings one finds a variety of different uses for the word, such as value in use, value in exchange, social value, objective value, subjective value, and so on. Many writers define the word as we have defined price, but price implies an exchange whereas value does not.

This term is not limited to objects which are for sale. The following are valuable things, although not for sale: Government reservations of natural resources; public buildings, as the capitol, jail, or schoolhouse; parks and highways; libraries, museums, zoological or botanical collections. Within this class, also, are many private possessions, as the picture of a deceased friend, grandfather's old pipe, one's clothing, and keepsakes of many kinds.

These things are not market facts, are not for sale, yet a definition that denies value to them would not, and should not, be taken seriously.

We shall define value as the importance which one attributes to an objective good or service. As such it is a very real subjective fact, but it is difficult to define it with exact quantitative or arithmetic exactness. An appraisal of things in their quantitative aspects is necessary as a foundation for exchanges where a definite amount of one thing is given in trade for a specified quantity of another. The idea of valuation serves this purpose; we will explain it shortly.

3. **Value Is an Individualistic Matter.**—Being the importance which the mind attributes to a good or service, value is in no sense to be considered a part of the good. It is an error to speak of intrinsic value, as though value were a quality of a good.

The same good varies in one's esteem with the change of desire; "witness the frumpy horror that was last year a coveted bonnet." We discover new qualities in goods, new services to which they may be put, and these lead us to attribute importance to them.

Around her flower-bed a lady had placed some odd-shaped rocks, which she had found at a river's side. A visitor was attracted to one of these, examined it, and made her an offer of $100 for its possession. This excited her imagination, and what to her had been but a worthless ornament became a rare and precious object. She refused the offer, and refused each successive offer, except the final bid, which was $5,000. A new quality was discovered in the rock—it contained diamonds. But this she did not know, for the visitor never revealed the secret of his find-

# 148 *Introduction to Economics*

ing. Her thought was that if it were worth thousands to the visitor, it must be of great importance for her. Thus value may be attributed either because we find a new quality or because we suspect such a quality to exist. In any case value is subjective; it is a quality imputed to an object.

Again, we may highly esteem a good under one set of circumstances, and a change of conditions, such as new inventions or styles, may largely diminish or destroy this value.

Moreover, we may highly prize an object when we believe it to have desirability, even if such quality is absent. At an auction sale a box was offered for what it would bring. The auctioneer declined to say whether anything was in it. He asked for bids and the highest offer was $3.75. On examination the purchaser found that the box was empty. That value was attributed to the box, however, cannot be denied. This but illustrates the fact that value is an attributed quality. It is natural for each and all to attribute less value to things which are plentiful. Were diamonds as plentiful as glass, one would then attribute no more value to the former than to the latter.

4. **"The Paradox of Value."**—If by magic the supply of necessities, comforts, and conveniences were increased until they became as abundant as air, they would cease to have value attributed to them and could command no price. When the total amount of any good is increased beyond a certain point, there is a decrease in its total price. This fact is termed the "paradox of value." Great abundance means great wealth whereas extreme scarcity may mean high price. If corn is scarce and sells at a dol-

lar a bushel, the total crop will be worth more than if it were twice as large and sold at forty cents a bushel, or four times as large and sold at eighteen cents a bushel.

When an individual (or corporation) controls a large portion of the amount of corn, wheat, or other commodity, it is to his interest to increase his output up to a certain point, and beyond that point his self-interest lies in destroying or otherwise limiting the supply in order to increase its price. The interest of the individual coincides with social welfare so long as it is to his interest to increase his output, but he comes into conflict with social welfare the moment that his interest lies in curtailing the supply. The paradox of value is a significant practical problem with which economists and lawmakers must deal in the regulation of monopoly power.

But in competitive industries the case is otherwise. If all crops are large the total amount of produce may have a less total price than if the crops were small. The individual farmer, none the less, finds it to his interest to make his output as large as is within his power. It would be unwise for him to produce no crop or a small crop, because that would avail him nothing. He would thus increase the price for his competitors at his own expense.

As for society, it is now clear that the per unit price of a good diminishes as the supply of it is enlarged; this makes it possible for a large to have a less total price than a small supply. As for the individual, we have seen that the marginal desirability of a good diminishes as one comes to possess more and more of it. It is in order to apply this principle in the study of exchange transactions. We shall now see that it limits and directs such transactions.

**5. Surplus and the Limit to Exchanges.**—Modern industry, as we have seen, is characterized by a division of labor, specialization, and exchange. One can specialize and devote his every effort to the making of hats because he can exchange these for the various goods he may choose to acquire. If there were no exchange it is clear that the manufacturer could not turn out five thousand hats a month. The division of labor and specialization are made possible by exchange. When one specializes in the making of hats it must follow that he will have a surplus of hats and a want for other things. But while he is anxious to exchange his surplus for other things, there is a limit at which he will cease trading. This is the limit of equal marginal desirabilities.

To illustrate: A has a bag of salt, and B has a bag of rice. They meet in trade. Each demands what the other has, and each supplies what the other has not. A hands over a pint of salt and B hands over a pint of rice; this is repeated time after time. As his supply of salt diminishes A finds that the remaining units have an increasing desirability; he attributes a higher value to them. And as he acquires additional units of rice, their marginal desirabilities diminish; he attributes less value to each unit of rice. Ultimately he reaches the point where the desirabilities of a unit of rice and a unit of salt are equal. When A reaches the point of equality of marginal desirabilities he stops trading on the old basis. B can push the trading further only by offering more than a pint of rice for a pint of salt.

This example illustrates that each buyer must also be a seller, and that each seller must also be a buyer. There are two suppliers and two demanders in every trade. It illustrates further that the limit to one's trading is reached at the point of equality between two marginal desirabilities.

**6. Decision in Directing Expenditures.**—Every purchase implies a decision to buy on the part of the purchaser. This decision may be the result of a whim, fancy, or impulse; it may be ill considered or well considered, none the less it is a decision. The psychologist may bother himself, if he wishes, as to the manner of its origin, but the economist takes the decision as a fact and proceeds.

Take, for example, the ladies at a bargain-counter. Some weigh light matters seriously, complaining that they cannot make up their minds. Others are all but incapable of decision, "like the ass between two stacks . . . simply stand and dodder." Still others have a penetration of mind, making them quick of perception and decision. Their decisions are of nice discrimination, are not ill considered because they are quick. One admires the quick, yet accurate decisions of noteworthy business men. Such ready decisions are usually the result of previous thought and experience applied to specific cases. Then, too, there are those in the market who jump at a decision, who decide like a flash without deliberation past or present.

Professor Hoffding tells how Jeppe, a character in a comedy, is addicted to drink. His wife has just given him money and ordered him to buy soap. He knows that if he squanders the money his wife will beat him. He deliberates over the longing in his stomach and the fear for his back. "My stomach says you shall, my back you shall not." Desire plays its part by minimizing the one and magnifying the other. Jeppe asks himself: "Is not my stomach more to me than my back"? I say, "Yes."

"Yes" forms the decision. It is of little consequence whether strong appetite, habit, hunger, cold, fancy, or caprice forms the decision; the fact of economic consequences is that decision determines man's economic behavior, determines the direction of his expenditure, determines his every purchase in the market.

Every good and service in the market is competing for the purchaser's dollar. And, unfortunately for him, he can spend his dollar but once. He deliberates between the marginal desirabilities of goods. The marginal desirability of a free good is zero, that is to say, it has no marginal desirability. Deliberation and choice as between marginal desirabilities of goods must be limited to scarce goods. Only goods that are valued, and not all of these, enter into an exchange economy.

The purchaser has a desire for goods; the different goods which he may purchase are the alternatives for the course of his action; he deliberates between these alternatives and the result of his deliberation (decision) is to acquire one good in preference to another. Briefly put, expenditures are directed by a comparison between the marginal desirabilities of different goods; such comparison leads purchasers to attribute different degrees of importance to goods, and to reach a resulting decision to buy one rather than another.

7. **Valuation.**—The last paragraph showed us the manner in which expenditures are directed. It is now in order that we inquire more particularly into the manner in which one comes to offer his own good or service for that of another. Of all the goods competing for the purchaser's dollar, let us assume that his preference is for a pair of gloves. How did he reach the decision to part with what

he has for what he has not, to give his dollar for the gloves? Subjectively he weighed the marginal desirability of the alternative use for the dollar against that of the gloves. If in his own mind the marginal desirability of some one of the goods which the dollar would buy had outweighed that of the gloves, he would have attributed higher value to it and would have decided to retain his dollar for the alternative good and to do without the gloves. On the contrary, should the importance of the gloves be uppermost in his mind, he at once comes to the decision to offer his dollar in exchange for the gloves. This subjective weighing of the importance of one thing against another is called evaluation, and the decision to offer what one has for that which he has not is the outgrowth of the evaluation.

A valuation, then, is a subjective weighing of the importance which one attributes to different things. It may take the form of a mere price appraisal. For instance, one has a violin with which he will not part for less than 100 bushels of wheat or $100 in money, either of these sums will be his price appraisal, despite the fact that there may be no purchaser for the violin. Or the poor man might be willing to pay $100,000, if he had it, for a string of matched pearls. In this case the valuation would be no more than a hypothetical price. Valuation, or price appraisal, then, is but the price one would be willing to pay under certain conditions, the maximum one would pay for a good, or the minimum which he would take in case he owned the good. From this it is clear that all valuations do not lead to a demand or offer to buy. One may evaluate goods whether he has or has not the means to buy them. Again, if I evaluate a good in my possession more highly than a good which another owns, I would certainly not offer to trade with him. But while all valuations do not lead to offers, all offers arise from valuations.

When A and B met in trade with the salt and the rice, each compared the marginal desirabilities of a unit of that which he had with a unit of that which the other possessed. Each of the two parties to the exchange of rice for salt first made a subjective valuation preparatory to making an offer. Thus, each trade implies two valuations, one on the part of each trader. The decision to make a demand or offer for a good is, let it be remembered, always the result of a valuation.

**8. Caution in the Use of Supply and Demand.**—"Market prices are determined by supply and demand"; this statement is so frequently encountered in the language of the business world that we must spare space to ascertain exactly what these terms mean. Demand must not be confused with desire. The humblest peasant may desire a luxurious home with as much intensity as if he were a millionaire, but he could make no demand for it. Desire must be coupled with purchasing power before it can become a demand. A hungry group of impoverished people may besiege a shop for bread, and yet be unable to demand a single loaf. One must have purchasing power before he can demand a meal, or a ride on a train, or a suit of clothes, or any other salable thing on the market.

To whom does a demand refer? This term is used with reference to the buyer, or would-be buyer, who makes a reasonable offer for a good. One never demands his own wares; the thing demanded must always belong to another. Demand must not be confused with the idea of the owner's withholding a commodity from the market for his own use, or for a higher price. Demand may be used with respect to an individual or to a group of buyers.

To what does demand refer? It refers to a certain article, be it potatoes, or cotton cloth, or iron, or any other particular good; there is no such thing as demand indiscriminately for shoes, steel rails, pianos, peanuts, and all other salable things in the market. Nor does this term refer to a good which is not for sale. It is said that there is an abundance of coal near the south pole. For this there is need, but no demand. The government is withholding coal from the market. There is a desire but no demand for this, for the single reason that it is not for sale.

On the other hand, *supply* refers to the person, or group of persons, who offer a commodity for sale at a reasonable price. It also refers to a particular good, and not to goods indiscriminately.

It would not be a demand should one offer 50 cents for a piano, nor would your corn be a portion of the supply, should you hold it for $10 a bushel. Such absurd figures are wholly without the reckonings of the market, they are not at all market facts to which the market terms of supply and demand refer. It must be remembered that supply and demand refer to a salable good which is offered at a figure neither too high nor too low for buyers and sellers to consider.

9. **Amount, Supply.**—Assume an isolated community in which ten farmers devote their wealth and labor to the growing of potatoes. Each of the ten produces 1,000 bushels, thus making a total of 10,000 bushels of potatoes. Without further ado, we may speak of the 10,000 bushels at the end of the season as the amount or stock of potatoes on hand.

Each of the producers will wish to retain, to withhold from sale, a portion of his stock for food and for seed. Assume that each withholds 100 bushels for his own use. Each will thus have 900 bushels for sale, and the ten will have 9,000 bushels for sale. Assuming that these 9,000 bushels are for sale (some at a reasonably high, and others at a reasonably low price), we may speak of them as the *supply*. Supply is that portion of the amount which is for sale at asking prices, such as will fall within the contemplation of buyers and sellers.

10. **Price-Making Illustrated.**—Will the whole supply of 9,000 bushels be marketed forthwith? This is very improbable. The market demand may be weak, and so, were the whole supply at once thrown upon the market, it could be sold only at a very trifling figure. It is more probable that those producers who have some money ahead will prefer to sell none of their stock until the market improves; others who are in need of money will sell only a portion of their supply. A weak market demand calls forth a small volume of sales.

It is evident that at a high price many would be willing to sell, but only a few would care to buy. Buyers are attracted by low prices, but these discourage sellers. The self-interests of buyers and sellers pull in opposite directions. The following table will serve to show these facts:

| At | | purchasers would buy | | | | and producers would sell | | | | | |
|----|----|----|----|----|----|----|----|----|----|----|----|
| At | $2.00 | purchasers would buy | " | " | 1,000 bu. | " | and producers would sell | " | " | " | " | 9,000 bu. |
| " | 1.80 | " | " | " | 2,000 " | " | " | " | " | " | 8,000 " |
| " | 1.60 | " | " | " | 3,000 " | " | " | " | " | " | 7,000 " |
| " | 1.40 | " | " | " | 4,000 " | " | " | " | " | " | 6,000 " |
| " | 1.20 | " | " | " | 5,000 " | " | " | " | " | " | 5,000 " |
| " | 1.00 | " | " | " | 6,000 " | " | " | " | " | " | 4,000 " |
| " | .80 | " | " | " | 7,000 " | " | " | " | " | " | 3,000 " |
| " | .60 | " | " | " | 8,000 " | " | " | " | " | " | 2,000 " |
| " | .40 | " | " | " | 9,000 " | " | " | " | " | " | 1,000 " |

**14. Elasticity of Market Demand.**—It is the experience of merchants that when the prices of certain commodities are lowered, even slightly, there is a marked increase in the number of sales, and that when the prices of these commodities go up there is a marked decrease in the market demand. In the case of other goods, salt for example, the number of sales or the amount sold is little affected by a movement in price. If one has a monopoly of salt, knowing full well that he will sell approximately as much at a high as at a low price, would his asking price be high or low? We can answer with certainty that it would be high.

Should this monopolist control the supply of a good for which there were adequate substitutes, should he control the supply of brick in the neighborhood of a stone-quarry, the case would be different. If his price were exorbitant, builders would buy stone. The elasticity of market demand refers to the extent to which the number of purchases varies with movements in price. Salt is an excellent example of a good for which there is an inelastic market demand; goods for which there are adequate substitutes (cotton for woollen, linen for silk, wood for cement, horses for mules or motor-trucks for either, one breakfast food for another, tea for coffee, etc.) are examples for which there are elastic market demands.

The market demand for tobacco or for other goods the use of which constitutes a habit is comparatively inelastic. The market demands of the wealthy are more inelastic than are those of the poor. When eggs sell at 60 cents a dozen the wealthy will diminish their volume of purchases but little, whereas the housewife of meagre circumstances will economize, substitute A-go-la, or go without eggs.

Production is constantly growing more varied, and this signifies a greater variety of goods or means of substitution. Because of substitutes the prices of different goods move sympathetically. The price of any good for which there is an adequate substitute cannot go disproportionately high. A consequence of varied production is that market demands are more elastic and monopolies have less power to fix high prices. Substitutes compete with one another, thus lowering the price and making it uniform.

Again, the larger the number of buyers at different price levels, the greater is the elasticity of market demand. Assume two cases:

| | | | | | | | | |
|---|---|---|---|---|---|---|---|---|
| First, | for X | at | 10 | cents | there | would | be | one buyer. |
| | " X | " | 9 | " | " | | " | " two buyers. |
| | " X | " | 8 | " | " | | " | " three buyers. |
| Second, | " Y | " | 10 | " | " | | " | " five buyers. |
| | " Y | " | 9 | " | " | | " | " fifteen buyers. |
| | " Y | " | 8 | " | " | | " | " thirty buyers. |

It is obvious that if the price drops a penny on these two goods, X and Y, the number of sales, or market demand, of Y will be larger than in case of X, *i. e.*, the elasticity of market demand is greater for Y than for X.

15. **Complementary goods** are those which work together in serving the same purpose. The following are examples: boilers and engines, sand and cement, the right and the left shoe, pen and ink, fiddle and bow, tobacco and pipe, horse and carriage. Do not confuse substitutes with complementary goods, for they obey different principles: goods in the one class *correspond in price* and goods in the other class *correspond in quantity*, as we shall now see. Cornflakes and oatmeal are substitutes, consequently their prices correspond.

Complementary goods, on the contrary, do not correspond in relation to price; they tend to maintain a constant ratio in relation to *quantity*. If one loses a left glove of a two-dollar pair of gloves, he would give the worth of the pair to get it back. Should we assume that there is a monopoly on automobile-wheels, and that the owner of a $2,000 car has a wheel smashed, it is evident that the owner of the car could be made to pay almost if not the whole price of the car for a wheel. Well-matched horses are worth more in a pair than separately, just as a matched string of pearls is far more valuable than would be the same pearls singly.

In the construction of a house there are many complementary goods, such as nails, cement, brick, lumber, hardware, and the like. A demand for a house is a *joint demand* for all the complementary goods entering into its construction. If it is a favorable time to build, if building materials and labor are cheap, it is evident that nails (being absolutely essential and but a small fraction of the total expense of building) must reach an extraordinary price in order to discourage building. It is not the prices but the *quantities* of complementary goods which tend to maintain a constant ratio to one another. Substitutes compete with one another; complementary goods employ one another.

16. **Prospective Prices and Present Demand.**—The demands of the people are primarily for consumable goods. But the demand for these places a demand upon labor and the industries producing consumable goods. In fact, a demand for the products of labor is an indirect demand for labor and for other productive agencies. It frequently occurs, as in December, 1916, or in the spring of that year,

that the pressure for finished goods becomes intense, with the consequence that production is crowded to the limit. Such periods, when there is not enough to go around, produce apprehension that supplies will be so limited as not to be had at a reasonable figure, and that still higher prices will prevail in the future. Buyers rush into the market, hoping to lay in a stock of goods before prices go up. The result is, of course, that market demand is quickened, thus causing prices to advance rapidly and out of proportion to a normal time.

At such times the newspapers are filled with resolutions of denunciations and urgent requests for investigations. Somebody must be blamed; storage-houses are denounced, middlemen condemned, coal operators and railroad officials are threatened with public ownership. Everything is censured, excepting the right thing—an excess of demand at the old price. In time the true remedy is accomplished through the great body of consumers themselves. If a drought shortens a crop, or grubworms take the corn, or boll-weevils ruin the cotton, they may vote one administration out and another in, yet despite this unwitting confidence in an administration they come in time to find the cure. They begin a substitution of cheaper products for dearer; they are actuated by an added stimulus to production and enlarge the acreage sown to wheat, oats, barley, and planted to potatoes, corn, and cotton. They produce more cars, spray the orchards better, and in many other ways augment production. This increased production allays the apprehension, brings about a new and less present demand, and thus lowers the price.

**17. Demand Curve.**—A demand curve is a graphic representation of the individual demands; it reports the number of units of a supply that would be bought at different prices. Note the different circumstances of the individual demanders for some common necessity, tea, for example. Some buyers are of the "cheap rich" type given to extravagant expenditures; others who are wealthy calculate their expenditures with discrimination; some are spendthrifts; others have the temperament to save; still others are poor and can spend but little; some are in the habit of using tea, while others care little for it. Thus there are many conditions causing as many subjective valuations.

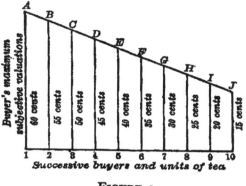

FIGURE 2

The marginal desirability of the dollar (*i. e.*, alternative goods which the dollar would buy) differs among the several buyers, as does that of a unit of tea.

According to Figure 2, A would be a marginal buyer at 60 cents, *i. e.*, he would go without tea rather than pay more. At a lower price it is probable that he would buy a larger quantity. Assume that the market price is, as a rule, about 55 cents, what would be the effect on the number of sales should the price drop to 35 cents? It is certain that the market demand (the demand would not be affected) would be increased in two ways: (*a*) There would be a larger number of buyers, and (*b*) each buyer on the average would take more tea. There would be more buyers: first, because buyer *F* would come into the market, and, of course, since the buyers A, B, C, D, and E are willing to pay more than 35 cents they would welcome the opportunity to buy at that price; second, the users of coffee, cocoa, and the like would take to the use of tea in many cases. The lowering of the price, furthermore, would form an inducement for each consumer to buy tea in larger amounts. This reasoning is based upon the supposition that the marginal desirabilities of the buyers with respect to both the alternative use for money and the tea remain unchanged. Such a supposition is fairly accurate for short periods of time.

**18. Demand: Questions and Answers.**—Some of the more important questions suggested by the previous discussion will now be stated and answered.

(*a*) Can one logically ascribe marginal desirability to money?

I answer in the negative. Money is but a half-way house in a trade. If I give you my cap for your pen the transaction is complete, but if I trade the cap for a dollar and hand it over for the pen, it is obvious that the transaction is only half complete when it reaches the half-way house—the dollar. Money is only a medium of trade, only a means or agency in the exchange of the cap for the pen. Perchance one expends his money for a ride on the train. Why this? Why did he not buy a ticket to the ball-game, or buy a painting, or some other good? Because in weighing the marginal desirabilities of the different things his money would buy he attached greatest importance to the ride. As the check for your coat enables you to take the coat from the cloak-room, so your money enables you to take whatever good you prefer from the market. The check and the money have no marginal desirability in themselves; they merely reflect the marginal desirability in something else. To define money as a "medium of exchange" is to foreclose the ascribing of marginal desirability to it.

(*b*) How may the demand for a good be increased?

There are two, and only two, ways in which the demand for a good may be increased. These are: *first*, when there is the same number of demanders as formerly, but each is willing to pay a higher price, *i. e.*, when no more goods would be bought, although the different bidders would be willing to offer a higher price for them; *second*, when there are more bidders than formerly at the different offers, *i. e.*, more goods would be bought than formerly at the different price levels.

The first: Assume five bidders for a certain kind of automobile who would be willing to pay:

```
Bidder 1 would not pay over $1,000 for one automobile.
  "    2   "    "    "    "      800  "    "      "
  "    3   "    "    "    "      600  "    "      "
  "    4   "    "    "    "      400  "    "      "
  "    5   "    "    "    "      200  "    "      "
```

These figures represent the maximum which each of the several bidders would pay. Each one would welcome any less price than this maximum. At $1,000 there could be only one purchase, for no other bidder would give so much for a machine; at $800 there would be two purchases, at $600 three purchases, at $400 four purchases and at $200 there would be five purchases. The following curve (Figure 3) shows the number of machines that would be taken at the different prices.

Assume now that·the sellers undergo an expensive advertising campaign, that they cover the market with skilful salesmen, and provide excellent service for customers.

The advertising, the work of salesmen and demonstrators, the exhibits, etc., educate the buyers relative to the qualities of the machine and to the new uses which it may serve. Through this extension of good-will for the automobile, the buyers come to impute a higher value to it, and are willing forthwith to pay a higher price. Suppose

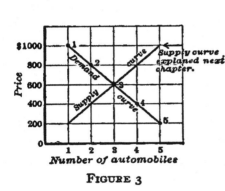

FIGURE 3

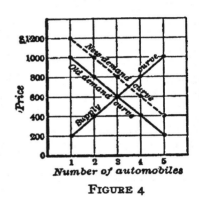

FIGURE 4

that each bidder places an additional valuation represented by $200 upon a car. This means a new and higher demand for the car; there are no more sales, but the price offers are higher. This situation may be represented by Figure 4.

*The second way* in which demand is increased: Assume that the effect of the advertising campaign will be not to cause higher offers, but to cause four times as many bidders at the several figures above given.

Instead of one there are four whose valuation would be $1,000.
"     "   "    "    "    "     "       "         "    "   800.
"     "   "    "    "    "     "       "         "    "   600.
"     "   "    "    "    "     "       "         "    "   400.
. "    "   "    "    "    "     "       "         "    "   200.

This means an increase in demand by an increase in the number of demanders at the different price levels. The following figure (Number 5) shows both the old and the new or increased demand.

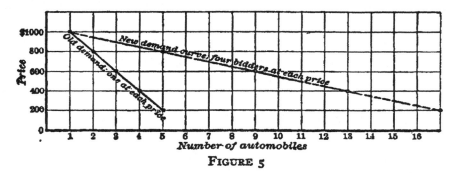

FIGURE 5

Again, a demand may increase in both ways because of an increase in the wealth or average purchasing power in the community. Farmers, for example, are always more liberal in their expenditures just after a remunerative crop season. Enlarged purchasing power increases one's demands both in size and variety.

(c) Assume that no change has been made in the valuations of bidders, would the demand for automobiles be increased should the price be dropped from $600 to $200?

We may say that the number of purchases would increase from three to five, but there being no change in the valuations of purchasers, the demand could not be increased. For should the price be again fixed at $600 the sales would be as before—only three. It would be correct to say that a fall in price increases the *market demand*, for it always expresses the number of purchases at the market price. Demand must not be confused with market demand: the former refers to the quantity of a good·that would be bought at a series of different prices; the latter refers to the quantity of a good that would be bought at the market price.

19. **Recapitulation.**—We have seen that desirability is individualistic: There is no such thing as social desirability. Demand arises out of the comparisons of marginal desirabilities. If one has, say, a dollar, and there are three goods, A, B, and C, any one of which sells for a dollar, he makes comparison of the marginal desirabilities of the different things the dollar will buy. He will retain the dollar if the marginal desirability of some alternative use outweighs that of each of the three goods mentioned, or he will spend it in case the marginal desirability of any good outweighs that of the alternative use for the dollar, for as the marginal desirability of a good is high one attaches high value to it. The explanation of the demand and the forces back of it are found only in the analysis of marginal desirability. Somewhat elliptically speaking, the order of thought is: desire as a motive of acquiring the means of gratification ➞ scarcity of the means of gratification ➞ desirability of these means ➞ relative marginal desirabilities ➞ value ➞ valuation ➞ demand.

20. **Exercises.**—1. Define price. Does the process of reasoning that would lead to the exchange of a cow for a horse differ from that which would result in the exchange of $100 for a horse?

2. Define value. Why has the term "intrinsic value" come into disrepute? Is the value which one attributes to a good varied because of the following: Change in fashion? New discovery? Increased amount?

3. What is meant by the paradox of value? What bearing does it have upon the fact that the self-interest of a monopolist may be contrary to the welfare of society?

4. In the above example, why was A unwilling to trade all of his salt for rice?   What determined the limit of his trading for rice?

5. The idea of valuation must precede that of demand. Explain this fact.

6. Distinguish between desire and demand.   To whom and to what does demand refer?   To whom and to what does supply refer?

7. Construct a supply and a demand curve to represent the figures on page 156, and explain why the price could be neither above nor below $1.20.

8. What is the difference between amount, supply, market supply?   Between demand and market demand?

9. What is meant by the elasticity of market demand? With respect to what kind of goods is this elasticity most pronounced?   Is this elasticity different as between the poor and the rich?   How does the number of potential buyers at different price levels have a bearing upon the elasticity of the market demand?

10. Is the elasticity of market demand for substitutes governed by the same principle as that which operates in case of complementary goods?   Explain why or why not.

11. The Dutch East India Company used to destroy part of the spice-crop in order to enhance its profits.   Was there a fallacy in the proceedings?   (Sumner.)

12. Criticise the following:

(a) "The marginal desirability of money varies as people have more of it."   Does marginal desirability refer to a unit or to the whole amount of a good? to all persons or to an individual? does it refer to money at all?

(b) "The demand will be larger when prices are low, and *vice versa.*"   Do you agree with this?   If not, reword the sentence to agree with your thought.

(c) "A low price causes a large demand, but a small supply."   If this is true, would it also be true that "supply and demand are always equal to each other"?   Does price determine supply and demand, or is just the opposite true?

# CHAPTER IX

## SUPPLY

**1. Supplies; Their Variety, Adjustment, and Limitations.**—He who visits a great city for the first time beholds a variety of supplies quite beyond his powers of comprehension. He sees goods of innumerable kinds, shapes, contents, and sizes. He sees a supply provided for the gratification of every want, desire, whim, and fancy that the imagination can invent. What impression must the backwoodsman carry away who is privileged to witness the variety of products within a large centre of trade, or who beholds the maze of sample commodities which at a world's fair are assembled from all trades and nations for exhibition? Well might he believe that the golden age of which men have always dreamed is at hand.

This variety of supplies could not exist apart from differences in productive capacity. Coal, gold, iron, silk, apples, salt, or any other product, is the output of a particular type of productive power. As with natural re-

172

sources and artificial agents, so with labor—it exists in great variety.

Mining is hard work, so why should any dig coal when there are such agreeable occupations as that of pitching a few games of baseball each summer at a salary of $10,000? Why do the majority of laborers go into the positions that pay low wages, while so few enter the more remunerative employments? The laborer's choice is limited by his aptitude for the tasks. According to their different capacities, producers are divided into many classes, and are adjusted accordingly to the unlike tasks within the division of labor.

But the variety of supplies is not alone due to different forms of productive capacity, for differences among demands furnish the motives for the production of all supplies. Should all turn vegetarian, those who grow swine would have to find another occupation. Should none want pork, no one would demand it, and so none would be produced. In every case there is a demand back of supply.

*Supply Adjustments:* Not only do supplies exist in great variety, but also they tend to hold, to the degree of a mathematical nicety, a proper economic apportionment to one another at innumerable different prices. Strangely enough, there are many persons (none of them economists) who would have the government take charge of production and manage it. They would have it dictated that so much of this, that, and the other shall be produced. Fortunately this industrial imperialism is uncalled for, because, in obedience to natural economic laws, there is a tendency for the various supplies to maintain a perfect economic adjustment. There is no boss and no need for any to dictate this adjustment; it is the outgrowth of natural forces which, under free competition, operate through the agency of market price.

Why are there not innumerable mistakes in the relative outputs of the different lines of supply? Why do we not have twice or three times as much productive power turned to the growing of wheat, and but a half or third as much given to the manufacture of shoes? Why is the total productive capacity apportioned as it is among different fields of endeavor, why not some other apportionment?

Were there a relative overabundance of wheat, its cost of production would exceed its market price, and many would abandon its production. Were there an insufficiency of shoes, their market price would so exceed their cost as to attract many new producers. As water seeks a common level, so through market prices competition tends toward a uniformity of profits (selling prices less costs), and hence toward a proper economic apportionment among the different supplies.

*Supply Limitations:* What determines the limitation to the volume of the different supplies? Productive capacity is limited, *i. e.*, it is incapable of furnishing us all that we wish. If our desires did not extend beyond a few simple lines of consumption, they could be fully satisfied. But when we demand a thousand things, rather than five or six, productive capacity is incapable of meeting in full the numerous drafts made upon it. Each person so directs his limited energies that there is a tendency, but only a tendency, to keep his numerous desires equally gratified. As a result no desire can be fully satisfied, and each supply limits every other supply. In our impatience we complain of the "niggardliness of nature," for it does not furnish all that we want; we might equally condemn our unbridled desires, for they are such that we cannot have all we want. These thoughts on supply will be more fully presented in the following discussion.

**2. Purchasing Power and Supply.**—Supply and demand are closely related ideas. Referring again to the example of A and B with the salt and rice; A's salt, together with his desire for rice made a demand, and B's rice together with his desire for salt made a demand. It is always the demand which fosters the production of supply.

Every good finds a sale because some one desires it and has another good or service to exchange for it. Great production means abundant purchasing power that opens a demand for other products. The greatest vent for one's wares is found in those places where the most wealth is produced. A salable product is no sooner created than it, from that instant, affords a market for other products to the full extent of its own price. A good harvest is a blessing, not only to the agriculturist, but likewise to the dealers in all commodities. Industries are so interdependent that the success of one has á wholesome effect upon all the others. To-day we regard Voltaire's dictum as sheer nonsense, that "such is the lot of humanity, that the patriotic desire for one's country's grandeur is but a wish for the humiliation of one's neighbors; . . . that it is clearly impossible for one's country to gain, except by the loss of another." We are interested in the prosperity of others because their success causes a demand for our own goods.

In the progressive state talent is turned to account; in the retrograde state it goes unrewarded. Compare the merchant's opportunities in a rich town with those of the merchant in the district of indolence and apathy. There is no gain from dealing with a people that have nothing to pay. Large purchasing power brings forth large demands, and in response to demands supplies are produced. An exception to this must be made for fixed supplies.

3. **Fixed Supplies.**—There is no cunning or device by which we may multiply the paintings of a dead artist. Antiques, rare jewels, meteoric stones, and select building sites are fixed in volume of supply. The present valuation of such supplies is affected in no way by their original cost. One would as readily pay $100 for the autograph of a famous seventeenth century author as for an antique, the production of which cost days of toil. The meteoric stone, the nugget picked up by chance at a river's bank, stand in one's valuation upon precisely the same basis as does the old sculptor's product costing months of sacrifice and labor. It is not the labor or expense of their original production, but it is the relative marginal desirability of such goods that determines one's price appraisal (valuation) of them.

4. **Senior's Statement.**—It is not to be implied, however, that cost has no bearing upon the valuation of a good, for most emphatically it does have such a bearing in the case of most goods. I shall say in the case of all reproducible goods on the market. Whatever influence, cost or other, that limits supply must affect the valuation and ultimately the price of a commodity. Bear it in mind that one's valuation and consequent demand for a good are derived from its marginal desirability in comparison with the marginal desirability of that which he would pay in exchange. But the relative marginal desirability of a good is high or low, as the supply is small or large. So we say that unfavorable labor conditions, ill-adapted machinery, a poor crop year, a shortage of cars, a panic, a heavy cost of production, or a limitation in the necessary

agencies of production—any form of influence which shortens a supply does increase its marginàl desirability and in consequence increases the price.

Professor Davenport makes this most illuminating quotation[1] from the writings of N. W. Senior: "Any other cause limiting supply is just as efficient a cause of value in an article as the necessity of labor in its production. And, in fact, if all the commodities used by man were supplied by nature without any intervention whatever of human labor, but were supplied in precisely the same quantities that they now are, there is no reason to suppose either that they would cease to be valuable, or would exchange in any other than the present proportions."

Cost, then, bears on the price of a good only as it influences the supply, but so important and far-reaching is the influence of cost upon supplies that we must not spare a thorough analysis of it.

5. **Cost Defined.**—Cost is the antithesis of income; it is outgo—the outgo made to get an income. If I enjoy the income of a man's labor, it is at the cost of paying him a wage; if I enjoy the income of your house it is at the cost of paying you a rent; if I enjoy the income of a farm it is at the cost of paying for the uses of that farm.

Should I own the farm, the house, and do. my own work, I would pay neither a rent nor a wage to another. Can it be said that I enjoy income free from cost? The cost of my income is not less real because I own the agencies of its production. I could have let the house and farm for a rent, also I could have received a wage by working for some one else. If this farm and house could be let to another for $1,500, I simply give up the receipt of $1,500,

[1] " Value and Distribution," p. 44.

by retaining them for my own use. And so with the wage relinquished; it is a cost.

The ideas of cost and sacrifice are closely related. We hear it remarked: his victory cost him his life; that painting cost tireless effort; he drained the swamp at the cost of his health. Strict accuracy would require the use of the word sacrifice rather than cost in these remarks.

Cost is an outgo and is expressed in terms of money. It may be regarded either as a sum paid to another or as income foregone. It is a mere word quibble, worthy of no serious attention, not to use the word outgo in the case of a relinquished income. I no longer have it if I pay out $1,500, nor do I have that sum if I refrain from accepting it.

The cost or price outgo necessary to get twenty bushels of potatoes may be divided into several parts. You may rent some land, hire some tools, hire a horse, hire a laborer, and buy some seed. With these the twenty bushels of potatoes are produced. The aggregate of all these prices is the cost. In case you own these different agents of production and do your own work, you are out of pocket, *i. e.*, your cost is the aggregate of all the prices you might have received by letting them to other people. Or suppose you could sell these for $1,000. It costs you, if the rate is 5 per cent, the interest on this sum or $50 to hold it for your own use.

6. **Cost and Limitation of Factors.**—There is much difference between the cost which one must undergo if he get a good, and the cost which he is willing to undergo in order to get it. What determines the cost which the business man must pay to produce a good? As a bushel of corn is the product of land, seed, labor, and tools, so any other product is the output of a number of agencies.

Should the productive capacity of these several agencies exist in such abundance as does air or sunshine, their services would be free and could command no price. But unfortunately the productive agents are limited, some of them very narrowly limited, and so their services are scarce and command prices. Demand fixed, the cost which the business man must undergo to produce a good depends upon the limitation of the productive factors back of that good. If there be a large demand for the product of a narrowly limited factor, the cost outlay for the services of that factor must be high. If there be a small demand for the product of a factor, the cost outlay for the services of that factor will be low. Demand remaining the same, the cost or price paid for the services of an agent varies with variations in the supply of the agent. Let us now turn to an answer of this question; what determines the cost which the business man is willing to undergo to produce a good?

7. **Cost and the Price of Product.**—The amount of costs which the business man is willing to undergo is determined by the price which he expects the product to bring. One will not pay a cost of $3 to produce a bushel of corn which he would expect to sell for $2. One makes the outlay to grow corn on the poor hillside, or to construct a shaft far into the ground for a ton of coal, or he pays a wage sufficiently high to induce the laborer to risk his life in dangerous enterprises, because the price of his product will be high enough to justify the cost. Pearls are not high-priced because men dive for them, but men dive for them because they are high-priced. Cost does not determine the price of commodities, but the price of commodities determines the cost one will undergo to get them. The cost of pro-

ducing any good is the total price of everything entering into its production, and the reason for paying these prices is that the good will sell for a price higher than its cost.

8. **Cost a Price Expression of Limitation of Agents.**— Productive factors are priced in keeping with the price of their anticipated yields. A security will bring a high price if it promises to pay a high return. Land, mines, steamships, and other productive agents are high-priced or low as their anticipated incomes are large or small. With certain omissions, the order of thought may be indicated as follows: Demand fixed; any productive agent, say land ➡ amount of yield or product ➡ price of yield or product ➡ price of land. This schematic showing of the causal sequence makes it obvious that it is the scarcity of the agent (demand taken for granted) which explains the limited supply of the product. They are the limitations of agents relative to the drafts made upon them which cause the costs that must be made by an entrepreneur to produce a good. If factors A and B are essential to the production of a commodity, and if A may be had in great abundance while B is scarce, evidently the business man will have to pay high for the use of B and little for the use of A. Cost becomes simply the price expression of the scarcity and productivity of agents.

9. **Supplies Limit Each Other.**—Because of limited productive capacity there is a limit to the total supply of all goods. But in the market there are various demands calling for the production of a variety of goods. The relative strength of the different demands causes a larger cost outlay in the production of some goods than of others. If the market price for corn is considerably higher than for wheat, farmers will use more land for corn and less for wheat. An increase of the one may mean a decrease of the other.

If demands so multiply that ten classes of commodities must be supplied whereas formerly five were supplied, other things remaining equal, the supply of each class of commodities must be less than formerly.

In Figure 1, let the total length of the five lines $a\ a'$ to $e\ e'$ be equal to the total length of the ten lines $f f'$ to $o\ o'$. Now,

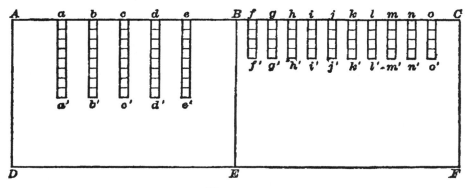

FIGURE 1

if the length of one of these lines represent the total volume of any one class of supply, it will be obvious that, other things equal, in the latter stage a supply is but one-half as large as in a former stage. When the production of ten units rather than five is undertaken, it follows that but a half of the former labor and other productive capacity, on the average, can be given to any one supply.

10. **Competition of Supplies.**—Another way of putting this thought is to say that supplies compete for the same productive agents. The same field may be used for grazing, for the growing of hay, corn, or for the most valuable fruits. Lands for the growing of such fruit are rare and expensive, and so the growers of the cheaper commodities mentioned could not compete with the fruit-growers for

such land because the price of their product would not justify it. With the discovery or improvement of more such land, however, the price of fruits would be lowered and the growers of the cheaper commodities may come into effective competition with the fruit-growers. Thus it is apparent that the cost which one producer must undergo for an agent is influenced by other competing uses for the same agent. The cost outlay of the corn-grower is influenced by the other competing uses for the land. The land will go to the highest competitor; to the extent that land is used for other products corn will be scarce and high-priced, but the more this corn is worth the higher is the cost which the corn-grower can pay in competition with others for the land.

11. **Increasing cost** per unit of output has been erroneously used by able thinkers, who ought to know better, as a synonym for the law of diminishing returns. This latter concept will be given discussion under the caption, " Proportionality." Increasing cost is a blanket term covering a number of ideas. We shall make brief mention of (*a*) exhaustion of basic wealth, (*b*) monopolization of a factor, (*c*) malapportionment of factors. Although America is a new land, yet, due to improper rotation of crops and to want of adequate fertilization, the productivity of the soil in many places is being exhausted, with the consequence that, other things equal, it requires a greater cost to secure a unit of supply. And this greater cost will be met only in case demand is such as to justify it. The choicest timber has been cut away in places and in other places exhaustion is threatened, so it must result that supplies are secured at an increasing cost. As coal is removed train-load after train-load, year in and year out, we must go farther and

farther from the mouth of the mine. In many other ways the constantly increasing cost of production is due to reduced supplies of basic wealth.

Again, the business man finds certain factors essential to the output of his product. What if a monopoly or other restriction controls the supply of a factor? He must pay the monopoly price or quit business. Thus a producer may suffer increasing costs through the artificial monopolization or restriction of others.

The malapportionment of factors must wait its turn for fuller treatment. We may say here that we have increasing costs or decreasing costs as the malapportionment of factors is becoming worse or better. It is this phase of increasing cost, and this only, which will find discussion under the heading of diminishing returns. A manufacturer finds that he must work out an adjustment of factors to factors within his plant and, furthermore, that the size of the whole plant must be adjusted to the extent of his market. To the degree that he reaches an ideal adjustment his costs of production decrease, and *vice versa*. We shall see that, although a factor may be kept in a perfect state of repair, yet, because of diminishing returns, the costs per unit of output will increase.

**12. Opportunity Cost.**[1]—If one goes to a theatre in the evening he cannot spend that evening at home with his family. If he has a dollar and wants a cap costing a dollar as well as a pair of gloves, it follows that if he buys the gloves he must forego the cap. The real choice determining the direction of his effort is not between the dollar and the gloves, but between the gloves and the cap, there-

---

[1] For best discussion of this topic see Davenport's *Economics of Enterprise.*

fore the gloves cost him the cap. One may use his field to grow either corn or cotton; to grow cotton costs him the opportunity to grow corn. If one has a coal-mine, it can be used only for the output of coal, yet its owner must give up recreation if he works it and sacrifice the alternative income on the capital which he must put into the mine. In the choice of an occupation the young man has an open field. He hesitates in his selection, knowing full well that his choice closes the gates between him and other promising alternatives. Getting into a profession or occupation is like getting into the rapids—it's difficult to turn back. Were there no alternatives there could be no choosing, and a choice made implies other opportunities relinquished. Opportunity cost is truly significant in the explanation of supply, because business men do weigh opportunities against each other in deciding to produce any one variety of supply.

13. **Kinds of Opportunity Cost.**—One may be capacitated for large earnings in the business world and yet choose to devote himself to research or to a learned profession with a small monetary return. Personal pride or public opinion may operate to direct one from the field where the monetary income is to be found. In numerous cases such as these, choice is not dictated solely by a price consideration; nevertheless, these choices directly affect supplies.

The choice between recreation and the sacrificing of wages presents some curious examples. It is a rule that the higher the price for a commodity the larger will be the production of that commodity. But a higher wage per hour does not necessarily mean that laborers will work longer hours. High wages, generally speaking, lead workmen to agitate for an eight-hour day, rather than for a twelve-hour day.

The end-of-the-day margin expresses the fact that fatigue

increases as one works longer until finally a point is reached when the worker prefers recreation to the extra income. If the worker is getting 40 cents an hour, his income will be considerably larger than his sacrifice for the first hours of the working-day, but the margin of difference will diminish as the day advances, until finally his sacrifice will equal his income and there he will wish to end the day's work. Each added 40 cents diminishes the desirability of money, and each added hour's labor increases his sacrifice.

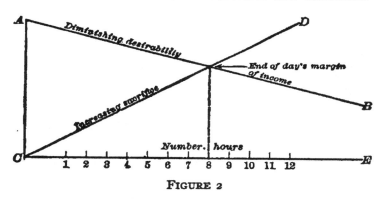

FIGURE 2

As we have presented Figure 2, the sacrifice curve is steeper than the desirability curve. If the laborer's standard of living is low, his desires will be easily gratified, consequently if the wages per hour are high the curve *AB* would be much steeper than *CD*. If his standard be high, his desires of a high order and varied, *CD* would be much steeper than *AB*. In any case the end-of-the-day margin will be reached; this is a significant fact in the limitation of the supply of labor, and consequently of the supplies which labor produces.

**14. Past Cost and Present Supply; Present Cost and Future Supply.**—Consumption goods and present supplies are not as a rule the products of current industry. Apples are gathered from trees planted twenty-five years ago. Trace a pair of shoes back to the leather, the leather to hides, the hides to cattle, the cattle to land and its products, the land back to its preparation, the preparation to the tools and these on back—the origin of current supplies could, in large part, be traced far back. It is estimated that not one-tenth of current supplies is wholly the product of current industries. Current supplies, then, are limited by the estimates which business men in the past have made of the prices which we should be willing to pay to-day.

At any one time men are planting orchards, preparing land, building new factories, and extending old ones in anticipation of future prices. Merchants buy ahead, builders make future contracts, farmers allot certain amounts of land to cotton and sugar-beets, depending entirely upon their estimate of future prices. Thus, it is seen that current supplies are largely determined by the estimates which business men in the past made of present prices, and, further, that present estimates of future prices are now shaping industry so as to determine future supplies. Bearing directly on the present volume of different supplies is the fact that we limit current supplies by shaping our efforts to the end of production for the future. Should we convert the labor and capital now employed in the construction and extension of factories, railways, and other productive agencies into the making of consumable goods, we should have a present feast at the expense of future hunger. All costs are forward-looking; the provision of supply looks to the future. This fact makes opportunity costs singularly significant in the supply problem.

It should be clear that it is supply, not the cost, which

determines present price. If at great cost a railroad is constructed in a region of few resources it will be of little worth. There are idle factories stocked with the best equipment known to man, valueless because they are idle and idle because of the miscalculation of their builders.

In a West Virginia oil-field a Mr. Clay sank a well within ten feet of the boundary-line of his land. He struck a gusher worth several thousands of dollars. His neighbor, anxious to tap the same pocket or pool of oil, sank a well but six feet on the other side of the boundary-line. His cost was $3,200, and that for a dry hole. It is not the cost but the price of the yield which determines the price of a productive agent. The cost of producing a good is the total of all the prices paid for the services of the agents that produce it. But how do these factors—the labor, raw materials, land, tools, etc.—get their prices? This we have answered previously: from the expected income or prices of their yield. The business enterpriser is a middleman who buys to sell again. He buys all the services of the factors and converts these into a product which is sold at such a price as it will bring. Does he make a profit? Only when his costs are less than his selling price. Assuredly it is not his costs which fix his selling price; rather it is the selling price which justifies and determines the amount of cost which the business man will make to get a good.

15. **Selling below cost** is sometimes advisable. When Congress was considering the measure to appropriate $11,000,000 for a manufactory of armor-plate, the Bethlehem Steel Company fought the measure chiefly because it would render their equipment for the same purpose worthless, or practically so. It seems that stockholders

had invested some $7,000,000 in the plant for the output of armor-plate. This company, in my judgment, overcame every reasonable contention of the Government by offering to produce armor-plate at any price which the Government itself might set. Why such an offer? Simply because it is better to get something than nothing out of the huge investment made in good faith by the stockholders, and made, too, at the behest of the Government. It is good sense to sell below cost rather than to suffer a total loss. Many obstinate or otherwise foolish merchants have been marked with ruin because rather than do this they prefer to hold goods until out of season.

Although prices are not determined by cost, yet cost may affect prices by affecting supply. When the producer anticipates a high future price for hats he will undergo a large cost in the construction of equipment to produce hats for sale at the high prices. The result of this large equipment will be a larger supply of hats. Cost of present construction, though determined by anticipated prices, cannot but bear on future price. The anticipated price determines cost, which in turn has an effect on supply and price.

16. Joint cost[1] is found in the numerous examples where the same operation which turns out one commodity turns out others also. One cannot produce mutton without growing wool, nor produce cotton fibre without cottonseed. If one grows beef, he cannot but add to the supply of hides, horns, bones, fat, etc.

If there be no material change in the demand for cottonseed, how would a growing demand for the fibre affect the price of the seed? A growing demand for the fibre would push its price up, would cause an increase in its produc-

---

[1] F. W. Taussig, "Principles of Economics," I, ch. 16.

tion, with the consequence that the increased supply of seed relative to the demand would lower the price of the seed.

The effect of the same cost outlay is both fibre and seed. The combined price of both products determines the amount of cost one will make to produce them. On the average there is a dollar's worth of seed to ten dollars' worth of fibre, so by utilizing the seed one gets eleven dollars every time he would get ten dollars were the seed wasted. The planter can afford a larger outlay to get the eleven dollars. In other words, the saving of the seed causes a larger output and consequently a lower price of fibre. Every chemical discovery or mechanical device which increases the joint products or the by-products of a plant tends to lower the price and to increase the supply of any one of the joint products.

17. **Movements in Market Supply.**—It is now clear that a rise in price causes an increase in market supply in two

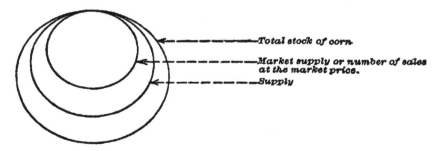

Total stock of corn.

Market supply or number of sales at the market price.

Supply

FIGURE 3

ways: more sellers are brought into the market, and each seller will convert a larger portion of his supply into market supply.

In the last chapter we saw that the market demand

may be increased in two ways: skilful salesmanship may extend the market demand and thus without lowering the price increase the volume of sales, or the market demand may be increased, due to an increase in price offers; these offers being higher, not more in number. Market supply may be enlarged in other ways than by an increase in price. If the owners of grain should anticipate a fall in price, they would convert a larger portion of their supply into market supply at the prevailing prices. Again, improved methods of production or a want of storage facilities would encourage them to extend the market supply. More frequently, however, the market supply is increased because of a rise in price.

18. **Movements in Supply Curve.**—A graphic representation of an increase in the number of sales which suppliers will be willing to make at the different levels of price will be seen in a shifting to the right of the supply curve (as in Figure 4).

Figure 5 shows a change in which suppliers will diminish the number of sales they would be willing to make at the different levels of prices.

Generalizing, as Davenport puts it, the language of plotting: With stationary supply, the demand curve moving up or to the right must mean higher prices; moving to the left or down, lower prices.

With stationary demand, the supply curve moving up or to the left means higher prices; moving to the right or down, lower prices.

With both curves moving, the possible combinations and the different price adjustments are indefinitely numerous.

19. **Recapitulation.**—Productive capacity or the source of supply consists of the co-ordinating of natural resources,

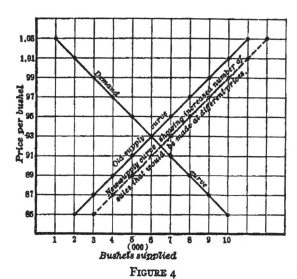

FIGURE 4

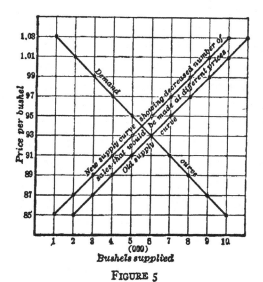

FIGURE 5

technological equipment, labor, and scientific knowledge. A large productive capacity brings forth abundant supply, and *vice versa.* Demands are the directing forces as to what classes of supply we shall produce, and productive capacity fixes an elastic limit to these supplies. If grazing-land is scarce there will be few cattle, few hides, and scarce leather. The different demands for leather affect one another. A large demand by the harness-makers means a smaller supply of leather for shoes. The various demands operating under a competitive price régime maintain through an automatic adjustment a grand proportion and balance among all classes of supply.

During the next moment our demands may change, but at the present moment they may be considered as fixed. To meet these is a large number of different limited supplies. These are physically limited by the physically limited productive powers in agents. Because of the physical limitation of these supplies, the goods of which they are composed command prices. It is the task of the entrepreneur to get together the essential factors to secure these marketable products. He can get together and control these factors only by paying such prices as their services will bring for the time he uses them. What he pays for them, expressed in terms of money, is the cost of producing the goods. If he sells below the cost of production, he fails in business; if he sells above, he makes a profit. Then, what determines the cost he can afford to pay? There is but one answer; it is the selling price of the product.

20. **Exercises.**—1. What effect upon the supply of automobiles would be caused by a large production of agricul-

tural and manufactured products? Were you a cabinet-maker, what would you care, so far as your personal interests are concerned, if the wheat-crop should fail?

2. What is meant by a fixed supply? Suppose that there are 2,500 pieces of a particular kind of seventeenth-century furniture, and that of these 1,000 are for sale. Is the fixed supply 2,500 or 1,000?

3. What theory of price is controverted by the above statement (paragraph 4) of Senior?

4. Does the cost of producing a thing determine its price, or is it the price of a thing which determines the cost that will be made to produce it?

5. Explain this statement: "Cost is the price expression of the limitation of productive agents." State the fundamental cause why champagne or copper is dear. In answering this, consider (*a*) the demand for these, (*b*) their cost of production, (*c*) the limited productive capacity.

6. How does the production of ships and munitions to meet war demands affect other supplies, such as cotton cloth, mutton, automobiles, and shoes?

7. Define opportunity cost; state different kinds of such cost; explain its effect upon the limitation of any supply; give its bearing upon the proper economic adjustment of supplies to one another.

8. How are present supplies related to costs in time past? Does it ever pay to sell below cost?

9. Define joint cost. The demand for hides remaining the same, what would be the ultimate effect on the price of hides should there be a vast increase in the demand for beef?

10. What is the relationship between limited pasture-lands and the price of beef? How might a sufficient rise in the price of beef affect the amount of land used for pasture? Is this a change in the *supply* of land? in the supply of pastureland?

11. A false bottom was put into an elevator-bin so that it held 50 bushels, when it was supposed to hold 10,000.

What was the effect on the market price of wheat?   (Sumner.)

12. Suppose a considerable rise in the price of wool to be foreseen, how would farmers expect the prices of mutton, beef, and hides, respectively, to be affected, and why? (Sumner.)

13. A manufacturer is prepared to produce a large amount of paper, but he decides to defer production even though his plant will be idle for a time, and his future cost will be larger.   He reasons that the market is not yet ready for the paper, that the effect of his having a large amount in store will be that buyers will defer their purchases and maintain a low price.   Buyers will try to ourwait him, knowing that he cannot afford to hold the idle stock indefinitely.

(a) Do you agree with his reasoning?
(b) What counter arguments might be made?
(c) What economic principle is involved?

# CHAPTER X

## MONEY AND ITS PURCHASING POWER

1. **Money and Price.**—Price, we have seen, is the amount of a thing, money or other, given in exchange for another thing. But prices are generally thought of and expressed in money. Reasoning on prices, then, must include an examination of the influences which determine the exchange powers of money. It is at once evident that if money is extremely scarce while corn exists in great abundance, very little money would be given for a bushel; that is to say, the price of corn would be low. On the contrary, were money abundant while corn is scarce, it would require much more money to buy a bushel; the price would be high. This does not differ in principle from exchanges in which no money is involved. If at the same time we have a scarcity of grain and the yards are congested with cars full of coal for which there is no market, a bushel of corn would command a large supply of coal in exchange.

In order to account for the money price of goods, account must be taken of the supply of money, as well as of the supply of goods. It will be the purpose of this chapter to point out some determining influences on the purchasing powers of money. The purchasing power of money is of such significance that we shall devote the following chapter also largely to this subject. The chapters immediately preceding this have had to do with influences which determine the supply of and the demand for goods. The money price of a good depends upon two things; the supply of and demand for the good and the purchasing power of money.

2. **Money in Exchange.**—In an economy of self-sufficiency the choice as to what one produces is determined by his personal wants. In an economy of interdependence and trade, such as we know, the choice as to what one produces is determined by abilities and aptitudes. The self-sufficing family produces its own clothing, food, and drink. The laborer in an exchange economy throws his product upon the market, let who will consume it. He, in turn, looks to the products of others for the means of gratifying his own desires.

The producers offer their several products for sale upon the market, these same producers become consumers, buying in the market such necessities, comforts, and luxuries as their desires, fancies, or caprices may dictate. In the market exchanges take place and the consequence of these exchanges is the division of labor. The virtue of exchange is that it brings about a division of labor, and the virtue of a division of labor is that it enlarges production. Exchange facilitates or, to speak more accurately, makes possible a minute division of labor with its consequences. Exchange in its turn is facilitated or, better yet, made possible by the great agent of exchange—money.

**3. Barter and Need for Money.**—Could a community in which no exchanging takes place enjoy a division of labor? Yes, but under an entirely different economic order from that in which we now live. It would be possible for the different members of a communistic society to follow tasks to which their talents are adapted, should they distribute the products of the community, giving to each according to his need. They would share the income of the community in the same way that the family to-day distributes its income without money and without price. The division of labor under existing circumstances requires persons to get together in exchange, or else go without needed supplies.

Exchanges there must be, but exchanges would in all instances be hampered and in many cases would be impossible without the use of money. Even in cases of barter, goods traded for goods, each of the goods traded is evaluated in terms of the money unit, in order to determine the ratio of exchange between these goods. For instance, suppose that the manufacturer of pianos could not resort to the use of money to effect his exchanges, he would find difficulty in trading his product for the inexpensive commodities of every-day use—salt, coffee, bread, and the small articles of merchandise. There would be many persons who would desire a piano, but who would not have the articles needed by the piano-maker. Or if one is found who possesses all or any of these articles it would be difficult, if not impossible, to work out an exact price equivalent as between the piano and the goods to be given in exchange for it.

Some goods are more barterable than others. Could the piano-maker first exchange his product for a very barterable commodity, one for which all would be willing to exchange whatever goods they might have for sale, he would experience little difficulty in obtaining the several commodities of his desire.

**4. What Is Money?**—We may first note how money may not be defined. It cannot be defined by telling what it is made of. It is no definition to say that the money unit—the dollar—contains 23.22 grains of pure gold. Different commodities have been used as money: Knives were formerly used as money in China; tobacco served the same function in Virginia; some other commodities that have served this function are wheat, bark, cattle, iron, and shells. These examples show also that there is no particular shape, size, or weight which money must have.

Money, furthermore, cannot be made by law. Tobacco in Virginia was money before it was so legally defined. A loaf of bread would not become a dollar should we affix a government stamp bearing these words: "This is a dollar —in God we trust." The law may declare a thing "legal tender" which will not be accepted as money. If the law declares some commodity to be money which debtors may tender in the full discharge of debts and which creditors are compelled to accept, the contracts between debtors and creditors may specify that payment shall be made in something else.

To declare a thing legal tender may not render it valuable. Continental notes were legal tender, yet they were so worthless as to give us the expression, "not worth a continental." There may be money which does not have the quality of legal tender. A slight error crept into the monetary bill for the Philippine Islands which failed to define small change as legal tender. The people were probably unaware of the oversight; or if they were it was a matter of no consequence. Small change was used at the post-offices, banks, and in general circulation. What is more, a commodity may be money in the full sense of that word, and at the same time be counterfeit, and everyone may know that it is counterfeit. The Philippines furnish another instance. Copper is found in an almost pure state in one place—for all I know, in several places—in the hills, and the natives, at the time of the American occupancy, had long been accustomed to mine, pound into shape, and use this copper as money. Centavas (a copper piece worth the half of an American penny) possessed the highest degree of acceptability, and was common currency, despite the fact that all knew it to be counterfeit.

Anything—counterfeit or of legal sanction, legal tender or not—which is generally acceptable carries with it a function beyond and in addition to its ordinary natural function. If copper becomes generally acceptable, it takes on a function in addition to the uses made of it in the industrial arts. And this additional function is the money function. Whatever acquires this function becomes a medium of exchange.

The word "medium" deserves particular emphasis here. The copper ceases to be an end in itself and becomes a means to an end, "an intermediate thing in the commerce between the producers and consumers of any and of every article." The seller accepts the copper with no other end in view than that of passing it on in payment to another seller.

The function described is the money function: money is the medium of exchange. How define it? *Money is that which passes freely from hand to hand throughout the com-*

*munity, in payment for goods and in full discharge of debts, being accepted without reference to the character or credit of the person offering it, and without the intention of the person who receives it to consume it otherwise than in tendering it to others.*

5. **The Definition Explained.**—The long definition just given embodies a number of points which deserve special mention. The money function is the kernel of this definition. That very able and gifted writer, F. A. Walker, had this in mind when he said: "Whatever performs this function, does this work, is money, no matter what it is made of, and no matter how it comes to be a medium at first, or why it continues to be such. So long as, in any community, there is an article which all producers take freely and as a matter of course, in exchange for whatever they have to sell, instead of looking about, at the time, for the particular things they themselves wish to consume, that article is money, be it white, yellow, or black, hard or soft, animal, vegetable, or mineral. There is no other test of money than this. That which does the money-work is the money-thing. It may do this well; it may do this ill. It may be good money; it may be bad money— but it is money all the same." [1]

Some writers say that money must be of full commodity value, but the above definition pays no regard to what money is made of, says nothing of the exchange power of the commodity used to make money. It defines money in terms of what money does—it would know the doer by what it does. It would include all media of exchange whether paper or coin—it is enough that it be generally acceptable. It would not include checks, because they

[1] Political Economy, Advanced Course, p. 123.

are not generally acceptable, do not pass freely from hand to hand, are not accepted without reference to the character or credit of the person offering them. The definition is not burdened with overrefinement, it corresponds to popular usage, and is workable.

6. **Functions of Money.**—What does money do? To answer this question is to give the functions of money. To serve as a *common medium of exchange* is its *primary function*, other functions are derivative from this. A pen or a watch performs a specific service and is wanted for no other purpose. Money likewise is a simple tool desired for the one purpose of making exchanges and none other. Money is no mysterious thing, no mystic principles veil or obscure it; it is a tool for making exchanges, just as a hammer is a tool for driving nails.

Money is a standard or common denominator of value or, more accurately, a standard of the relative prices of goods. This is a derived function, although many writers class it with the first-mentioned, and speak of these as the two primary functions. This error is easily disposed of, for a thing could not serve as a standard of value unless it be a medium of exchange. Strictly speaking, money is not a standard of value as between persons. It would be a curiously poor yardstick, which is two feet long in one man's hands and ten feet long in the hands of another. But something comparable to th's is true in the case of the dollar, for it reflects large marginal desirability for the poor and little for the rich. Considered from the standpoint of one person, the dollar does serve as a measure of the comparative worth of different commodities. The individual measures the relative valuations of corn and wheat by bringing these in comparison with the value he attributes to a unit of money. If for him the marginal desirability of a bushel of corn and the alternative use of a dollar are equivalent, while the marginal desirability of a bushel of wheat would be the equivalent of two dollars, he would here have measured the values attributed to two commodities, finding the one to be double that of the other. As between persons, however, money serves simply as a measure of price.

The third function of money, likewise derived from the first mentioned, is that of a storehouse of general purchasing power. When we speak of value being stored in money we do not imply that value is something intrinsic in money; we mean that money is a durable thing and that it is always salable.

The fourth function of money is very similar to the third: it is a standard of deferred payments. The purchaser defers payment when he buys goods on credit; the borrower defers payment when he borrows from a bank; in any case payment is deferred when a debt is made. If one borrows $1,000 for one year's time, he agrees simply to return the $1,000 plus the interest; he does not, except in rare instances, agree to pay back as much purchasing power as he borrowed. As a little reflection will show, this introduces a point of great significance. Let us suppose that one had borrowed in the year 1915 $1,000, which he agreed to repay in 1920. Assume further that in this five years prices double, that in 1920 it will take $2 to buy the same goods which $1 would have bought in 1915. What would be the consequences? As much money would be returned as was borrowed; the debt would be paid in legal tender and, therefore, legally cancelled. The obligation would be cancelled, dollar for dollar returned, while but one-half of the purchasing power would be repaid. But this is not all, for the creditor has been affected with a serious injustice, and the debtor has enjoyed an unearned benefit.

Money (and this is the last function to be mentioned, although it certainly is not a distinct function) is used as the reserves of banks. Notes and checks are based on bank deposits or reserves. Bank reserves form the basis of the credit structure.

**7. Credit, Currency, Cash.**—Popular usage makes money, credit instruments, currency, and cash synonymous, but there are differences in the meanings of these terms.

*Credit:* There could be no credit apart from confidence. When a buyer of goods or services makes a promise to pay at a later date, he is trusted or given credit. This credit is evidenced by written promises or contracts to pay, these written contracts being called credit instruments. Credit instruments are unconditional promises to pay money on demand or at a specified future time. Certain credit instruments, bank-notes for example, become generally acceptable throughout the community; and since they come to do the money-work, they are therefore the money-thing. This type of money is called "representative money" by some and "fiduciary money" by others.

*Currency:* Certain goods acquire through custom a high degree of marketability; these are money or closely approximate it. Goods or instruments with a high degree of marketability serve as circulating media or currency. Currency includes primary money (gold in the United States, which is back of all other forms of money), fiduciary money (which is backed by primary money), and bank deposits.

*Cash:* Some forms of currency such as checks drawn against bank deposits are of limited acceptability. Cash always means "ready money." Generally speaking, cash is a synonym for currency.

**8. Qualities of Good Money.**—An essential quality of good money is *stability*, because movements in the purchasing power of money are always troublesome. If a commodity maintain the same exchange power through time, its money price will vary with every variation in the purchasing power of money. If wheat is priced at one dollar the farmer borrows the equivalent of 1,000 bushels of his product when he borrows $1,000. Assume the exchange power of wheat relative to other goods to be stable for the period of a loan, yet it is possible for the price to drop from a dollar to fifty cents, because of an increase in the purchasing power of money. In this case the farmer would have borrowed the equivalent of 1,000 bushels of his product and would be compelled to return in payment the equivalent of 2,000 bushels of his product. Or assume that two bushels represent a day's labor; he would have borrowed the product of 500 days' labor, paying for it the product of 1,000 days' labor. On the contrary, should the purchasing power of the money unit be diminished by one-half, the wheat would double in price, and the farmer would return the product of only 250 days' labor.

Money should also be *uniform* in purchasing power. If there were no fixed relationship in purchasing power of coins, or should there be a lack of uniformity in the purchasing power and appearance of notes coming from banks in different sections of the country, there would be no end of confusion, both in current transactions and in deferred payments.

Money should be *elastic* in order that it may be adjusted to the varying needs of trade. Inelasticity has been the most serious defect in our monetary system. Hard money cannot be coined, thrown into circulation, and withdrawn with the changing demands of trade. Elasticity is to be looked for through the expansion and contraction of notes.

Money should be in *convenient denominations* in order that it may be adaptable to all transactions, to large business deals and petty purchases. Many have argued in favor of a half-cent piece in order to still further adapt money to current needs.

Money should be *convenient to handle*. If the dollar were made of iron it would be too bulky. We no longer coin the single gold dollar, because it is too small for general convenience.

Money should be *beautiful*, easy to *recognize, difficult* to *counterfeit*. It should be made of substance which is *impressable*, or capable of taking and holding the impression or die. It should be of such shape and hardness as to make it difficult or impossible to remove a portion of the metal without defacing the coin. Coins are made harder by the addition of alloy. Small coins should contain a large per cent of alloy, because they get more wear than large coins. In a dollar's worth of small coins there is much more surface exposed to friction and wear than in a single dollar-coin.

Money should be *durable*. No perishable commodity could serve as a standard of deferred payments or as a storehouse for saving.

9. **Coinage** is the process of converting bullion into coin. When a government stamps a piece of metal, certifying its weight and fineness, the process is known as

coinage. Coinage is a matter of convenience; no questions are asked when one tenders a gold coin in payment. The people accept a coin by tale or count when the government by means of its stamp has certified as to its weight and fineness. One would appreciate the necessity for coinage were he compelled to carry around the necessary acids, retort, and scales to test and weigh the proper amounts of the precious metals used in his current purchases. The fact that coins are accepted at face value furnishes temptation to the counterfeiter, because he knows that a similar stamp on a baser metal would pass current. The clipper, likewise the sweater, is also tempted, for if he can abstract part of the metal in such a way as not to disfigure the coin, it will continue to pass at full face value. Improvements in the art of coinage have been stimulated by the presence of potential counterfeiters. At first coins were stamped on but one side, later both sides were stamped, so that the stamp would be defaced in a process of removing a portion of the metal. The edges were milled to defeat the work of the clipper. The sweater's task is made hard by a provision for the recoinage of pieces showing natural wear, so that a worn coin is an object of public distrust.

The medium of exchange must have universal acceptability, and this it cannot have unless it maintains the full confidence of the people. A country's monetary system pervades the whole life of the community. So significant is coinage that governments everywhere single out coinage as a particular process to be monopolized by the sovereign power of the State, and counterfeiting is made an act of treason.

10. **Free, Unlimited, Gratuitous Coinage.**—Many people have the idea that free coinage means simply that a person

may have his bullion converted into coin free of charge. This would be true in case of gratuitous coinage, but not in case of free coinage. We are said to have free coinage when any owner of bullion is at liberty to have it coined on the same terms as the government, or as any other citizen. There may or may not be a charge for the operation. We have the free coinage of gold in the United States.

Unlimited coinage has, of course, just the opposite meaning of limited coinage. If we had limited coinage of gold the government would specify a limit to the amount of coin which one might have struck. We have the unlimited coinage of gold in the United States.

Gratuitous coinage, as above implied, means that the government makes no charge for converting bullion into coin. We have the gratuitous coinage of gold.

11. **Money Exchanged by Weight and by Count.**—In ancient times the precious metals were not always coined. They were used as money in bulk. Exchanges involving money must have been difficult to make and only approximately accurate, for the metal had to be weighed and tested. Even in antiquity there was some coinage; "pieces of silver" are spoken of in Genesis (20 : 16, 37 : 28). Also in Genesis reference is made to "money in full weight" (32 : 21); another reference is to "land worth four hundred shekels (224 grains troy) of silver . . . and Abraham weighed to Ephram the silver" (Genesis 23 : 15, 16). "And I . . . weighed him the money in the balances" (Jeremiah 32 : 10). Reference is made in the Bible also to the use of gold (Genesis 44 : 8) and brass (Matthew 10 : 9) as money. The probability is that a number of metals were used as money and that they passed for the most part by weight.

In our day gold bars are used to settle international balances.

The exchange of coins (exchange by count) is in reality an exchange by weight, for coins are but pieces of metal stamped to indicate their weight and fineness. The American dollar is 23.22 grains of fine gold stamped. In 1816 the English Parliament defined the pound sterling as being 113 grains of pure gold, and that definition still holds. The American gold coin is nine-tenths fine and the English sovereign, the "pound," is eleven-twelfths fine. The par of exchange (the ratio of fine gold in them) is 4.866; that is, that number of dollars contains the same amount of fine gold (113 grains) as an English pound.

**12. Seigniorage** is the charge which the government makes for converting bullion into coin. This charge may be barely sufficient to cover the actual cost of coinage, or it may be large enough to leave a surplus above the cost of coinage. That part of seigniorage covering the actual cost of coinage has been termed *brassage*.

Should the purchasing power of a coin be computed according to the amount of the bullion contained in it, or should the cost of mintage be added? That is to say, if it costs 5 cents to coin a $5 gold-piece, should it contain 500 cents' worth of gold, or should it contain only 495 cents' worth of bullion, and should the cost of coinage (5 cents) be added in to make up the $5? Those who answer that it should contain only 495 cents' worth of bullion argue as follows: The distinct need for money gives an additional purchasing power to gold which has taken the form of coin. As a piece of furniture is worth more than the crude lumber of which it is made, so a coin is worth more than the bullion contained in it. If a pair of shoes is worth more than so much leather, why is not a coin worth more than so much bullion?

What is more, if a gold coin, say $5, has five dollars' worth of bullion in it, what is to prevent its being melted down when occasion arises? The metal would be alternately coined and melted down, recoined and again melted as necessities dictate.

It is evident that if the bullion-owner were asked to give 500 cents' worth of bullion and to pay in addition 5 cents (making 505 cents' worth of bullion), he would either have no coining done, or else a $5 coin would be worth more than 500 cents.

In connection with foreign trade another question would arise, for a coin containing 495 cents' worth of bullion might be kept in circulation at its face value (five hundred cents) in the country of its issue, but it would buy only 495 cents' worth of goods from another country.

**13. Seigniorage and the Purchasing Power of Money.—** This topic suggests a significant monetary principle, and in order that this principle may stand out more boldly I shall avoid confusing it with a multitude of considerations by limiting the discussion to a single assumed country. Assume that in a certain country the monetary transactions remain about constant, and that 1,000,000 coins, each containing 100 grains of fine gold, are required. This would involve the use of 100,000,000 grains of gold as money. If the government decides to charge a seigniorage of 1 per cent, it may take one grain out of each coin, thus leaving 1,000,000 coins in circulation, each of which contains 99 grains of fine gold. Would a coin now purchase as much as when each contained 100 grains? It would, for there would be no increase in the number of coins, and no decrease in the demand for purposes of exchange.

"But suppose the sovereign proceeds further, and takes, not 1 grain but 10 from every hundred, issuing 1,000,000 pieces of only 90 grains each. Will the purchasing power of each piece be affected? Not in the least. There is the same demand for pieces, the same supply. People still want pieces of money; can only get them by giving commodities for them; have as many commodities and no fewer to give; and there are just as many pieces and no more to be obtained in this way." [1]

Now, assume that the government goes to the full limit of seigniorage and takes out 100 per cent of the bullion in a piece of money. Will a piece of money now purchase as much as before? Yes, on one condition, and one only, namely, that there be no alteration in the supply relative to the demand for money.

The reasoning found in this paragraph was clearly stated by the great thinker, David Ricardo, over a century ago, and through all these years not a single first-rate writer on the subject has deviated from his thought. To present the whole matter in a word: the purchasing power of money is determined by the demand for relative to the supply of money.

14. **Other Illustrations.**—Assume that this government charge a seigniorage of 25 per cent, and that it provides that the bullion content of coins should not be diminished. What would be the immediate effect on prices? Inasmuch as there would be the same amount of money and the same amount of money-work to be done, there would be no immediate change in prices. Would the bullion-owner be

---

[1] Walker's Political Economy, Advanced Course, p. 147.

encouraged to take his bullion to the mint? No, because he could get in exchange for his bullion only 75 per cent as many coins as before the enactment of the law. What would be the effect on the purchasing power of a coin should the monetary demand increase, due to the normal business growth of the community? I answer, it would increase. The purchasing power of a coin would continue to grow beyond and above its bullion content with the growth in the monetary demand. When the purchasing power of a coin becomes 25 per cent larger than its bullion content, would men be induced to have their bullion coined? They would be under precisely the same inducement as if no seigniorage existed; they would receive from the mint coins whose purchasing power would be the full equivalent of the bullion they brought to the mint.

Let us change the assumption: The government decides to debase the coins 25 per cent (*i. e.*, have them contain 25 per cent less gold), and to hoard the 25 per cent seigniorage. This would, of course, cause no increase in the rate of coinage. A light-weight coin would now cost the same that a full-weight coin had cost before the seigniorage charge, and since the charge would not cause an increase in the number of coins, there could, under this assumption, be no rise in prices.

Would prices fall? This would happen only in case the light-weight became more valuable than the full-weight coins, and they could become more valuable only by a diminution in the number of coins struck. And since men would give no more bullion for a light-weight coin, and since it would buy as much as a full-weight coin (for we have seen that prices could not rise), the rate of coinage would not be diminished.

Let us suppose that after accumulating a large fund of seigniorage the government adopts the policy of coining its fund of seigniorage, and thus adding largely to the supply of money in circulation. How will this affect the purchasing power of money? So long as this 25 per cent seigniorage was hoarded it had no more effect on prices or (what is the same) on the purchasing power of money than if it were non-existent. But the very moment this large additional sum of money enters into circulation, the supply of money relative to the demand for it is increased, so the purchasing power of coins will diminish; in other words, prices will rise. Demand remaining the same, so long as the quantity of money is limited, a debased coin will circulate not according to the amount of the metal actually contained, but at the purchasing power it should bear, were it of full weight and fineness. Depreciation of money (rise in prices) can result only from an excess of it.

It has been said that prices would rise (the purchasing power of money would decline) at the time when this large additional volume of money enters the market. Let us now consider the permanency of this decline. We have assumed that men have been bringing 100 grains of gold to the mint in exchange for coins which (though they contain 75 grains) are worth the full 100 grains. If coins are now worth less than 100 grains of gold, it will be evident that bullion-owners will no longer give 100 grains for coins worth less than 100 grains. After this extra supply of coins has been absorbed in the market, there will be little or no gold offered to the mint for coinage. As the monetary demand of the community grows, prices will decline (the purchasing power of money will rise). This will continue until the money unit reaches a purchasing power equivalent to that of 100 grains of gold, when the bullion-owners will again offer their gold to the mint.

15. **Seigniorage in the Monetary System of the United System.**—The following table will show the main features of our monetary system. Gold is the only kind of money which is not artificially limited in amount; it is the only metal subject to free, unlimited, and gratuitous coinage. Minor coins are issued only in exchange for other money; men get change from the bank, and the bank obtains it from the government mints. Small coins are redeemed on demand at the treasury and at the banks. Their convertibility maintains their parity. As the following table will show, the bullion content of these coins is small.

The variety of uses for money necessitates a number of different denominations, there being an elastic limit to the amount needed in the different denominations. If there be a shortage of dimes, traders would be glad of the privilege of exchanging other money for dimes; if too many dimes, traders will be anxious to exchange dimes for the more needed denominations. Relative to all forms of money, there is a point of greatest convenience for any one denomination, and this point is called the saturation-point. This point marks the upper limit to the supply of any denomination. The dime, for example, is convertible into other forms of money, and when too many dimes get into circulation they will be offered for redemption. But while the bullion content of the dime (silver subsidiary: gold :: 14.958 : 1) is small, the government issues it at face value, thus making a profit. It is therefore to the interest of the government that these coins remain in circulation. The government maintains their circulation by using its monopoly power over coinage to limit their output.

## 16. Monetary System of the United States, 1915.

| Metals | Weight, grains | Fineness | Ratio to gold |
|---|---|---|---|
| 1. Gold coins | 25.8 | .90 | 100 |
| 2. Silver dollar | 412.5 | .90 | 15.988 to 1 |
| 3. Silver, subsidiary | 385.8 | .90 | 14.953 to 1 |
| 4. Nickel (5 cents) | 77.0 | .25 | .......... |
| 5. Copper (1 cent) | 48.0 | .95 | .......... |

| Metal | Limit of issue | Legal tender for private debts | Receivable for public dues |
|---|---|---|---|
| 1. Gold coins | Unlimited | Unlimited | For all |
| 2. Silver dollar | Ceased in 1905 | Unlimited | For all |
| 3. Silver, subsidiary | Needs of the people | $10 | $10 |
| 4. Nickel (5 cents) | Needs of the people | 25 cents | 25 cents |
| 5. Copper (1 cent) | Needs of the people | 25 cents | 25 cents |
| *Paper* | | | |
| 6. Gold certificates | Unlimited in exch. for gold coin | No | For all |
| 7. Silver certificates | In exchange for silver dollars | No | For all |
| 8. U. S. notes | No new issues | Unlimited | Except customs |
| 9. Treas. notes of 1890 | No new issues | Unlimited | For all |
| 10. National b'k notes | Capital of banks | No | Except customs |
| 11. Fed. Reserve notes | Per cent of gold reserve | At banks of res. system | For all |

| Metal | Exchangeable at Treasury for | Redeemable at Treasury in | In circulation Oct. 1, 1915 |
|---|---|---|---|
| 1. Gold coins | Gold cert. U. S., Tr. or Fed.Res. notes | | 616,000,000 |
| 2. Silver dollar | Silver certificates | | 65,000,000 |
| 3. Silver, subsidiary | Minor coins | Lawful money (a), in sums or multiples of $20 | 162,000,000 |
| 4. Nickel | | Lawful money (a) in, sums or multiples of $20 | 62,000,000 (d) |
| 5. Copper | | Lawful money (a), in sums or multiples of $20 | |
| *Paper* | | | |
| 6. Gold certificates | Subsidiary and minor coins | Gold coin | 1,172,000,000 (e) |
| 7. Silver certificates | Silver and minor coins | Silver dollars | 482,000,000 (f) |
| 8. U. S. notes | Subsidiary and minor coins | Gold | 337,000,000 |
| 9. Treasury notes of 1890 | Silver and minor coins | Gold | 2,200,000 |
| 10. National bank notes | Subsidiary silver and minor coins | Lawful money (b) | 761,000,000 |
| 11. Fed. Reserve notes | Gold (c) | Gold (c) | 133,000,000 |
| Total (g) | | | 3,792,200,000 |

(a) "Lawful money" includes gold coin, silver dollars, U. S. notes, and Treasury notes.
(b) Redeemable also in lawful money at bank of issue.
(c) Redeemable also at Federal Reserve banks in gold.
(d) Not usually included in the estimates of total money in circulation.
(e) Represented dollar for dollar by gold kept in the U. S. Treasury.
(f) Represented dollar for dollar by silver kept in the U. S. Treasury.
(g) Besides, there were about $312,000,000 in the U. S. Treasury not offset by outstanding paper. The total money stock (in circulation and in the Treasury, eliminating certificates representing gold and silver) was about $4,233,000,000, of which 70 per cent was metal (largely represented in circulation by paper certificates) and 30 per cent·was paper. Of the 70 per cent 50 was gold, 18 was silver, and 2 was copper and nickel.
The foregoing table is taken from Fetter's Modern Economic Problems, vol. II, page 57.

**17. The Mint Price and the Market Price of Gold Bullion.**—The weight of a gold eagle must not vary more than half a grain from the standard weight prescribed by law. Smaller gold coins must vary not over one-fourth of a grain. This allowable variation is called the "tolerance of the mint." The American gold dollar contains, allowing for the tolerance of the mint, 23.22 grains of fine gold. In the United States 23.22 grains of fine gold is worth as much in the form of bullion as in the form of a coin. Why is this so? The answer is that we have free, unlimited, and gratuitous coinage of gold. The owner enjoys the privilege of offering his gold bullion to the mint in exchange for gold coin. There is no limit to the amount that he may so offer, and no seigniorage is charged him; he gets as much metal in the form of coin as he offers in the form of bullion. A dollar could be worth neither more nor less than 23.22 grains of gold, because the mint stands ready at all times to give gold coins for the amount of bullion they contain.

Furthermore, the market price (the price of gold bullion in the open market) cannot vary from the mint price (the amount of money which a given weight of gold will produce when coined) of gold bullion. Before the bullion-owner are two competing markets, the arts market and the money market. On the one side stand the manufacturers of jewelry and other articles made of gold, these manufacturers being the middlemen through whom are expressed the demands of all purchasers of gold products. On the other hand stands the mint, likewise an intermediary institution through which are expressed the demands of the whole people who are offering their goods in exchange for money. To which market will the owner sell his bullion? The answer is a simple one; to the one offering the higher price. Let us assume for the sake of illustration that the arts market offers a slightly higher price. Gold bullion would drift from the money market to the arts market. This would limit the output of money, thus causing its purchasing power to rise; relatively speaking, it would enlarge the gold supply in the arts market, thus causing its money price to decline. The change of demands in the two markets would now cause gold to drift in the opposite direction—from the arts to the money market. The precious metals are very sensitive, very responsive to even slight variations in demand—so much so, indeed, that virtually no difference exists in the price of gold as between the two markets.

Now that gold coined and gold uncoined are worth the same, we may say that there can be no change in the money price of gold. A dollar, regardless of changes in the prices of all other commodities, will always exchange for 23.22 grains of fine gold, no more and no less. Gold is the primary money of the United States; all other forms of our money are automatically regulated by the purchasing power of gold.

18. **Convertibility of Money.**—Any one kind of money is convertible when it is capable of being exchanged for or redeemed in another kind of money. In a broader sense we may speak of the convertibility of any good into money; land is convertible into money and money into land. Convertibility is used generally to exchange other forms of money for primary money. Convertibility may be either implied, as in case of our silver, or it may be and usually is expressed. It is expressed, for example, on a $10 gold certificate in these words: "This certifies that there have

been deposited in the Treasury of the United States of America ten dollars in gold coin, payable to the bearer on demand."

The purchasing power of fiduciary money will be maintained by the primary money, even though it should have little or no bullion content when a large amount of it is in circulation. It is conceivable that 100 pennies might be made worth more than a one-dollar piece. They perform a very necessary function in our petty transactions and were their supply narrowly limited, they would surely rise in purchasing power. After 1893 British India restricted the coinage of their rupee, and the monetary demand of the community grew until the money worth of the rupee surpassed its bullion worth. When the rupee reached 16d., for instance, it would have produced no effect for the government to offer to redeem it at 15d. in gold. This reasoning leads to this conclusion: Convertibility determines a limit below which the purchasing power of fiduciary money cannot fall, but it can go above that limit.

This conclusion suggests another important consideration: If under our system the purchasing power of a fiduciary dollar cannot go below (under certain conditions might even go above) the gold dollar, does it follow that a large issue of fiduciary money would have no bearing on the purchasing power of a dollar? This does not follow. Every additional dollar thrown into circulation has the effect of lowering the purchasing power of every other dollar. If for every dollar of fiduciary money we add to our circulating media we should withdraw a gold dollar from circulation, placing it in the treasury to redeem the fiduciary, there could be no change in prices (the purchasing power of the dollar would remain the same). Prices, the demand for money remaining the same, could not change, because there would be no alteration in the supply of money. But we do not deposit gold, dollar for dollar, back of all the circulating media. Long experience has demonstrated that there is need for a gold redemption fund which is small in comparison with the total circulating media. It is rare that some forms of fiduciary money are offered for redemption. This fact leads to the conclusion that a large issue of fiduciary money adds to the supply of money, and, therefore, the demand for money remaining the same, the purchasing power of a dollar will decline (prices will rise).

19. **Exercises.**—1. If there were no exchanges would there be any money? If there were no money would there be any exchanges? State the causal sequence between the following: large production, money, minute division of labor, exchange, price.

2. Tobacco is not money. Why? Tobacco would be money under certain conditions. What are the conditions? What is meant by "that which does the money-work is the money-thing"?

3. What is meant by "legal tender"? Could a commodity serve as money which is not legal tender? Give an example to prove your answer.

4. What is the primary function of money? Mention five other functions which are derivative from this?

5. Are the following synonyms: money, currency, cash?

6. What are the qualities of good money? Would the qualities of money which is good for a poor society accustomed to petty transactions, be the same as those of good money for a wealthy society in which there are large monetary transactions?

7. In many markets the laws require that the exact quality and weight of goods be stamped upon the container; coinage laws require that metal be stamped, thus

certifying its weight and fineness. The objects of the law in the two cases are not precisely the same. Explain.

8. In the United States we have the free, . . ., and . . . coinage of gold. Fill in the blank spaces and define the terms used.

9. This chapter states that money would not depreciate in purchasing power under certain conditions, even though 100 per cent seigniorage were taken out. Is this true, and if so, under what conditions?

10. The mint price and the market price of gold tend to remain the same in the United States. Tell why.

11. Nations as men are wealthy in proportion to the amount of money possessed. Criticise.

12. Assume that a gold-mine in California is owned by citizens in the same community. Would there be any difference in the increased wealth of that community whether $10,000 worth of gold were mined or $10,000 worth of wheat were produced? Would there be any difference in the total wealth of society as a whole?

# CHAPTER XI

## MONEY AND ITS PURCHASING POWER

### (CONTINUED)

**1. Can the Government Make Money?**—The beginner in economics believes, and will state without fear of contradiction, that not only can the government make money by law, but also that it does actually do so. He believes that it is in the prerogative of the all-powerful sovereignty of the state to declare what is and what is not money. That the government makes money seems to be a truism; no statement is more likely to command universal assent among the uninformed, for they see about them different kinds of money, some pieces made of gold but many more made of paper, and all possessing the same purchasing power. And the uninformed think this is because all bear alike the government stamp.

But after a study of the question the student will realize that it is in a very limited sense that the government makes money; that in a broader sense the government can no more make money by law than it can make grape-juice by law. The government prescribes the conditions under which money may be issued, and here its powers end. The government can make money only in the sense of making itself a servant of the laws of money. Public officials must understand the principles of money and define, subject to these principles, the conditions which regulate the issue of money.

Suppose that the government could arbitrarily make money by law, that it could place its stamp upon bits of paper, and that these bits of paper, inscribed "This is a dollar," would pass current in exchange for the products of the world. There would be no reason why Montenegro might not establish a government press and print enough paper money over a week's end to buy such an abundance of goods as would make it as wealthy as the United States. A political speaker said, with reference to the American silver dollar: "If the government can make a dollar with 48 cents' worth of silver and 52 cents' worth of law, why should a poor man be compelled to pay $10 in hard-earned money as taxes? Put 100 cents' worth of law in a dollar, print a note and give the tax-payer a rest."

The above are the ideas of extreme fiat theorists who preach the doctrine of the unlimited power of the state to make money and maintain its purchasing power. Fiat means "let there be made," and extreme fiat theorists believe that the government in its magic power has but to say "let there be made money" in order to convert stones, bark, paper, or anything else into money. The chief example of fiat theorists in the United States were the "Greenbackers" who wished to retain and to increase the greenbacks issued during the Civil War. Many of them saw in greenbacks an exhaustless source of national income, a ready means of paying the national debt, a liberation from the burdens of taxation, and better yet, a source from which citizens might borrow at will money without interest. Irredeemable government paper and luxury for all was their dream.

**2. A Conservative View of Fiat Money.**—Fiat money has no promissory relationship to other money. The government definitely promises to redeem certain forms of money in gold coin, and because of this promissory relationship this money cannot be depreciated below the purchasing power of gold coin. Fiat money need suffer no depreciation; on the contrary, it may be made to appreciate, but from an entirely different reason from that of a promissory relationship. Its purchasing power, whatever that may be—low, medium, or high—depends upon the degree to which it is artificially limited and the demand made for its use. If its output is wisely restricted, if confidence be maintained in the integrity of the government issuing it, it will serve all the functions of money; through its use as a medium of exchange it becomes the standard of price, the basis of credit, and the standard of deferred payments.

Those writers are in error who claim that money always derives its purchasing power from the metal constituting it. Any cause limiting the supply of money relative to the demand for it is as efficient a cause of its purchasing power as is the metal constituting it. Gold coin may be fiat money, and is fiat when the money worth of the coin exceeds its bullion worth, due to the artificial limitation of its supply. Then, why squander the precious metals in making money?

There is a sound reason why every civilized nation makes use of the precious metals in its monetary system. The precious metals have been produced from antiquity to the present; they are so precious and durable that they have been saved, and they exist in great abundance. Current losses from them or additions to them from the mines make relatively little difference in their total supply; they, therefore, maintain a relatively stable, definite purchasing power. Note that the word was *stable*, not *fixed* purchasing power. *Stable* implies relativity; that which is stable is so by comparison with that which is of less duration. Money made of the precious metals cannot have a lower purchasing power than that of the bullion content. The supply of such money under free, gratuitous, and unlimited coinage is automatically regulated by the market price of the bullion constituting it, whereas money containing no bullion is left to law, to the miscalculations and changing opinions of lawmakers. There can be no business stability when there is a lack of public confidence in the money system.

3. **Greenbacks and Prices.**—In 1861 gold was the money in common use throughout the country. In that year the secretary of the treasury negotiated with the banks of New York City a loan of $150,000,000. The brilliant successes of the South on the field of battle, together with financial incapacity at Washington, weakened Northern credit and rendered these bonds all but unsalable. Depositors, becoming alarmed, withdrew gold from the New York banks, and forced them to suspend specie payments. Other banks throughout the country (excepting banks in California) followed the New York banks in the suspension of specie payments. Bank-notes became the money of the country.

The government could not get gold, and this gave the fiat theorists their opportunity, of which they did not fail to take advantage. In February, 1862, the first greenback law was passed, and in less than a year's time $400,000,000 of United States notes (called greenbacks because of their color) were issued. The government promised to redeem these notes some time in the future, but set no date for their redemption. They were legal tender and served as the standard money of the North. Public confidence in their worth was shaken by the large and frequent issue of these notes, and they declined in purchasing power until $1 in gold would exchange for $2.50 in greenbacks. It follows, of course, that there was a corresponding rise in prices.

But this increase in price was not due wholly to the great supply of greenbacks. Only one-half of the country demanded greenbacks, whereas formerly the whole nation used gold; this meant that there was probably a decline in the demand for money. The lessened demand for money caused a decline in its purchasing power, and, the commodity prices of goods remaining the same, money prices increased. The Confederacy issued $500,000,000 in notes, which may be considered, in their bearing on prices, a part of the money supply of the whole country. Lastly, the government issued treasury notes to the extent of $400,000,000. These were largely used as bank reserves and thus became a basis of credit. Since credit does exactly the same work as money, whatever serves to increase credit would have the same bearing on prices as an increase in the supply of money.

When greenbacks were issued, they were from the beginning worth less than gold. In this way debtors profited, because they could pay their debts in cheap money, could pay to creditors less purchasing power than they had received. The largest single class of debtors were the bankers, who were forced to take these legal-tender notes in payment of loans, and so were forced to pay them out to depositors; thus greenbacks quickly reached every channel of commerce. The greenback displaced at once the old standard and became itself the new standard of prices. Upon becoming the standard of prices it must be the basis of credit, because promissory notes, checks, book credit, and other obligations were cancelled by the payment of greenbacks. The greenbacks became the object of the country's monetary demand; they came to have a purchasing power independent of the old standard; as this purchasing power was less than that of the former standard money, prices (the amount of money in greenbacks) would rise. When $1 gold exchanged for $2.50 greenbacks, the farmer cared not at all whether he sold a bushel of potatoes for a price of $1 in gold or for a price of $2.50 in greenbacks; depreciated money and high prices are convertible terms.

4. **Fiat Money a Monopoly.**—The whole charge for fiat money may be considered as seigniorage, seigniorage being the monopoly price which the government charges for the issue of fiat money. In the case of a fiat issue, the government has complete monopoly power, but the government, as in the case of any other monopolist, can control the supply only; no monopoly has power to dictate what the demand shall be. The expression of the needs of the people for money is the demand for money; it is the amount of money-work to be done in the community. He who fails to give as full weight to the demand for money as to

the supply of it is ignorant of the purchasing power of money and wholly unfit to discuss the subject. The purchasing power of money will not be altered, will move neither up nor down, unless the government alters the quantity of money, so long as the demand remains unchanged. It makes not a feather's weight of difference whether the government takes out 1 per cent of seigniorage or 10 per cent or 100 per cent.

"But," objects one, "former issues of such paper have depreciated; history repeats itself." This objection is beside the point; this argument is not in behalf of a fiat system, its purpose is to point out the principles according to which the purchasing power of money is regulated. Nowhere is a better exemplification of these principles found than in the history of fiat issues. Valuable lessons are gained from the history of monetary systems, even when the results are wholly negative. History may reveal the nature of monetary principles by showing the conditions under which they will *not* work. Some conspicuous depreciations of fiat money are recorded in history, and insight into the causes at work in these cases acquaints us with monetary principles and the best utilization of them. We learn how to do by learning how not to do.

As early as the twelfth century China had a pure fiat money cut from the inner bark of the mulberry-tree. It was issued by the sovereign power of the people with as much solemnity as if it were of pure gold; it was strictly limited in accord with the principle of monopoly control; it maintained the full confidence of the people; it performed all the functions of money and was, therefore, money in the full meaning of that word. In the thirteenth century Persia imitated this Chinese money, but attempted to enforce artificially its circulation. After a trial of three days business closed down, the officials were massacred, and the money disappeared. The Persian money had been made in imitation of the Chinese piece; why was one a conspicuous success and the other a conspicuous failure? China adhered to the principles of money by restricting its issue to the amount of money-work to be done; Persia attempted to prosper by law and to enforce artificially the circulation of their issue.

During the French Revolution, the authorities issued "assignats," fiat paper money, which at first performed well the functions of money. Seeing these favorable results the authorities were encouraged and continued the operation of the printing-press until forty-five thousand millions of franks were issued. Failure, due to overissue, was the result. Continental currency in the United States was issued in such volume that even the treasury ceased to keep a record of the issue. Failure, due to overissue, was the result.

**5. Marginal Desirability and Value: a Restatement.—** We are coming now to a statement of the marginal desirability of the alternative uses of money, and preparatory to that statement a brief review of the general principle is called for. For a fuller discussion of the principle see the chapter on " Desire, Desirability."

Desirability is a quality of goods or services which is calculated or fitted to excite a wish to possess. It varies with persons, goods, places, and times.

Diminishing desirability expresses the principle that as supply increases the total desirability increases at a diminishing rate. As one adds unit after unit to his supply of a good, the total desirability of the supply will increase, but as the supply is enlarged, as unit after unit is added, each portion of the supply will have less and less gratifying power.

Each additional unit of a supply causes the owner to be less dependent upon each and every preceding unit. And every unit maintains an equal desirability with every other unit of a supply. Should one add orange after orange until he had a supply of twelve, any one would have a desirability equal to that of any other.

If the desirability of one unit is equal to that of any other in the supply, can the total desirability of the supply be obtained by multiplying the desirability of one unit by the number of units? Not at all. If a Crusoe had twelve guns he could not utilize so many and would be willing to throw one away; its desirability would be zero, but it does not follow that ($0 \times 12 = 0$) zero would be the desirability of the whole supply. How, then, can we measure the total desirability? We can do it by subtracting unit after unit and adding the desirabilities of the different units, in this way obtaining the sum of all the desirabilities—the difference between the total desirabilities of twelve guns and no guns.

The tendency is for supplies of different commodities to maintain equal marginal desirabilities. One ceases to buy bread, not necessarily because he would have no more of it, but because the money he would spend for additional bread will gratify a more intense desire if spent for some more highly desired commodity.

The dollar cannot be a common measure of marginal desirability as between persons, because it does not itself reflect the same desirability for all persons.

Valuation is the price appraisal of a good or service; it

may be expressed as the amount of a thing one would be willing to give for a good or service. Valuation is, therefore, a direct outgrowth of the comparison of the marginal desirabilities of different things.

6. **The marginal use of money** differs from that of other goods in this way; the services of other goods are more narrowly limited, whereas money is universally exchangeable and thus capable of serving all desires. The marginal use (it of itself has no marginal desirability) thus comes to express the general level of the marginal desirabilities of goods. Any particular good, bread for example, diminishes rapidly in per-unit desirability to each owner with additional increments; the desire for money diminishes slowly with additional increments, for the purchasing power of money spreads out over the broad area of goods in general. When water is poured into a hollow pipe, the level will rise rapidly; but it will rise slowly when poured upon a broad surface. Just so rapidly will desirability decline when increments, say bread, are applied to the gratification of a particular desire, and as slowly in the case of money, which spreads itself out to gratify all desires. When a good is offered for a dollar, it is offered in competition with all other goods, because a dollar is readily exchangeable for all other goods.

7. **It is the Exchange Function Only that Imparts Desirability to Money.**—The rich may be enslaved by their wealth, they may have more than they can advantageously expend, but the poor must calculate their expenditures with care, must weigh this necessity against that in order to get the greatest total desirability. It is simply untrue that the dollar is a common measure of desirability as between the rich and the poor. One will say that the poor

and the rich pay exactly the same prices in the market; bread is not 10 cents a loaf to the man worth $10,000 and 5 cents to the man worth $5,000.  Both may be marginal buyers of bread at the same market-price, and this, it is argued, proves that a piece of money has the same desirability for the two classes.   In fact, no such thing is proved. The desirability reflected by a piece of money may be ten, or twenty, or one hundred times greater to the poor than to the rich, yet both are willing to pay the same price for a loaf.   But, suppose that both are marginal buyers of the same thing at the same price (*i. e.*, neither willing to pay a penny more), how account for the fact that the desirability reflected by money is higher to the one than to the other?   The simple truth and complete reply to this question may be stated as follows: If the marginal desirability of a unit of money is ten times greater for the poor, and if the marginal desirability of the loaf is likewise ten times greater for the poor than for the rich man, both must be marginal buyers at precisely the same price.[1]

How much of any one commodity will the buyer, rich or poor, take?   Each and every individual will continue to buy until the point is reached where the marginal desirability of that commodity comes to equal the marginal desirability of its money price.   If oranges are 5 cents each, a buyer will continue to buy oranges until an equality is reached between the marginal desirabilities of something else the 5 cents will buy and one orange.   This point of equality of marginal desirabilities is the stopping-point of the purchaser.

Let us answer this question: What determines the mar-

---

[1] See last paragraph in chapter on "Desire, Desirability." *Cf*. Davenport's Economics of Enterprise, ch. VII.

ginal desirability of the alternative use of a unit of money? Through a simple exchange the purchasing power in the form of a coin may be given the form of an orange, of a loaf of bread, or of any other thing on the market. Money serves no end in itself, it is a means to an end, and its desirability is to be thought of in terms of the goods for which it will exchange. Its desirability is not an independent thing, because it is derived from that for which it will exchange. For what quantity of other commodities will a dollar exchange? The amount of anything for which a dollar will exchange depends upon the price of that thing; and the concept of the general purchasing power of a dollar depends wholly upon the general level of prices.

To state the argument briefly: The importance attributed to a dollar differs among persons; the purpose of the dollar is to buy things, therefore its desirability for a person is the desirability of a dollar's worth of goods to that person. The dollar's worth of goods depends upon the general or average level of prices, and the level of prices is at the point of equality of ratio between money and goods. Marginal buyers, rich and poor, pay the same level of prices in the market, not because they have the same marginal desirabilities, but because they have an equality of ratio as between the money and the goods bought.

**8. The Purchasing Power of Money.**—A dollar will buy 10 pounds of sugar at 10 cents a pound, 20 pounds at 5 cents, and 50 pounds at 2 cents a pound. It is but a common truism that the purchasing power of money is large when prices are low, and small when prices are high. The average or general purchasing power of money depends upon the general average or level of prices. The words, "depends upon," in the last sentence do not express the exact idea; it is strictly accurate to say that "the purchasing power of money" and "the general level of prices" are convertible terms. Neither depends upon the other, both mean one and the same thing.

The average weight of a baseball nine is the total weight of the members divided by nine. No member may weigh exactly the same as this average. The weights of the different individuals will be distributed about this general average—some below and some above. Likewise, if we compare the prices of particular goods with the general level of prices, we will find them distributed about this general average—some above and some below, some high and some low. Professor Irving Fisher aptly compares the level of prices to the level of a lake. The surface of the lake is not smooth, there are waves and for every wave a trough. Below the general level are the troughs, and above are the crests of the waves. The individual waves and troughs will not vary far from the general level of prices. If prices are low the purchasing power of money is high. This would cause each person to be anxious for money and would make him willing to sell his product for a low money price. On the contrary, if the purchasing power of money is low, the seller will require more money, a higher price for his product. The prices of particular commodities are influenced by and tend to vary with the general level of prices.

**9. Real Income and the Price Level.**—We have defined valuation as a price appraisal, or as the amount of one thing which an individual would be willing to give for another thing. From this definition it is clear that one's valuation of a piece of money is the amount of something else which he would be willing to give for it. Thus the valuation of money comes to be expressed in terms of commodities in general, and so we can express one's valuation of money in terms of the general level of prices.

The level of prices (the purchasing power of money) determines for the individual what he can get in exchange for a unit of money. The various classes of people, such as farmers, laboring men, and professional men, buy those goods which are suited to their needs. Engineers do not buy plows and farmers do not buy dentists' chairs. The real income of the individual depends upon his money income and upon the prices of the things he buys. But the prices of the things he buys depend upon the general level of prices. To illustrate: Will the housewife pay 90 cents for a dozen eggs? Yes, if she desires the eggs more than something else the 90 cents would buy. She weighs in her mind the eggs against the alternative use of the money. If the level of prices is low the purchasing power of her money will be high; she will highly regard her 90 cents and so will pay but a small price for eggs. The seller of eggs will be more eager for the money because of its high purchasing power, and, in consequence, he will part with the eggs for a low price. Hence, if the price level is low, the price of eggs or the price of any other particular good, will be low. Because individual prices conform, more or less roughly, to the general price level, one's real income—whatever class of goods he buys—depends upon his money income and the level of prices. Some modifications of this statement will be noted under the topic "Price Movements Not Uniform."

10. **Two Meanings of the Purchasing Power of Money.** —Two meanings may attach to the expression, "the pur-

chasing power of money." We may have in mind either a unit of money or the total supply of money when speaking of the purchasing power of money. In this discussion we have reference to the purchasing power of each integral part of the circulating media, for to speak of the total purchasing power of money would serve no practical purpose. Moreover, the total purchasing power of money is neither increased nor diminished by adding to or subtracting from the amount of money. The total money-work to be done determines the purchasing power of the amount of money used to do that work, be that amount large or small.

If an isolated society requires $100,000 to carry on conveniently its money-work, this sum would perform all the functions of money, would transact all the exchanges requiring money; it would, in short, supply the total demand for money. Were this amount doubled no additional money-work could be done and no additional demand supplied. Two dollars would be used to do the work formerly done by one, and two dollars would take on the same purchasing power which was formerly held by one. This reasoning holds with equal force for the entire world.

We have seen that the total price of a large crop may be smaller than that of a small one, but, as above pointed out, the same reasoning does not apply to the total purchasing power of the quantity of money. The total purchasing power of money, be it remembered, is determined by the money-work to be done, and this work, other things being equal, is not altered by a change in the quantity of money. Again, every bushel of wheat added, even though it decrease the total price of wheat, is an increase of wealth, but the same cannot be said in case of the added dollar. On the one hand, money exchanges against all commodities; on the other, wheat is but one of a number of commodities to exchange against money. If a large supply causes wheat to decline in price as compared with other commodities, it will represent a less portion of the total demand for money, and its price will fall per bushel and in sum. But the total supply of money, on its side, stands alone in the demand for goods and, other things remaining the same, can neither rise nor fall in purchasing power.

11. **Effect of Increasing Gold Production.**—Due both to the discovery of new fields and to improved methods, there has been an enormous increase in the output of gold in the last few years. There are two world markets for gold; the arts market and the money market. It has large value in little bulk, is durable, and is universally acceptable. These qualities, together with a world demand, give it a world market at a virtually uniform world price, so whatever effect there may be from an increase of its output, it will be world-wide. If it affects prices, not one nation but all nations share the consequences.

If there be no material change in the volume of business or in the methods of trade, an enlarged output of gold will enlarge the supply of this commodity relative to other forms of wealth, thus lowering the valuation of a unit of it in terms of other goods. What use will be made of this increased output? It will be used in the industrial arts, or for the coinage of money, or for both of these purposes. If at first the arts market bids higher for its use, the supply of money will not be increased, while many additional articles, made partly or wholly of gold, will be thrown upon the market. The money price of these goods will decline, and this will cause a part of the increase to be diverted to monetary uses. For the reasons stated in the discussion of free, unlimited, and gratuitous coinage, the bullion value of gold will be the same in the two markets. A portion of the additional output of gold will go into the arts and a portion will be converted into coin. The demand for money remaining the same, there will be a transition from lower to higher prices. We are now prepared to summarize our discussion with a statement and explanation of the economic theory accounting for these price phenomena.

12. **The Quantity Theory of Money.** — Logically the quantity theory should have been discussed near the beginning of the preceding chapter, because it embodies the foundation principle of all reasoning on the purchasing power of money. But I have tried to follow a more pedagogical order of topics in order to prepare the way for a clearer insight into this theory. By placing it here it will serve as a review in part of principles already given and these in turn will make clear the quantity principle.

The quantity theory of money may be formulated as follows: Other things remaining equal, the purchasing power of a unit of money falls as the quantity of money increases, and *vice versa*. To express this differently: Prices will rise and fall in direct proportion to changes in the quantity of money, providing other things do' not change. What do we mean by other things? They are two: the rate of turnover of the money itself, *i. e.*, the average number of times a year a dollar is exchanged for goods, and the number of goods per year exchanged for money.

The supply of money and the quantity of money are different concepts. The supply of money includes the quantity of it and, what is equally important, the velocity of its circulation. "The nimble sixpence does the work of the slow shilling." A dollar that turns over or is exchanged for goods five times a day does as much money-work, no less and no more, as the five-dollar coin or paper which turns over once a day. Let M symbolize the amount of money and R its rate of turnover, then M (money) multiplied by R (rate of turnover) gives us the supply of money. Let N symbolize the goods exchanged for money and P the price at which these goods are exchanged. Then N multiplied by P gives us the demand for money. The equation of exchange algebraically expressed: MR = NP or

$$P = \frac{MR}{N}$$

In order that P may be increased there must be an increase in M, or in R, or a decrease in N. On the other hand, P is decreased by a decrease in M, or in R, or by an increase in N.[1]

**13. Misunderstandings Answered.**—Does the quantity theory teach that if the amount of money is increased prices will increase? It teaches nothing of the kind. Writers who ought to know better have erred at this point. Suppose that M (quantity of money) is doubled and that its rate of turnover (R) is reduced from twenty to ten times a year; there would be no movement in price, for, in the light of our reasoning above, the supply of money (the product of M and R) is unaltered. Suppose, again, that M is doubled, that R is unchanged, and that N doubles; here again there would be no price movement.

If India has $3 per capita and the United States $45, does it follow that prices will be fifteen times as high in the latter country? This would have to be answered in the affirmative, if money in both countries circulated at the

[1] See *Money and Prices*, by E. W. Kemmerer (2d ed., 1909), pp. 15 *ff*.

same rate and if the amount of goods exchanged for money were the same per capita. But in India money circulates less rapidly and the number of goods per capita exchanged for money is less than in the United States.

What effect does barter have upon money prices? To the extent that people trade by barter they lessen the demand for money. If N is diminished, MR remaining the same, P must increase.

What effect does the use of checks have upon prices? They substitute directly for money and thereby lessen the demand for it. The purchasing power of money declines and prices rise. As in the above case N (the number of goods exchanged for money) declines, and, MR remaining the same, P rises.

What effect does hoarding have upon money prices? Hoarding is a matter of degree, for exchanging is a series of hoarding. Money is hoarded except at the instant it is doing money-work. Its circulation cannot be compared with the flowing of a stream through the channels of commerce, it could more aptly be compared, as some one has put it, with the jumping of a rabbit. It jumps and rests a while, then jumps again, and so on. But to the extent that money is hoarded it diminishes the supply of money which is doing the money-work. R in the equation of exchange is diminished, that is to say, the supply of money is diminished; M and N remaining the same, P must diminish.

Does an increase in the quantity of money decrease its rate of turnover? History shows that there is no perceptible change in the velocity of circulation when the quantity of money is increased. In case of the discovery of a gold-mine the miners at first convert their product into money, and in this way obtain bags of surplus money above their needs. They will either spend it for goods or put it in the bank. If large amounts of surplus money suddenly come into the market, there will be a rush upon the stores. The demand for goods relative to the supply will push the price up. If this surplus finds its way into the bank it will not be held idle; the banks will find a means of forcing it into circulation. Its rate of circulation will not be diminished and the goods exchanged for it will take on a higher money price.

What is the effect of book credit upon the rate of turnover and therefore upon prices? If we have goods "charged" we need keep little money on hand. If we pay at the time of purchase we must have the money in advance of the purchase. In the first case we may have no money until pay-day, and then turn it over to our creditors all at once. In the second case we pocket our wages on pay-day, and pay it out gradually. The first throws the wages into circulation immediately; the second has the effect of hoarding (holding out of circulation) on the average at least half the wages. We have seen that hoarding diminishes the supply of money and, other things equal, lowers prices. Again: when one pays as he goes, he usually pays in money and when he pays at the end of the week or month he pays by check. When the use of checks substitutes for that of money, the demand for money is lessened and prices rise.[1]

**14. The Number of Goods.**—We have spoken as if a good exchanges but one time in the market and, therefore, makes but one demand upon the money supply. In one sense this is literally true. But the student may

[1] See Fisher's Economics, pp. 242–247.

take an example, say, of a hat worth about $5, to show that our assumption is not well founded. He may show that it is sold by the manufacturer to the jobber for $4, by the jobber to wholesaler for $4.50, by wholesaler to retailer for $5, by retailer to consumer for $6. ($4 plus $4.50 plus $5 plus $6 equals $19.50.) This would show that the hat makes a demand of $19.50 rather than a demand of $5 upon the supply of money.

If we have grasped the full meaning of production, however, it is clear that the hat as such is not fully produced until it is in the consumer's hands. At each productive stage it holds a new and different economic relationship and may be considered as a different economic good with respect to the demand it makes for money. In any one stage it exchanges but once and at a different price from that of any other stage. How, then, is the number of goods counted? The number of goods exchanging against money is counted by the number of exchanges just as the number of passengers on a railroad is counted by the number of fares collected. The Subway in New York City carries about 1,500,000 passengers a day, or approximately 547,500,000 a year. The number of different persons carried would be but a small fraction of the number of passengers.

15. **Price Movements Not Uniform.**—At any one time the prices of certain commodities will be rising and the prices of others will be declining. But when speaking in general terms of price movements reference is made to the general average or level of all prices. Some objectors to the quantity principle argue that if an increase of money is a cause of rising prices, it will have the same influence on the price of all goods; if the cause is general its effect

will be general. But any right-thinking person should know that if the worth of certain goods declines more rapidly than does the purchasing power of money (*i. e.*, a rise in general price level) these goods must fall in price.

Certain goods maintain the same price, even with large movements in the purchasing power of money. Prices that are fixed in advance by contracts cannot change. Interest or the price paid according to a contract for the present over the future use of capital will not change. The price of gold bullion will change not at all, and the price of goods made of gold will vary little, if any, when there is a change in the value of money. Goods sold under the principle of price maintenance will not vary. Charges such as rates and fares on public utilities, and other prices subject to legal restrictions will remain the same, whether the purchasing power of money varies up or down.

Monopoly prices, for example, steel rails, tend to maintain a uniform price, irrespective of the general price movement. Articles will vary little in price which fully substitute for other goods which maintain a fixed price. If two articles directly substitute for one another they can differ but little in price, for if one becomes cheaper buyers make little market demand for the dearer, thus causing its price to decline; they make a large market demand for the cheaper, thus causing its price to rise. This principle causes substitutes to sell at about the same price.

Certain goods decline in price at the same time that the price level is rising. Perishable food products decline in price at those times of the year when the market is full, or approaching a glut, and this despite a decline in the purchasing power of money. The same is true of goods passing out of style. New processes and inventions are all the while sending machinery to the scrap-heap in some cases, and forcing down the prices of machinery in other cases. The level of prices could not rise unless the total increase of prices outweighed the total decrease. And the prices which rise do not go up uniformly. For instance, the wages of labor move very slowly. Employers fear to raise wages because it is difficult to lower them in case of necessity, and when wages are high laborers fight every move to lower their income. Real estate, advertised goods, and others move very slowly. But a decline in the purchasing power of money means that average prices rise; to the extent that some prices decline, others remain stationary, and others rise slowly, the prices of some commodities must rise rapidly.

16. **The Price Level Determined by Means of Index Numbers.**—As above pointed out, the purchasing power of money is expressed by the quantity of other things which a unit of money will buy. It varies inversely as the general level of prices. If the level of prices is high a given amount of goods or services will cost a large amount of money; the money cost of these would be low if the price level be low. It would be an easy task to determine the price level if all prices moved uniformly, but individual prices, like the different bees in a swarm, move with seeming independence in divers directions, though the general movement be upward or downward when taken as a whole. The different movements of individual prices make the determination of general prices extremely difficult. General prices are determined by index numbers.

17. **Simple Index Numbers.**—The prices of a large number of commodities are determined in some year, and these prices are called 100 as a basis of comparison. If in the

year chosen, say 1900, the price of salt is 10 cents a pound, that price will be 100 per cent of itself. Now, in order to get a broad range of prices, take the prices of, say, one hundred different commodities so selected from the several fields of industry as to represent the general average of the purchasing power of money. As in the case of salt, each of these prices will be 100 per cent of itself. The index number for all these commodities will be 10,000. This, divided by the number of commodities, will give 100 as an average. Suppose at the end of the following year the prices of the same commodities be again determined, with the following results: ten have risen 50 per cent, ten have risen 40 per cent, ten have risen 20 per cent, twenty have risen 10 per cent, forty have remained the same, ten have diminished 20 per cent. By adding these prices we get 11,200 as the index number for the whole group for the second year. This, divided by the number of commodities (100), will give 112, representing a rise of 12 per cent in the general level of prices. This method of simple index mumbers is obviously deficient in one particular. Our next method will take account of this shortcoming.

18. **Weighted Index Numbers.**—Some commodities make far heavier demands upon money than others. The amount of indigo sold is insignificant in comparison with the volume of wheat sold. If the price of indigo drops 50 per cent, and that of wheat increases 10 per cent, would it be fair to state that the cost of living has declined 20 per cent? Weighted index numbers are used to avoid this difficulty. They give to each article an importance proportionate to the quantity marketed, as recorded in trade statistics. Or commodities may be weighted according to the amount produced, as determined by the statistics of

production. Let us take the price (100) in the year 1900 as a base, and assume that the price of wheat has gone up 25 per cent by 1905. The index number for it would then be 125. We may assume that in the meantime indigo has diminished in price 25 per cent, or that its index number is 75. Assume that the production of wheat has been 10,000 times that of indigo. How shall we weight these prices? Multiply the index number for indigo by 1 and that for wheat by 10,000, because relatively it is 10,000 times as important (75 × 1 = 75 and 125 × 10,000 = 1,250,000), and divide the sum of these products by 10,001.

When Professor R. P. Falkner, of New York University, was constructing index numbers for the United States Senate Committee on Wages and Prices, he followed a method slightly different from that here indicated. He assigned commodities their relative importance not on amounts sold or produced, but on the basis of amounts used by the typical working man's family. Although this method does not reveal changes in the general level of prices, it is of great sociological importance. While the Falkner Index Numbers are easily the best means yet devised for determining real wages, they are open to the criticism of taking wholesale rather than retail prices.

Simple index numbers are easier to construct than the weighted and, despite appearances to the contrary, there is ordinarily very little difference in the results obtained.

19. **The purposes of index numbers** are numerous. New uses are arising all the time to which this instrument or indicator of price movements may be applied. Private businesses as well as governments use index numbers. We shall point out only a few of the more important uses. They are used by governments to aid in public arbitration

or otherwise settling labor disputes. If unions demand a 20 per cent advance in wages at the time when general prices are remaining constant or diminishing, their position is weak. But when prices are increasing, if the employer is receiving a high and increasing price for his product and paying a low price for labor, the laborer's real income is diminishing and the employer is making a net gain at the laborer's expense. If labor asks an increase sufficient to take up this slack, it has a strong position. Then, too, the government cannot establish an equitable system of taxation without respect to real incomes. These are determined by means of index numbers which make possible accurate comparisons between the expenses of doing business and the money incomes from businesses. To levy a tax without considering expenses works injustice, for if some assessments are too low, other taxpayers are unduly burdened. In many instances such taxes prove prohibitive. Furthermore, the government must have a basis of judging price movements over long periods of time when introducing remedial measures to improve the standard of living. We read of low prices in times past and of high prices in the present. Any conclusion from the statistics of past and present prices is hasty and unwarranted unless carefully interpreted through the agency of index numbers.

Index numbers may be used by individuals: If one is considering a change in the location of his business, say from Boston to Galveston, he would want to compare the purchasing power of money in these two places. Business men are continually comparing their expenses of doing business (raw materials, labor, rent, advertising, salesmen, and so on) with the selling prices of their output. Their price movements and selling policies rest in large part upon the price movements of the items making up the expenses. Railway officials resort to index numbers to establish the necessity of raising rates. If the Standard Oil Company is accused of fixing its prices too high, it might prove that, although its money prices are rising, its real prices are declining. Index numbers are used in making such comparisons, and in cases at law, which turn upon questions of fact, index numbers play an important part.

Of course, index numbers, as other figures, may be juggled. Some say, "Figures won't lie," but the statisticians know better. Courts may be effectively deceived by a skilful manipulator of index numbers. In order that index numbers may properly show the facts, they should be so selected as to compare things under like conditions.

This may be shown by the considerations involved in the answer to this simple question: Has the price of coal advanced during the past year? In the first place, there is a seasonal demand for coal; it is more in demand during cold weather. It would be an error to compare the July price of 1918 with the November price of 1919. The situations are not comparable. Like periods of the year should be selected for comparison. Secondly, due regard must be given to place. Coal on the Pacific coast is much higher than in the East. If one finds that in November, 1918, coal is $10 a ton in Scranton, and that at the same date in 1919 it sells for $15 in San Francisco, he has no basis for the conclusion that coal has advanced in price. The Scranton price should be compared at the two dates. Again, local conditions such as fires, floods, and strikes may so affect prices at particular places that no general conclusion can be drawn. Also the same kind and quality of coal must be compared at the two dates. No safe conclusion can follow a comparison of the price of a good grade at one date with that of a poor grade at another date.

General index numbers should be given such a balance as to represent fairly all prices. If, for instance, forty commodities are selected and intended to be representative of general prices, they would fail of their purpose were several commodities chosen from one group of products. The prices of commodities of one group tend to move sympathetically. If ten out of the forty commodities were different kinds of fish, a movement in the price of fish would have disproportionate weight in making up the average.

Lastly, the interpretation of the figures representing price levels would be aided, and comparisons in different years simplified, if the unit for measuring any commodity be taken as a "dollar's worth." Let every price in the base year be a dollar, then the average of all prices would be a dollar. If in the base year a dollar's worth of bread be ten loaves, and if during the following year ten loaves sell for $1.50, we have a ready comparison of prices at the two dates. In the same way take a dollar's worth of coal, shoes, wool, and so on, throughout the selected list, and make an average of the movements of the several prices to determine variations in the purchasing power of money.

20. **Exercises.**—1. Is the value of gold due to the action of government? Was tobacco in early Virginia money because the government declared it so? Had a law been passed against the decline of continental currency, would this have arrested its decline?

2. The law which regulates the purchasing power of money is not made by Congress. Is this true? Legisla-

tion on the money question is good or poor to the degree that it conforms with ...... ...... ...... ......
Finish the sentence, and tell why you so finish it.

3. What is fiat money? Could its purchasing power be made to appreciate? How? If all the different denominations of media of exchange were doubled in number, would all money be fiat?

4. What were the reasons pointed out in paragraph 3 of this chapter for the increase in prices following the issue of greenbacks?

5. Does a dollar possess the same purchasing power for the poor man and the rich man? Does it reflect the same marginal desirabilities?

6. The "general level of prices" and the "purchasing power of money" are two ways of expressing the same idea. Explain. In what way is the price of shoes related to the general level of prices?

7. Professor Fetter puts the question, "Why does nearly all the gold produced in California leave the State? What keeps any of it there?" Answer it.

8. If at the same time wheat is selling at $2 a bushel in San Francisco and Philadelphia, would any be shipped from one of these places to the other? An ounce of gold, 900 fine, is alike at San Francisco and Philadelphia, $18.604. Why is gold ever shipped from California to New York?

9. A dollar contains 25.8 grains of standard gold—that is, gold nine-tenths fine. An ounce contains 480 grains. How many dollars will an ounce make? 100 ounces? A government officer says that the value of gold is constant because it is fixed in price. Is this true?

10. Does the price which a dentist pays for his gold remain the same because gold is stable in value?

"Gold is stable in terms of itself and in terms of itself only." Explain. Would this be true of corn were we to make it the standard?

If the money price of gold can neither increase nor decrease, shall we regard gold as an exception to the law that prices are fixed by supply and demand?

11. Dr. Scott Nearing says: "Theoretically, if the amount of the circulating medium is in any large sense a cause of the increase in prices, the prices of all commodities should have risen in approximately the same ratio." Criticise.

12. Why might an increased resort to barter have the same effect upon money prices as an increase in money?

13. A country using gold money as its sole medium of exchange, under free and gratuitous coinage, makes the following changes: it imposes a seigniorage charge of 10 per cent, but without giving up free coinage or reducing the amount of fine gold in the coin. To what extent and in what direction will the value of money change, if at all—
(a) If the number of goods exchanged gradually increases 5 per cent?
(b) If the number of goods exchanged gradually increases 25 per cent?
Give your reasons clearly. (Fetter.)

14. How may long-time contracts retard the adjustment of prices?

15. "The nations in this great war can never pay their debts for the very simple reason that they owe more than the total of all money on earth." Criticise.

16. Assume that there is twenty dollars' worth of wealth in the United States for every dollar in money, should we increase the money twentyfold would the discrepancy between money and wealth disappear? or decrease? or increase? or remain the same?

17. Criticise these statements: "There is not enough money in the world to do the money-work." "The money is not coming out of the ground fast enough to meet the new conditions of life." "The railways of this country could never have been built in the early fifties had it not been for the lucky discovery of gold in California in 1849, which provided the means by which we could pay for the construction of the railways."

18. What is the difference between simple and weighted

index numbers? Mention different purposes which index numbers serve.

19. If you were to make a set of index numbers for the purpose of determining the real wages of labor, would it make any difference as to the kind of commodities you might select as a basis for your index numbers? Why or why not?

Suppose you select 50 commodities for this purpose, would it be fair should 10 of these commodities be different varieties of breakfast foods?

20. At a given time the following commodity prices prevailed: Cotton (raw), $0.10 per lb.; wheat, $1.00 per bu.; sugar, $0.07 per lb.; potatoes, $1.00 per bu.; beef (for roasting), $0.25 per lb.; shoes, $5.00 per pair; cotton cloth of a standard grade, $0.12 per yd.; woollen cloth of a standard grade, $1.25 per yd.; men's hats, $4, and coal, $7 per ton.

At a later date the prices of the same commodities were respectively as follows: $0.13, $1.05, $0.06, $1.10, $0.30, $5.75, $0.15, $1.20, $4.50, and $6.50.

Tabulate these facts and compute index numbers, which will show:

1. Changes in the price level of all ten commodities.
2. Changes in the price level of the articles of food.
3. Changes in the price level of the articles of clothing. (Fetter.)

# CHAPTER XII

## MONEY STANDARDS

1. **Money Movements Automatic.**—The money of a country circulates in the land of its issue, not according to weight but according to the stamp it bears. The grocery-man does not weigh a piece of money offered him in payment for goods, he looks at the inscription upon the coin offered and accepts it at face value without further ado. But if a gold coin, marked ten dollars, is offered to a foreign creditor, it is accepted, not according to its face value, but according to its bullion content. Were American gold coins so worn as to be diminished five per cent in weight, it would take ten dollars and fifty cents in these coins to pay a ten-dollar obligation to an English creditor.

So much for the basis of international money payments; let us now inquire as to the movement of money between countries. Should Canada enjoy a bumper crop and, as well, a large output from her forests, mines, and fisheries, she would doubtless enjoy an abundance of goods at low prices. If at the same time unfavorable weather, pests, and labor disputes work against the production of supplies in the United States, her people must pay high prices, and can enjoy a large consumption of goods only by securing

251

commodities from Canada or elsewhere. But two sets of prices, the one high and the other low, cannot under normal trading conditions long remain side by side. The situation resembles that of two reservoirs side by side, the one full and the other half full of water. So long as they are independent of each other the water in the two will remain at these unequal levels; but once a connecting pipe is introduced between the two, automatically the water's flow will leave but one level.

The wise old saying holds true here: "A good market to sell in is a poor one to buy in, and a good market to buy in is a poor one to sell in." Canada will find the United States a good market to sell in, and the United States will find Canada a good market to buy in. The buyer in the United States, finding that his money has a higher purchasing power across the line, will send his money thither for goods. Good will continue to flow one way and money the other until prices are equalized in the two countries. No investigator will make the discovery that Canada has proportionately less money, and no formal negotiations will be inaugurated to equalize the money supplies in the two countries. Individual traders, prompted by the principle of self-interest, and knowing little and caring less about relative money supplies, will so trade as to level automatically prices between these countries. The workings of this automatic regulation were formerly slow and obstructed, as traders depended upon weekly letters and price-currents. To-day the principle works with a freedom and fulness of movement, trade news being flashed far and wide, daily and even hourly.

2. **Selection of Coins.**—While a local overstock of gold coin is flowing into foreign markets, it will also be flow-

ing into the arts market—both local and foreign. Slack business and a shortage in the production of wheat, beef, and coal will cause a relative oversupply of money, so money will go to the melting-pot as well as to the other markets of the world. The two sources of outlet for a local oversupply of money are foreign markets and the melting-pot.

Will coins be exported and melted indiscriminately? The answer is in the negative, and it involves one of the most significant laws in Economics. Coins are not selected by chance, not sent out because they are closest to the place of export, not melted because they are nearest the manufacturer of jewelry. We shall now inquire as to the principle of selection. They are not the fittest coins but the unfittest which shall remain in circulation.

3. **Gresham's law** teaches that the bad money drives the good out of circulation. Let the student commit this: "Bad money always drives out good money, when issued in abundance." Despite her vanity and many administrative blunders, Queen Elizabeth, as above remarked, was an able ruler, the one element of strength that distinguished her being her keen judgment of men, that enabled her to officer the administration with the ablest thinkers and advisers in England. Sir Thomas Gresham, founder of the Royal Exchange of London, was the chief financial agent under Elizabeth. He investigated for his government the condition of coins in Amsterdam, and found that the old and worn coins drove out of circulation the new coins of full weight, which were issued in abundance. This principle, that the bad money tends to drive out the good, was noted by so ancient an observer as Aristophanes (B. C. 444–380), but it was discovered anew and brought prominently

before the English-speaking world by the noted adviser of Elizabeth.

The original formulation of this law made no reference to the exportation of gold coin as caused by an issue of fiat money. More than a few writers have erred at this point. Gresham referred to coins of the same metal but of different weights on account of wear, clipping, and abrasion. If in a gold-using country exportation or conversion of money into the arts takes place, the heavier coins will be selected for these purposes. As money, heavy coins are worth no more than abraded coins, but when sold by weight, as they are in the arts and export markets, they are worth more. While this law was originally formulated with reference to coins made of the same metal, the principle involved is easily applied in any case where bad and dear money circulate in the same market.

4. **When Gresham's Law Will Not Work.**—A Virginia fruit-grower permits his family to use only the sortings— the green, knotty, inferior apples, and his neighbors call him penurious. He answers the charge: "We can't afford to use good apples when there are plenty of poor ones." And this is the way the nations act with respect to their money. Poor money serves the functions of the home market as well, and good money serves the other functions better; there is great economy in Gresham's law. But this law will not always work, for were it a bald truth, without exceptions, that the bad money drives out the good, then a deficient penny would deplete a treasury.

No one would melt a new ten-dollar gold coin into bullion, if that bullion were worth less than the ten dollars, as no one will intentionally convert metal from a more valuable to a less valuable form. Gresham's law will never work, in the sense that the best coins will find the melting-pot, when the supply of money is so small relative to the demand for it that the metal will be worth more in the form of a coin than in the form of bullion. It will not work when money is worth more than its bullion content.

We now know that metal will not be transformed from coins to bullion when the purchasing power of such coins is superior to that of their bullion content. But would this prevent the operation of Gresham's law in the sense that the lighter coins cause an exportation of the heavier ones? No, the heavier coins may be exported when they are in no danger of the melting-pot.

To return to the supposition regarding Canada's abundance and our shortage of goods, her need for money was in excess of the supply. Canadians might have cheap money and dear circulating side by side, the bad money driving the dear money neither to the melting-pot nor to the United States or any other country. The good money would not be driven to the melting-pot, because it would be worth more in the form of money, and it would not be driven out of the country because its purchasing power in Canada would be higher than if it were sent out of the country.

A knowledge of Gresham's law introduces a discussion of bimetallism, for the operation of this law will maintain a fixed ratio between the purchasing powers of gold and silver. Should either metal become cheaper debtors will be eager to pay with it. This will at once increase the demand for the cheaper and lower the demand for the dearer metal, thereby making them equal.

5. **Bimetallism** means the free coinage of two metals at a fixed ratio, the coins of either being legal tender as the

debtor may elect. Monometallism is a monetary system where one metal is given the right of free coinage. Bimetallism as well as monometallism may be thought of as a single standard. Two metals maintained at a parity perform precisely the same functions; they lose their independence in a monetary sense and become one and the same. A country may have the bimetallic standard based on gold and silver, and coin other metals, as copper and nickel. Coins of other metals, however, are token and not primary money.

The common man of this generation thinks of bimetallism as a mere theory—something nice to talk about but dangerous and unworkable if established. He is not informed that mankind has had far more experience and, may I add, more satisfactory experience with bimetallism than with monometallism and that prior to the nineteenth century no nation definitely adopted monometallism. England broke the rule in 1816, but neither the United States nor European nations followed her example until after 1870. Bimetallism is workable and it is not involved in mystery as many are led to believe. It rests upon a single definite and simple principle which explains the extraordinary permanence of the ratio of exchange of gold and silver under bimetallism.

6. **The compensatory principle** is the fundamental fact in bimetallism. This principle recognizes two great demands for both gold and silver; their use in the arts and in the coinage of money. The monetary demand is large and any change in it reacts quickly upon the purchasing power of these metals. This very fact—the quick and sensitive response of the purchasing power of these metals to changes in demand—makes it impossible for either gold

or silver, under bimetallism, to fall much below the other, and impossible for them to remain separate in price. After the gold discoveries in California and Australia, John E. Cairnes, the eminent English economist, wrote (and I give this illuminating quotation, because it shows the nature of the compensatory principle): "The crop of gold has been unusually large; the increase in the supply has caused a fall in its value; the fall in its value has led to its being substituted for silver; a mass of silver has thus been disengaged from purposes which it was formerly employed to serve; and the result has been that the two metals have fallen in value together." If, according to Gresham's law, gold tends to drive silver out, less silver and more gold will be used in coinage. This decrease in the demand for silver will lower its purchasing power; this increase in the demand for gold will increase its purchasing power; the result will be a coming together of the two. This interaction of the forces of supply and demand which maintains a fixedness of the ratios between gold and silver is known as the compensatory principle.

7. **The Meaning of Terms.**—When a coin is adopted the government determines how much gold or silver to put into it. The gold dollar contains 23.22 grains of fine gold, and 2.58 grains of alloy to harden the coin so that it will stand wear; the total or standard weight is fixed by law at 25.8 (23.22 + 2.58) grains. The silver dollar contains 412.5 grains, which is 90 per cent fine (371.25 grains of fine silver plus 41¼ alloy). The ratio of silver to gold in our coins is 371.25 : 23.22 :: 15.98 : 1. This is so near 16 : 1 that we speak of it as such. 16 : 1 means simply that there is sixteen times as much fine silver in a silver dollar as there is fine gold in a gold dollar. But it must not be concluded

that we are on a bimetallic standard because we coin these metals at the ratio of 16 : 1. When is a nation on a bimetallic standard? When it declares for the free and unlimited coinage of both metals and gives to both equal debt-paying power.

Let us next inquire the meaning of the terms, "market ratio" and "mint ratio." When gold and silver bullion change in price with respect to one another and to other commodities, independent of their exchange power in the form of money, their "market ratios" have changed independently of their "mint ratios." If one grain of gold in the form of coin is made by law to exchange for sixteen grains of silver in the form of coin, their "mint ratio" is 1 : 16. But if a rich silver-mine is opened, silver bullion will fall in exchange power, and if it falls until one ounce of gold bullion will exchange in the open market for thirty-two ounces of silver, the "market ratio" has fallen to 1 : 32.

**8. When Bimetallism Will Not Work.**[1]—Assume that a country has a bimetallic standard at a ratio of 16 : 1, and that meanwhile the market ratio is 32 : 1. How would Smith, a gold-bullion owner, pay Jones an obligation of $10? He can pay this debt in either of two ways: He can take 232.2 grains of gold (the bullion content of $10) to the mint, exchange it for $10, take this $10 and pay the debt. Or he can take but one-half of this gold (116.1 grains) to the bullion market and trade it for enough silver bullion to exchange at the mint for $10 in silver, and with this pay Jones in full. All debtors would pay their obligations with silver; gold would go out of circulation; business transactions would be adjusted to the money in circulation; there would be bimetallism legally and monometallism in fact.

An excellent discussion of bimetallism is found in F. A. Walker's Political Economy (advanced course, 3d ed.) pp. 463–475.

It must be observed, however, that as gold in this example loses its monetary demand, it tends to decline in purchasing power; also, the demand for silver and consequently its purchasing power is increased, because it must fill the place made vacant by the withdrawal of gold. The establishment of bimetallism in a few unimportant money-using countries will have the effect of making the purchasing power of these metals more nearly equal. But bimetallism will not work so long as the monetary demand for gold and silver is not large enough to bring the purchasing power of these metals to the ratio established by law. In all such cases Gresham's law operates to the defeat of bimetallism.

9. **When Bimetallism Will Work.**—Bimetallism will succeed when Gresham's law ceases to operate or to expel the dearer metal from circulation. This, of course, will be when there is no longer a cheaper and dearer metal, but when gold and silver are equal to one another in purchasing power at the legal ratio. The compensatory principle will hold them at this equality in purchasing power when the mint ratio is fixed reasonably near the market ratio, and when there is a reasonable monetary demand for the metal.

Assume the nations of the world to be divided into three approximately equal groups of four countries each, and that one group is composed of silver-using countries, another is composed of bimetallic countries holding the ratio 16 : 1, and that the remaining group consists of gold-using countries. They may be represented thus:

| Silver-using countries. | Bimetallic countries. | Gold-using countries. |
|---|---|---|

What will be the effects of a large increase in the output of silver? This will cheapen silver relatively to gold. The owners of silver bullion will hasten to take advantage of the situation in the bimetallic group, where they can exchange their silver for gold at the rate of 16:1. The gold thus displaced by the new silver will pass into its best market, the gold-using countries. Gold will decline in purchasing power because of the diminished need for it in bimetallic countries, and because of the largely increased supply in gold-using countries. Forces are in operation meanwhile to increase the purchasing power of silver. It has to supply the place made vacant by the departure of gold from 'the bimetallic group; then, too, it will be demanded in the silver-using countries. A sudden increase in the supply of silver will cause the price of the bullion content of coins to be less than their purchasing power in the form of money, thus making it profitable for silver-owners to have their bullion coined in the silver group as well as in the bimetallic group.

Should the cheapening effect on silver be large at a time when commercial forces are advancing the purchasing power of gold, there will be a rapid substitution of silver for gold in the bimetallic group. If there be an unusual need for additional gold in the gold-using countries, they can draw for their additional needs only from the bimetallic states. Will the gold become exhausted in these countries? Such is possible but not likely. The increased supply of silver will find a market covering two-thirds of the money-using world—the silver-using and bimetallic countries. This extensive demand will not permit a rapid decline in its purchasing power. The displaced gold will find a market in but one-third of the money-using countries, and these countries already have a normal gold supply. It is all but certain that the compensatory principle will make these metals equal to each other in purchasing power at the legal ratio long before the bimetallic group finds its more valuable metal exhausted.

Assume that states from each of the monometallic groups change to the bimetallic standard, leaving two countries in each of the monometallic groups and giving eight countries to the bimetallic group. It may be represented thus:

| 2 Silver-using countries. | 8 Bimetallic countries | 2 Gold-using countries. |
|---|---|---|

Beyond question, the bimetallic standard is now safe. The base of the system is broadened to cover two-thirds of the money-using world; if the cheaper threaten to drive the dearer metal from this extensive area, it can go to only two states already normally supplied; these two states would be surfeited with the metal long before the great bimetallic area is drained. The extensive area demanding the metal tending to decline will retard or arrest its decline; the limited area demanding the dearer metal is soon fully supplied, thus causing that metal to decline.

The reasoning under the last two headings leads to the conclusion that national bimetallism cannot succeed, but that international bimetallism, if sufficiently broad, will succeed.

10. **Arguments for Bimetallism.**—National bimetallism is unworkable and there is no defense for it. International bimetallism would be workable. Two primary arguments, to say nothing of minor arguments, have been advanced

for it. These are: Bimetallism would give to the world a more stable standard; it would facilitate exchange between gold standard and silver standard countries.

The needs for a stable standard are apparent. If the purchasing power of money rises, debtors are injured because they must pay back more purchasing power than they have received, or if the purchasing power of money declines creditors must take in payment less purchasing power than they have given. Rising prices disturb industry because price movements are not uniform; declining prices throw a blanket over industry. One hesitates to invest his money in business when prices are declining, for he buys at a higher and sells at a lower price. Rising prices stimulate most branches of industry, because capitalists hasten to invest their means at the lower to sell out later at the higher price.

*How would international bimetallism stabilize the purchasing power of money?* The two metals will be tied together in one system; the volume of gold and silver when combined would be so large that temporary movements in the supply of either would have little effect on the purchasing power of money. The probabilities are (and the history of the metals bears out the point) that gold and silver will not together advance or decline in purchasing power in the same degree. If gold tends to rise rapidly, while the tendency is for silver to move as rapidly in the opposite direction, since they are tied together, the purchasing power of money cannot vary. If silver tends rapidly downward while gold tends downward but slowly, the gold will retard the decline in money. The purchasing power of money varies with the average variation in the volume of the two metals. The production of gold and silver are not related, and there is no reason why their output should vary equally in the same direction; in fact, they have in the main tended to vary in opposite directions.

Professor J. F. Johnson closes his discussion of this topic with these words: "Since stability of the standard is the most important quality it can possess, the argument is in favor of bimetallism." [1]

*How would international bimetallism facilitate exchanges between silver-using and gold-using countries?* It would simplify trading and all kinds of contracts between these countries. At present exchange relations of gold and silver fluctuate constantly. If a New York merchant is quoted the price of silk in China (a silver-standard country) he is puzzled to know how much gold he must give. If he sells to a merchant in Shanghai he is paid in silver, the gold price of which may vary considerably before the transaction is completed. He may lose or he may gain, depending upon the turn in the relative purchasing powers of the metals.

Dealers in foreign exchange speculate in these variations of money; they assume the risks. Because dealers in foreign exchange assume the risk, the New York exporter may know exactly how much American money he will receive for his draft on the silver country. The risk, none the less, exists regardless of who assumes it; it makes trade inconvenient and expensive. Moreover, long-time contracts can be little more than a gamble between gold and silver using countries.

The fluctuations between the metals discourage a normal flow of investment funds between nations of different monetary standards. Tariff walls and unstable monetary

[1] Money and Currency, revised ed., p. 222.

systems removed, capital would seek the best profits the world over. The American financier fears to invest in a country of another standard lest his investments return to him in depreciated money.

Silver-standard countries fear to contract obligations in gold-standard countries. England formerly made loans of enormous sums in pounds sterling to British India (a silver-using country prior to 1893). The interest alone on these loans amounted to about £16,000,000 in gold which they were compelled to pay annually in London. The Indian government noted two significant facts: (1) The purchasing power of their money in the home country varied but little through time. (2) Silver continued to decline in terms of gold. It took just twice as many rupees (the Indian coin) in 1893 to buy a pound sterling in London as it took in 1873. Their foreign debt grew more and more burdensome because it took more and more of their money to pay London; and this despite the fact that, in terms of gold, her annual dues to London were not increasing and her money retained about the same purchasing power at home.

A similar situation arose after the Boxer troubles in China, when that country was required to pay considerable indemnities to gold-standard countries.

11. **Argument Against Bimetallism Considered.**—There are eminent authorities on the money question who object to bimetallism. One such authority states: "Whenever two kinds of money are legal tender, the cheaper will be used, and the other will disappear." This question begging assertion assumes what is to be proved, namely, that a cheaper metal exists under bimetallism. This assertion, moreover, embodies the very principle which would pre-

vent the metals from separating in purchasing power at the legal ratio. W. S. Jevons, who justly ranks as one of the two or three most brilliant economists England has produced, understood well the compensatory principle, yet he was a monometallist. His objection to bimetallism is based upon the belief that there is a strong prejudice against silver. In his well-known work, Money and Banking, Horace White expresses the same opinion. If silver were as desirable, he thinks, it would be put on an equal footing with gold. "Even the most elaborate system of exchanges through banks and clearing-houses leaves a residuum of payments to be made by the transfer of metal, and here the question of weight becomes decisive. A bank which has to receive $1,000,000 of metal will always prefer, say, 4,000 pounds of gold rather than 140,000 pounds of silver. It can afford to pay a premium for gold equal to the difference in the cost of handling and storing the two masses. The earliest sign of a premium on gold, after a bimetallic agreement had been made, would render the agreement itself inoperative."[1]

No one has ever proposed such a ratio as that here assumed, and nothing is proved by an argument based upon a single and minor function of money. Gold will serve better in some functions and silver in others. Both will serve alike for bank deposits; certificates backed by silver would be no less desirable than those backed by gold. If gold be more desirable to settle trade balances with gold-standard countries, silver will be more desirable to settle these balances with silver-standard countries. If a silver dollar is inconvenient because it is too large, a gold dollar is inconvenient because it is too small.

[1] Money and Banking, third ed., pp. 76–77.

There is no natural "preference of mankind for gold." A large portion of the world is on the silver standard, a number of countries since 1893 having changed from the silver to the gold standard. They changed, not because of a natural preference for gold, but because of their commercial relations with the gold-using countries of the United States and Europe. The prejudice, if such it be, in most of these countries is against gold, for, although virtually forced to the gold standard, silver is the only money used in circulation. It is found difficult "to educate these peoples to the use of gold."

12. **Historical Summary.**—Space will permit no more than the briefest outline of American monetary history. The great financier, Alexander Hamilton, was the first secretary of the treasury. He found the people thinking in terms of English money, but really using a medley of coins—Spanish, Mexican, and others. He weighed the situation as best he could in this and other countries in order to strike the proper ratio between gold and silver. Upon finding the ratio to be about 15 : 1, he recommended the bimetallic standard at this ratio to Congress. Congress trusted the judgment of Hamilton and gave his report the form of law in 1792. Thus America began with a bimetallic standard of 15 : 1, the gold dollar containing 24¾ grains and the silver dollar containing 371¼ grains.

*Difficulty arose;* the new silver dollar slightly outweighed the worn Mexican and Spanish dollars which were in circulation. Money-brokers assumed the profitable task of exchanging the worn Spanish and Mexican coins for the new dollar, which they exported to the Spanish colonies in exchange, and at 1 per cent profit, for old coins. The latter were brought back and offered at our mint for new dollars, and again the rounds of exchange would be made, thus "forming an endless chain." President Jefferson put a stop to this in 1806, when he ordered the mint to strike no more silver dollars, and this act remained in force thirty years. The presence of underweight Spanish coins, together with the small monetary demand, brought our first experience to failure. This cheaper metal drove gold from circulation.

*The next important date is* 1834, for in that year a new coinage act was passed, and a new ratio of 16 : 1 between the metals was chosen. This is sometimes called the "Gold Bill"; it did not disturb the bullion content of the silver dollar, but reduced the bullion content in gold coins some 7 per cent. This made gold coin slightly inferior to silver and Gresham's law played its part expelling the silver. This law operated slowly at first, but later its operation was hastened by the production of Russian gold-mines about 1840 and by the extraordinary discoveries of gold in California and Australia in 1849. An increase in the supply of gold, never before equalled in the history of the precious metals, lowered the purchasing power of that metal and hastened the expulsion of silver from the market.

Creditors declared the law unjust, for it lowered the bullion content of coins which they were compelled to accept in payment of debts previously contracted. These objections were easily disposed of, because gold had not been in circulation and, therefore, no debts had been contracted in terms of it. Moreover, prices were declining and the purchasing power of money remained about the same.

*The next significant date was* 1853. This act gave us for the first time a settled money of our own. We had in circulation no silver dollars of our minting since President Jefferson's order of 1806 to stop their coinage. Smaller silver coins were of full weight and were driven out by light-weight foreign coins. The Act of 1853 reduced the bullion content of minor coins which ever since have remained in circulation. The coinage of silver "change" was limited, otherwise we should have gone to a silver basis, and our hard money would have consisted entirely of small "change." This law was followed by an Act (1857) denying legal tender to foreign coins.

*The Act of 1873* gave the sanction of law to the single gold standard, and stopped the free coinage of the standard silver dollar, making it legal tender to only five dollars. Little did the people care about this restriction on the silver dollar, for "to Americans it was an unknown coin." Nor were the people enthusiastic concerning the gold standard, for, excepting in Oregon and California, the money in circulation consisted of greenbacks, bank-notes, and silver "change." Conditions soon changed, however; silver dropped in purchasing power; had we kept bimetallism, silver would have become the money of the country. The silver interests branded the act "the crime of 1873." Contentions arose which led to the next important measure.

*The Bland-Allison Act of* 1877 was a compromise measure, providing for the purchase and coinage of not less than $2,000,000 worth nor more than $4,000,000 worth of silver each month. The bill passed over the veto of President Hayes and became law in 1878. In 1890 it was repealed when the Sherman Act took its place.

*The Sherman Act was passed in* 1890 and repealed three years later. It provided for an indefinite amount of legal-tender notes for the purchase of silver bullion. It was a party measure; not a Democrat voted for it nor a Republican against it in either House of Congress. The only restriction on the rate of this note issue was that a sum should be issued necessary to buy 4,500,000 ounces of silver each month at its market ratio. About $156,000,000 notes were issued. Being legal tender, they were, although redeemable, in effect a fresh and unlimited issue of greenbacks. Inflation followed, the gold standard was seriously threatened, and the panic of 1893 followed.

13. **A summary review** of the events following the passage of the Sherman Act in 1890 will be found instructive. The act led to the issue of $156,000,000 new treasury notes within three years, and to the exportation of $160,000,000 worth of gold in the same period. In 1893, therefore, the country held at least $150,000,000 less gold than it would have had if the Sherman Act had not been passed; the gold reserve, while the act was in force, declined from $184,000,000 to $84,000,000 (October, 1893). The depression following the panic of 1893 was accompanied by a shrinkage in the need for currency, while at the same time continuous inflation was resulting from the treasury deficit, the excess of expenditures from July 1, 1893, to December 1, 1895, amounting to $130,000,000. Continuous inflation gave rise to a continuous demand for gold for export. The treasury, having lost most of its gold during the preceding three years, was obliged within three years to add $262,000,000 to the funded debt, receiving in cash thereby $293,000,000."[1] During the seven years 1890 to 1896, inclusive, the total exports of gold exceeded the total imports by $273,160,658.

The "limping standard" is a name applied to a situation

[1] Johnson's Money and Currency, revised ed., pp. 358–359.

which arose in France, Germany, and the United States when these nations surrendered the free and unlimited coinage of silver. The mints were closed to silver, and thereby the demand for silver was lowered; but the silver coins were neither recalled from circulation nor made redeemable in gold. Although the bullion in a silver dollar was worth much less than the bullion content of a gold dollar, yet, being limited in issue, it hobbled along at the same purchasing power of its stronger associate.

Since there is no free coinage, new silver supplies cannot become money and thus increase the supply of money, or, what is the same, lower its purchasing power. The coinage of incoming gold supplies is not so restricted, and the demand for money remaining the same, additional supplies of gold coins tend to lower the purchasing power of money. Should the face value of silver coins drop below their bullion content, such coins will readily find their way to the melting-pot. Bullion is not free to become coin, but coin is free to become bullion.

Were there a sufficiency of money in the form of silver, paper, nickel, or copper to do the money-work, it would oust gold money. But the limitation of such moneys enables gold money to circulate. Silver, of course, did not maintain its parity with gold on any other ground than that of a limitation in its supply. It is fiat and its purchasing power was maintained, as in the case of the birch-bark money of China, upon the principle set forth in discussing the "quantity theory."

The limping standard, despite the opinion of competent writers to the contrary, passed out of existence in this country with the incoming of the Sherman Law of 1890. According to the letter of this law, silver dollars are not redeemable in gold on demand. "However, in ordinary times, the holder has no difficulty in exchanging them for gold; and in extraordinary times, if non-redemption should threaten depreciation, the secretary of the treasury would be obliged to redeem them."[1] This statement, summarizing the facts of the subject, shows that they are truly redeemable.

The primary money of the United States is gold; ours is a gold standard, the value attributed to all money other than gold rests upon the confidence of the holder, that he can exchange it upon demand for gold.

14. **Free-Silver Agitation of 1896.**—There should now be no doubt that a well-established system of international bimetallism would work; this is confirmed by the reasoning on the subject, and it has been proved in fact in every case when it has been given a fair trial. It would steady prices and facilitate international commerce and the normal distribution of capital. The fluctuations in the production of the single metal—gold—make it a very imperfect standard.

Serious objection was urged against the single gold standard in the United States and in European countries, prior to 1896, lest the supply of gold would prove inadequate to satisfy the needs of all gold standard countries. Gold prices fell with alarming persistency, and with ill effects upon the business temper of the people. When conditions were at the worst (1896) W. J. Bryan came forth with a radical proposal for national bimetallism at 16 : 1; he was nominated for the presidency and, with "free silver" as a paramount issue, was given nearly one-half of the popular vote of the country. The bullion in a silver

[1] Johnson's Money and Currency, revised ed., p. 364.

dollar, at the time, was worth about fifty cents, and, had the United States alone adopted bimetallism, the effect would have been a shift from the gold to a silver standard. The Republicans met the issue with a vague indorsement of international bimetallism; but this indorsement was for political effect only, because all informed persons knew that the European nations would not agree to it. Both parties favored international bimetallism, and both knew it to be impossible of accomplishment, but the Democrats, rather than suffer the effects of the limited money supply under the gold standard, were willing to assume the risk of national bimetallism.

But after 1897 an enlarged supply of gold caused an upward movement in gold prices which has continued to the present time. It was not long before Mr. Bryan was able to remark that the Republicans wanted the gold standard and got it, and the Democrats wanted more money and got it. Both got what they wanted and both should be happy.

The problem has changed from one of scarcity to one of an increasing oversupply of money. As previously noted, there is no problem in uniformly low or in uniformly high prices, nor would uniformly rising or declining prices present difficulties; the problems difficult of solution arise out of the maladjustments occasioned by the inequality of price movements. Problems we now have a plenty, but how to increase the money supply is not one of them, consequently bimetallism is for the time a dead issue. History is being made rapidly, however, and the dead issue of to-day may be the burning and paramount issue of to-morrow.

**15. The Gold Standard on Trial.**—Stability stands out as the single most important feature money can have. If the gold standard fails it will fail upon the ground of instability. Gold combines, as does no other metal, all the features necessary for the making of money. What of the prospects of its stability in purchasing power? Declining prices prior to 1897 threatened the continuance of the gold standard, as have rising prices since that date. The history of the subject does not make us sanguine, yet important influences are becoming active which may steady gold prices.

It is argued that transition to the gold standard bids fair to cover the whole commercial world in the near future, and this extensive demand will arrest, it is thought, the rapidly declining purchasing power of gold. But this argument is less convincing when we remember that a large portion of the earth, including important money-using countries, have within the last few years substituted the gold for the silver standard. At the very time when the gold standard was becoming securely established in these countries, gold prices have made the most rapid advances. This extensive demand has been more than offset by increased gold production. The growth of the business of the world, bringing about an expansion of exchange transactions, must mean that growing demands will be made for money. Supply being aside, the greater the demand for money the lower will be general prices.

Let us inquire into the prospects on the side of supply. From present indications the supply will be sufficiently large. The production of gold, like that of any other manufacturing industry, has a precision made possible by the inventions and processes now used. Costs can be accurately estimated and output normally regulated to demand. Costs promise to be the chief limiting agency of the supply. And these costs of production will tend to be automatically regulated by the purchasing power of gold. The various items of cost, such as wages, tools, and machinery, will go up as the purchasing power of gold goes down. The decline in the purchasing power of gold will arrest its production at the point where the cost of production equals the worth of the gold produced. New gold discoveries aside, we may expect a more stable gold output throughout the next decade than we have had during the half-century now ending.

**16. Different Standards Defined.**—All writers on money agree, if in little else, upon the one fact that the money standard should be stable. Their reasoning teaches them, in the first place, and the history of previous experiences confirms their reasoning, that no one commodity, gold or other, can maintain perfect stability in the purchasing power of money.

The *multiple* or *tabular standard* was the first suggestion made to remedy the instability of the value of money. This suggestion attempts to answer the question: How maintain a uniform purchasing power over goods? If Smith lends Jones $500, the loan in reality amounts to the command over a certain quantity of goods which that sum of money would buy at the time of the loan. The tabular (multiple) standard provides that Jones shall return to Smith the same purchasing power borrowed, be that $500 more or less. But how are debtors and creditors to determine the equivalence of the purchasing power borrowed and returned? This suggests the necessity of a government commission which shall make frequent estimates of price changes, and with such estimates in hand it will be easy to calculate the amount of money necessary to cancel a loan. If, during the life of the loan index numbers should rise from 100 to 110, Jones would return to Smith not $500 but $550. Or if the index of prices drop to 90, Jones would return the same purchasing power he borrowed by handing back $450 instead of $500.

Other writers say there can be no stability with respect to goods. Changes in styles, methods, and inventions make the expression "command over a certain quantity of goods" difficult of interpretation. Formerly the articles of common necessity—and such articles must enter into an interpretation of the purchasing power of money—would include goods now obsolete. Tallow candles, spinning-wheels, and flint-lock rifles were once common necessities; where they now exist they hold a different economic relationship. Goods have but the one purpose of gratifying desires; justice, therefore, requires not an equivalence in command over a certain quantity of goods, but an equivalence in, to use an awkward expression, desire-gratifying power. This has been called, but erroneously so, a *utility standard*. It is worthy of no further consideration, in that it is impossible of attainment.

Others say: "Let us have the *labor standard*." This is based upon a hodgepodge of theories now discarded. Pay back a sum of money which will buy the same amount of labor as the money borrowed would have bought at the time of the loan.

The *commodity standard* is the name given to the standard now in use throughout the civilized world. The world's money is made of gold and silver; long-time contracts are made in terms of gold or silver money, depending upon the standard under which they are made. If one borrows $1,000 when prices are low and pays when prices are high, he pays back $1,000. This is not the most just, but the most practical standard, and is universally accepted.

The *compensated dollar* has, within the last few years, been the subject of numerous articles in different languages. The thoughtful consideration of the subject and its wide acceptance by statesmen, business men, and economists are due to the very able and attractive manner in which it has been presented by Professor Irving Fisher.

This plan does not claim to be ideal. This fact alone entitles it to discussion. He who comes forth with an "ideal standard" is unworthy of being heard, for in the very nature of things such a standard is impossible. Under this plan the gold standard would be constantly maintained in conformity with a multiple or tabular standard. A tabular standard, as pointed out a moment ago, is far from ideal. If prices go up we cannot say whether the worth of goods has gone up, or the purchasing power of money down, or whether both of these phenomena are causal. Those who defend the idea of the compensated dollar do not allow themselves to be drawn into a harangue over the tabular standard, accepting this standard for better or for worse; they say, simply, the plan is to vary the weight of the gold dollar or other unit from time to time in such a way as to maintain always substantially the same purchasing power.

There would be no recoinage of gold money from time to time. It is suggested that all circulating gold be called in and paper certificates issued therefor, and that a varying quantum of gold bullion be held in reserve for the redemption of these certificates. It is thought that such a change could be easily made because we now use paper, for the most part, rather than gold coin. Regardless of its changing worth, we now hold 22.23 grains of gold per dollar, back of a certificate; the new plan would not define how many grains of gold must back the dollar; it would require that a varying amount of bullion back the certificate, this amount to be so varied as to keep the purchasing power of a dollar the same through time. The dollar now has an unvarying bullion content and a varying purchasing power; it would then have an unvarying purchasing power and a varying bullion content. If during the year the exchange power of a unit of gold diminish one-half, a gold certificate could be redeemed for twice the amount of gold at the end as at the beginning of the year.

All the plans given for improving the standard have their defenders, but the gold standard is here to stay, so far as we can now see, indefinitely.

**17. Exercises.**—1. In a poor community there is little money. Is the community poor because there is little money in it, or is there little money because the community is poor?

2. A good market to sell in is a poor market to buy in, and a good market to buy in is a poor market to sell in. How is this fact related to the movement of money from one nation to another? What limits the extent of the movement of money from one place to another?

3. What is Gresham's law? When will it not work?

4. Define bimetallism. Explain the compensatory principle. Would you vote for national bimetallism? For international bimetallism?

5. Assume that in 1896 the market ratio of gold to silver was exactly 32 : 1, and that the United States had adopted bimetallism at a ratio of 16 : 1. Would both gold and silver coins have come into and remained in circulation? If not, in what money would debts have been paid? Which

money would have become the standard? What would have become of the other?

6. Summarize the arguments for and against international bimetallism.

7. Define these terms; mint ratio, market ratio, gold points, "bad money," "good money," inconvertible paper money.

8. "Should all prices rise uniformly or decline uniformly, no one would be either benefited or injured." Is this true?

9. Because prices do not increase uniformly some classes are benefited and others are injured. Is this true? If so, what classes are injured? And what classes are benefited?

10. Tell what occurred at each of the following dates in the monetary history of the United States: 1792, 1806, 1834, 1853, 1857, 1873, 1877, 1890.

11. Make an argument either for or against the idea of the compensated dollar. Would it work with respect to foreign exchange? Why or why not?

# CHAPTER XIII

## CREDIT AND BANKING

**1. Credit as a Substitute for Money.**—In our reasoning upon the law of substitution, it was made clear that when commodities will readily substitute for each other, the prices of these commodities will tend to be uniform. If two kinds of building material will supply the same demand or readily substitute for each other, their prices will vary but little. If a large increase in supply tends to diminish the price of pork at the same time that a shortage in production is tending to increase the price of beef, an increased demand for the former will arrest its decline, while a decreased demand for the latter will arrest its advance. The two are competing to fill the same demand and this competition tends to level their prices.

Credit substitutes directly for money; in performing the same function both supply the same demand, and an increase of credit affects the purchasing power of a dollar no less than an increase in the supply of money itself. So close is the relationship between money and credit that in many instances they come to perform precisely the same functions; here their identities fuse and the two become one. Bank-notes; are they credit instruments? Yes, they bear the promise to pay to the bearer on demand. Are they money? That which does the money-work is the money-thing, and this work they do in full.

Credit liberates wealth when it substitutes for primary money. An isolated community worth $100,000 can enjoy but $80,000 worth of necessities and conveniences should it be compelled to set aside $20,000 in gold coin to facilitate its exchanges. Could it substitute credit for gold coin, and convert its gold into necessities, its well-being would be increased to the extent of $20,000.

2. **All Classes Use Credit.**—Formerly the debtor class consisted almost entirely of the poor, who were forced in times of stress to borrow from their more favored brethren. To-day the debtor class consists, for the most part, of the wealthy who borrow for investments. But the distinction must not be drawn too sharply, for all classes use credit.

Improvident working men spend their wages before they are earned. Always dependent upon credit stores, they pay extortionate prices to be carried on the books. The rule of these stores is low prices for cash and high prices for credit, the credit prices being made high enough to counterbalance bad debts. Those honest enough to pay, pay enough to square the account of the dishonest customer. Improvidence, as a cause of credit, makes the commercial system uncertain.

A very poor community must have the necessities of life; the pressure for goods causes idle money in the drawer to be regarded as an unnecessary luxury. So their cash reserves are reduced to a minimum; they resort to credit and trust to luck that they will get more money somehow when it is needed.

Provident persons starting into business or desiring to enlarge operations will have little money in reserve. The need of funds to construct large productive establishments may require more money than is in circulation. This necessity, whether for purposes of consumption or of production, will lead to the establishment of a credit system which shall serve the place of money.

**3. Credit Defined.**—What has been said indicates that credit is a readily acceptable thing, which performs the essential function of money, but it has a broader application. If we speak of the public credit of Mexico, we have in mind the ability and readiness of that government to fulfil its pecuniary obligations. Credit is trust given or received; expectation of future payment for property transferred or promises given; it applies to individuals, corporations, and nations.

Credit is used at times to signify a person's ability to contract a debt. "A good pay is master of another man's purse." "A good way to make debts is to pay them." William Roscher, a German economist, said: "Credit is the power of disposition over the goods of another, voluntarily granted in consideration of the mere promise of the counter-value."

A more accurate statement is that credit refers to the obligation which exists between a debtor and a creditor during the interval of time between the two parts of a complete act of exchange. The economist, for the most part, thinks of credit simply as a substitute for money.

This credit obligation may or may not be legally enforcible. If Smith makes a note to Jones for $1,000 for value received, it could be enforced at law; but if Smith and Jones gamble, the obligation or credit given is non-enforcible.

Credit is to be distinguished from a credit instrument, the latter being a promise to pay money which is written or printed or in tangible form.

Credit is not a commodity; it creates only indirectly; it is merely an agency of transfer.

4. **The basis of credit is confidence.** There must be confidence in the honor and probity of the debtor, but his personal honor is not enough; there must also be confidence in his ability to pay. Confidence as a basis of credit refers both to the disposition and the ability to pay.

If an irresponsible tramp tender his note the maker of the note has neither the will nor the ability to pay, and his note, properly speaking, is not a credit instrument. Credit must have reference to the ability of the persons contracting debts. This fact is recognized by the law, for the contracts of idiots and, in many cases of minors, are non-enforcible. The merchant who would sell "on time" to the irresponsible tramp would be incapable of giving credit; or if mentally sound he would be merely "taking a chance."

There are cases where credit is given without reference to the honor of the debtor. In real-estate transactions, for instance, the record in the county clerk's office is the only worth-while witness. If Smith executes a land contract to sell to Jones mortgaged property, Jones must receive it according to contract and at the agreed price, even if Smith declared it to be free from obligation. Here credit is involved and Jones must pay even if against his will, and must receive the real estate, even though Smith falsified.

**5. Credit Facilitates Production.**—It is common knowledge that people who borrow money on credit really borrow the use of the wealth which that money will buy. No one pays interest on borrowed money for the sake of keeping it; on the contrary, it is at once exchanged for ripe goods or for productive wealth.

There are active capitalists who productively employ such means as they may have or may borrow; there are also passive capitalists—women, children, retired business men—who, having no productive use for their means, loan at interest to active capitalists. Credit facilitates the transmission of capital, the control over agencies of production, from passive to active capitalists. Thus credit serves to place the productive agencies of the community at the proper place and in the most enterprising hands. By the transfer of productive power to the vigorous and energetic class of people, public welfare is promoted. This makes active agencies more active and gives motion to idle agencies. It concentrates industries and makes possible the advantages of large-scale production.

Credit, then, is a means to the end of larger production and is, therefore, itself productive. All the numerous agencies, facilitating and other, which co-operate in their organized capacity to create utilities, are productive. No one agent alone is productive. Land, or labor, or machinery, or credit, or any other one agent, considered separate and apart from others, is non-productive. A productive agent is a composite unit, and every essential element necessary to compose it is productive. Credit is such an element and it is idle to deny, as many do, its productivity.

**6. The Danger of Credit.**—Credit ties firm to firm and business to business throughout the industrial life of the people. No misfortune can attend one branch of industry which is not of vital concern to every other. For instance: A large corporation is forced into bankruptcy; its outstanding obligations are large and numerous; its creditors have reckoned these obligations among their assets and have contracted with other concerns upon the strength of these assets; but, this basis of credit failing, they in turn cannot pay their debts and so the effects of the one big failure are passed on. The failure of one firm gives effect to a succession of failures throughout industry. Its effect has been compared to that produced when a stone is cast into a pond; one circular wave leads to another until the farthest edges of the pond are reached.

Credit is most sensitive; being based upon confidence, it is as changeable as human thought. It unites with money to facilitate exchanges and every extension of it is an added possibility of disaster, for if any considerable portion of the intricate mechanism of trade should fail, confidence is shaken. An impairment of confidence results in the withdrawal of credit, and this in turn causes stringency in the money market. This condition, accompanied by a nervous and unreasonable rush on the part of each to save himself, ruins many and may injure all.

Production is roundabout and is becoming more so with the development of civilization. If the primitive man wanted a drink of water, he lay down by the brook and drank directly from it. Later on he made use of a crude receptacle which we may call an economic good with an indirect use. The water was no longer attained directly, but indirectly through the agency of the receptacle.

Should the average city-dweller trace the whole roundabout process step by step of his getting a drink of water, he would be amazed at the complexity. The water is obtained only at the end of a long succession of technical steps—mining, smelting, shaping, transporting, merchandising, and other. This indirect or roundabout process is the most effective way of getting what we desire, but it requires time to obtain thus the objects of desire. The more roundabout the process, generally speaking, the longer is the lapse of time between the beginning and the end of the productive process. Credit facilitates this complicated process; it enables probable future goods to exchange against those actually present; it provides the basis of a continuous working policy, thus giving temporal solidarity to business. At the same time, however, it lengthens the forecast which producers must make of the market, and thereby increases the uncertainties of time. Credit further increases the uncertainties of time, because through it the number of interests involved are increased.

In his Economic Crises, a book deserving careful study, E. D. Jones writes: "The abuses of credit may manifest themselves in many forms. At one place they may centre in the banking policy, at another in joint-stock companies; at one time the fault may lie in bankruptcy laws, at another in a reckless issue of paper money. The use of credit is particularly dangerous when the tone of business is unusually optimistic. It is also dangerous in lines of trade in which estimates are unusually speculative and results are uncertain. The history of mining, invention, and foreign trade is replete with failures due to easy credit. And the modern growth of credit has for the first time made speculation socially dangerous." And further:

"The convulsions of modern business would seem to indicate that the credit structures which have been raised in the business world are too lofty for the basis of integrity we have at present to offer. The remedy lies at every man's door. Civilization cannot merely migrate from country to country as it has done in the past; we must learn how to intensify the economic and social bonds without self-destruction and without the increase of those economic wastes of which crises form a part."

7. **The General and Limited Acceptability of Credit Instruments.**—A credit instrument has general acceptability when all persons in a country accept it without question in payment for goods and services. Such an instrument must be negotiable; there must be general confidence in its maker; it must be difficult to counterfeit, easy to recognize, and in convenient denominations. Notes of this character are issued by banks and governments; if non-interest bearing, they serve as money, whether legal tender or not.

A credit instrument is said to have limited acceptability when it will serve as a means of payment only within a restricted field. A non-negotiable promissory note is most limited as to acceptability. If made payable to order or bearer, it is negotiable and its acceptability is broadened. Other instruments of limited acceptability are book accounts, bills of exchange, various forms of bank credit, and emergency currency such as "pay checks."

All such instruments are based on confidence in the individual or firm which makes them, and since the maker is not generally known, confidence in his promise to pay is limited.

During the panic of 1893 confidence was at a minimum

and little personal credit was accepted, and the need for money to take the place of credit exceeded the available supply. People lost confidence in one another, but large corporations were able to maintain the people's faith in certain localities. The corporations issued "pay checks" as a sort of emergency currency. They have been called "community credit money," but one should not speak of a credit instrument of only a community reputation as money.

8. **Bank credits** form by far the most important form of credit and have, therefore, a most significant influence on prices. Banks are institutions which deal in credit; they make their income by selling their credit to customers. This credit is more convenient than primary money, and is so universally acceptable as to become the common medium of exchange in the business world. A bank sells its credit by simply giving its promise to pay. The written evidence of an individual's promise to pay is a promissory note; the written evidence of a bank's promise to pay takes the form of a bank-note or an entry in what is known as a "pass-book." But why such confidence in a bank that its mere promise comes to serve as the common medium of exchange throughout the business world? This confidence rests upon so many pillars of support that a mere. enumeration of them becomes tedious. They are: the bank's paid-up capital; its surplus and undivided profits; its reputation and good-will; the character of its loans and securities held; the liability of stockholders; the prestige of its officers, directors, and stockholders; and, finally, the people's confidence is strongly supported by faith in the control and inspection by expert official examiners.

Banks perform various functions useful to their customers; some of these are performed by institutions other than banks. They maintain deposit vaults, change money, sell securities, and serve as trustees. But the one essential and true banking function is that of dealing in credit.

9. **Banks as Reservoirs of Capital.**—A bank may be likened to a reservoir from which capital (purchasing power) flows in the form of credit. Surplus funds flow into the bank and become the basis of credit issues, which flow out to the places where capital is needed. Thus banks become equalizing agencies of finance throughout the community. Small driblets of idle capital are collected by the banks and consolidated into huge funds capable of meeting the demands for large capital on the part of great industrial establishments. In this way the banks put idle capital to work and they arrange capital in such volumes that it can work most effectively.

10. **Deposits.**—Individuals might retain their own funds, might disappoint the burglars by hiding them in unsuspected places, or at enormous expense keep burglar-proof vaults, but a division of labor is better which allows one man to make it his business to provide a place of safekeeping and so do this work for all. Those who intrust their funds to a bank are called *depositors* and the funds so intrusted are *deposits*. The bank holds itself ready to pay the depositor at any moment, or "on demand." Individuals would rather leave their means "on deposit" than to bear the risk and inconvenience of carrying them about. Consequently, even the most wealthy carry little money with them; they carry instead the right to draw money. Thus risks and inconvenience are reduced to a minimum.

But the money deposited is small in comparison with the deposits made through discounting. A simple illustration will show how deposits are thus made. A merchant who sells on time furnishes a farmer with tools, fertilizer, and seed, taking in exchange his note for $500, which will mature four months hence, when he sells the crop. The merchant cannot exchange this note to distant commercial houses for goods, as such houses would not take the note of a man, though of high moral honor and financial ability, who is unknown except in his home community. But such houses make it a practice to accept the credit of banks. The merchant wishing to use in his business the $500 called for in the note will wish to trade this promissory note to the bank for its generally accepted credit. He indorses this note and presents it to the local banker, who (knowing both the maker and indorser to be honest and able to pay, and knowing further the power of the law to compel payment) is willing to trade the credit of his bank for it. Inasmuch as the note will not mature for four months he will not give in exchange the credit of the bank to the full face value of the note, but accepts the instrument at its present worth ($500 less interest for four months). The merchant is now at liberty to take his pay for the note, for instance, $490, in either of two ways—he may take the cash, or he may leave it with the bank as a deposit and take away a pass-book which evidences the deposit, and a check-book which enables him to draw in such amounts and at such times as he finds convenient. The latter is the usual method followed in this country, therefore in discounting a customer's note the bank increases its own deposits. What does this illustration show a deposit to be? From the standpoint of the bank, a deposit is the bank's promise to pay money to a person or corporation. From the standpoint of the depositor, a deposit is the right to draw upon the bank.

In this illustration the discounted note becomes the property of the bank. The merchant, though called a borrower, has sold to the bank his right to secure money in the future, just as he sold agricultural equipment to the farmer. He indorsed the note, thus promising to make it good just as he guaranteed the plows and other equipment sold to the farmer. What did the bank give in exchange? This transaction simply involved an exchange of rights; the bank sold the merchant a right to draw at will for his right to a future income.

No new principle would be involved in case the merchant has a note, made by himself, discounted at the bank. His note evidencing the right to collect a certain sum of money in the future is sold to the bank in exchange for the right to draw on demand.

11. **Deposits Lower the Purchasing Power of Money.—** Business men meet their obligations for the most part by drawing on their bank accounts. Professional men and the wealthier classes avail themselves most generally of this means of payment. On the other hand, the poorer classes and, for the most part, those who live in the country districts use money. Again, bank credit is used in case of large payments and money is used by all classes in so-called "petty transactions." It is both convenient and customary to use money and bank credit in transacting the people's business. The demands for each are fairly established in practice, and the amounts of each in common use hold a more or less constant ratio to each other. In other words, there is a rather constant ratio of money

in circulation to money in the form of deposits. This means simply that an increase in the supply of money causes a proportionate increase in bank deposits. Compared with these deposits the bank credits (substitutes for money) issued upon them are many times larger. Consequently deposits have the effect of lowering the purchasing power of money or of raising prices.

12. **Time Deposits** are carried by savings-banks, as well as by separate departments of commercial banks. These deposits are not drawn (as are deposits in commercial banks) on demand. Upon making a time deposit the customer agrees not to draw for some specified minimum time, or until a certain number of days after he shall have notified the bank of his intention to withdraw funds. Because the banker knows in advance when withdrawals will be made he can prudently invest a large portion of the funds intrusted to his safe-keeping. There is no danger of a "run" upon the bank in times of panic. He has to maintain but a small fraction of the deposits to meet the demands of his customers for cash. The Federal Reserve Act of 1913 requires that only 5 per cent shall be kept as a reserve against time deposits. The depositor receives interest on time deposits and regards them as investments and not as demand credit available for current cash transactions.

Demand deposits are spoken of as checking accounts; they are payable at any time and the demand for payment is made by the personal check of the depositor.

13. **Liabilities and Assets.**—Thus far we have seen that bank discount amounts to this: the bank buys the right to collect a specified sum of money at a certain future time, and gives in exchange its promise to pay on demand a sum

of money equal to the present worth of the money it acquires the right to collect. A liability (debt) is that which one is under obligation to pay. The bank has a right to receive, at its maturity, the face value of a note which it discounts; there is a corresponding duty to pay on the part of the debtor or maker of the note. That which is a right of the bank is a debt or *liability* of the debtor. On the other hand, the depositor has a right to receive on demand the funds deposited at the bank; this right on the part of the depositor is a debt or *liability* on the part of the bank. The liabilities of a bank embrace its total indebtedness to stockholders, note-holders, and depositors. But in return for every liability assumed the bank gets something, and this which the bank receives is called its assets. The bank gets as much as it owes and owes as much as it gets; its assets and liabilities weigh the same—they balance. A bank is a corporation, a legal person; it is unlike a natural person in this: it can own no more than it owes.

14. **The Operations of a Bank.**—We have said that a bank is a legal person, a corporation, and that it can own neither more nor less than it owes. This may be seen when the liabilities and assets of a bank are arranged side by side. A bank, as any other corporation, must have capital with which to begin business. Let us assume that five persons agree to establish a bank, that they secure a charter, and subscribe $50,000. The bank will be capitalized at this sum, and the ownership of it will be divided into 500 parts, called "shares," each of which will be worth $100. If each of the five men subscribed $10,000, each would come to own 100 shares of stock. When this money is turned over to the bank, it owes or is liable to

the stockholders for it. The paid-in capital is a liability of the bank, and the bank holds the $50,000 cash as an asset against its liability. The statement stands thus:

| Assets | Liabilities |
|---|---|
| Cash................$50,000 | Capital...............$50,000 |

The bank cannot do business without real estate, furniture, and fixtures, which it buys at a cost of, say, $5,000. This sum will be deducted from cash, leaving the statement thus:

| Assets | Liabilities |
|---|---|
| Cash................$45,000<br>Real estate, furniture...   5,000<br>———<br>$50,000 | Capital...............$50,000<br>———<br>$50,000 |

Both the purpose of the bank and its obligation to the stockholders require it to earn profits; and, since it is an institution which deals in credit, it will seek to convert its idle cash into interest-bearing securities. There will be in the community a number of merchants and other business men who desire bank credit. Their customers in payment for goods have made over to these business men notes varying in amounts and dates of maturity. Suppose that the bank is offered an aggregate of $20,000 worth of these promissory notes (securities). The bank will discount these in the manner above described. Should the average time for their maturity be 90 days, the bank will deduct the discount of, say, $300 and give *deposits* of

$19,700 for the notes. The value of the notes at maturity would be $20,000, but the depositors are willing to forego $300 for the present right to draw $19,700. The $300 discount becomes a liability, under the item "undivided profits," to the stockholders. The $20,000 worth of securities are the property of the bank and are entered among the assets under the item of "loans." In this transaction there appear some new items changing the statement to read thus:

| Assets | | Liabilities | |
|---|---|---|---|
| Cash.................. | $45,000 | Capital............... | $50,000 |
| Loans (securities)....... | 20,000 | Undivided profits...... | 300 |
| Real estate, furniture... | 5,000 | Deposits........... | 19,700 |
| | $70,000 | | $70,000 |

15. **The value of a bank's liabilities** must rest upon the value of its assets. The major part of the assets consists of the liabilities which the bank holds against its customers. These liabilities are backed in part by the houses, land, and other wealth of these customers, and they may also be backed in part by the liabilities which these customers hold against other persons. But these in turn are backed by tangible wealth. So we may say the ultimate basis of a bank's assets is the real wealth of the community. *The bank is merely an agency for giving the quality of liquid currency to unsalable forms of wealth.* One may be wealthy yet have no purchasing power, such is the condition of an owner of unsalable land. He turns to the bank for aid, offers it a note backed by his land, and this is converted into the form of readily acceptable bank credit.

**16. Capital Items.**—A bank as a corporation or legal person is distinct from the shareholders who own it, and intrust their funds to it. To the shareholders it owes the original capital received from them, as well as all the earnings of the capital. It is understood, however, that any claims held against the bank by shareholders cannot be enforced until after all other creditors are paid in full. The "capital" item represents the bank's liability to its stockholders; therefore the capital is what is left after all other liabilities are subtracted from the total assets of the bank. It is evident that the value represented by the "capital" item is constantly changing. Bookkeepers, however, keep the "capital" item unchanged; they characterize any increase not as "capital," but as "surplus" or "undivided profits." Why? Because bookkeeping is simplified by keeping the capital at the same figure; because the history of a bank's net capital accumulations is shown at a glance when the original capital is kept separate from the later accumulations; because, finally, the certificates which represent the stock have an engraved face value which cannot be changed conveniently to keep pace with the fluctuating money worth of the stock.

The items of "surplus" and "undivided profits" are simply bookkeeping devices for recording the variations of capital. As the "capital" is maintained at the same figure, so bookkeepers also hold the item of "surplus" at the same figure for considerable periods of time. The main reason for this is simplicity. How can this be done, it will be asked, since the additions to the original capital must fluctuate with the normal operations of the bank's business? This is made possible by the creation of a third item, also a part of capital, called "undivided profits." This item consists of a varying amount in addition to surplus. "Capital" (the original sum put in), "surplus" (an accumulation of earnings maintained in round numbers for considerable periods of time) and "undivided profits" (an irregular and varying sum in addition to surplus), are but three parts of one and the same liability of the bank to its stockholders.

17. **Reserves.**—He is a poor banker who holds large surpluses of idle cash. Funds must be loaned at interest, and deposits created through the discount of notes far in excess of the cash which a bank keeps on hand. If it fails in this, a bank neither serves its function nor makes a reasonable profit. What would happen if all these deposits were immediately called for in cash? If the governor did not declare a legal holiday (as governors have done when banks were threatened with a "run"), the bank would become insolvent. Then, is it not dangerous for a bank to contract obligations beyond its cash reserves? This is to be answered in the negative. Would the notes which the bank has discounted maintain its solvency? *Legal insolvency* exists when a bank's cash assets are insufficient to meet its liabilities as they fall due. The demands upon a bank are for cash and cannot be met by an offer of even the best securities. The moment a bank is unable to meet the demands of the depositors in cash, that moment it has failed; and the moment a depositor has to accept securities in satisfaction of his claim, that moment begins a division of the property of the bank among its creditors. The real banking reserve consists of those assets of the bank which are cash (ready purchasing power) or immediately convertible into cash. Such assets are specie, cash items (demands on others immediately collectible in cash), and legal-tender notes.

To return to the above question, bankers are in no danger who increase the deposits subject to call far beyond the amount of the reserves. Skilful bankers so order their discounting of notes as to have a more or less regular inflow of money with the maturity of these notes. Suppose that a banker discounts 300 notes a month, or an average of 10 each day. Should all these mature on one day, the banker would be embarrassed with surplus and idle cash for a day or two; he would have to carry a large reserve to tide him over until his next income period, thirty days hence. But should the discounting of securities be so ordered that there will be an approximately equal number of maturities each day, fewer idle reserves will have to be held, because the inflow of funds to the bank would approximately equal that of the outflow from the bank. The demands on reserves run more or less steadily from day to day and observing banks soon learn what ratio of reserves to deposits to maintain.

The proportion of reserves to demand liabilities is weakened in two ways—by an increase of liabilities, or by a decrease of cash. In a conservative bank there is a careful watch kept over the demand liabilities and the cash, so that they are maintained at a ratio well above the danger-line. In an unsafe bank, too much stress is laid upon the point that "idle cash is a loss," the possibility of financial storms is disregarded, all possible sail is spread, the reserves are imprudently reduced below the danger-line. In behalf of depositors, laws have been made to define minimum reserves requirements.

Under the national banking laws of the United States this minimum was fixed at 25 per cent for city banks and 15 per cent for country banks. It is left to the banker to determine how much, if any, may be required in addition to this minimum. The size of the necessary reserve varies from place to place; generally speaking, it is larger in the city than in the country districts.

Payment by checks do not necessarily make demands on the reserves of banks. Smith, Jones, and the other business men of the community are customers of the same bank, and when they make their payments to one another through checks upon the bank, these credits are turned back to the bank for deposit. Smith hands to Jones his check for $100 in payment of a debt; Jones takes this to the bank for deposit, and the bookkeeper deducts $100 from Smith's account, adding the same to the account of Jones. No cash is required, there is merely bookkeeping. If Smith decides to pay Jones $100 cash, he will withdraw this amount from the bank, but as soon as it is received by Jones he will return it to the bank. These examples are typical of the ordinary transactions carried on through banks; they are of such a nature that banks are enabled to keep reserves that are small in comparison with their liabilities.

**18. Other Assets.**—Banks are coming more and more to loan on *collateral;* that is, borrowers pledge some form of salable property to the bank, which may be readily converted into cash by the bank in case the loan is not promptly paid. Stocks and bonds are the most desirable form of collateral, because if the bank is embarrassed for funds, these securities may be sold quickly on the stock exchanges. Banks, especially those in the vicinity of stock exchanges, carry a considerable proportion of their assets in the form of stock-exchange collateral. Loans made on this basis are usually payable at "call"; that is, no definite time is set at which they mature, but they are payable at any time the bank demands payment.

Other quick assets, of growing importance in American banking, are such securities as government, state, and municipal bonds. English banking-houses will go so far as to treat consols as if they were cash.

"Outside paper" is a technical name given by a bank to the promissory notes of business firms which are not among its own customers and depositors. When a bank has surplus funds over and above the requirements of its clientele it may find an outlet for them in the purchase of outside paper. A group of middlemen called note-brokers make it a business to search out and sell to banks desiring such paper. This practice is commendable on condition that the bank knows the financial standing of the firms backing this paper, because it has the effect of distributing the risks of the bank over a broader business circle. It is not well for the bank to restrict its loans to a few customers or firms, for, these failing, the bank fails. It is better not to carry all the eggs in one basket.

**19. The Leading Safeguard of a Bank.**—*Real insolvency* means that an institution owes more than it is worth. *Legal insolvency* is reached when an institution is not able to pay on demand, although its assets are equal to its liabilities. When a bank receives a commercial deposit it agrees to pay on demand; when it fails in this, the bank has failed despite the sufficiency of its assets in forms other than cash. While a bank's failure does not necessarily imply that it is really insolvent, yet it must make safe its depositors. The leading safeguard of a bank against real insolvency lies in the strength of its capital, surplus, and undivided profits. These represent the stockholders' interests and the claims of all other creditors of a bank are prior to those of the stockholders. The greater the ratio of their interests to those of the other creditors, the less is the danger of real insolvency.

But the standing danger which threatens the safety of a bank is the right of depositors and the holders of its notes to demand funds at any instant. Bankers may increase reserves relative to liabilities by (1) care in the selection of securities to be discounted; (2) so raising the rate of discount as to discourage borrowers; (3) refusing to renew loans or to make new loans; and (4) collecting loans subject to call.

**20. The Agency of Clearing-Houses.**—Should Smith patronize the First National while Jones deposits with the Second National Bank of the same city, they could still pay each other by means of checks as effectively as though both deposited in the same bank. If both carried deposits in the same bank, a check paid by one to the other would mean that the bookkeeper would simply deduct the amount of the check from the deposit of the payer and add the same to the deposit of the payee. In the case now assumed the transfer of the check would be effected through the agency of a clearing-house. Smith, for example, hands Jones a check or order on the First National, to pay Jones $100; Jones indorses the same, making it payable to his bank (the Second National), which in payment adds $100 to his deposit. He surrenders his title to the check; it becomes the property of his bank, which gives Jones in exchange a right to draw $100. Now the First National Bank owes the Second National $100. Throughout the day each of these banks has collected from the numerous business men of the city a large number of checks against the other. Were there a large number of banks in the city, they would accumulate numerous checks against one another. These checks or credits are sent to the clearing-house, which settles the accounts between banks just as a bank settles accounts between customers. Suppose that the First and Second National Banks hold equal amounts against each other. The obligations would cancel out. But if the orders were in favor of the First National to the extent of $1,000, it would be credited with the surplus and the bank or banks owing this would be debited with the deficiency. The aggregate of these differences over a considerable period of time will be small. By paying these small differences to the clearing-house, there will be but little cash used in transactions which would otherwise aggregate large sums.

21. **Payments by Checks between Different Communities.**—Should Smith live in Hoboken and Jones in St. Joseph, Louisiana, they could still pay each other by means of bank credit. Smith may draw a check on his bank in Hoboken and send it to Jones. The Hoboken bank now owes Jones $100. Jones indorses the check, takes it to his bank in St. Joseph in exchange for a corresponding sum to the credit of his deposit account. Now the bank in Hoboken owes the bank in St. Joseph $100. The St. Joseph bank indorses it and sends it for collection to a New Orleans bank with which it maintains a deposit. The New Orleans bank now owns the check against the Hoboken bank, and it has paid for it by simply adding a corresponding sum to the credit of the deposit account which the St. Joseph bank carries with it. The New Orleans bank carries a deposit with a New York bank, so it indorses the check to the New York bank. The New

York bank buys the check by adding a corresponding sum to the deposit account of the New Orleans bank. The New York bank now owns the check, and sends it to the clearing-house in New York for collection from some other New York bank, with which the Hoboken bank has a deposit account. In the clearing-house $100, the amount called for in the check, is added to the account of the bank presenting the check, and the same amount is deducted from the deposit account of the correspondent[1] of the Hoboken bank. This correspondent bank deducts $100 from the deposit account of the Hoboken bank, and sends the check to the Hoboken bank, which deducts $100 from the deposit account of the customer, Smith, who originally signed it.

22. **Bank-notes** are credit instruments so exchangeable that they do the work of money and are, therefore, to be classed among the forms of money. They are so convenient that they take the place of metallic money in many cases, and thus lessen the amount of it used in effecting exchanges. A bank-note is simply a promissory note issued by the bank. The holder of a note has a right at any time to demand payment by the bank, and the bank's obligation to a note-holder is not unlike its obligations to a depositor.

23. **Exercises.**—1. "The basis of credit is found in the tangible wealth of the world." Explain. "The basis of credit is confidence." Are these statements contradictory?

2. What effect will an increase in the supply of cotton have upon the demand for woollens? What effect would an expansion of credit have upon the purchasing power of

---

[1] When one bank carries a deposit account in another they are called "correspondent" banks.

money? What economic principle is suggested by these two questions?

3. Point out the dangers connected with credit in the modern business world.

4. Why will bank credit substitute for money more readily than will the credit of a good citizen?

5. How may deposits be made in a bank? Describe in detail how deposits are made through discounting.

6. What effect do deposits have upon the purchasing power of money?

7. "A bank statement is a summary of the bank's assets and liabilities.

"(a) The assets and liabilities are always exactly equal. How do you account for this?

"(b) If the assets and liabilities are always equal, how can the statement indicate the strength of the bank?

"(c) If you deposit $100 in gold, does this affect the bank's assets? Its liabilities? Explain. Answer similar questions assuming the deposit to be in the form of a $100 check on this bank; assume it to arise from your giving your note for $100 to the bank?" (Hayes.)

8. "(a) Why is it that for 'every asset there is a liability?'

"(b) If men in organizing a bank put in $20,000 in gold, the statement will then stand: Assets, cash, $20,000; liabilities, capital stock $20,000. Why is capital a liability?

"(c) How will the statement be affected if $10,000 is spent for a site and building?

"(d) If Mr. X deposits $200 in gold?

"(e) If Y cashes a $50 check drawn by X?

"(f) If Z opens an account by depositing a $100 check written by X?

"(g) If Z, wishing to borrow, gives his note for $300 to the bank and has this amount, less $2.45 interest, deposited to his account?

"(h) If the bank spends $1,000 for bonds?

"(i) If the bonds are later sold for $1,100?

"(j) If Z pays his note at maturity?" (Hayes.)

9. After the following operations, how would you arrange the several items under liabilities and assets? The bank begins with a paid-up capital of $150,000 and has a surplus of $30,000. It discounts for customers $300,000 of four months' notes, and bills receivable at 6 per cent, the borrowers take one-third of the proceeds in cash and leave two-thirds on deposit. Customers deposit $50,000 in cash, $25,000 in checks drawn on this bank, and $25,000 in checks drawn on other banks.

# CHAPTER XIV

## BANKING LEGISLATION IN THE UNITED STATES

**1. Introductory.** The function of banks, as well as their operations, have been pointed out in the chapter on "Credit and Banking." In a great commercial community these functions reach beyond the welfare of individual customers; they are national and international in scope. Banks are the agencies through which currency systems operate. In proportion to their ability to distribute properly, to expand and contract the currency as need arises, to make their services readily available to all classes, agricultural and other, they do their work well or ill. Coins cannot be struck and recalled to meet the varying contractions and expansions of business, but some kind of elasticity of currency is necessary to meet the ups and downs in the money demand. This elasticity is to be found in bank credit, through the expansion and contraction of either bank-notes or deposits. Notes may be issued by numerous and competing banks, or they may be issued by one bank or under one central supervision.

305

2. **Centralized Banking.**—Prior to the Civil War there were different kinds of banks which issued notes. These notes were easily put into circulation; they passed as money, though not always at par; their redemption at the banks was postponed, for certain banks evaded their redemption when called upon, and they continued to pass from hand to hand; reckless issues led many banks to collapse. This sad experience led to the advocacy of a unified control of note issues, but as a "let alone" policy prevailed, a decentralized note issue accompanied it. Decentralized note issues in Scotland, England, and the United States led to recurrent bank failures during the first half of the nineteenth century.

On the European Continent a different and more praiseworthy experience is recorded. There the issue of notes has been regarded as a public function, and generally has been permitted only by institutions connected with or supervised by the governments.

Two policies have taken root: (1) Decentralization, manifold note issue, government supervision, and (2) centralization and quasi-public note issues.

Typical of the latter policy are the three noteworthy central banks: the Bank of France, the Bank of England, the Reichsbank of Germany. These institutions are not alike in all respects, but they have one lesson in common. Attention will be given here only to the Bank of France: It is simple in operation, and will show the functions of a central bank.

3. **The Bank of France.**—Although the Bank of France is privately owned, and pays dividends to private stockholders, its manager is appointed by the French Government, and it is under the virtual control of the state.

Nevertheless, it is little hampered in its operations, since there is no special regulation of its banking functions, no separate provision for the safety of its notes, since it has a monopoly of the note issue.

*Public Duty:* The Bank of France is the fiscal agent of the government, keeps the public funds, administers and records the public debt, and lends funds to the government. ₁ Always, in time of need, the treasury of France turns to this bank for advances. Since 1914 as well as after 1870, the services of the bank in financing the government cannot be overestimated. It issues notes and lends to the government. So large was the issue during and after the war of 1870–1, that it was decided to suspend specie payments, but so great was the confidence in the bank's power and willingness to meet its obligations that no depreciation occurred prior to the date of redemption, 1878. That was a period of enormous note issue, yet conservative in comparison with the great demand for currency, and this conservatism sustained public confidence.

*Specie Reserve:* In normal times this bank, relative to its demand obligations, carries the largest reserve of any bank in the world. The large and growing specie reserve is composed of both gold and silver—mostly gold, and so the bank is able to maintain a low rate of bank interest. Moreover, this large reserve is never in danger of exhaustion, and enables the bank to maintain a policy of low and uniform discount rates. It changes the discount rate on the average about once a year—from 1875 to 1908 there were only thirty-six changes. American bankers would object to holding a large reserve of idle specie, but the Bank of France is not primarily a money-maker for its stockholders. Its main purpose is to render the best public service, to hold the government's finances to impregnable strength. Because of this it has even been accused of collecting a huge war reserve in this form.

*Deposits:* There is little deposit checking in France; the people use specie and bank-notes almost altogether. The tendency for notes to remain in circulation for long periods of time, together with the fact that they are more convenient than hard money, causes gold to flow into the bank in exchange for notes and to remain there. Notes are not issued in small denominations, however—not less than 50 francs, few less than 100 francs—and this compels the use of hard money for petty transactions. The money system and habit of the people are such that the average per capita use of money is very large.

*Branch Banking:* Provision has been made for the establishment of 337 branches of the central bank. By the decree of 1808 branches were established plainly with the design of centralizing the banking interests of the empire under the lead of the great bank in Paris, but the Bourbon ruler in 1817 and 1818 closed these branches. In 1882 branches were again established. There are some objections to these branch banks; their capital is allotted by the central bank; they are supervised by the parent bank in Paris; they must secure special permission to do business with other banks; their rates of discount are determined, not by the local needs where they are, but by a policy fixed in Paris; their directors are selected by the governor of the bank; the real authority is in the hands of a manager appointed by the government, frequently a stranger, and assisted by subordinates sent from the capital. The objections to branch banking in the United States are that small banks fear they will be swallowed up by the large banks in New York City, and that local interests will be served best by independent local banks. Our system has advantages over the rigid uniformity required for the whole of France. That system lacks adaptability to local needs. On the other hand, branch banking has many advantages. Branch banks facilitate the collection and distribution of loanable capital from and to different parts of the country. Such a system keeps its fingers on the business pulse of the whole country and makes easy the circulation of money from places of surplus to places of need. Such an acquaintance with the needs of the whole country cannot but add to the solidarity of business. While it is true that a small branch may afford adequate banking facilities for isolated places, one system effects a comparatively uniform rate of interest. This is an appealing argument to the American business man who has suffered the needless burden of wide differences in the interest rates between different sections of the country. A bank with branches reaching every section of the country does not face ruin by local business depressions. Many towns are built around a single industry, and the banks serving these towns go down with the failure of the industry. Branch banking also secures superior executive ability at the head. Inasmuch as a central policy guides the whole system, the necessity of spreading rare ability over the individual branches is spared. But when such ability is revealed in any branch it is, through a system of selection and promotion, advanced to a higher ranking. Branch banking lends efficiency to capital. The small nation with facilities for marshalling and transporting its troops from front to front may withstand a foe far superior in all but these facilities. Likewise a nation with an adequate banking system **that** penetrates all sections may give to a small volume of capital adequate powers to do the nation's work.

*Elasticity:* There is a maximum legal limit to the notes the Bank of France may issue. But this limit is virtually a dead letter as it is far in excess of the usual issue, and is modified in times of need. We may say that it issues notes as far as it sees fit; they fluctuate from week to week, depending upon the market needs; when they come back to the bank they are not reissued. It discounts ordinary commercial paper for its customers. Its accommodations are for the poor as well as for the rich; it will discount paper worth five francs (one dollar). It does a large rediscount business for other banks. Seventy per cent of its paper bears the signature of some other bank as an indorser. This privilege of banks to have their commercial paper rediscounted enables a bank with limited means to make loans.

This bank gives to France a strong centralized financial system, so organized as to reach all sections of the country, and to apportion the nation's capital to the local needs. It furnishes an elastic system; through rediscounts it enables other banks to supply the credit and monetary needs of those who hold good commercial paper; it does not discriminate between rich and poor in extending its accommodations. It does business for the people, for other banks, and for the government. In marked contrast with this centralized system is the decentralized national banking system of the United States.

4. **Banking Prior to National Banks.**—It is beyond the scope of this book to trace through the several types of banks and banking which preceded the national banking system. At some periods in the history of ante-bellum

banking inconvertible notes existed in weltering chaos; the secretary of the treasury could not, within several millions, estimate their amount; they were termed "heterogeneous rags" as they poured forth in great volume from "wild-cat" or "coon-box banks"; they took, at times, the form of unchartered scrip in denominations from six cents upward; redemption, if at all, was at times enforced by "lynch law"; Secretary McCulloch spoke, in disgust, of the system, at one time, "as a compound of quackery and imposture." During these "good old days" the pickpockets and unscrupulous rogues had a free license. When Congress refused to recharter the second bank of the United States (a worthy institution), a large number of state banks sprang up, of the "joint-stock" and limited liability type. In not a single state were they subject either to effective regulation or supervision. It was the system, not the banks—the government, not the bankers—that are to be censured. But there were praiseworthy characters among bankers, and some illuminating examples of banking.

5. **The free banking system of New York** deserves special mention as a forerunner and model for the national banks. "The wildly extravagant issues of really inconvertible paper money," says F. A. Walker, "supplied the motive and the means for every species of extravagant, wanton, and irresponsible speculation. Words could scarcely exaggerate the extent to which the distortion of production and the misapplication of capital were carried. The whole head was sick and whole heart faint. The retribution came in the panic of 1837, and in the second and heavier shock of 1839, and in the long and dreary prostration of industry which followed."[1] These experiences led

[1] Political Economy, pp. 441–442.

to legislation designed to place banking on a sound basis. Before 1838 in New York banks had special charters, with the consequence that a bank was a privileged monopoly. Special charter institutions, banking or industrial, have always been a cause of political corruption and bribery of legislatures. The Act of 1838 was an enabling act. It enabled any person or group of persons to engage in banking on certain prescribed conditions. One condition was that no bank-notes could be issued until security for their redemption was placed in the hands of the comptroller of the state. This security had to consist of United States or New York stocks or bonds, and of mortgages on improved real estate. This scheme of *secured circulation* is known as the New York system. The system was not perfect in two respects: (1) It provided certain but not immediate convertibility of notes; (2) the nature of the securities to back notes did not prove a most fortunate selection.

Different states undertook to follow New York's example, but these attempts ended in failure, due to the character of securities with which they backed their notes. Improvements which pointed to success, however, were under headway when the Civil War began, and they were superseded by the National Bank Act.

6. **The National Bank Act** was advocated in the report of Secretary Chase in 1861, but it did not take the form of law until February 25, 1863. In its behalf the following arguments were urged.

*Market for bonds:* A prohibitive tax was placed upon the note issue of banks other than national banks; thus the new banks were to issue all bank-notes. They were required to buy government bonds and deposit them at the Treasury Department in Washington as a guarantee of the notes issued. The treasury was in great distress, and the demands upon it for war purposes put the department in search for new sources of revenue. It was thought some hundreds of millions in bonds could be sold to the banks to back their note issue. Moreover, each bank, whether it issued circulating notes or not, was required to deposit in the treasury a certain amount of registered bonds of the United States. To sell bonds to meet the exigency of war was the first and primary object of the National Banking Act; it was truly a war measure. But as a fiscal resource it failed. Not until after the war and when the government was on its feet—able to borrow at home and abroad—did the national banks begin to call for bonds in large amounts.

*Uniformity in Currency:* We now come to the most redeeming feature of the act. Notes, uniform in appearance, in value, and in acceptability, came in the place of a great variety of notes—worthless, altered, forged, and other. Every holder of a national bank-note is backed by the credit of the government. A note from a bank in Maine will pass as readily in California as in its home state, and that, too, without regard to the stànding of the bank which issues it. No longer is the holder of a note annoyed from the refusal to receive bank-notes by those unacquainted with the bank of issue.

*Curb Inflation:* State banks, during the Civil War period, were redeeming their notes in greenbacks. These went down in purchasing power with the greenbacks and added largely to the circulating media. Could national bank-notes supersede state bank issues and be limited in amount to the capital stock of the national bank, the public credit would be strengthened. This would clear the market of state bank-notes, leaving only greenbacks and national bank-notes. The latter being restricted, the purchasing power of greenbacks would be strengthened.

*Public Deposits:* The banks would provide a place of safe-keeping for the government's funds. A number of banks have been designated by the secretary of the treasury as depositaries of public money. These are especially convenient for making local disbursements.. The deposits of the government are running accounts like those of private customers. If the government wishes to restore funds to the money market, it makes what is known as special deposits. To withdraw these advance notice is given, and upon them interest is to be paid at a rate prescribed by the secretary of the treasury.

*Tie People to Government:* It was argued that a large distribution of bonds would tie up the people's interest with that of the government. When the national banks come to own millions of bonds they will use their agency in behalf of the credit of the government. Likewise the people who hold bank-notes supported by government bonds will make effort to safeguard the public credit.

7. **Provisions of the Act.**—The original act and its later amendments provided that every national bank should deposit registered United States bonds in the treasury, whether it issued circulating notes or not. Every bank may receive notes equal to the par value of the bonds deposited by it, but not exceeding their market value. Bank-notes thus rest on the credit of the government; this security remains if the issuing bank fails. Banks are required to redeem their notes at their own counter. And in addition to the bonds deposited, each bank must keep

on deposit in the United States Treasury, in lawful money, a sum equal to 5 per cent of its circulation. This is to redeem notes when presented in sums of $1,000 or multiple thereof. What if a bank fails? The comptroller pays the note-holder in lawful money, and declares the bonds which the defaulting bank has deposited to be forfeited to the government. He may cancel or, at his pleasure, sell bonds equivalent to the notes he redeems. Suppose the bonds do not fully reimburse the government for the notes it redeems for the failed bank? It has first lien on the assets of the bank, and a right against stockholders who are held to double liability. When the notes are paid they are cancelled.

In order that country districts may have banking facilities, provision is made that a town having less than 3,000 population may have a bank with a capital stock of $25,000. The amount of capital required to establish a bank ranges upward as follows: When the population is from 3,000 to 6,000, at least $50,000 capital is required; when the population is from 6,000 to 50,000 at least $100,000 capital is required; when the population is over 50,000 at least $200,000 capital is required. Bank shares must be $100 each, at least 50 per cent of the capital must be paid in before the bank begins business, and the remainder must be paid in monthly instalments of not less than 10 per cent each.

The legal reserve is not the same for all banks. Banks are divided into three classes: Central reserve city banks, reserve city banks, and all others, commonly called country banks. Prior to the Federal Reserve Act the country banks (banks outside of certain large cities) were required to have as a reserve a sum of lawful money equal to 15 per cent of their deposits, but three-fifths of this 15 per cent (or 9 per cent) might be deposited in a reserve city bank. Then, a country bank was not required to keep in its own vaults a reserve of over 6 per cent. Reserve city banks were required to keep a reserve of 25 per cent. One-half of this (12½ per cent) might be kept on deposit in a central reserve city bank, where it was counted as part of the depositing banks' legal reserve. There are three central reserve cities—New York, Chicago, St. Louis—and the banks in them were required to hold in their vaults a reserve of lawful money equal to 25 per cent of their deposits.

8. **Defects of the System.**—The national banking system accomplished much good for the country, but it had certain defects which were largely responsible for the panics and financial strains which business has recurrently suffered. The banks were not equal to the situation during the panics of 1893, 1903, and 1907. There was demand for reform; why should the wealthiest nation have the poorest banking system in the world? Yet, what was there to do? The subject was intensively studied after 1903, and in the year following the severe panic of 1907 Congress appointed a National Monetary Commission. This large commission, with its corps of eminent scholars and experts in finance, submitted a comprehensive report in 1912. A summary of that report (Report National Monetary Commission, 62d Congress, 2d Session; Senate Documents 243, 6–16) should be carefully read by all students of economics. The chief faults of the system were: (1) Decentralization; (2) inelasticity of credit; (3) poor distribution of banking facilities over the country; (4) no American banking institutions in foreign countries, and (5) no rediscount system.

**9. Decentralization of Banking.**—A national bank could have no branches, as does the Bank of France. Consequently, there was no really national banking institution. Each national bank was a local institution, doing a local business, and depending upon its own resources. Each depended upon its own reserves to meet its demand liabilities. In dull times country banks deposited a portion of their reserves in reserve cities. Reserve city banks in turn sent their idle cash to New York City banks, which paid a small interest for it. Thus the idle funds of the country drifted to New York, the commercial and financial centre of the country. But New York banks were not paying interest on cash to hold it idle; they loaned it out at call for use on the stock and produce exchanges, carrying the required reserve of 25 per cent. During a revival of business—generally at crop planting or harvesting time—the banks in the South and West were called upon by depositors for cash, these banks called upon the reserve city banks, and these upon New York banks. The New York banks having loaned down to the required reserve were forced to call in loans, but the borrowers had this invested and found difficulty in liquidating immediately. Just this order of circumstances is largely responsible for the recurring panics in this country, and explains why they have been more acute than in other countries. The year 1913 was fairly normal as respecting banking conditions, and in that year the banks owed depositors $20,000,000,-000, when the total currency of the country was about $3,-600,000,000. Less than one-half of this was in the banks, and that centred, as above described, largely in New York. Should fright seize a fair portion of depositors and they make sudden demands on banks, the banks affected must close their doors.

A partial remedy is suggested in Mr. Paul M. Warburg's illuminating remark that we must treat our money reserves as a city does its water-supply—accumulate it in one or more large reservoirs and be able to send it at once to the spot where it is needed. France has long since learned this lesson and practises it in the manner above indicated. A banker in Lyons does not fear his depositors, for the Bank of France will furnish him gold or notes in exchange for his assets. "Depositors do not want money when they know they can get it"; they make a run on the bank because they fear they cannot get money.

Not only were the national banks local in organization, but also their assets were of a local and non-liquid character. A bank's discounts are for the most part in the form of the promissory notes of its customers, and the bank officials are local men, on confidential terms with their customers. Borrowing is a matter of private business, a promissory note a personal matter, and the borrower would regard it a personal offense should the banker attempt to raise money on his note. This is called *rediscounting*—the bank discounts a note for a customer, and has this same note discounted again by another bank. That is, the bank buys the note from its customer, and sells the same to another bank, taking its pay in cash or in the form of an increased deposit at the other bank. Rediscounting is a common practice in Europe, and a very helpful one in distributing among the people the total loaning capacity of the banks. In this country it has been regarded as a confession of weakness on the part of the bank.

In Europe the seller of wares draws a bill of exchange or draft upon the buyer which the buyer "accepts" or attaches his signature to. The creditor also indorses this and has it discounted at the bank. These are freely bought and sold by banks, thus enabling a bank to increase its liquid assets at will. This furnishes a discount market for the obligations of business men which works as freely as do our own markets for stocks and bonds. Want of a discount market has made more pronounced the local character of our banks.

10. **Inelasticity of Credit.**—The rigid requirements for bank reserves (15 or 25 per cent), together with the tendency of banks to keep their funds loaned to the limit, has already been commented upon. At crop-planting or crop-moving seasons banks whose reserve percentages are at the minimum, are not permitted to extend their accommodations. " A fixed reserve is to credit what a stone wall is to a prisoner: thus far, but no farther."

But the bond-secured note issue is the chief difficulty. A national bank can issue notes to the market value or to the par value, whichever is the smaller, of the government bonds which it buys and deposits in the treasury. As the price of bonds goes up the profits of the bank must go down, and *vice versa*. If the par value of a bond is $100 and its market value $110, the bank must pay $110 for the privilege of issuing $100 in notes. When will banks issue a large amount of notes? Assuredly, when the price of bonds is low. When is the price of bonds low? Always when the market rate of interest is high. The income on a bond is a fixed amount. A 5 per cent bond whose par value is $100 yields the owner $5 a year, no more and no less; it yields this fixed sum whether the market rate of interest be 1 per cent or 10 per cent. What would a permanent annuity of $5 a year be worth when the market rate of interest is 10 per cent? Fifty dollars, because $5 is 10 per

cent of that sum.   What if interest changes to 2 per cent?
It will be worth $250 because $5 is 2 per cent of that sum.
As the rate of interest goes up a bond (a fixed income instrument) goes down in price, and *vice versa.*   When will
the interest rate be high?   On two occasions: (*a*) With
few exceptions, when prosperity abounds and prices are
rising; and (*b*) always during the sudden fright of a panic.
Thus, in times of great prosperity, at the very time when
the market is not in need of more money, bond prices are
low and notes are thrown in large volume upon the market.   But the panic period is short, and banks, in self-
preservation, are collecting cash rather than buying bonds.
Yet many notes are issued during the flurry of panic.
When the interest rate is low bonds are high and note
issues few.   When will this be?   During depressions and
periods of dull business, when additional notes are most
needed.   The expansion of notes is not always at the
wrong time; fortunately, it sometimes occurs in time of
need.   But note the direction of such elasticity afforded
by the national banks; it is always out, not in.   We can
get notes out, but in slack seasons they do not return.

   11. **Distribution of Banking Facilities.**—Banking facilities have developed with respect to the urban centres,
while agricultural districts have had their prosperity re-
tarded for want of banking accommodations.   No adequate
agency has been provided for supplying them with funds
for their busy seasons; they have had to pay higher interest rates than prevail in the industrial centres.   National
banks, before 1913, were forbidden to make loans on real
estate.   The banking machinery was devised for money
to drift from small banks to the large banks—from country districts to financial and urban districts.   Deposits

did not travel in the opposite direction, and when city banks were called upon to return borrowed funds to country banks it was calculated to cost a panic. What is more: "We have no effective agency," reports the National Monetary Commission, "covering the entire country, which affords necessary facilities for making domestic exchanges between different localities and sections, or which can prevent disastrous disruption of all such exchanges in times of serious trouble."

12. **Banking and Foreign Trade.**—To quote further from the commission's report: "We have no American banking institutions in foreign countries. The organization of such banks is necessary for the development of our foreign trade." European countries maintain such banks, much to their advantage. These banks extend accommodations to the financial and business interests where located, enlist good-will, and attract attention to home products; they study local demands, inform their countrymen of prospective sales, report on the credit of importers, negotiate trade, arrange and make it easy to effect foreign payments. Foreign banks handling American trade in South America and the Orient naturally favor their own countrymen.

Competitive or decentralized banking cannot protect or regulate a nation's gold supply. There are times when a country has an oversupply of gold and to export it is profitable, and at other times when the supply is short it is necessary to attract gold from abroad. A central institution to dominate the control of foreign exchange is needed to raise its rate to hold gold in the country or attract it from abroad, and to lower its rate to dispose of a surplus. A central bank controls the expansion of credit which is an essential factor in depleting a nation's gold supply.

When credit expands prices accordingly rise, and it becomes profitable to buy in other countries where prices range lower. Exports fall and imports increase, thus leaving an unfavorable balance which must be paid in gold.

**13. New System Demanded.**—When you add to these difficulties the constant meddling, to the displeasure of many, of the national treasury, there is little wonder that a complete overhauling of the whole system was called for. The Aldrich plan, committed to the principle of a central bank, was brought forth and intensively debated. At this time the Democratic party came into power, pledged against the plan bearing the name of the champion of high tariff. None the less, the new administration adopted the essence of the plan, but provided, as we shall now see, twelve central banks instead of one.

**14. The Federal Reserve Act** became law December 23, 1913. It created twelve regional banks, each of which is to keep the reserves of the district in which it is located. In each of the districts, designed as 1st, 2d, 3d, and so on to the 12th, the regional banks are located as follows: No. 1, Boston; No. 2, New York City; No. 3, Philadelphia; No. 4, Cleveland; No. 5, Richmond; No. 6, Atlanta; No. 7, Chicago; No. 8, St. Louis; No. 9, Minneapolis; No. 10, Kansas City; No. 11, Dallas; No. 12, San Francisco. The districts have undergone slight modification as to boundary and may be further modified. Missouri is the only State having two regional banks.

**15. The Federal Reserve Board.**—The whole system is under the supervision of a governing board, called the Federal Reserve Board, with headquarters in Washington. There are seven members of the board, two of whom are *ex-officio*, the secretary of the treasury and the comptroller of the currency. Five members are appointed by the President of the United States, for a period of ten years, and at a salary of $12,000 a year. As head of the whole system this board is charged with heavy responsibilities. Committed to its direction are the following powers: To protect the national gold supply; to provide an elastic currency through the contraction and expansion of notes; to provide a systematic pooling of reserves of existing banks, thus securing economy in and an effective utilization of the money supply; to provide a free and general discount market for commercial paper. The law provides that this central board may (1) compel one regional bank to rediscount commercial paper held by other regional banks, and may determine the rate at which such rediscounts are made. Thus the privilege of one bank to rely upon others so organizes banking facilities that their resources are denied to no section, and are at the disposal of all who can offer paper measuring up to a certain standard. A marked contrast is this to the old decentralized system where each bank must deny credit, and in self-defense call in reserves when expansion is most needed. The board may (2) suspend reserve requirements, thus effecting an economy in gold, and adding to the lending power of banks. It may (3) suspend for cause any officer or director of a regional bank in its exercise of general supervision over the whole system. It may (4) regulate the issue and retirement of Federal Reserve notes. Regarding this means of providing an elastic currency more will be said a moment later.

16. **The reserve banks** are banks for bankers in their respective districts. Every national bank in the district is required, and State banks and trust companies are

privileged, to subscribe for stock to an amount equal to 6 per cent of the subscribing bank's capital and surplus. Thus, reserve banks are owned by other banks, which are known as *member banks.* Their dealings as a rule are limited to member banks, but these stockholders or member banks do not get all the earnings in dividends. Part of these earnings go to the United States as a franchise tax.

*What They Do:* A regional or federal reserve bank may accept deposits from the government (and from non-member banks for exchange purposes); discount notes, drafts, and bills of exchange indorsed by a member bank and drawn for agricultural, industrial, and commercial purposes; discount acceptances based upon the importation and exportation of goods; deal in bills of exchange; deal in gold coin or bullion; deal in government obligations and short-time obligations of States and municipalities; carry balances with other regional banks for exchange purposes; establish branches in its own district and in foreign countries; and, subject to the approval and determination of the Reserve Board, fix its rate of discount.

*Directors:* Over each regional bank are nine directors who are divided into three classes of three men each. Class A are chosen by the member banks and are presumably bankers, class B are chosen by the member banks but must not be bankers, class C are chosen by the Federal Reserve Board to represent the general public, but two of these must be bankers.

17. **Federal Reserve Notes.**—Provision is made in the act for the gradual withdrawal of national bank-notes. But these notes may, if national banks so desire, continue in circulation.

The notes issued by the regional banks may be in denominations of $5, $10, $20, $50, $100, $500, and $1,000. They are receivable by all member banks and regional banks, and for taxes, customs, and other public dues.

These notes are not secured by government bonds, but by a deposit either of gold or commercial paper; furthermore, they are obligations of the United States, and they are also secured by the assets of the issuing bank. They are redeemable in gold at the treasury and in gold or lawful money at the regional banks.

A regional bank must send to the treasury or return to the issuing bank, and not reissue any notes of other regional banks which it may receive. This brings notes back to the issuing bank, limits their circulation in other reserve districts, and shortens the time during which they remain in circulation.

18. **Reserves of Federal Reserve Banks.**—A regional bank must carry a reserve in gold of not less than 40 per cent against its notes, and 35 per cent in gold or lawful money against its deposits. Any deficiency is subject to a graduated tax.

A tax of 1 per cent per annum is charged upon each such deficiency until the reserve is lowered to 32½ per cent, thereafter 1½ per cent tax is added for each 2½ per cent deficiency or fraction thereof. The following table will show this:

| When the reserves against notes are: | The tax rate upon the total deficiency shall be: |
|---|---|
| Below 40.0 to 32.5 per cent. | 1.0 per cent. |
| Below 32.5 to 30.0 per cent. | 2.5 per cent. |
| Below 30.0 to 27.5 per cent. | 4.0 per cent. |
| Below 27.5 to 25.0 per cent. | 5.5 per cent. |
| Below 25.0 to 22.5 per cent. | 7.0 per cent. |
| Below 22.5 to 20.0 per cent. | 8.5 per cent. |
| Below 20.0 to 17.5 per cent. | 10.0 per cent. |

The bank paying this tax must add an equivalent amount to the interest and discount charged member banks. This enables a necessary expansion of the note issue in times of emergency. The heavy tax paid upon a deficiency below the required reserve will encourage banks to withdraw their notes from circulation when the emergency calling them out is over. Professor Fetter illustrates these facts thus: "Suppose for example that the circulating notes were in normal times $1,000,000,000, and the reserves, therefore, were $400,000,000 and the rate of discount 5 per cent. Then the circulation might be doubled with the same reserves, the proportion thus falling to 20 per cent of outstanding notes, and the rate of discount to customers rising to 13.5 per cent (5 plus 8.5)." [1]

The Federal Reserve Board may, in times of emergency, reduce reserves against both notes and deposits, and in both regional and member banks, down to the last dollar. This affords an opportunity to provide sufficient credit for any emergency.

19. **Reserves in Member Banks.**—The act makes a wise distinction between the reserve requirements for time deposits and demand deposits, in case of all member banks. They are required to keep no more than a 3 per cent reserve against time deposits. The purpose of this requirement is to encourage banks to establish savings departments.

The reserve required for banks in the central reserve cities is reduced from 25 to 13 per cent, in reserve cities from 25 to 10 per cent, and in other banks from 15 to 7 per cent. We have seen that the depositaries of funds that might be counted a part of a bank's reserve were in the

[1] Modern Economic Problems, p. 124.

reserve and central reserve cities. The regional banks are now such depositaries, and all legal reserves of member banks must be on deposit with them, no reserve in vault being required of member banks.

**20. Noteworthy Features of the Law.**—The law would break down a monopoly control of the money supply by large banking syndicates, and give the advantage of credit to all worthy investors. It would insure the pooling or co-operant use of reserves, thus putting adequate lending power at the disposal of banks in all sections of the country and at all seasons of the year. To this end regional banks are empowered to maintain branches, and interdependence among all banks has been established. Banks are not now compelled to withdraw currency from the market and hoard it as a means of fortifying themselves against danger. Centralized reserves will also secure an economy in gold. Adequate provision for acceptances and rediscounts is provided, a judicious use of which will make slow-moving securities liquid, give the widest employment to local resources, and facilitate the movement of goods into and out of the country. This will create new and convenient types of paper, giving them stability and certainty in the market. But more important, an adequate distribution of funds in time and place will equalize the interest rate over the whole country. The most noteworthy features of the law are those which add to the elasticity of deposits and notes. We have seen how the expansion and contraction of notes, as well as liberality in reserve requirements, work to effect this elasticity.

*The Transmission of Funds :* American commerce has suffered because of the excessive charges made upon business men for the collection and transmission of their funds.

Prior to the Federal Reserve Act country banks carried this type of extortion to the point where some of them made fully one-half of their earnings from such charges. Provision is now made for clearing checks through the regional banks and for collecting drafts. Member banks may charge clients a fee sufficient to cover the actual cost of collecting funds, but these charges are under federal control.

*Foreign Branches:* Americans heretofore, who have engaged in foreign trade or operated branch houses abroad either have financed themselves or depended upon foreign banks. South America is a developing field for our business. Until branches of American banks were established there, our business men depended largely upon branches of European banks. The charge has been made that such banks, working as they did in close harmony with merchants of their own nationality, were often unfaithful to their American clientele, allowing competitors to know their business operations, and, when disposed to do so, cutting off their credit in favor of such rivals.[1] Banks may now establish branches abroad, with the permission of the Reserve Board, which will be operated subject to very liberal terms. This will provide the needed foreign banking accommodations to place American business men upon a footing of equality with foreign competitors.

21. **Exercises.**—1. If in France prices are rising owing to an inflation of currency, there will be a tendency for imports to increase and for gold to be exported. What could the Bank of France do to remedy the situation?

2. A *central bank* with *branches* in different sections of

---

[1] *American Economic Review*, IV, p. 22.

the country is more desirable than a *decentralized system* such as have been the national banks in the United States. Define the terms italicized.

Make an argument for, and an argument against this statement.

3. What is meant by the elasticity of currency? What are its advantages?

4. Compare the free banking system of New York with the national banking system.

5. What arguments were made for the National Banking Act prior to its adoption? Were these arguments correct?

6. How was the financial situation affected by the custom of banks to deposit a part of their reserves in New York banks? (Foster.)

7. What was the chief problem that grew out of the seasonal demands for currency?

8. Tell why note issues under the national banking system run counter to the requirements of business?

9. An item in the financial page:

> The rediscounting of commercial paper at the Federal Reserve Bank of New York by some of the city's largest banks on Wednesday had the effect yesterday of improving general money market conditions. Call loans which were made at 15 per cent on Monday, and as high as 10 per cent on Tuesday, and touched 7 per cent Wednesday, were placed yesterday at from 3 to 5 per cent. Most of the loans were made at 4½ per cent, the renewal rate, and the closing quotation was 3 per cent. Time money rates were easier.

Explain the process of rediscounting here referred to. In just what way did the rediscounting operations relieve the call money market? Do you consider that this use of the rediscounting facilities provided by the Federal Reserve System was in accord with sound banking principles? Was it the best possible use of the rediscounting mechanism?

10. A financial stringency is felt in the ninth and tenth Federal Reserve Districts owing to the fall-crop movement.

Cash is scarce. What action may the Federal Reserve Board take to remedy the situation? (Foster.)

11. The Federal Reserve Board desires to force up the market rate of interest as a means of checking overspeculation and inflation. The banks have large reserves on hand. The rediscount rate is raised. In your opinion, will this achieve the desired result? Explain.

If your answer to the preceding question is in the negative, outline in detail what plan may be followed. (Foster.)

12. Explain carefully why Federal Reserve notes cause a greater elasticity of currency than was secured by means of national bank-notes.

13. In times of emergency the Reserve Board may furnish relief through its power to regulate the reserve of a member bank. Explain how this may be done.

# CHAPTER XV

## THE ORGANIZATION OF PRODUCTION

1. **National Forces Co-operate in War.**—During a great war nations are organized into vast fighting machines. One purpose guides and shapes these organizations—to overpower the enemy. Into one complex whole the powers of the nation are integrated so that they operate successively and simultaneously. That is to say, the forces of the nation under one supreme command are knit together, so as to form a compact harmonious whole of all the related branches and necessary processes of the belligerent powers of the nation. These forces operate successively, so that step by step raw materials in the ground are extracted, transported, and through many processes shaped into finished forms.

These forces operate simultaneously, so that all the necessary divisions of labor are at one time joint or co-operant forces to a common end. The organization embodies divisions of infantry, cavalry, artillery, ammunition columns, engineers, and transporting facilities to furnish supplies at the front. But the war would be of short duration were this all. Whence these supplies? From the shops, mills, and factories that shape raw materials into ripe goods. Whence the raw materials? From the mines, forests, fisheries, and farms. This vast system embraces: All laborers, from the miner in the shaft to the soldier in the trench; all materials, from the minerals embedded in the crevices of rocks to the shell exploding over the batteries of the enemy; all the comforts from their elemental forms, through the many processes, till they come to clothe, feed, amuse, instruct, and otherwise provide the personnel of the nation.

These forces, so integrated into a vast fighting machine, are but the elements of one composite unit that is subject to orderly regulation. The seat of authoritative regulation is in the all-powerful sovereignty of the state. From this source power is delegated to a commander (though chief servant he is) with general supervision over all the forces in the field. This power is further redelegated to commanders of divisions and so on down to the squad corporals.

The roar of musketry and the strategy of officers may obscure the vision as to those who are extracting, transporting, and shaping materials. But in fact these silent workers co-operate in the common plan to serve the common purpose of the state. All the forces of men and materials are not separate units, but under a structural organization they fuse into one productive system.

What the people want they produce, and they produce nothing else. Desire is the motivating force which shapes a system and sets it in operation. If you would know what a people produce ask, first, as to the nature of their desires. It took mastership to bring productive power to its present height, and it could not be maintained at that height one year without it.

**2. The Co-operant Forces of Industry.**—As in time of war so in time of peace, industries are shaped in obedience to the demands of the people. What the people want they produce, and changes in desires affect the shape of industries and bend the direction of human endeavor into new lines.

Productive capacity embodies all the agencies which supply the means of gratifying desires. It consists of natural resources, of the scientific knowledge of the ways and means of utilizing these resources, of the technological equipment through which this knowledge operates.

But there may be capacity which lies dormant. The most effective utilization of this capacity is the most fundamental industrial problem. A solution of this problem is to be found in the method of analysis and co-operation. The productive process is analyzed into its constituent elements; tasks are divided into difficult and easy, mechanical and intellectual, skilled and crude. Men are, according to their fitness, set to the numerous tasks which make up the industrial process. There are tasks for each and all; the miner, the transporter, the manufacturer, the middleman, the lawyer, the artist, the comedian, and the rest.

The scope of the industrial process is larger than the worker, or the resources, or the organization—it is a co-operation of all these in one composite whole. No one division of industry is independent of other divisions carried on elsewhere. Any one division of the productive process presupposes the proper working of many others; it follows some, precedes others, and operates simultaneously with others. Each fits into and becomes a part of the industrial order. The line of work followed by each is adapted to and determined by the other divisions of the whole process. There is no severalty of processes; they are interlocked.

3. **The Automatic Adjustment in Industry.**—The producer invests his labor and means according to the principle of comparative value. Why, for example, do not farmers sow their lands wholly to wheat? They produce for the market, and their self-interest causes them to plant such crops as will yield the largest net money return. Should all turn to the production of wheat, that product would be cheap and others dear. The demands of the people operating through the self-interest of the farmers thus cause a variety of crops. Apply this principle to the whole industrial order, and we have the explanation of variety in the processes of production.

The principle of comparative value, where competition is unobstructed, explains why there is a tendency for profits to be uniform throughout the industrial process. As the farmer would shift from wheat production to the growing of swine in order to increase his net income, so would productive energy in any line be shifted to another and more remunerative field. But all producers are actuated by the motive of largest gain, and this causes productive power to shift from places where it exists in largest abundance (where money returns are small) to places where it is scarce (where money returns are large). In this way the shifting of the means of production tends to equalize returns throughout the industrial system.

4. **Adjustments Never Complete.**—Immobility of productive agencies retards and, I may say, defeats a perfect equilibrium of returns throughout all industry. Assume that a community has a most intelligent population, that in alertness, prosperity, and inventiveness it ranks second

to none—even such a people are slow to adjust themselves to new needs. If such a people are suddenly called upon to construct new ships to counterbalance the destruction by a fleet of submarines, it takes many months to make the necessary readjustments of the productive power which is ordinarily devoted to the arts of peaceful industry.

Capitalists invest their means in forms that are more or less fixed and can convert their wealth into new forms only after much delay. If one has invested in or constructed a mill which utilized power from a waterfall, he could change the place of his mill or reconstruct it to take advantage of steam-power, only against great resistance and at heavy cost in time and money.

The risk involved in a change of investment lends to the immobility of productive agencies. The differentiation, specialization, and localization of trades vastly increase productive power, but the risk of loss from a misadventure is large in proportion to the chances of gain. To enlarge productive equipment is to enhance the risk of loss. If Smith has specialized in the shoe trade—knows that trade and none other—his risk is large if he attempts to transfer his means to the hat trade, of which he is ignorant. Or through no fault of his own a new invention may reduce him to penury over a week's end. This is an era of specialists; specialists are ignorant of advantages in other fields and helpless if the opportunities for working in their own field are taken away. And this may be done by a monopoly entering the field, or by an invention, or by a change in demand. So many are the risks of loss that the less adventurous are willing to "go slow and let well enough alone."

Backward peoples follow in the footsteps of their fathers century in and century out; advanced peoples not infrequently find that readjustments are not fully accomplished in the generation that first feels the necessity of them. The mobility of productive power is a matter of degree, less pronounced among backward peoples and more tardy where investments are of a fixed nature. There is always a tendency to bring about a well-ordered proportion and balance among all branches of industry; but such is never fully accomplished.

5. **Quantitative precision** is another characteristic of the industrial process. This is an age of machinery, whereas prior to the industrial revolution, except for a few simple tools belonging to workmen themselves, work was done by hand. With the introduction of steam-power large and expensive machinery made competition by hand processes impossible, and the cost of such machines made it possible for only capitalists to own them. Thus the introduction of steam-power brought about a distinct class of owners, a distinct class of workers or hired men, and congregated labor. The use of machinery is found in all industry; it has so subdivided work as to break up labor into simple movements, and it has made of all industry one balanced mechanical process.

As the unerring time-piece requires exact functioning on the part of each cog, wheel, and spring, so the machine process requires quantitative precision and accurate functioning in point of time and sequence. Mechanical accuracy requires uniformity of processes, standardization of tools, and staple grades of output. Mechanical standardization has taken the place of the craftsman's skill that adapted the output to any style, cut, and trim which the fancy of the user might dictate.

It would be difficult, costly, time-consuming, and I shall say impossible to equip an army with rifles were each made after an individual pattern to suit the fancy of the soldier who might use it. But if standardized to one pattern and the several parts made of a definite size, shape, and gauge, then high-power machinery will be constructed for the specific purpose of making rifles and, without undue delay, will produce them in the needed abundance. Consumers object at times to standardization on the ground that one's individuality cannot show itself, since all must buy goods made according to a common pattern. Standardization applies to the agencies which transport us, which transport our goods, and which transport our messages. The tools and machinery of production are made according to a definite grading in size, shape, and gauge. The articles of consumption—clothing, food products, home-furnishings, and the like—are standardized and stamped as to grade, weight, and content. This has led to uniform systems of weights and measures.

**6. The services of men** are standardized. A standardized machine process works with automatic precision. Maladjustment in one department affects the smooth working of the process as would the disorder of a spring defeat the accurate time-keeping of a clock. Any part can perform its function in full only when the other parts are rightly adjusted and properly working. The nature of the workman's job is determined for him by the machine which he is to operate, and a pace or rapidity of work is set for him by the rapidity of the movements which work in sequence throughout a plant, and the quality of his work is set by the standard or grade of excellence which the output is required to reach. The worth of a laborer is measured in units of output.

**7. The Test of Production Not on Moral Grounds.—** To this point reference has been made only to the external form of the productive system. We have seen that productive forces interlock and work co-operantly. This, it has been pointed out, requires that a proportion and balance must exist among the several parts to guarantee their smooth and harmonious joint operation. The introduction of machinery results in the congregation of labor, and brings about the rather distinct classes of capitalists and workers, as well as another class to be considered a moment later—the entrepreneur. We have also seen that the most marked characteristic of the productive order is standardization, which is a consequence of the comprehensive use of machinery.

It is now time to inquire what this is all about: What is production, and what the thing produced? It has been stated that people produce that which they desire, that they intentionally produce nothing else, that desire is the motivating force of production. All productive energy is directed toward the gratification of desires, and production is itself the creation of the means of gratifying desires and needs. Production is the creation of desirabilities and utilities.

Competitive production consists in so changing things that they command a price. Production, for the most part, redounds to human well-being, but it may also work to the injury of man. Acts are not judged as productive or unproductive on moral grounds. The outfit for the gambler, the equipment for the highwayman, liquor for the drunkard, and opium for the drug fiend are economic products, and that which produces them is productive.

**8. The Test of Production Not Tangibility.**—Acts are not judged as productive or unproductive with regard to tangibility. The preaching of a sermon, the dancing act, the work of the menial servant or of the musician do not result in tangible products as does the work of farmers, carpenters, and cabinetmakers. But they gratify desires directly; the cabinetmaker gratifies desires indirectly, his labor taking the form of a cabinet which in turn gratifies the user.

Production and destruction are antonyms, yet all production involves destruction. Fire destroys fuel in firing an engine, chemicals are used up in making medicines, building materials are consumed in the erection of a house, and so on through all production. Labor, time, materials are requisites of and are used up in production. But skill in production minimizes the necessary wastes. Should the untrained hand attempt to draw a cartoon the result would be an awkward grouping of marks—a waste of time, paper, and ink. But give the same equipment to an expert, Bud Fisher, for instance, and the pen marks are converted into the amusing characters of Mutt and Jeff. Will his act be productive? Apply the test: society, through the newspapers as middlemen, is paying this cartoonist a high salary, his product gratifies desires, and that is the end of production. In a cartoon the author had Jeff claim exemption from service in the European War. The officer questioned, and Jeff answered, as follows: "Does a wife depend on you?" "No." "Children?" "No." "Relatives?" "No." "Then upon what grounds do you claim exemption; who does depend on you?" "Bud Fisher." The idea here expressed is literally true. The cartoonist produces and markets his product for a living. He is productive in the same sense that the farmer is productive. To produce is to provide the means for supplying the demands of the people, regardless of the character of these demands. Production may take tangible form or it may not. The thing produced is desirability whether it be in the form of a skirt-dance or of a loaf of bread. But it should be emphasized that the large portion of productive enterprise has to do with tangible commodities. Science has demonstrated the inability of man to add or detract a single atom of matter; production must, therefore, concern itself with such changes in matter as will create desirabilities and utilities in things. Such changes consist in giving a proper composition to things, of putting them in such form, time, and place that they may serve the desires and real needs of the people.

9. **Social production** refers to *amount* rather than to price. It has been pointed out that social production is not the creation of price gain. It is not true that production is always the response to price-paying disposition. Value and price are high in proportion to the scarcity of goods, that is, in proportion to the niggardliness of productive capacity. The high price of goods and limited production of them are almost convertible terms. Social production is great to the extent that the output approaches the stage of free goods.

10. **Individualistic and Social View-Points.**—Individualistic or competitive production must not be confused with social production. The individual may grow wealthy at the expense of society. He may (if a monopolist) withhold or destroy a portion of his supply in order to raise the price of the remaining portion. In any case, his one interest is to get the highest price. His interest oftentimes runs counter to the interest of society; the competitor in the refining of sugar would like to see the failure of every refinery excepting his own.

The interest of society lies in the production of general abundance. Since the economic welfare of all is the primary problem, the economist must concern himself primarily with social production. But although the viewpoints of social and private production differ, it does not follow that a system of private or competitive production works, on the whole, contrary to the public interest. On the contrary, experience demonstrates the reverse of this, and throughout the civilized world competitive production has been adapted as the means, or rather as the form of productive organization, to secure the largest social production.

In other words, society as a whole, through the agency of governments, is master and manager of its productive machinery. There are different ways in which this machinery may be organized and society will adopt the manner which the majority believes will yield the largest social production. And at the present it has chosen the private or competitive form of organization. Competitive production is to be regarded as a means to that which is first, foremost, and primary in consideration—social production. The economist who rests his case with a discussion of competitive production does not grasp the problem, mistakes the means for the end, cannot see the town for the houses.

Private production is, in nature, acquisitive; its command is to acquire possession of that which will buy or otherwise obtain from others the objects of individual desire. To get possession is the individual producer's idea in competitive production. Social production asks not who owns, but what new desirabilities and utilities are created? It consists in so changing materials by compounding, shaping, or placing them in time and location as to create in society new utilities and desirabilities. It consists further in rendering services which do not take material form.

The productive system, above described, operates under the guidance of the entrepreneur.

**11. The Entrepreneur.**—The French term, *entrepreneur*, has a meaning very similar to that of the English words undertaker or enterpriser. Many authors prefer to use one or the other of the English terms, but these are in common use in the street and market-place, and are therefore encumbered with different shades of meaning—we think of the undertaker as a funeral director, and of the enterpriser as some type of adventurer. The entrepreneur may be one man or many, may make an income or may not, may own capital or may not, may perform the several tasks in his business or may hire others to do them. The word entrepreneur is a title (as is sheriff, minister, or president), which is given to the person or persons who perform a particular set of functions. What are the functions of the entrepreneur?

**12. Functions of the Entrepreneur.**—Upon his own initiative and at his own risk the entrepreneur assumes the ownership and mastery of a business. This may be a newly promoted business or an old and established business. A business is an opportunity harnessed or so correlated with industrial agents as to be productive. The entrepreneur is the central figure in production who correlates the agencies of production and acquisition; labor comes to him for employment, and all forms of wealth come to him for direction and utilization. Entrepreneurs determine what and how much shall be produced, hire workmen, and determine what they shall do, borrow money and invest it.

The entrepreneur's relations with others are contractual in nature; he pays wages and salaries according to contract, the interest paid for capital, the rent or hire paid for other productive agents, the price paid for raw materials, and all of his other costs which go to other people are paid according to contract. He has other costs which are not contractual, such as the rendering of his own services (wages relinquished) and the interest which must be allowed for his own capital invested in the business. When he sells the product and subtracts all the contractual costs the net residue is termed profits.

13. **The Entrepreneur is a Self-Employed Middleman.** —He buys to sell at a profit. The jobber in the line of food products is an entrepreneur who buys commodities in bulk; he sorts, packs the products according to grade, prepares the goods for the market, receives orders, and sells if fortunate at a price sufficient to cover all costs and leave a fair profit.

It has been a much-debated question as to whether the directors of boarding-houses, hotels, restaurants, and cafés are middlemen. These directors, together with wholesale houses, have taken the affirmative, have insisted that these institutions are intermediary agencies in the same sense as are retail grocerymen, and, therefore, should have the benefit of wholesale prices. Retail grocerymen have taken the negative, insisting that eating-places must be regarded as final consumers, that wholesalers must not supply them, that this profitable field must be left for the retailer. But, in fact, there is no room for argument, for just as the retailer buys meats and cuts, prepares, and distributes them to the trade, or as he buys coffee, grinds, prepares, and distributes it, so the hotel proprietor buys goods, prepares, and distributes them to the trade. Both must undergo the costs of maintaining a place of business, of paying for food products, of hiring help, of preparing and selling.   Both as self-employed middlemen for a profit are entrepreneurs.

The factory-owner as entrepreneur is a self-employed middleman who buys raw materials and undergoes the costs of preparing and selling them, in the form of finished goods, to the trade for a net gain.   He may buy iron ore and, through several processes, convert it into steel products of different forms and shapes to suit his purpose; may buy logs and convert them into handles, spokes, axles, and so on to suit his need; may buy paint ingredients and compound them into durable form and bright color—when all is done and the different parts assembled, these crude materials will have taken the finished form of wagon, mowing-machine, or what-not that he cared to produce.

As middleman, or in the capacity of entrepreneur, he is owner of the materials he handles.   If as entrepreneur this man uses his own money, we may say that in a sense he borrows it from himself in his other capacity as a capitalist.   And he must count this interest relinquished as a cost equal to that which he would secure in the capacity of a capitalist, should he loan this money to another.   With this capital (owned or borrowed) he constructs a plant, rents land and other needed agencies, buys equipment, hires labor, and lays in raw materials.   All these outlays are money prices paid for the services of men, for the use of capital and other agents, and for the raw materials bought outright.   These things and services are his own private property to do with as he will for such time as he has contracted and paid for them.

14. **The Entrepreneur as Servant of Demand.**—This introduces another point: though independent owner, with the liberty to dispose of his possessions at will, is not his

course of action, after all, determined for him rather than by him? I answer, it is. His business is a privately owned public intermediary through which the forces of supply and demand operate. If a change in season lowers the demand for straw hats, the cheapening effect is passed back to the entrepreneur, who, in turn, passes it back, in the form of lower prices, to the earlier producers who furnish raw materials. These will diminish their output, and finally cease producing if the prices they receive become less than their costs. This will be true of every commodity which becomes unfavorably affected by changes in styles, seasons, or by the substitution of other goods. If on the supply side favorable weather, new inventions, improved methods, or new discoveries of raw materials, should lower the costs of output, this cheapening effect is passed to the entrepreneur and, through him, transmitted to consumers in the form of lower prices.

The entrepreneur is servant, not master, of these natural forces of demand and supply. His ability to forecast changes and make contracts to take advantage of them is his source of profits. Changing demands affect, through the medium of entrepreneurs, corresponding changes in the organization of productive agencies. But the output of these agencies is restricted because the agencies are themselves limited. The equating-point between supply and demand is price. Thus the entrepreneur fixes prices and determines what shall and what shall not be produced only in the sense that he is a self-employed agent to direct the operations of the limited productive agents to meet the demands of consumers.

15. **The Uses of Materials.**—We have seen that production is used in two senses—competitive or acquisitive, and

social. To get purchasing power, by creating it or otherwise, is the competitor's aim. His selfish aim, however, generally redounds to the public welfare. Social production works to the end of greater abundance. The individual with purchasing power may remain idle and buy what others produce. But society, taken as a whole, must produce or starve.

Material production creates, as above stated, not an atom of matter, but new uses in things. A few examples will make this clear. The pen is one thing, and the uses which flow from it is another. Apples are one thing, the tree or agency giving them another. In the economic sense the difference between a draft-horse and a dead horse is that one can and the other cannot give off uses. All that one wants with a house is the uses it will bear. No one would pay for a house located in a desert or polar region beyond the reach of man. A sunken ship at the bottom of the sea may be as physically perfect as the swift French liner, *Rochambeau*, yet it could command not a penny in exchange. The only difference between gold in the moon and gold in a national bank is that one is worth zero and the other one hundred cents on the dollar—and this solely because the one is at the proper place to render uses, whereas the other is not. It is wholly because of the uses of things that they have desirabilities and utilities.

16. **Direct and Indirect Uses of Money.**—The coal-mine, the well of water, the storage plant full of goods, and the money-bag contain uses in the form of goods which they yield up at the will of man. Likewise the tree, the horse, the farm, and the engine contain uses in the form of apples, services, crops, and power which they yield up at the will

of man. All economic goods or agents contain uses either actually or potentially, and it is for this reason, and this only, that we value them, work to produce them, and deny ourselves to save them. Be it remembered, the only reason why we care for goods, why we undergo hardship for them, why we value and price them, is the uses which they actually or potentially contain and will surrender to our needs.

As the years come and pass out during the life of man, so with his desires. And he must make provision to meet the desires that will be, as well as those that are. The uses of durable agents ripen through time. No ingenuity can get all the uses of the field in any one year, but its potential uses become actual as time passes and needs arise. As we sever the maturing coupon from the bond at the interest-paying date, so we must await the proper season to sever grass from the field and fruit from the tree. Productive agents mature their yields in recurring order: The fleece of the sheep and the crop of the field recur annually, milk from the cow, and eggs from the nest recur daily. What the bond is to the coupons attached, productive agents are to their recurring yields. And as the bond is priced according to the number, size, and maturing date of its attached coupons, so durable agents, the parent stems of future yields, are priced according to the number, size, and maturing date of their recurring uses. In capitalizing durable agents, we are, so to speak, pricing the services locked up in them.

We capitalize these services whether direct or indirect. Clothing is valuable for the warmth it yields, wool for the clothing it makes, sheep for the wool they produce, and pastures for the feed they supply. The steaming cup of coffee has direct uses in the hands of the final consumer, but a moment previous to that they belonged to the restaurant-keeper, and were to him what a hoe is to a farmer —simply a means of obtaining a livelihood. As such they were an agency or means of getting something else; that is to say, indirect.

Note further: it took heat, pot, water, and coffee-grain to make that cup of coffee. The uses of these several agents were compounded into one final use. And these several uses were themselves the joint product of different agents; as such they were compound uses. The agents producing them worked successively as land, coffee-tree, coffee-grain, transportation facilities, grinding-mill, middleman, and so on. In this case the land uses are most indirect. Thus the productive process proceeds from simple uses to compound, and from most indirect to direct. The productive agents work successively and simultaneously in transforming indirect into direct uses.

With the development of civilization production takes a more circuitous, roundabout, or indirect method. In attempting to analyze this process the older economists attempted to classify concrete material agents as direct and indirect. Their labors were in vain; they might as well have reasoned regarding a perpetual motion. All the uses of a hoe are indirect and it may be, therefore, an indirect good. The uses of bread at the time of final consumption are direct and, at that time, bread is a direct good. But other goods render both direct and indirect uses at the same time.

As an ornament pleasing to the eye, Velvet Joe's big pipe bears direct uses, but as a means to the pleasure derived from the "glowing weed" it is an indirect good.

The train carrying both freight and passengers is rendering both kinds of uses.

The purpose of the owner makes goods both direct and indirect. The farm wife has two buckets of milk, alike in all respects; she will use the one directly and fatten the pig with the other.

The same good may be direct at one time and indirect at another. If you ride the horse his services are, for the time, direct, but if you hitch him to the plow, his services are indirect—an agent to get a crop. The uses of goods may be classified as direct and indirect, but goods themselves cannot be so classified. We think, deal in, and appraise goods according to their uses, therefore there is no significance in a classification of goods were this possible.

**17. The agencies** which the entrepreneur uses for producing these desirable changes in materials are of many kinds and used for many purposes.

(*a*) *Composition:* All are familiar with certain agencies for compounding materials so as to add to their uses. Among these agencies are the materials used in making medicines, explosives, liquors, in cooking foods, in converting iron into steel or hides into leather. All chemical and biological agencies are of this class, which alter the chemical content and material composition of things.

(*b*) *Form:* A change in form, such as converting a briar-root into a pipe or a log into a piano-case, does not involve a chemical or organic change in matter. The lace-knitting machine that arranges gossamer into fantastic shapes, machines for spinning, weaving, tools that extract coal from the mine, stone from the quarry, and water from the well, form implements to gather grain, dig ditches, and split rails—these are agencies for changing the form of things.

(c) *Place:* Every transporting agent—cart, horse, train, hod-carrier, or other—that removes a thing from a place where it has little use to where it is more needed, is a productive agent adding to the desirabilities of materials.

(d) *Time:* There are agencies which add to the uses of things by preserving them to such time as they are most needed. Granaries, cellars, cold-storage plants, jars for canning, and other preservative agencies are exemplary. Also, there are agencies for producing things before their normal season, for instance, greenhouses, ice-factories, and incubators.

All these agencies may play a part in furnishing the same good. There is a change in composition when ice is frozen, a change in form when it is cut into cakes, a change in place when it is put into the ice-house, a change in time when kept until the warm summer months.

18. **Exercises.**—1. Operations of nations which are at war are carried on successively and simultaneously, and the same may be said with respect to the operations of industries in times of peace. Explain fully the meaning of this statement.

2. What is meant by the statement that industries are established in obedience to the demands of the people?

3. What is meant by the automatic adjustment of industries to one another throughout society?

Is such adjustment made upon a physical basis or upon a basis of profits?

4. Would it be correct to say that there is always a tendency toward a complete adjustment of industries to one another, but that such adjustment is never fully attained?

If the statement is correct explain why such adjustment is never reached.

5 Why does the extensive introduction of machinery into industry bring about quantitative precision?

6. What forces are now operative in industry that cause the services of men to be standardized?

7. Define production. Is the test of production materiality of result? Commendability of result? Useful service?

8. Is a franchise productive? The lawyer who gets guilty men acquitted? A counterfeiter? A whiskeymaker? A painter of obscene pictures? A roulette-table? A burglar's jimmy? A burglar? Explain. (Davenport.)

9. What are the functions of the entrepreneur?

Is the entrepreneur in a large factory the manager? The board of directors? The stockholders?

10. Can the entrepreneur tell how much he can afford to pay for the use of a factor? Is this the same as telling what its separate service is? How may a thing in its actual use cost the entrepreneur more than he pays to get it? (Davenport.)

11. If entrepreneurs generally get more skilful, what is the effect on their profits? On the wages of laborers? (Davenport.)

12. An economic good, such as a pen, a horse, a car, or a food-product, cannot be classified for all purposes, either as a direct or as an indirect good. Why is this so?

13. They are only the economic uses of goods which may be classified as direct or indirect. Explain this statement.

# CHAPTER XVI

## THE LAW OF PROPORTIONALITY

**1. Complementary Agents.**—When agents unite or work together in performing a function, they complement or fill out each other and are called complementary agents. For instance, the boiler is worthless without the engine, and the locomotive is valueless without the track. The wheel and belt complement each other, and so with saw and carriage, soap and water, knife and fork, lock and key. A group of complementary goods is valued as a whole; if the hook is missing the eye is worthless, and the hook will be worth the same as both hook and eye.

In a study of the technical productive process, we are studying the best quantitative relationship of complementary agents. All such agents employ or make necessary the use of others. As each member of a baseball nine complements every other member in the co-operant group of a well-balanced team, so the building, land, raw materials, labor, and varied parts of technological equipment complement each other and become one large composite productive agent.

Any product—whether it be shoes, loaf, cloth, hat—is the product, not of one, but of a number of agents working together. Pens alone cannot write; they must combine with ink, paper, operator. Land alone cannot produce wheat; it must combine with water, seed, labor, and tools. There could be no ride in the automobile were a wheel missing, or the engine out of repair, or the gasolene wanting, or the chauffeur absent—each complementary agent must contribute its bit in the production of a good or service.

**2. The Principle of Resistance.**—Productive agents will not render their services gratuitously; they resist our efforts to compel them to supply our needs. And the more effort we exert upon an agent the greater this resistance becomes. In order to grasp the significance of this principle it is necessary to hold two things in mind: a limited agent and static conditions.

A given area of land will yield more and more as more and more labor, tools, and seed are applied to it. But while the total yield from this land is increasing, the returns per unit of expenditure upon it will diminish. The resistance of the land will increase with the increased pressure upon it for more products. This may be illustrated as follows:

LIMITED AREA WORKED

| | | | | | | | | |
|---|---|---|---|---|---|---|---|---|
| By 1 man yields | 15 bushels, or | 15 bushels per man | | | | | | |
| " 2 men " | 40 | " | " 20 | " | " | " | | |
| " 3 " " | 54 | " | " 18 | " | " | " | | |
| " 4 " " | 56 | " | " 14 | " | " | " | | |
| " 5 " " | 60 | " | " 12 | " | " | " | | |
| ", 6 " " | 66 | " | " 11 | " | " | " | | |
| " 7 " " | 66½ | " | " 9½ | " | " | " | | |

This illustration shows that two men are the most appropriate number to work this specific tract of land in order to get the highest commodity return per man. At this point begins increasing resistance on the part of the land to the further application of labor. The commodity returns to each successive laborer grow less and less.

What is true of land is true of other productive agents. If a manufacturer installs too much machinery, a part of it will be habitually idle. The other portions of his plant are too small to employ fully the machinery; too much machinery is applied to the other portions of the plant, or, what is the same, too little of other things is applied to the machinery. Machinery is the long factor, other factors are short. Because of the increasing resistance on the part of the short factors, the physical or commodity returns to each additional machine grow less and less. If the building is the long factor each foot of idle space is physically an excess and is, when translated into price terms, carried as an unnecessary cost. Again, an excessive office force makes this the long factor, and the resistance to further production on the part of the short factors causes a diminishing return of the physical product for each addition to the office force.

If there were no physical resistance on the part of agencies to produce, one hammer would drive all the nails in the community; one farm would feed the world; one laborer could do all the work; one productive agent along any line would be a national supply.

Resistance limits the supply of products coming from any one agent. Thus resistance is the cause of the scarcity and consequently the price of commodities. The greater the resistance of a productive agent, the greater, of course, is the cost of getting additional uses.

**3. Physical Intensive Utilization.**—If we take a limited agent, as a planing-mill, it will become the short factor as we add more and more to the labor force, to building, to other machinery, and to raw materials. This short factor becomes unable to back up the longer factors, and they produce a diminishing commodity return. It may be possible to get still further uses from the planing-mill by working it more intensively, but, to speak in terms of price, the resistance may be such that the cost of harnessing further uses from the machine will outweigh the price of such uses.

Getting more and more commodity returns from any agent—farm, engine, horse, laborer, house, or other—by applying more of other things to it is called *physical intensive utilization*.

**4. Turgot's Statement.**—The early resistance of an agent is comparatively difficult to overcome. Productive agents are "like a spring which is forced to bend by being loaded with a number of equal weights in succession. If the weight is light and the spring is not very flexible, the effect of the first load might be almost nil. When the weight becomes sufficient to overcome the first resistance, the spring will be seen to yield perceptibly and to bend; but, when it has bent to a certain point, it will offer greater resistance to the force brought to bear on it, and a weight which would have made it bend an inch will no longer bend it more than half a line."[1] And the same noted author goes on to remark on the cultivation of the soil as

---

[1] This was, I believe, the first illustration of the principle by an economist. It was written about 1768 by A. R. F. Turgot, on a prize essay submitted to him. See Cannan's Theories of Production and Distribution, pp. 147–148.

follows: "If it were once tilled the produce will be greater; tilling it a second, a third time, might not merely double and triple, but quadruple or decuple the produce, which will thus augment in a much larger proportion than the advances increase, and that up to a certain point, at which the produce will be as great as possible compared with the advances. Past this point, if the advances be still increased, the produce will still increase, but less, and always less and less until the fecundity of the earth being exhausted, and art unable to add anything further, an addition to the advances will add nothing whatever to the produce."

This illustration shows that the initial resistance of agents is strong, that after the initial advances are made resistance grows less and less up to a point (maximum commodity returns) where it again grows stronger and stronger as further advances are made.

**5. These Facts Expressed in Money Terms.**—The facts brought out by this study of the physical adjustment of factors relative to commodity returns may be expressed in terms of money cost and price returns. Put differently, an agent gives off few uses for the first expenditures upon it, after which it gives off more uses per unit of expenditure up to a point where it begins to give less and less money returns for each additional expenditure. The entrepreneur will not make further expenditures upon an agent when the point is reached where the use given off by the agent is no larger than the expenditure made to get it. This point, where the price of the income from an agent is no larger than the outgo to get it, is called the *intensive margin of utilization*. It marks the edge, point, or margin at which the utilization of the agent will cease.

**6. Intensive Margin of Utilization.**—Land is intensively cultivated by erecting higher buildings upon it, or by digging further down into it, or by any other means which tends to get more and more returns from it. But there is a definite economic limit to the height of building, or to the depth of digging, or to the care of cultivation. We stop at the point where loss would be incurred by going further, where the increasing cost comes to equalize the diminishing price return, or, in other words, at the margin of intensive cultivation. A use is valueless which would be worth no more than the cost of harnessing it. Then, the marginal uses of an agent are valueless, but man will undergo no effort for a valueless use, therefore marginal uses are not cultivated. Theoretically, cultivation extends down to, but does not attempt to harness the uses on or below the intensive margin.

**7. Extensive Margin of Utilization.**—It was the principle of resistance in the cultivation of land which caused Abraham to depart from Lot. "The land was not able to bear them, that they might dwell together." Were there no principle of resistance in land, a small area would provide for all. There would be no land rents, no transportation costs, and every economy of localized industry would be enjoyed. Why migrations, and why are all inhabitable parts of the globe occupied? The one answer is the principle of the increasing resistance of land.

If a colony settles in a new country, it will (fertility, location, and all things considered) occupy the best grades of land first. As the population increases, or as foreign markets develop, or as increasing standards of the people call forth higher prices for goods, this land will be more intensively cultivated. Increasing resistance will make it more and more difficult to supply their needs from this land. Rather than cultivate this one tract at too large an expense it will be more profitable to occupy the next best tract. And with further demands for land products poorer and poorer tracts will be cultivated. Extending cultivation out to cover additional tracts of land is called *extensive cultivation*. The outer edge or margin to which cultivation extends is the *extensive margin of cultivation*.

**8. What Lands or Land Uses are Cultivated?**—All land under cultivation is valuable. Men do not labor to harness a valueless use, and this they would do should they cultivate valueless land. The heaviest expenditures are justified only upon the most valuable land. One is marked as a poor business man who makes lavish expenditures upon cheap land. The least valuable land of all can command the least application of labor and capital upon it. Worthless land, like the scrap-heap machine, is abandoned, not because there are no possible uses in it, but because the cost of harnessing these uses would be more than they are worth.

Those who object to this view make this well-sounding fallacy: "Yes, men will cultivate worthless land, so long as they get a fair return from the capital applied to it." This, I may say, is the only point of any significance favoring the contention that valueless land is cultivated. And it is easily set aside. We have seen in the reasoning on complementary agents that land, tools, seed, and labor jointly produce. Any one of these agents alone is non-productive. And a return from their joint action is to be attributed, not to one or two but to all the causal factors. Why attribute the whole return to capital when land is an absolute essential in production? These complementary agents unite into one composite productive unit, as do the parts of a clock into one timepiece, but no one would be so foolish as to attribute the time-keeping quality to the dial, and value it to the exclusion of the other parts. Now, the tools, seed, and labor applied to this land are valuable solely because of what they produce, and for precisely the same reason the land is valuable, for indeed it is joint partner with the other factors in producing exactly the same thing.

The point at which cultivation ceases or the line, so to speak, which marks off the valuable from the valueless land, is called the *extensive margin of (cultivation) utilization.*

There is an extensive utilization of all forms of productive agents. The intensive utilization of a planing-mill grows more and more inconvenient and costly. As its resistance increases the other (long factors) show diminishing returns. This will justify the installation of another planing-mill. And so for all productive agents.

**9. Equality of Intensive and Extensive Margins.**—If a farmer has an extra hundred dollars, will he bring more land under cultivation or more intensively utilize land now under tillage? His desire to receive the largest net return will cause him so to distribute his expenditures as to keep the two margins at an equality. Should the field intensively cultivated offer the larger returns, it will pay to continue investing upon it until its margin is lowered to the point where its money return equals that of the extensive margin.

Again, one attempts to withdraw his capital from the less paying occupation in order to invest it in the more remunerative occupation. By withdrawing capital from where relatively too much is employed he raises the margin and thus increases the returns from each unit of capital remaining there. And by applying this capital to the more remunerative field the margin will there be lowered and the returns to capital diminished. In any case, the attempt to employ capital in its most remunerative employment tends to equalize the returns to capital in all employments.

10. **Substitution.**—During the course of production entrepreneurs find it necessary to substitute one thing for another, one type of labor for another, new inventions for old, a larger machine for a smaller, or *vice versa*, and so on. The purpose of substitution is to bring about a better apportionment or adjustment of the factors of production. This is also concerned with such problems as lengthening short factors, or of eliminating waste by shortening factors which are unnecessarily long.

A certain factor is found to hold a monopoly position, at times, and all the other factors must be adjusted to it. The flow from a mineral spring is limited and the other factors employed to utilize this water must be adjusted to the size of the flow, for it cannot be so enlarged as to accommodate itself to the size of the other agents. The same idea holds with respect to a building site in a crowded city, or with respect to a factor which relatively is very costly, or with respect to a factor limited by franchise, or monopoly right.

To work out proper substitutions in order to maintain a proper proportion and balance in the business is the primary problem in business management. When such an adjustment is reached there is no reason for further substitution, and it would be sheer waste to enlarge or further improve any of the productive factors without improving all. But, unfortunately, such an ideal adjustment is at best only temporary.

11. **The Law of Proportionality.**—We have now come to the most important topic in economics. This law simply states facts regarding quantitative relationship from which most facts concerning price relationships are derived. There is a best adjustment of parts to make a bridge, automobile, or machine, and, any part lacking, the mechanism works poorly or not at all. There must be a proper mixture of ingredients to produce a paint, and a proper mixture of paints to give us a painting. These are physical facts illustrative of physical adjustments.

Industry consists of mental processes and the movement of physical things. Back of the existing structure are the movements of materials which gave it form, and back of these movements were the thoughts and plans of where and how to move these materials. The principle guiding these thoughts and shaping these materials into finished structures is the law of proportionality. This law teaches how to add to the serviceability of things by giving them proper combination. The work of farmers, merchants, cooks, chemists, engineers, transporters, and miners is to move or combine things so that natural forces may operate to give desired results.[1]

There is an old saying that "too much of a good thing is bad." Water is so good as to be an absolute essential to life, but too much of it fills the cellar, floods the valley, and makes swamps. No crop could be produced without it, but too much of it destroys the crop. If a dry plain

---

[1] The reasoning and some of the illustrations used in this paragraph are most admirably expressed in, and are taken from, Professor Carver's Essays in Social Justice. See particularly his chapter XI.

fails to produce for want of water, a swamp refuses to produce for the opposite reason—too much water. The owner of the dry plain would like to buy water, whereas the swamp-owner would regard it a privilege to give it away. Its price or want of price depends upon the physical fact of proportionality. The swamp-owner reasons: "More water less crop; less water more crop." The remedy for both of these cases is to move water; move it from places of abundance to places of scarcity. The entrepreneur constantly deals with substitutions to bring about the proper adjustment. The proportions with which he deals are variable, and a chief duty of his is to redistribute his resources from time to time so as to cut down long factors and add to the short ones. If he is a manufacturer of gunpowder, he knows that his product results from the mixture of charcoal, saltpetre, and sulphur, and further, that *the short factor will be the limiting factor.*

He may have enough charcoal and saltpetre to make 20,000 kegs of powder, but if he has only enough sulphur to make 500 kegs, the short factor—sulphur—will limit his total product to 500 kegs. He might double or quadruple the long factors, but to no effect on the final output. Should he double the short factor, however, the forthcoming product would be doubled. In this case the increased product would be attributed to the short factor. This manager could well afford to pay a high price for sulphur, but he would not be justified in a large outlay for the other two factors. It is thus shown again that the market conditions respecting productive agents are based upon the physical fact of proportionality. Davenport's statement, "The ultimate determinant of the high price of any product is to be found in the scarcity of the productive factors upon which the forthcoming of the product is conditioned."[1] But this lacks strict accuracy in that it is the relatively short factor which limits supply and thus accounts for high price.

12. **Bearing of Proportionality on the Distribution of Wealth.**—When we speak of the distribution of wealth we mean, strictly speaking, a distribution of income. And a study of economic distribution is an attempt to account for the comparative size of the shares of income which go to the different agents (or their owners) which produce the income. It attempts to answer the question, Why do some agents get so much of the income while others get so little? All shares of distribution are not governed by the same economic principles. With respect to the principles governing them the shares are divided into four classes— Rent, Interest, Profits, and Wages. They may be indicated with respect to the agents producing them as follows:

$$\left.\begin{array}{l}\text{Rent} \longleftarrow \text{Wealth} \\ \text{Interest} \longleftarrow \text{Capital}\end{array}\right\} \text{Things and Men} \left\{\begin{array}{l}\text{Entrepreneurs} \longrightarrow \text{Profits} \\ \text{Laborers} \longrightarrow \text{Wages}\end{array}\right.$$

For the sake of clearness let us repeat a statement previously made: The order of thought is from the price of the product to the price of the productive factor. If the product is scarce and high-priced, then a high price will be paid for the use of the productive factor. The causal sequence runs from product to agent; it never runs

---

[1] Economics of Enterprise, p. 435. This is quoted from Davenport's chapter VIII, which is recommended to the readers of this book as, in my judgment, the most clear-cut analysis in print of the relation of cost to value. To use his own words to express his line of thought: "The causal sequence on the supply side of the problem runs from the relative scarcity of the product, thence to the relatively high price of the product, thence to the relatively high remuneration of the factor" (p. 111). Note his application of this to wages (p. 115).

in the opposite direction. If a productive agent is very scarce, it would be vicious reasoning to hop directly to the conclusion that it is, therefore, very high-priced. The order of thought is: Supply of productive agent ➡ supply of product ➡ price of product ➡ and, lastly, to price of productive agent.

Because the scarce factor limits the product, the high price of the product will, in turn, cause a high price to be paid for the use of the short factor. Again, to increase the short factor has the effect of increasing the product; unit for unit the short factor is most productive and the long factor less productive. The greatest productive need is met by adding to the supply of the shortest factor, and he who adds most to the short factors adds most to production. The high price for scarce products reflects a high price back to the short factor; thus he who produces most gets most. If sulphur is the short factor in the output of gunpowder, he who adds most to sulphur adds most to the gunpowder, and the high price of gunpowder will reflect the highest reward back to the producer of sulphur. And in all cases where desirabilities and utilities coincide, he who gets most is worth most to society.

If a capital instrument is the short factor and labor the long, the capital instrument will secure more of the product as its share. Similarly, different grades of labor are needed in production. If skilled labor be the short factor and unskilled labor the long, then the larger share will go to the skilled labor. Or if unskilled labor were the short factor, its share would be larger than that of skilled labor.

Land was the long factor, whereas labor was short in this country prior to the Civil War, so the result was a small share for landowners and high wages for labor. At the same time in England land was the short factor and the labor supply was disproportionately large. The result was the reverse of conditions in America—labor was cheap and land rents dear. The same is true throughout distribution—long factors and low returns, short factors and high returns.

13. **How the Price of Agents Affects Proportionality.**— We have so far, for the most part, studied proportionality as a physical fact. It takes a best quantitative technical combination to produce the largest commodity returns. But nature has not distributed her bounties equally; some, like air, she has oversupplied, and others she has supplied sparingly. We may be very saving of short factors, may make every possible substitution for them, yet they are limiting agents, and the high price of their products gives them a large share in distribution. The scarcity and cost of these agents makes it unprofitable at times to carry out the best technical proportionality of factors. "The patent-office at Washington," says Professor Fetter, "is a veritable graveyard of ingenious inventions that are not commercially profitable. The inventor, in order to gain material rewards and at the same time to benefit mankind, must study not only the technical side of his problem, but the question of value as well."[1]

Mention was made above that a certain factor may hold a monopoly position and others must be adjusted to it. This factor may be so limited and high-priced for some purposes as to defeat a best technical apportionment of factors for other purposes. When there are a number of uses for a limited agent, it will be put to the most remunerative use, and thus denied to the others. Hay is not grown

[1] Economic Principles, Vol. I, p. 109.

on the rare wine-lands of France. In working out an apportionment of factors, regard must be paid to the selling price of the product and the extent of the market for it, and to the relative cost of factors as well as to the price which is offered for these factors because of their use in other fields of employment.

Suppose that X is a limited factor and, further, that the production of articles A and B is conditioned upon the use of X. If A is very high-priced, and is in such general demand that it requires all of X in its production, it must follow that if B is a low-priced good it cannot be produced. Thus the high price of product A and the physical limitation of productive factor X defeat the production of B. The large demand for one commodity oftentimes precludes the existence of other commodities, and this is true solely because of the limitation and high cost of certain factors of production. Apportionments will be made that will produce the output which commands the highest income.

Many writers say that the price of a product is high because the cost (money outlay) of the factors to produce it are high. This type of shallow instruction does not get below the surface. It simply accounts for one price by another price. What we want to know is how to explain the price thing. To explain price two things are to be kept in mind: the one is demand, and the other is the limitation of the short factors of production which makes necessary a large cost outlay to secure the use of them.

14. The Elastic Limit of Factors.—When we speak of the physical limitation of certain factors, we do not mean that the services which we can get from them exist in a mathematically fixed quantum under all conditions. A

few words of explanation are called for. The quantity theorists, for instance, tell us that a dollar which turns over ten times a week does as much money-work, has the same effect on the price level, and is as large a part of the supply of money as is a ten-dollar piece which turns over once a week. By like reasoning, the employer would as willingly pay a skilled workman $4 a day who can turn out four pieces a day as to pay $4 to two inferior workmen who combined could produce four pieces a day. The one man who turns out four pieces is as large a part of the labor supply as are two men who combined could do no more. One will pay as much rent for an acre that produces 100 bushels as for two acres which combined could produce 100. Put differently, the supply of productive factors is not measured, in the economic sense, by bulk, size, or area; it is measured in terms of yield.

Consider land for the purpose of illustration. A group of English writers, known as the Maltho-Ricardian School, taught that land is fixed in supply, while population tends to double every twenty-five years. The conclusion from these teachings was most pessimistic; population must pass subsistence and be cut off by starvation. But the lapse of a century since this teaching began shows the error of this doctrine. The growth of population is regulated by other causes than those supposed, and the land supply (in the economic sense of a productive agent) has been vastly increased.

If a non-productive thing is made productive, the economist calls it a truism that the supply or productive capacity has increased. In keeping with this truism, if swamp lands are drained and set to growing crops, the land supply is increased. If dry plains are made productive through irrigation, the land supply is increased. If new inventions, discoveries, or methods cause an increase in the yield of land, land is more productive—the land supply is increased. Any means of getting more from land—building, tillage, and rotation of crops—is from the standpoint of production and, therefore, from the economist's view, to add to the land supply. Despite the simplicity of this truism some economists have joined company with the single-taxers in denying it.

At a given time or at a given stage of improvements in the industrial arts there is more or less fixity in the supply of productive agents. The law of substitution at any given stage of industrial development is operative to secure the best apportionment of forces at that time. The better the apportionment the greater is the supply of productive capacity. The problem of proportionality has to do with variable factors. It would add to simplicity could we definitely tie down certain factors and regard them as fixed, but such would be an unreal simplicity.

15. **Extent of Market.**—To this point we have considered proportionality with respect to the proper adjustment of factors to one another. The other phase of the problem, in its broader sense, is to adjust the size of the plant to the extent of the market for its output. The best technical adjustment of factors may leave the plant too large or too small for the demand made for its products.

In an exchange economy, such as we know, where all produce for the market every commodity produced is in reality a demand for another commodity. If there is too large an output of one class of goods relative to others, its price will be low in terms of other goods. This is what is meant by overproduction. There can be no overproduction along all lines, for all of our desires are never fully gratified. There is a tendency for man to spend his means so as to keep his desires equally gratified, and if there be a disproportionate supply of goods along one line, it can be sold only at such prices as shall tap a lower level of "price-paying disposition."

In a well-balanced industrial community there is a tendency for the size of plants to be apportioned to each other as are the productive factors in a single plant. If one line of industry is relatively short its products will sell at a high price. This will induce investments from other fields where the plants are relatively large. Thus there is always operative an automatic adjustment of the lines of industry to one another. Then, proportionality is a broader concept than the adjustment of parts to one another in a single plant; it embodies the idea of the balancing and adjustment of industries to one another throughout industrial society.

16. **Quantity and Money Returns.**—What has been said but emphasizes a point made in an earlier chapter, namely, that there is a limit to large-scale production. An entrepreneur may reason that by maintaining a good technical apportionment of factors it will pay constantly to enlarge his plant. By so doing he will enjoy decreasing costs per unit of output. But such a policy would, if continued too far, bring him to ruin.

To the extent that he buys up productive capacity in the enlargement of his own plant, he somewhat reduces the available productive capacity in other lines of industry. Thus, while disproportionately enlarging his own output he causes a diminution in its price. Consequently his output will bring a lower price in terms of other goods, because it will be disproportionately large, and others will have relatively fewer goods to give in exchange for his product. So if one directs a large business or has a monopoly he may at the same time enjoy increasing returns with respect to the *quantity* of his output and suffer diminishing returns with respect to the *money income* from his output. This recalls the kindred point, namely, that a producer's success depends largely upon the wealth, prosperity, and purchasing power of his neighbors. One never grows rich by selling to those who have nothing to pay.

But those rare cases, where an increasing physical return causes a decreasing money return, simply reflect a maladjustment in industry as a whole. It means merely that some branches of industry are proportionately too large. Should the output from all lines of industry increase uniformly, elasticity of market demand aside, the ratio of exchange among products would not change, therefore the increased quantity return would mean also an increased purchasing power or money return. Where a right adjustment is kept a curve describing the money incomes will represent uniform profits. We have seen that in competitive industry there is a tendency to uniformity of the extensive and intensive margins, and to uniformity in the rate of profits. We now see that the whole tendency of competitive industry is to maintain automatically a uniformity of commodity and money returns or exchange power.

For the average competitor, but not for the monopolist or large producer, the total money product always varies in proportion to the quantity of his output. The amount which he can produce is too small to affect perceptibly the general market price of the product. For him the market price is a fixed thing.

**17. Summary Conclusion.**—On the demand side: Man's desires are numerous; he attempts so to expend his means as to gratify the most intense desire; as he adds unit after unit to the gratification of a desire the desirability of the added units diminishes; when the desirability of a class of goods diminishes to the point where other classes of goods hold for the purchaser higher desirabilities, he will transfer his expenditures. The effect of this order of expenditure is the tendency (though far from realization among the poor) to maintain an equality of the desirabilities of different classes of goods.

On the supply side: Products come from a combination of complementary agents, which agents are limited in amount and resist our efforts to compel them to supply our needs. Some of these agents are scarcer than others, and some show increasing resistance more readily than others.

These facts call into play the principle of substitution which is of first importance to business managers. It is based directly upon the principle of resistance, and so it has to do with the amount of agents that should be combined with this factor or that; it is concerned with the diminution of long factors and the extension of short ones. In brief, the substitution of factors is a means to the end of the best proportionality of factors.

The proportionality of factors is their physical combination and adjustment (in certain proportions) which render them jointly productive. Thus proportionality is a consequence of substitution. The law of proportionality covers all productive factors in their various combinations; it determines the physical fact of productivity. It is the organization of productive capacity.

While proportionality is a physical fact, it is worked out according to the price of products and the cost of factors. Men will form productive establishments only when the selling price of the products is large enough to leave a reasonable return over all costs. The high cost of certain factors often makes impossible the best physical apportionment of them.

Each of the factors which go to make up a plant is subject to the principle of resistance, consequently the whole plant obeys the same principle. This causes the product to be scarce and valuable. The price of the product makes the producer willing to pay a price for the services of the productive agents, both severally and in combination. But the price paid for the services of a productive agent is rent, hence the relationship between the principle of resistance and rent.

**18. Exercises.**—1. If one man should own New York harbor, could he obtain rent for it? If so, what now becomes of the rent he could get for it? Is that harbor now wealth? Would it be wealth were it owned by some man?

2. If there were no principle of resistance, would there be any difference in the amount of land needed? In the number of laborers needed? In the number of houses needed?

What has this principle to do with the scarcity of grain grown in a field? With the size of a load hauled on a wagon? With the number of chairs needed by a family?

3. Is there any relationship between the facts noted in Turgot's statement (paragraph 4, this chapter) and the price of corn?

4. What lands or land uses are cultivated? (Paragraph 8.)

"Under certain conditions it would pay to carry on

cultivation beyond the intensive or the extensive margin of utilization." Why does this statement contradict itself?

5. "The law of proportionality is based directly upon the principle of resistance which causes an elastic limit to the output of each individual factor." Explain carefully.

6. Land may be physically productive in the sense that it has the physical properties for growing a crop, meanwhile it may be economically unproductive. Explain.

If economically unproductive, would any farmer work land?

Would it add to the wealth of society if a crop should be grown upon such land?

7. Explain how land economically unproductive might be made economically productive by a decrease in the wages of labor. By superior management. By new inventions or improvements in farm implements. By an increase in the price of farm produce.

8. The physical fact of productivity is determined by the great law of proportionality which states a physical relation. The physical apportionment of factors to one another is conditioned upon the cost or price of the different factors. Explain why the two statements are consistent with each other.

9. An analysis of the distribution of wealth must be based directly upon the law of proportionality. (Paragraph 12.) Explain.

10. What economic principle explains why buildings are so high in Wall Street? Why are they not much higher?

# CHAPTER XVII

## THE RENTING CONTRACT

**1. Introduction.**—Chief among the politico-economic problems of the nineteenth century were these: the tariff, the pressure of population upon the means of subsistence, the advantage of landowners in the distribution of wealth, and the single tax. The arguments, pro and con, upon these problems were based directly upon the theory of differential land rent. It has been said that a tariff would force a population to feed from its own soil. This would bring inferior lands under cultivation and increase rents, thereby enriching landlords and impoverishing tenants. It has been said that whereas the supply of land is fixed by nature, there is a natural tendency for the population to multiply rapidly. Thus the increasing numbers of people must cause pressure upon the earth for food, must increase the landlord's rent and impoverish the tenant. It has been said that the land is the source of all supplies and the field of all labor, that the puniest infant who comes wailing into the world in the squalidest room of the most miserable tenement-house becomes at that moment seized of an equal right with the millionaires. And it is robbed if it is denied equal access to the land. Place a tax, a single tax, upon the land so large as to absorb all land rents. This would have the effect of making public property of what is now the private ownership of land.

Until recent years the literature upon the subject taught that rent forms no part of the cost of production. The business man who paid rent knew full well that this was a part of his outgo or cost of doing business. Yet he read in the books that rents were not costs. The economists now, though not without exceptions, teach that rent is a cost.

Within recent years another change has been made in the thought on the rent problem. Rent was formerly defined as a payment for the use of land and for the use of land only. To-day rent is defined as a payment for the temporary use of a house, horse, automobile, plough, land, or any other durable productive agent other than man. Rent is now studied as one of the primary shares in distribution, as a leading cost in the production of wealth, as the greatest obstacle to clear thinking on taxation, and as the source of numerous social problems.

**2. Definition of Rent.**—If a farmer tills his own soil, he gets an income but cannot be said to receive a rent. When one occupies his own dwelling, or drives his own team, or uses his own tools, he gets services (usances), but receives no rent. Rent is the price paid by one person to another for the temporary use of productive agents. Rent is but a special application of the general problem of price—it is the price of the temporary services of agents.

Rent implies private property. Where there is no private property there can be no rent. There could be no buying or selling, consequently no rent, apart from ownership; the only reason why you cannot rent or lease to another a public park is because you do not own it. Rent also implies legal contracts. You cannot discharge the tenant at will, because you are bound in contract to fulfil your agreement with him throughout the renting period. To rent is to contract with an owner for the use of an agent.

3. **Durable Goods Rented.**—One does not rent a pound of beef, a loaf of bread, or a ton of coal, because these objects are destroyed by the uses made of them. Rented agents are returned intact to their owners after the renting period. If one pays $1,000 a year for the lease of a house, he is said, in popular usage, to pay that sum as rent. But in strict usage, the cost of such repairs as will leave the house in as good condition as when leased, must be deducted from the $1,000 in order to find the *net* or *true rent*. Rent is a net sum over and above all repairs; only those things may be rented which remain practically intact through the renting period.

Goods which serve their purpose only by entering into permanent combination with other goods are not rented. One would not rent steel beams, or nails, or bricks to be used in the construction of his house. One does not rent the thread with which to sew a garment, because it could not be returned intact to the owner. Such goods lose their identity by becoming a part of other goods. Only durable goods which maintain their identity are well suited to the renting contract.

The tenant who rents a farm does not rent separately

the land, hedges, fences, ditches, and durable improvements on the land. These combined make the farm, and the farm thus composed of land and durable improvements is well suited to the renting contract. The different factors cannot be separated for rent or for purposes of taxation.

4. **Buying or Renting.**—It has been pointed out that the only reason why one desires a good or is willing to pay a price for it is because of the services which it is capable of rendering. You will pay no price for a house which you are forbidden to enter, rent, sell, or otherwise use. The price you will pay depends upon the price of the services you expect to get from the house. You buy the house when you pay for its services *in toto;* you rent the house when you buy the services for a limited period of time.

It is not always wise to buy a dwelling or building for one's business, even though it is offered at a reasonable figure. One may have difficulty in disposing of his dwelling to advantage if he is called elsewhere to a more remunerative position; or one may use his capital funds to better advantage by investing them in something else. If one does not know the neighbors and surroundings in a community, it is better to rent for a time in order to determine whether permanent residence is desirable.

The entrepreneur of a new enterprise cannot be sure that his business will succeed. The beginner, by renting for a time, can test his possibilities for success in the building of another, so that in case of failure his burden is less, because less fixed capital is involved. On the other hand, if he is successful his business will grow. With the expansion of business, larger quarters will be needed, and possibly a move to a better neighborhood or trade centre would be advisable. Such changes can be more easily made by the renter. When a business has become firmly established, especially if it requires a large amount of room, it may be desirable to own the building in which it is housed.

If one's business requires only an office, it may not be wise to buy or build. It is more economical to rent office space in a building constructed for the purpose. Such buildings furnish every convenience, are easily accessible, and are well-known. An office in the Woolworth Building may be had for a reasonable rent, but to buy land in an equally advantageous location and build an office as fully equipped would call for a large investment.

One will rent rather than buy in order to gratify a temporary need. One will rent a taxicab rather than buy it, to get home on a rainy day. If the farmer's mowing-machine is in the repair-shop temporarily, he will prefer to rent for the short period of time.

5. **Use-Value Derivative.**—There is a difference between the use and the product of an agent, a difference between the uses of a farm and the corn, wheat, or potatoes which that farm produces. The use is the origin of the product. One cannot buy the uses of potatoes unless he buys the potatoes, because the potatoes are destroyed in the process of rendering their uses. But one may buy the uses of the farm for a given time without buying the farm, because the farm is not destroyed in the process of yielding a crop. The farm remains intact after a period of cultivation; it is, therefore, as above stated, subject to the renting contract.

To rent a farm is to buy the uses of it for a given period of time. The rent is the price paid for these uses. The purpose of renting or of buying the uses of the farm is to secure the products or yield of the farm. How much rent will you pay for the uses of the farm? As you are willing to pay the merchant a high price for a valuable good, so you are willing to pay the landlord a high price (rent) for the opportunity of a valuable crop. In a sense the rent is the advance purchase price of the crop. The price of the farm, or of its total uses, is derived from the anticipated valuation of what it will produce through time.

The products of uses vary in nature. Some uses give off a tangible return, *e. g.*, the corn from the field. Some uses give off intangible returns, *e. g.*, the sound of a musical instrument. The product of a corner lot is location, or relativity to the market. The product of an accountant's outfit is to facilitate the workings of other agents. *In the rent problem the nature of the product is of no consequence. To explain rent is to explain the price of the uses of rent-bearing agents.*

The uses to which agents are put determine the relative supplies of goods. If the price of corn increases while that of wheat declines, more land will be turned to corn and less to wheat, with the result—more corn, less wheat. But productive agents, all things considered, will be turned to their most remunerative employment. The rich to-bacco-farm in Kentucky will not be used for grazing purposes any more than would the luxurious mansion on Fifth Avenue be used for a tobacco-barn.

**6. The Renting Contract Prospective.**—The renting contract is made before the renter takes possession. This fact subjects the renter to risk. Smith leases a dwelling, expecting to live in it, and so he must pay the rent, even though he cannot occupy it as when a turn in business calls him to another town. Corporations rent coal, oil, or timber lands at times, years in advance of operations. The tenant contracts to pay a high rent because he expects a valuable crop, but pests or a drought or a flood may ruin his crop. He may secure a large yield in bushels, but the market price may be low.

The rent paid is fixed by contract at the beginning of the renting period. If the merchant agrees to pay $500

a month for a building over a period of five years, his rent outlay remains the same irrespective of his earnings. Rent depends not upon past earnings but upon anticipatory earnings.

Because anticipatory earnings are not definitely known, the renter may either suffer a loss or enjoy a net gain. Whereas rent is the purchase price of the temporary uses of an agent, the purchase price of the agent is the sum paid for all the future uses of the agent. Then, if risk is involved in the purchase (rent) of the uses of the agent for the immediate future, certainly a greater risk is involved in the purchase of all the future uses.

We see now that present contract rents are based upon the prospective or future yields of agents. No one will contract to pay rent for an abandoned mine because of its former yield. Rent emerges only in case of a gain-promising opportunity.

7. **The Time Element in Rent.**—If one rents an agent which will yield an income immediately, he will be willing to pay a rental approximately equal to the price of the

yield. But if the income will not be secured before the lapse of one, two, or five years, the case is different. Men prefer the present over the future possession of goods. You would rather have $1,000 to-day, than twenty years from now. The average man holding a note of $106 due a year hence would be willing to sell it at the present for $100. Assume that the income from a rent-bearer will mature a year hence; its present worth (future price discounted to the present) will be less than its price at maturity. The further the income is removed in time, the less is the rent of the producing agent. Present rent is derived from the present worth of income.

**8. Short Factors and High Rent.**—In working out the best proportionality it was found, in the preceding chapter, that certain factors may hold a monopoly position. For instance, the available land space may be limited. A corner lot, a franchise, or natural conditions may fix the area at the disposal of the entrepreneur. A monopoly right by another may definitely limit the supply of certain factors essential to his business. Wherever, for any such reason, a factor is limited, the entrepreneur must work out his adjustment of factors with respect to this factor. Or if the price of one factor is far in excess of that of the other factors, the adjustment will usually be made with respect to this one.

This is but another way of saying that short factors determine the capacity (ability to produce incomes) of productive establishments. These factors are high in price by virtue of the fact that they are short factors. As short factors they limit the output of goods; they are most productive and, therefore, command the largest rent.

**9. What Is High Rent?**—If a lot on Wall Street rents for $50,000 a year, while a potato-patch of the same area in Kansas rents for $5, shall we say that the one rent is high and the other low? Not in strict accuracy. One dollar for 20 cakes of soap is no higher price than 5 cents for 1 cake. Likewise $50,000 for 10,000 units of productive power is no higher rent than is $5 for one such unit. Before we say a rent is high we should inquire the productivity of the agent rented. Where competition is active and free the rents or prices of productive services are reduced to equality.

If one rents a farm and pests or drought spoil the crop, he has paid for non-remunerative services—the rent is high. If he rents a business house or a factory and an unforeseen panic injures the business, he has paid for non-remunerative services—the rent is high.

Superior management increases the productivity of land as does increased fertilizer. But competition is such that the inferior manager must pay the same rent as the most skilled manager. Under inferior direction the yield of the land may be small as compared with rent, and a high yield relative to rent may reward the efforts of the wise manager. For the inferior the rent would be high and for the superior it would be low. Rent is high or low always in comparison with the price of the yield.

**10. Monopoly Rents.**—Monopoly rents obey the same principle as do monopoly prices which have already found discussion. Monopoly rents are one kind of monopoly prices, for the monopolist will rent his wealth at that figure which will yield him the largest net return. Monopoly rents are not without limit.

One limit to monopoly rent is the selling price of the

product; in no case will a tenant pay a rent that is higher than the anticipated price of his crop. Another limit to the rent of an agent is the rent of other agents which will readily substitute for the monopolized agent. Automobile trucks and draft-horses may be substituted for each other in most cases. Should there be a monopoly on draft-horses the rent could not be made excessive because of the available substitute for them. Again, the monopolist must endeavor to preserve the renter's prosperity. Should the owner of a waterfall demand a ruthlessly exorbitant rent, he would kill the business of the renter. The renter can go into some other business and would do so if a monopolist exact his profits in the form of rent.

**11. Product Returns vs. Money Returns.**—It is now clear that one rents wealth in order to get returns from that wealth. But of what do returns consist? It is evident that the tenant of a farm may speak of his return as so many bushels or as so many dollars' worth. For some purposes it is best to think of returns in weight and tale; for other purposes it is best to calculate returns in terms of money. For purposes of trade and distribution we are forced to think of returns in their price aspect. If one is calculating his profits or losses on the year's operations, he can compare his income and costs only by reducing them to their money equivalents. But if one is reasoning on the problem of social well-being, if he is estimating the current supplies to meet the needs of the people, he must think in terms of product rather than in terms of money. The supply of a good—as sugar, salt, or other—may be least when its price is greatest.

Let us consider, for example, all competitors who are growing corn. As each one endeavors to grow such an amount as will render him the greatest net gain, the total number of bushels produced will be greatly augmented; but the larger the product return, the less the price of each bushel produced. After a certain point is reached, the total price of the corn-crop will diminish as the number of bushels increases. The producing competitor will suffer because of the decline in the price of his corn, but the same facts—abundant corn at a low price—will add to social well-being.

Assume now that a monopoly controls the available salt factories. It may well be that by a better physical adjustment of factors the volume of output is augmented at a diminishing cost, that is to say, the cost per unit (per bag) of output is diminished as the volume of output increases. But the demand for salt is inelastic. The price must be very low if more than a normal supply is sold. Then, despite the fact of increasing volume returns, there will be decreasing money returns. It will be to the producer's interest to curtail physical output; his interest will conflict with the interest of society.

The view-point of each competitor is now to be considered. Any one grower of corn will find his crop so small in comparison with all the corn produced that his output will have an insignificant effect on the market price. Consequently, the larger the amount of his product the greater will be his money return. It is then to the interest of each competitor to make his commodity ·return large. This being to the interest of all competitors, causes the maximum total output in society. The competitor's interest in this case is in keeping with the interest of society.

From the above reasoning it is clear that the rent paid

for the use of an agent may be diminished in certain cases by virtue of the fact that improvements in the agent may increase the volume of its physical output.

**12. The Tendency Toward Diminishing Money Returns Universal.**—When more and more productive factors are expended upon a limited agent that agent will show increasing resistance to further output. This was made clear in the preceding chapter with respect to a limited area of land. Additional expenditures upon the limited agent show a decline in both the commodity return and the money return.

Let us now consider a factory or a railroad. Here we find a tendency for the cost, per unit of output, to diminish until a certain point is reached, as the volume of output increases. If the railroad moves 100,000 passengers a month, its costs per passenger will be less than if it moved only 1,000 passengers. It will cost the sugar-refinery less per hundredweight of output when it produces a large volume, until a certain point is reached, than when it produces a small volume of sugar. But such institutions (sometimes erroneously called institutions of increasing returns) will see the total price of their output decline when the volume of output has grown beyond the normal needs of the market. Ultimately receipts will fall below costs despite the fact that the per-unit costs themselves are diminishing.

Thus we find diminishing money returns generally applicable, but there are two unlike causes for this general tendency. (*a*) Money returns diminish in one case because of a decrease in product returns relative to costs. (*b*) Money returns diminish in the other case because of an increase in product returns.

**13. Large Production and Monopoly.**—Agriculture furnishes a good example of the tendency of money returns to a competitive producer to diminish with a decrease in commodity returns. There is a definite paying limit to the amount of expenditure justified upon a field. This fact renders large-scale production upon a limited area impossible and maintains competition by keeping productive units small and scattered.

But, as explained previously, the institution which diminishes the costs per unit of output by enlarging its scale of production has a tendency to monopoly. In case of a number of competitors in the manufacture of sugar, each will desire to reduce his productive costs below those of his competitors. In order to do this he must have the largest output, and this is made possible by lowering the price to drive competition from the market.

**14. Conditions for Study of Principle of Increasing Resistance.**—If the student is following this reasoning carefully, he finds two unlike view-points in what has just been said. The one has to do with a given situation, with a limited agent (in the above case a limited area of land). One can see the principle of increasing resistance, can isolate it from a heterogeneous mass of details, only when he limits the study of it to a given agent at any one time. The words "at any one time" are important. Should I study the comparative returns from a given field in 1815 and 1915, I should observe a large increase in returns, but I should be reckoning with unlike situations. During the century marked improvements have been made in labor, inventions, and in the arts of husbandry generally. There would be a change of situation which would becloud the reasoning with respect to the increasing resistance of a factor.

But if I take, for the reckoning on returns, a given time in which no perceptible changes take place in the arts of husbandry, if I further confine my study to a limited area, I can then and then only observe the true working and significance of the principle of resistance. The like conditions are termed *static* conditions. The principle of resistance is always and everywhere operative in industry, but the point here made is that under static conditions only can this principle be isolated, seen, and scientifically studied.

In case of growing large-scale production, we find that there is rapid change from old to new, from small to large, from antiquated methods and machinery to the newest and best. With these changes the cost per unit of output diminishes. But it is clear that such changes are but transitions from one set of conditions to another. The factors are changeable and the mind cannot clearly grasp the true workings of the resistance of any factor.

There can be no compromise; it is absolutely essential for clear thinking on rent that the student grasp this fact —at any given time the yield of a productive agent cannot be indefinitely increased without increasing costs. In a given time there is an elastic limit to the returns from any productive agent—be it horse, engine, house, field, or other.

**15. Rent a Deduction from the Principle of Increasing Resistance.**—All economy begins with scarcity. Apart from scarcity, there would be nothing to work for, no increase of material blessings to inspire further activity; life would not be worth living. To acquire valuable things is the incentive to effort and the value one attributes to things (demand assumed) is determined by their scarcity. The resistance of agents to further production causes the scarcity of goods. We are, therefore, willing to pay a price or rent for the services of agents to produce these scarce and desirable goods. We attach value to the field because of the valuable crops it yields, and to the horse because of the valuable services it performs, and to the boat because of the valuable transporting it does. Products are valuable because they are scarce, and they are scarce because of the resistance of agents to the further production of them. Thus the scarcity of goods is traceable to this basic economic thought—the increasing resistance of agents. The rent we are willing to pay for the temporary services of productive factors is determined by the so-called "scarcity value" of these products.

16. **Proportionality and Rent.**—Proportionality or the adjustment of productive factors to one another, as we have seen, is based upon the law of resistance common to each and every factor of production. It does not pay to apply too many or too few factors to any one factor—there is a best adjustment or proportionality. All of the agents— mill, belts, fuel, building, and so on—which unite to convert a log into lumber must be reckoned as one composite productive unit. As you attribute value to a horse as a whole, so you attribute value to a composite productive unit as a whole. As you would not attribute value to the legs, eyes, and stomach of the horse separately, so you would not attribute value to the engine, belts, fuel, and building of a sawmill separately. Where factors must co-operate to produce a good, it is impossible to assign to any one agent a product based upon the supposition of separate productivity. No separate product can be ascribed to any single factor.

Well does this writer remember the first question put to

him on his oral examination for the degree of Doctor of Philosophy. It was: "In a large wagon-factory, what part of the value of a spoke should be attributed to managerial ability?" His guess was most fortunate: "It can't be done. All the factors back of that spoke are united into one composite unit and must be valued as such."

The supply side of the price of a good is found in the comparative advantage of various combinations of factors of production. If the price of structural steel rises, the entrepreneur will undertake to increase the supply. His problem is: "What changed proportion of the several factors will most easily turn out the increased supply?" Should more labor be applied to the same plant, or should the plant be enlarged relatively to the existing labor force, or what should be the conjunction of additional factors? The best technical or physical adjustment of factors to one another is always conditioned upon the cost of the different factors. If land is cheap and abundant, while labor and tools are scarce and high-priced, farmers will not be sparing of land—it will pay to "skin" the land in order to conserve and more intensively utilize tools and labor. Were land, tools, and labor of the same degree of scarcity and price, their intensity of utilization would tend to be the same.

The yield of any factor depends largely upon the other factors applied to it. Land can reach its maximum yield only when the agents—tools, fertilizer, seed, labor—are most advantageously applied to it. Therefore, the usance of an agent will be largest and its rent highest when there is a best adjustment of other factors to it.

17. **Rent Limited by Income.**—The rent which the entrepreneur does pay for agents is vastly different from

what he would pay if he had to. One pays two cents for the morning paper, but he would pay, say, ten cents rather than go without it; so the owner of the sawmill may be willing to pay an annual rent of $5,500 for an engine rather than do without it, but he does pay for it only the normal competitive rent. It is a matter of much concern to him whether certain essential factors are owned by a monopoly. The limit to the rent which he could permanently pay for a monopolized factor would be determined by all of his other costs and the selling price of his product. He would lose if he paid more rent for one factor than the difference between his income and other costs.

Concerns are sometimes forced to run their business at a loss for short periods of time. It is better to get something out of the plant than nothing. Rather than disband an organized laboring force during a dull period in the market and pay interest and depreciation upon an idle plant it may well pay to rent an essential factor, although such a rent exceed the difference between income and other costs. But it is impossible for costs—rent and other —to exceed incomes over a long period of time. Should income remain small, the plant would be capitalized at a lower figure. Or if costs could not be reduced the factory would either quit business or transfer to a new line of production. In the long run, maximum rents cannot go above income.

**18. Rents Limited by Cost of Reproduction.**—Should one control the only thrashing-machine in an agricultural community, he could temporarily command a high rent for the use of it. But the neighbors, seeing this large rent, will begin the purchase of thrashers. This will push down the rents until they pay only a competitive return on the cost of a thrasher. Where goods are freely reproducible, rents will tend to a fair return on cost of reproduction.

19. **Differential Rent.**—One group of thinkers have taught that there would be no rent were all lands equally accessible and uniform in fertility. Let us examine this idea. No one claims that oxen are valuable because they differ in weight; in the same way, it would be in the highest degree absurd to claim that houses are valuable because some are better than others. Is land valuable because some is better than other? Certainly not. The price of land is derived from the price or price equivalent of its yield. Whether land is the same or different in quality is of no consequence in explaining why land yields rent. Differences in quality explain why some land yields more rent than other, just as differences in diamonds explain why some are worth more than others.

If the net yield of one field is 50 bushels, while that of another is 100 bushels, the tenant would pay twice the rent for the one that he pays for the other. Differences in land may serve as a measure of rent, may explain why one field rents higher than another. Differences in land do not explain the cause of rent. The "differential theory of rent" is a misnomer. A theory is the explanation of a fact. To explain why some rents are higher than others is vastly different from an explanation of the fact or existence of rent. It may well be that inferior lands are unused and valueless, while superior lands command a high rental; but this is nothing peculiar to land. The best apples may command a fancy price, while the knotty green ones are left to rot on the ground. But the best apples are not valuable because there are inferior ones, nor is superior land valuable because there are swamps and bleak summits beyond the margin of cultivation. Men rent land and the land is valuable, not because inferior land exists, but because of the scarcity and desirability of the services it renders.

20. **Differentials which measure** rent must be distinguished from the cause of rent. If the net yield of acre Number 1 is 100 bushels, while that of Number 2 is 50 bushels, the differential or difference in yield between these two acres of land is 50 bushels. Acre Number 1 will command a rental larger by the price equivalent of 50 bushels than will Number 2. This difference measures the difference in rent. But it is no theory or explanation of rent, because a theory of rent must explain why rent exists. It must answer the question why a rent or price is paid for the temporary productive services of a house, horse, machine, acre of land, or other productive agent. The differential idea is important, however, in the explanation of why some land or houses or horses rent higher than others.

*Business Sites:* A corner lot usually holds a differential advantage and commands a higher rent than an inside lot. The store on the corner is more accessible to customers because twice as many people pass by it. The accommodation of customers is a primary consideration in the location of a retail shop. This idea explains why country stores are located at the cross-roads, and why small shops go to the residential districts of cities.

In wholesaling the differential advantages depend mostly upon nearness of shipping facilities. Nearness to wharfs, side-tracks, and stations will command a high rent from the wholesaler.

*Residence:* Who are the neighbors? is the primary question in selecting a residence site. A few years ago in a particular section of a Southern city the houses were of excellent construction and commanded a high rental. Some undesirable families settled in that section, with the consequence that some of the residences are vacant, while others rent for a nominal sum. In another case a noteworthy citizen of this country secured control of the real estate in one section of a small city, and later on moved there. This attracted men of means to that neighborhood, and thereby largely increased his land rents. Other factors making for differential rents on residences are improvements such as water, gas, electricity, street-railway facilities, schools, and churches.

**21. Differences in Fertility.**—A colony settling in an uninhabited country finds more land than is needed. Because of its great supply land is a free good, no one has to pay a price for the use of it. The land being of various grades of fertility, the more productive grades will be occupied first, and with the increase of population the growing demand for food will bring less useful lands or less useful qualities of land under cultivation. Suppose that there are four grades of land. The best quality (Number 1) will be first cultivated, and the second grade (Number 2) will be used when the growing demand for food can no longer, except at a high cost, be supplied from the first. And the further growth of population will necessitate the cultivation of grades 3 and 4.

Assume, now, that the yield per acre of these four grades of land is 100, 90, 80, 70 bushels respectively, and, furthermore, that the cost per acre of cultivating the different grades of land and of getting their yield to the market is the same. With these assumptions in mind, the amount of rent can be accurately indicated. At first no rent would be paid because land is a free good. But when grade 2 comes under cultivation, the first grade will command a rent of the price equivalent of 10 bushels per acre. It will be immaterial to the farmer whether he cultivates grade 1 and pays a rent equivalent to 10 bushels per acre, or cultivates grade 2 free from rent. When grades 3 and 4 are cultivated, the rent per acre of grade 1 will be 30 bushels, of the second grade 20 bushels, and of the third grade 10 bushels.

**22. Differences in Costs.**—Let us now assume that the gross yield per acre of these four grades of land is the same, say 100 bushels. Number 1 may be well kept and ready for the plough; Number 2 requires a considerable outlay for fertilizer; Number 3 must be fertilized and cleared of rocks; Number 4 must be drained, hedged, fenced as well as fertilized and cleared of rocks. The gross yield is 100 bushels in every case, but should you be willing to pay as high a rent for Number 4 as for Number 1? Certainly not. Let us put the case in the form of figures.

Number 1 yields 100 bushels, less 70 for costs—rental, 30 bushels.

Number 2 yields 100 bushels, less 80 for costs—rental, 20 bushels.

Number 3 yields 100 bushels, less 90 for costs—rental, 10 bushels.

Number 4 yields 100 bushels, less 100 for costs—rental, o bushels. (See figure 2, page 395.)

**23. Differences in Location.**—We shall now assume that the four tracts of land each produces 100 to the acre, and that there are uniform costs of 50 bushels an acre for the cultivation of the different tracts. Let us further assume

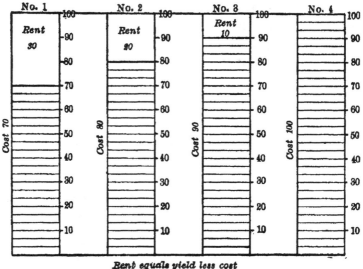

*Rent equals yield less cost*

FIGURE NO. 2

that all the products are marketed in Liverpool, that Number 1 is in the United States, Number 2 in Canada, Number 3 in Argentine, and Number 4 in Russia.

The Russian tract could pay no rent, because the cost of cultivation plus the cost of transportation (50 bushels) leaves no surplus. The Argentine tract could pay a rent of 10, the Canada tract 20, the United States tract 30.

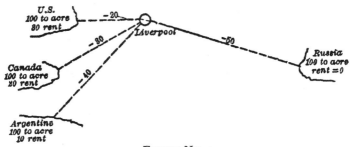

FIGURE NO. 3

As world markets develop, lands everywhere compete. Differences in location have the same effect on rents as have differences in the quality of land.

We may conclude from the above illustrations that the rent of a productive agent tends to equal the present worth of the net yield for the renting period of that agent (the net yield being the gross yield less all costs).

**24. The Owner's Income.**—We have seen that rent is contractual in nature, that the rent problem is a part of the general price problem, that rent is always a price paid by one person to another for the temporary uses of a rent-bearer. The owner of a rent-bearing agent has before him two alternatives: he may use the agent himself; he may let it to another for a rent. In either case he enjoys an income. The prices or price equivalents of all the anticipated incomes—contractual or other—discounted to their present worth give the present capital value of the agent. The term "usance-value" has been used to signify the return which the owner gets from operating his own agent. The term "economic rent" has been used in this same sense. It is well to have a definite term for this non-contractual return as well as to have the term rent for the contractual return. I have preferred at times to employ the more common terms—yield and income—to signify the non-contractual return.

**25. Exercises.**—1. Jones lets his house to Smith for $1,200 a year. Jones pays for up-keep $20, for taxes $200, puts in a new furnace costing $500, makes a plantation of shrubs on the lot costing $100, bores a well costing $300, grades the lawn, costing $80.

Does Jones get any rent? If so, show what outlays should be deducted from the $1,200 received in order to determine the rent.

2. Which of the following are rent-bearing agents: Loaf of bread, ham, plough, farm, dollar, lubricating-oil, house? Tell why in each case.

3. Generally speaking, would it be expedient to buy a house or to rent during a period of great building activity? Defend your answer.

4. During the World War there was little building in New York, but it was thought that there would be much building immediately following the war. Would it, generally speaking, have been better during the war to have signed a long lease or to have rented for a year at a time?

What other facts than those given must you have before answering the question just given?

5. "When the franchise was granted for a surface line the rent on dwellings along this street declined, but the rent for business houses increased." Why might this be true?

6. "The big stores on Fifth Avenue must sell at a high price because of their enormous rents. We are not so conveniently located, yet due to low rents we can sell at much lower prices." Criticise.

7. Does rent as a price paid by one person to another add anything to the wealth of society as a whole?

Does the income (usance or economic rent) which one gets from working his own land add anything to the wealth of the community?

Is it the owner who tills his own soil, or the owner who rents his soil, who suffers in case of floods, drought, pests, or low prices for the product?

Why can we not call both the contractual and the non-contractual incomes rents?

8. Short factors command large rents. Why?

9. What effect did the opening up of Western lands have upon the land rents in New England States? Why?

10. Suppose a new and inexpensive chemical should double the yield of any land upon which it might be used. What influence would this have upon land rents in general? Would any less land be used than at present?

11. Should American farmers cultivate their soil as intensively as do the Belgian farmers?

12. Why is the tendency toward diminishing money returns universal?

13. Rent is a deduction from the principle of resistance. Explain.

14. "Were a new process discovered that would double the products of all cultivated lands, rents would double." Why or why not?

15. Trace the sequence from rare land to high land rent.

16. Under perfect competition the total costs to the tenant of producing a bushel of corn is exactly the same whether he rents good land or poor land. Why?

17. Place the following in proper sequential order: Limited land area, increased demand for córn, larger production of corn, lower marginal land, higher price of corn, increased cost of production, increased land rent, increased price of corn land.

18. Should the landlords forego all land rents the price of corn would not be diminished. Is this true?

19. Why is the cost of production the same for any one tenant at the extensive margin as at the intensive margin?

20. Why is the average farm getting larger in the United States?

# CHAPTER XVIII

## POPULATION AND THE SUPPLY OF LABOR

1. **The Supply of Labor: Location.**—The problem of the supply of labor may be local, or national, or international in scope. Let us consider the local problem. We frequently speak of our cities as being overcrowded at the very time when crops in the Central West are going to waste for want of harvest hands. If wages are at a subsistence basis in New Orleans and at a premium in St. Louis, we may conclude that workmen are few in the one place and too numerous in the other. Where jobs hunt labor, workmen are scarce; where working men hunt jobs, labor is in oversupply. The problems suggested by these examples are local in scope.

*National:* For the purpose of our present illustration, Canada and Australia are considered different nations; in these nations and in America high wages prevail, for the population is scarce relative to the abounding resources. Contrast these with Sicily, where numbers are so dense that only a marvel of patient toil enables the people to live. In that country there is little machinery, for so low are wages that human toil is cheaper.

Imagine a Texas ranchman being compelled, as are the Swiss, to allow the cattle to stand in a stable while he cuts their food and brings it to them, lest they may trample down the precious grass. Translate a dense population into terms of human labor and again the Swiss are exemplary. "In the haying season," says Professor Fetter, "the harvester clings with one hand to the steep mountainside, cutting the grass by the handful and piling it in little bunches loaded down with stones to keep it from blowing away, until it can be carried down into the valley on the backs of men and women."

Differences in the density of populations in the several countries suggest many problems, among others: differences in per capita wealth and wages; unlike social conditions; migrations from overcrowded to less crowded countries. These are studies in the national supply of labor.

*International:* Prior to the occupation of the Americas and Australia the growth of population in England and Europe had, considering the stage of industrial arts at the time, begun to press upon the means of subsistence. Many observe the rapid multiplication of numbers in our time and predict an overpopulation for the whole world. The theory of population is a systematic study of the forces, positive and negative, which account for the number of people. As such it is primarily concerned with all men; it is international in scope.

**2. The Supply of Labor: Industrial.**—The supply of labor may also be studied from the standpoint of different industries. Because of the division of labor and specialization, the skilled artisan is limited to a single line of manual dexterity. This skill being the result of many years of application, the artisans of to-day are those who began their preparation years back, and the artisans of the not distant future will consist of those now in training. At any one time the supply of skilled labor depends, not upon the current demands, but upon previous lines of training.

This makes the choosing of a career a hazardous undertaking. The young man may see that plumbers and fitters are scarce and highly paid, whereas jewellers are plentiful and work for low wages. Influenced by this observation, he becomes a plumber rather than a jeweller; perhaps thousands of other young men have made the same observation and followed the same course. After the lapse of years, however, when these men have attained proficiency in plumbing, the demands in these two employments may have changed about. There may be a large demand and high reward for jewellers, for the reason that skilled men are few in the trade. The opposite of this condition may prevail in the plumbing business. The wisdom of a present choice depends upon future demand rather than upon relative present incomes.

The introduction of new inventions, the substitution of one thing for the use of another, and changes in demand, make it impossible to foresee the future and adjust labor. Where supplies are slow to meet a rapidly changing demand, there is always maladjustment. Labor is unlike other goods in the length of time required to provide it, consequently its adjustment to other things is most imperfect. One industry is blessed with an abundance of labor, another has little help and must limit the output, still another is forced to substitute inventions for labor in order to continue business, and so on throughout the industrial world.

3. **The Supply of Labor: Non-competing Groups.—** There is no line sharply distinguishing skilled from unskilled labor. But for the most part skilled labor is found in the more remunerative positions, and these are the positions where ability and long training count for most. Many bricklayers have neither ability nor skill and some hod-carriers have both, but the assumption is that men are adjusted to tasks proportionate to their aptitudes, and are classified accordingly.

It is well known that the wages of the skilled exceed those of the unskilled. But since common labor for the production of our every-day supplies is indispensable, why this difference in wages? As scarcity makes diamonds more precious than bread, so the relative shortage of supply explains the higher wage for the skilled. Reverse the case, and the higher reward would go to the unskilled. Could labor move freely from one grade to the other, wages would come to equality, as water, when unobstructed, attains a common level.

4. **J. E. Cairnes**[1] further divides the labor supply: "What we find, in effect, is not a whole population competing in-

_____
[1] *Some Leading Principles of Political Economy*, chap. III, pp. 66–67. Although the exact wording of Cairnes is here given, we use the quotation to serve a vastly different theory from the one Cairnes had in mind. He regarded the idea of non-competing groups as a rare exception to the "labor-theory of value"; we regard it as a particular case of the theory to be developed shortly, namely, the wages of labor are determined by the discounted marginal product of labor.

discriminately for all occupations, but a series of industrial layers, superposed on one another, within each of
which the various candidates for employment possess a
real and effective power of selection, while those occupying the several strata are, for all purposes of effective competition, practically isolated from each other. We may
perhaps venture to arrange them in some such order as this:

"*First*, at the bottom of the scale there would be the
large group of unskilled or nearly unskilled laborers, comprising agricultural laborers, laborers engaged in miscel-
laneous occupations in towns, or acting in attendance on
skilled labor.

"*Secondly*, there would be the artisan group, comprising
skilled laborers of the secondary order—carpenters, joiners,
smiths, masons, shoemakers, tailors, hatters, etc., with
whom might be included the very large class of small retail
dealers, whose means and position place them within the
reach of the same industrial opportunities as the class of
artisans.

"The *third* layer would contain producers and dealers of
a higher order, whose work would demand qualifications
only obtainable by persons of substantial means and fair
educational opportunities—for example, civil and mechanical engineers, chemists, opticians, watchmakers, and
others of the same industrial grade, in which might also
find a place the superior class of retail tradesmen; while
above these there would be a *fourth*, comprising persons
still more favorably circumstanced, whose ampler means
would give them a still wider choice. This last group
would contain members of the learned professions, as well
as persons engaged in the various careers of science and
art, and in the higher branches of mercantile business."

It goes without saying that no hard and fast line divides one class from another, and that there is much seepage constantly going on among them.

5. **The Supply of Labor, Peculiarities of.**—Large families are expensive rather than remunerative for parents. Salable live-stock is bred for the market, but there is no commercial motive in rearing children. There is some evidence of an exception to this statement on the early American frontier. There the cost of rearing a family was at a minimum; meanwhile wages were prohibitively high. The economist, F. Bowen, says that a motive in rearing children was to secure their labor.

*High Pay and Short Hours:* The supply of labor is not wholly a question of the number of workmen. The skill and dexterity of labor, together with its application, are important in reckoning the labor supply. One man that turns out two units of product a day supplies as much labor as do two men who each turn out one unit.

Especially among those whose standard of life is low, a higher wage causes less application. Irving Fisher's example of the basket-makers is at point: "In South America, for instance, traders from Europe were once buying native-made baskets of a peculiar kind. In order to increase the supply of baskets, which was far less than they could market in Europe, the traders decided to raise the price that they would offer to the makers, thinking to stimulate the production of baskets by inducing the men to work more hours. Exactly the opposite result followed. As soon as these workmen were offered high prices for the baskets, they worked fewer hours and made fewer baskets than before; they could now get more money even for doing less work, and they did not need or want more money. Their wants were so few and simple that the marginal desirability of money to them decreased very rapidly with an increased amount of it; and their disinclination to work was so great that, combined with the feeble desirability of its rewards to them, they would supply less of it when the rewards were great than when they were small. Similar instances have been cited among the Filipinos and among the negroes in the South. Recent experiments in coal-mines show that a slight increase in wages stimulates the men to work longer, but that a large increase (60 per cent beyond the ordinary wage) results in irregularity of work and the desire to reduce the number of hours."[1]

It is an accepted principle that a rise in price stimulates production and augments the supply of goods. If you would have an abundant crop of wheat, guarantee the owner a high price. In peculiar contrast to this general rule is the supply of common labor which decreases for the very reason that other supplies increase.

**6. Alfred Marshall,** the distinguished English economist, points out these peculiarities of the supply of labor: (1) The worker sells his work, but retains property in himself. (2) The seller of labor must deliver it himself. (3) Labor is perishable, and often sold under special disadvantages.

To comment on the third peculiarity first: The workman's labor is his source of income, and when he is unemployed the income lost cannot be recovered. Perishable in this sense does not conform to strictly accurate usage, for perishable implies liability to decay; a thing must have existence before it can decay, and labor does not exist where the worker is idle. If men lose time when idle, so

[1] Elementary Principles of Economics, chap. XVII, pp. 313–314.

does a machine, factory, or mine. Marshall did not do well in his choice of the term perishable. On the whole, the peculiarity is this: the seller of labor is commonly poor, cannot afford to dispense wholly with the wage-income, even temporarily. This puts him at a disadvantage in bargaining with his more wealthy employer. This very peculiarity has become a primary cause for the establishment of labor-unions with funds to support those who may be temporarily unemployed, and to give each member the distinct advantage of collective bargaining.

The second peculiarity is important, even though not always true. If you sell shoes your product may go far and near, but you do not present yourself where it is delivered. Your product may go to decorate the tiny foot of a winsome performer at the Winter Garden, or may serve in the sewer to protect the feet of the common laborer.

But the laborer must go with his labor. Whatever may be the temper of the employer and the character of the associates; whatever the nature of the pursuit, whether as a miner in the deepest shaft or as a painter upon the topmost pinnacle, whether as a flyer in the air or diver in the sea, whether the work is filthy or clean, unhealthful or healthful, whether dangerous as a TNT plant or safe as a pulpit—wheresoever labor goes, the worker must go.

The fact that the worker must go with his job is at the base of much legislation looking to safety appliances, sanitation, and moral improvement. The first peculiarity is significant, for he who rears and educates the laborer does not receive the price paid for his services. Producers of material goods may pocket the price paid for them. He who rears beasts of burden and builds factories or machines reaps the reward, whether these are retained for his own use or sold to another. The investor in private property takes the yield; the rearing of laborers is costly, but the yield goes to the one invested in rather than to the investor.

Through differences in the wealth and foresight of parents labor tends to be divided into two classes—the few who are well trained and the many who are without adequate preparation. The evil of this tendency is cumulative. Too often the poor are without vision for the future; their families are large and ill kept. These in turn beget large families, thus continuing a process which multiplies still further the number who are poor and inadequately trained. As a rule wealth belongs to those who appreciate more fully the importance of educating children. The few who inherit wealth and are educated by their parents in turn have few children. In this manner there is a tendency to maintain a comparatively small class of well-to-do and educated persons.

7. **The Order of Treatment.**—Certain peculiarities of the labor supply, together with its maldistribution among places and industries, have been pointed out. Because this subject matter sets forth in the beginning some of the more practical questions involved, it has been considered before the more theoretical aspects. The beginner should have an idea of what it is all about in order to appreciate the bearings of a theoretical discussion.

The student is well advanced toward a grasp of the population problem when he appreciates that it is a study in the proportionality of the number of people to the available productive resources. An ideal proportionality would have: (*a*) An adjustment of labor and resources proportionate to the requirements of the several lines of employment;

(*b*) a best adjustment of the population as a whole to the total social wealth. Any discussion of the density of numbers or of the labor supply is meaningless unless the number of people is considered in its relationship to the resources.

The fact that there are differences in the labor supply relative to resources throws much light upon the reason why there is such variance in rates of wages in different localities and in different industries. It explains the reason for intensive cultivation in old countries and extensive cultivation in the new. It furnishes the reason for the differences in per capita wealth in different countries. It accounts for the large tenant class in old countries where land is high. It is the chief cause of the migrations of people from one land to another. The proportionality of population to resources gives rise to many social problems. Birth-rates and death-rates, wars, pestilences, famines, etc., find their chief explanation in the numbers of people relative to the available resources.

We shall now turn from the distribution of numbers among trades and territories to the different views regarding the increase in the numbers of mankind.

**8. Population—a World Problem.**—When the tribes of old dwelt in isolated places it was possible for local famines to thin or destroy some tribes, while others, more fortunately located, enjoyed abundance. Then men were fed from the land upon which they dwelt; the want of transportation and trade imposed isolation and made of each community a self-sufficing world.

Transportation and trade, together with the dissemination of knowledge put an end to self-sufficiency. Want is not localized when, as Henry George would put it, "sheep killed in Australia are eaten fresh in England, and the order given by the London banker in the afternoon is executed in San Francisco in the morning of the same day." Were people forced to feed from the soil they occupy, a city, as London, would forthwith perish. But as individuals employed in their several tasks provide each the need of others, so, through the art of trade, localities and nations depend upon and serve one another. With money "I can even lay the fertility of both Indies and of the farthest corners of the earth under contribution to supply my personal wants." (F. Bowen.)

Transporting facilities will distribute not only products but also population; they carry people to the food as well as carry food to the people. If marked inequality arises between places, the localities in need will either import necessities from the lands having a surplus, or a portion of the people will emigrate. This tendency to equalize the conditions of men is world-wide, and it makes the population problem a world problem.

9. **Views of the Seventeenth and Eighteenth Centuries Favorable to the Increase of Numbers.**—Prior to the famous contribution of Malthus at the beginning of the last century, public opinion approved every increase of population. The Englishman, Joshua Gee, writing in 1729, said: "Numbers of people have always been esteemed the riches of a state." The first sentence in Goldsmith's Vicar of Wakefield reads: "I was ever of opinion that the honest man who married and brought up a large family did more service than he who continued single and only talked of population." In his justly famous essays of 1752 David Hume, after discoursing upon the unproductiveness of lawyers and physicians, declared the doctrine

that happiness and populousness are necessary attendants. William Pitt's speech of 1796 declared that those who rear children enrich their country; Samuel Whitebread replied to Pitt proposing a liberal premium for the encouragement of large families.[1]

10. **The Attitude in New Countries.**—In new and partially settled countries public opinion will give sanction to a rapid multiplication of numbers, for the vast potential power of idle resources only awaits the human hand. A golden situation without labor to exploit it makes a demand for population. As between the number of people and the supply of natural resources, maladjustments take two forms: in an old and overpopulated country, as Italy, labor is the long factor, while nature's bounty is the short factor; in a new country, as Canada, labor is the short factor and resources the long.

The first of these conditions gives rise to a pessimistic view which regards additional numbers as a cause of lower wages and a multiplication of mouths to be fed. The second type of maladjustment gives rise to an optimistic view which sees in additional numbers a cause of higher wages and a multiplication of hands to do work.

11. **The Limit to this Progress.**—A pioneer colony disembarking in America may be faced with the alternatives of starving to death or of making their return to the overpopulated land from which they came. Nature yields her bounties under resistance and where the human element is too feeble few provisions may be had. Let the numbers of people multiply into the thousands, and labor will acquire sufficient power partially to overcome this resistance.

[1] See Edwin Cannan's, Theories of Production and Distribution (second edition), 1903, pp. 124–125.

Let these numbers increase to a hundred million, and nature's resistance succumbs to the power of man. The feat of controlling the vast resources of America by the human will has made this the richest of all nations. The march of human progress is from the control of nature over man to the control of man over nature.

But this progress is not without limitation; its final limit is the point of best adjustment between the numbers of people and the amount of resources. Every increase in numbers up to this point means an increase of the average per capita income, and every increase of population beyond this point will decrease the average per capita income. Up to this point there is a demand for more people.

**12. Why Some Competitors Favor a Large Population.** —Competition is based upon self-interest, and it is to the interest of our entrepreneurs to produce goods at the least expense. If we would compete under favorable conditions with Europeans in the open markets we must produce equally as cheap. If the manufacturers of Great Britain produce cotton cloth at a lower cost than the American factories, we could not expect to undersell and capture their South American market for this product.

A primary cost in producing is the wages paid for labor, and it is to the employer's interest that this cost be lowered. Cheap labor is the entrepreneur's plea; his self-interest adapts him to the false view that a mass of half-paid workers would result in industrial advance and in national prosperity.

As is well known, this view of the entrepreneur has been most efficacious in maintaining the open-door policy of immigration in the United States. By precisely the same view they would welcome large families to augment the supply of cheap labor. It has been well said that, "foxes approve large families among rabbits."

**13. The Attitude in Different Forms of Government.—** Monarchies put first the augmentation of the power of rulers. "It is I who am the state," is the theory of an autocrat, and in obedience to that theory the land and its people are made subservient. In democracies the power resides in individuals who see to it that the welfare of persons comes to the fore. Self-interest is at liberty to exert itself in behalf of a better distribution of wealth. And the interest of first magnitude is per capita income rather than aggregate national wealth. Where the welfare of individuals is of first importance, self-interest operates against the pressure of over-numbers long before the senses revolt in disgust or pinch in hunger. In monarchies the self-interest of persons is subordinated to the power of the state. The ruling class is content to stand upon a substratum of general poverty if only a vast aggregate wealth is at its disposal. Rulers seek aggrandizement in the multiplication of the people, for their policy is imperialistic and their autocratic power seeks extension by the force of arms. Whence large armies but from the people? Hence the desire for a large population. The aggrandizement of a potentate is found in the multitudinous misery of his subjects, but the aggrandizement of the people is found in happy fewness where prevails the highest average in the ordering and furnishing of individual lives. The first scientific study of population was made by Thomas R. Malthus.

**14. Environment of Thomas Robert Malthus.—**Malthus was an unmarried English clergyman in a small country parish when, at the age of thirty-two, he published his first study (1798) on the population problem. At that time the people had begun to react against the extravagant desire for a large population. Reaction in France was intensified by the cynical selfishness with which the court and its adherents sacrificed the well-being of the people for the sake of their own luxury and military glory. The feeling became general that, whether an inordinate increase in numbers strengthened the state or not, it occasioned untold misery. It was insisted that the rulers of the state had no right to subordinate individual happiness to the aggrandizement of the state.

While Malthus was furthering his studies the social conditions of England, already gloomy, were becoming more unendurable. At that stage of industrial improvement, the population became so large as to strain seriously the productive facilities for support. An astonishing series of bad crops came at the very time when England was cut off from the markets of Europe from which she was accustomed to import quantities of grain. Meanwhile an exhausting war, a series of ruinous poor laws, the introduction of new inventions that threw artisans out of employment, were but aiding the evil forces of the time. The masses of England were reduced to the greatest misery recorded in the social history of that country.

While the seasons were such as to stunt the crops, the principle of resistance was in full force, still further limiting the yield of the intensively cultivated land. As if to add to the misery, the birth-rate seemed, without limit, to add to the overpeopled land. The price of wheat jumped from 37s. 1d. in 1790 to 83s. 11d. in 1810.

These were the conditions when Malthus, by nature a well-meaning pessimist, presented his theory of population, and that, too, with a darkness of prospect ending in evil, starvation, and death.

15. **The Malthusian theory** is, in brief, that population has a tendency to multiply faster than subsistence. The former perpetually outstrips the latter, with the consequence that everywhere arises the disease of overpopulation, with its accompaniments—poverty, starvation, and death. The author mentioned two checks to this tendency —"the preventive and the positive." The positive check kills after birth; the preventive check prevents birth.

Malthus, wishing to put a sharp edge on this argument, reduces it to a mathematical nicety. People understand figures better than abstract statements, and the notion that "figures won't lie" gives to the unreal an appearance of truth. His memorable formula shows the frightful rapidity with which population grows when allowed to progress unhindered, and the relative slowness in the growth of the means of subsistence. Population is shown to follow a geometrical series, doubling every twenty-five years, whereas the means of subsistence increase in arithmetical progression, each term also corresponding to a period of twenty-five years. Thus the increase:

| Population | 1 | 2 | 4 | 8 | 16 | 32 | 64 | 128 | 256 | 512 |
|---|---|---|---|---|---|---|---|---|---|---|
| Necessities | 1 | 2 | 3 | 4 | 5 | 6 | 7 | 8 | 9 | 10 |

In the table given the lapse of only 225 years is long enough for the population figure to grow to over 51 times the means of subsistence. Henry George has been patient enough to follow this geometrical series for 2,150 years. He goes to China for the solitary example of a family that has survived a great lapse of time. The descendants of Confucius still exist there, forming, in fact, the only hereditary aristocracy. According to the calculation the members of that family, 2,150 years after Confucius, should number 859,559,193,106,709,670,198,710,528 souls. Though the maxims of "the Most Holy Ancient Teacher" inculcate anything but the prudential check, yet there is a discrepancy between a Malthusian tendency and the actual figures for that family of only 22,000.

16. **The Persistence of the Doctrine.**—How brief is the history of America in point of time, yet its population has passed the 100,000,000 mark. The frontier is no more; the occupation of land free from charge has long since become history; already the superior resources are harnessed, and the ill effects of over-numbers is taking the form of diminishing real wages. Note the facts: In 1800 the population of this country was 5,000,000. Doubling four times (4 periods of 25 years each = 100) gives us a population of 80,000,000, which is actually the figure for 1905, only five years after the end of the century. Go to the lower East Side of New York, or to the impoverished sections of the great cities, and you see the buildings and streets teeming with pallid children who bear the marks of poverty. Contemplate an overcrowded land, as is Sicily, where "For days or months the peasants live on almost any sort of green thing they find in the fields, frequently eating it raw, just like cattle."

Do not these examples seem to support the dismal theory, to give some basis of fact for the tendency of population to outstrip the means of subsistence, and to show that the equilibrium of numbers with resources is brought about by misery, plague, and famine, which raise the death-rate to equality with the birth-rate? I simply put the question, deferring its answer, for the one purpose of this paragraph is to account for the persistency of this much-hackneyed doctrine.

I venture the belief, furthermore, that many put faith in Malthusianism for no other reason than the volume of criticism hurled against it, now for over a century. Is not the much-continued smoke an evidence of fire? The stinging sarcasm and unbridled abuse of half-baked scholars must disgust the thoughtful, for what argument is there in abuse? Derision has served to advertise the doctrine, and to make it famous rather than obscure.

Malthus, moreover, made his argument adaptable to a variety of views. All know that restraint there must be in some form, and if the misery-vice-death type of restraint is distasteful, you may be an equally devoted Malthusian by adhering to the moral or preventive type. Like Colonel Bryan's example of the stone fence in Nebraska, it is as tall as it is broad, and must therefore be as high after it is overthrown as before.

Many theories of population have contested for place and attention, but these have proved no more than flash-lights which for a time dazzle and blind us to the old doctrine to which sooner or later we are forced to return. But this we must bear in mind, that many modifying conditions have arisen which Malthus could not foresee. No one accepts the doctrine in unmodified form. Thoughtful students now confine their attention almost wholly to the preventive check as among advanced societies. Among backward peoples the positive check works in full force.

**17. Rates of Birth and Death.**—By the birth-rate we mean the number of births per 1,000 inhabitants per year. If the population of Blank City is 100,000 and the number of births there is 3,600 a year, the birth rate is 36 per 1,000. Statisticians sometimes speak of the refined birth-rate, meaning thereby the number of births a year per 1,000 women of child-bearing age, from fifteen to fifty. The greater the per cent of the population which are of child-bearing age, the greater, other things the same, will be the birth-rate. This explains why in some communities the birth-rate is so large among immigrants as compared with the native population. A large portion of the natives are either children or elderly persons, while the immigrants, especially the newly arrived, are wage-earners at a pro-creative period of life.

By the death-rate we mean the number of deaths per one thousand inhabitants per year. It is computed and expressed in the same manner as the birth-rate.

The difference between the birth-rate and the death-rate for any one year represents the rate of increase, or of de-crease, of population for that year. If the birth-rate is 36 per thousand, and the death-rate 16 per thousand, the increase of population is 20 per thousand, or 2 per cent.

The tendency of numbers to increase depends upon two things—propagation, preservation. Where the tendency to propagate is greatest, there may be, however, no increase in numbers. In backward societies record has been made of tribes in which it is normal that women forty years of age have given birth to twenty children. So low is the preservation of numbers, however. that the population is stationary in these tribes.

To preserve a child to manhood the parent must feel sufficient love for it to provide care and the necessities of life. Races have different tendencies to cherish and provide for their offspring. Premature death from disease, or want of parental care, or the niggardliness of nature to provide sufficient means, may tend as strongly to diminish population as does procreation to increase it. Inquiry into the nature and causes of increase must give equal regard to the forces preservative of population as to propagation.

18. **Malthus's Emphasis on the Positive Check.**—Since the writings of Darwin, who was influenced somewhat by Malthus, the thought of scholars has turned to the theory of development by natural selection or survival of the fittest. In consequence much has been read into Malthus that was not a part of his own thought.

At the time he received his education the laws of physical science and the methods of thought common to the exact sciences dominated thought and set the way of thinking for the social sciences.

His thought was on a material basis; the earth is limited in its power to supply physical means of subsistence, population can progress to the extent of this limit and there it must stop. By nature man's procreation is controlled, by nature the food supply is controlled, nature's consequence is through misery and vice to place a definite physical limitation which man cannot control and beyond which he cannot go. Consider Malthus's later work on political economy and this leaves no room for doubt; it shows beyond question that his thought was tuned to and ruled by the laws of exact science dealing with material things. Rent due to physical differences in soil and the natural law of diminishing returns; wages due to the procreative instincts and to the niggardliness of nature; interest fixed by the natural workings of self-interest—these were chief tenets of his. Malthus brought in enough of volitional control to save his doctrine from being characterized as predestination in its boldest form. The positive check was his main interest and the theory of his treatise was built around it.

**19. Progress from Pressure.**—Closely related to these checks is the dynamic influence which pressure seems to bring about. The poverty engendered by pressure acts as a powerful stimulus in the development of industry, science, and invention. It took the pressure of war to bring out numerous devices previously unknown, to perfect forms of organization and strategic moves with power to overcome the force of the enemy. Man must also invent, reorganize, and marshal anew his forces in his time-enduring contest with the niggardliness of nature.

Malthus, unwilling to give more credit than that of an arithmetical progression to human ingenuity, looked upon increasing numbers as deadening to progress. Were Malthus now alive he would doubtless admit that the experience of a century shows supplies to have outgrown the number of people. But, he would admonish us, experience is often a deceptive teacher; the past century must be regarded as a period of readjustment and of the occupation of new lands. The end of this period of prosperity is rapidly approaching.

**20. President Hadley's Statement.**[1]—"This pressure of population upon subsistence serves in no slight degree as a stimulus to improvement in the arts. It was this which forced hunting tribes to practise the domestication of animals. It was this which forced wandering pastoral tribes to settle down and apply themselves to the less exciting and agreeable arts of agriculture. It is this which has done much to accelerate the change from the military organization of society to the modern system of free labor. The attempt to provide for all children that might be born would, in the opinion of the Malthusian, not only prove

[1] *Economics*, pp. 45–46.

futile from the difficulty of finding food enough to go around, but it would also, first, take away the stimulus under which progress had been made; second, put a stop to the natural selection of the stronger individuals and families and reduce the race to a dead level; third, impair the capital of the community through increased consumption and diminished production so much that it could not maintain the stage of civilization which it had reached, and that its progress must give place to retrogression. The Malthusian therefore argues that society cannot undertake to relieve its members from the pressure and from the evils of poverty unless they will consent to adopt preventive checks to population."

21. **Doctrines Logically Following Malthusianism.**—Today there is no fear of universal misery, although our system of property may threaten the very existence of numerous families. But is it not the business of society to provide for its members? On the whole poverty is decreasing, and many who suffer want have but themselves to blame. None the less, the present system is criticised for falling short of its duty; when any man is willing to work, it is said, he should not be denied the privilege. Malthus made sharp criticism of this idea on the ground that society could not undertake to furnish employment, and that poverty grew out of the pressure of population upon the means of subsistence. He thought it no indictment against society that the struggle for existence should reduce some to poverty.

Would Malthus sanction the distribution of alms among the poor? The question of charity has always been a perplexing one; there are many who can produce large fortunes, but surprisingly few who can give wisely to charity.

Right or wrong, Malthus could have but one conclusion—to give charity adds to the evil of overpopulation. In criticism of an English poor law, he said: "Canute, when he commanded the waves not to wet his princely foot, did not in reality assume a greater power over the laws of nature." He thought that public charity, with particular reference to England's system of poorhouses, would encourage child-bearing. "The poor are themselves the cause of their own poverty," but if the state assumes the burden of this poverty there can be no limit to overpopulation short of reducing the whole people to the minimum of subsistence.

The population theory made a protectionist of Malthus. A system of international trade bringing into England an abundance of necessities only augments the ill effects of overnumbers. Let England limit her population in accordance with the provisioning of her own soil, he argues, and her difficulties will be less when international wars cut her off from the markets of the world.

This theory has stood in the way of social relief, has defended the capitalist, and shifted the responsibility for the maldistribution of wealth from human institutions to natural laws. To feed the hungry and clothe the naked is to run counter to the decree of Providence, for let the capitalist divide profits with the poor and no relief is given. Numbers multiply in proportion to charity given, only to press again upon the means of subsistence. Charity can only impoverish the giver, and it cannot aid the pauper; if it tends to equality, it is an equality of common misery.

22. **The Simplicity of Malthus's Basic Assumption.**—In many respects there is close similarity between the writings

of Malthus and Darwin. The struggle for existence is, said Darwin himself, Malthusianism applied to the whole animal and vegetable world. Despite the similarity of subject matter and lines of treatment, there was a vast difference in method between these famous scholars. Malthus reduced his problem to an unreal simplicity; he reasoned concerning man as he would concerning an Australian rabbit. He thought of either as having a few definitely fixed attributes unalterable by circumstances. Darwin's was a doctrine of adaptability. It was his thought that animals change characteristics in conformity with their environment, and that "reasoning man excels in adaptability." Briefly put, the view of Malthus was static, that of Darwin dynamic.

How did Malthus apply his simple notion of human nature to the question of marriage? He was willing for the rich to marry young, for in all respects his was a rich man's doctrine that made a public benefaction of the greed and self-interest of the upper class. But he admonished the poor to delay marriage, for he regarded early marriage and large families as convertible terms. His purpose was to shorten the procreative period of married life.

His characteristic error lay in the assumption that the procreative instincts of animals and men are essentially the same. He treated too lightly the moral and intellectual differences, but, most important, he virtually ignored the distinction between sexual and reproductive instincts. The two are in no wise similar and are governed by different motives. Gide well says: "Only to the first can be attributed that character of irresponsibility which he wrongly attributes to the second." They differ, indeed, as animal instincts differ from the social and religious.

23. **Private Property and Family Development.**—Private ownership tends to divide society into classes. This tendency calls for a restatement of certain outgrowths from private property. When a system of property arose to make men secure in their possession, the result was most beneficial yet an apparent violation of justice. It led to domination rather than extinction among successful fighters in an early age. If there were no right to hold in possession, conquerors would kill the conquered, whereas private property would preserve them as slaves. Security of tenure also stimulates the saving as well as the creation of wealth.

Private property divides families from one another as if they were in separate compartments. It places the house of have beside that of want, and enables Jones to rear his family in luxury while Smith, who lives within a stone's throw, must for want of means rear his family in indigence. There is no "keeping up with the Joneses" on the part of Smith, for the former has been more prudent than the latter. This individualizes the problem of overpopulation by bringing it within the discretion of each householder. It enables a progressive advance of the members of a family from generation to generation, and again it permits the poverty of a family to deepen from generation to generation.

But what of family progress were the burdens of poverty equally shared? In a social state the burdens of the improvident would drag all down to a common state of poverty. Private property then gives free play to the process of natural selection of the types most fit to survive.

"At this point, it is interesting to note one of the great economic paradoxes. They who call themselves socialists, and who might therefore be supposed to look at things from the standpoint of the group or the state, are the very people who are least inclined to do anything of the kind. To them the group or the state is only an agency through which individual rights and advantages are to be obtained. The kind of reasoning which necessarily follows from the conception of the group as an entity having interests more permanent and greater than those of individuals is peculiarly abhorrent to them. Such an idea as that the advantage should be given to the strong rather than the weak, in order that the herd, group, or state may become eventually a herd, group, or state of strong members, is diametrically opposed to all their ideals and ways of thinking." [1]

**24. The Influence of Freedom and Public Education.—** Common property implies a common burden, and whatever may be one's endeavor to act with prudence, he cannot emancipate himself from the burden of poverty caused by the imprudence of others. Private property tends rather to happy fewness; Jones is responsible both for the size of his family and for its provisioning. This gives motives, on the one hand, to have the family smaller, and, on the other, to produce wealth for its subsistence and to save wealth for its maintenance.

But men are imitative, and the craving to enjoy the status of the well-to-do affects the masses. In a state of private property and freedom, such as ours, this craving for the luxuries of the rich shows itself in an economy of off-spring. As Professor E. A. Ross says:[2] "The little stranger

---

[1] Thomas N. Carver, Essays in Social Justice, p. 321.

[2] Western Civilization and the Birth-Rate. Publications of the American Economic Association (3d series, vol. VIII, No. 1) Feb, 1907, pp. 80–81.

trenches on raiment, bric-a-brac, upholstery, travel, entertainment. Here the decencies, there the comforts, yonder the refinements and vanities of life compete with the possible child and bar it from existence." Our state knows no durable system of caste; "wide stairways are opened between the social levels, and men are exhorted to climb if they can." If children impede the climbers, prudence will take care that children are not born. From this I conclude that our free educational system is now a factor, and is destined to become a most powerful factor, in the prevention of families burdensomely large among the poor.

**25. Conclusion on the Limit of Numbers.**—The preventive and positive checks both operate, the latter among backward people and the former among the more cultured. In an advanced country, as France, where the population has been almost stationary for years, volitional control regulates numbers, whereas among the Eskimos, where "the girl is married in her teens and carries a baby on her back each summer," the population is stationary wholly because of the positive check.

We have found that in a state of free labor and private property the responsibilities of rearing children are individualized; they fall directly upon the parent and only indirectly upon society. We have found that with the spread of knowledge the reproductive instinct tends to divorce itself from the sexual instinct. These facts reduce the problem to its simplest form. Each parent, realizing the personal responsibility involved, and apart from sexual instinct, answers this question—how many children do I want?

Three considerations enter into his answer—his plane of living, his standard of living, and the devotion he would feel for the offspring. These influences vary from person to person.

The plane of living is his actual possession and enjoyment of goods—his actual level of subsistence and comfort. It is an objective fact. The standard of living is a subjective fact—a fact of thought, desire, and purpose.

If one's plane of living is above his standard of living, children are more likely to be welcomed. Children, too, are welcome if one is optimistic regarding the future of his plane of living. An intense love for children serves to cause a willingness to lower the plane below the standard of living.

In a larger sense the apportionment between the numbers of people and the productive resources must affect the individual planes and standards of living. If the average standard of living is low, the adjustment of numbers to resources will be fixed at a point where the plane of living will be low. The growth of numbers will be arrested where the proportionality between the numbers of people and the resources come into conformity with the standard of living. Numbers will increase as the standard of living is lowered, and *vice versa*.

I am aware that a full discussion of the supply of labor would carry us beyond a mere study of the increase of numbers; the strength, knowledge, inventiveness, and character of people bear upon the productive capacity of labor. Further than the slight consideration already given these important matters, however, the scope of this book will not permit us to go.

**26. Exercises.**—1. Real wages are higher in Europe than in China, and higher in the United States than in Europe.

Assume that you were asked to make an investigation to explain the differences between the real wages in these countries. What questions would you ask relative to the environment of labor in the different countries? What questions would you ask relative to the laborers themselves in the different countries? What questions would you ask relative to the political and economic institutions in the different countries?

2. During the World War doctors of medicine were so scarce that their services commanded a very high price, yet the supply of doctors could not be readily increased. Might there have been a similar situation with respect to painters? plumbers? ditch-diggers?

3. At a given time are artisans of equal skill paid the same wages in the different industries? Why or why not? Is the tendency in the long run for the wages of equally skilled artisans in different industries to be the same? Why or why not?

4. Point out some peculiarities relative to the supply of labor. (Paragraphs 5–6.)

5. How does the attitude in old countries relative to the increase in the population differ from that held in new countries? Explain the cause of this difference.

6. Write a brief account of the life of T. R. Malthus.

7. What was the Malthusian theory of population? Make an argument either for or against this theory.

8. What bearing does the institution of private property have upon the number of births?

9. With the spread of knowledge the reproductive instinct tends to divorce itself from the sexual instinct. One writer says that the effect of this truth is "a tendency toward the survival of the unfittest." What does he mean? Is he correct?

10. What is the limit to the number of rabbits in Australia? Do the same influences limit the number of people?

11. If the maximum human birth-rate were constantly maintained, what would be the effect on the average duration of life? (Fetter.)

12. The population of Blank City is ————. The number of births in that city each week is ————, thus the number of births a year is ————. So we say the birth-rate is ————. The number of deaths each week is ————, thus the number of deaths a year is ————. So we say the death-rate is ————. The birth-rate is $\frac{less}{larger}$ than the death-rate by ——— per cent. The annual $\frac{decrease}{increase}$ of the population of that city is ————. Fill in the blank spaces and cancel such words as may not be necessary.

13. "From the following and similar figures a German statistician formulated what is called 'Engel's law,' as to the proportion of the expenditures going for food."

PER CENT SPENT BY FAMILIES IN SAXONY

|  | Laboring | Middle Class | Well-to-do |
|---|---|---|---|
| Food........................... | 62 ⎫ | 55 ⎫ | 50 ⎫ |
| Clothing..................... | 16 ⎬ 95 | 18 ⎬ 90 | 18 ⎬ 85 |
| Shelter........................ | 12 ⎪ | 12 ⎪ | 12 ⎪ |
| Fire and light.............. | 5 ⎭ | 5 ⎭ | 5 ⎭ |
| Education.................... | 2 ⎫ | 3.5 ⎫ | 5.5 ⎫ |
| Public safety............... | 1 ⎬ 5 | 2. ⎬ 10 | 3. ⎬ 15 |
| Health........................ | 1 ⎪ | 2. ⎪ | 3. ⎪ |
| Labor......................... | 1 ⎭ | 2.5 ⎭ | 3.5 ⎭ |

How would you formulate the "law"?

# CHAPTER XIX

## LABOR AND MACHINERY

1. **Labor Defined.**—It seems waste space to define labor, for who does not know the meaning of this common term? Common terms are deceptive, however, and lead to difficulty when exposed to examination. "Much philosophy is wanted for the correct observation of things which are before our eyes." The actor, the musician, and the ball-player—do these labor or play? They both play and labor; enjoyable labor is play and remunerative play is labor.

Again, one may labor for another receiving a contract wage, or he may drive his own team, till his own soil, keep his own shop, thus laboring for himself for such income as he may acquire.

Furthermore, labor may take tangible form when the builder constructs a house, or the product may be intangible as the service of the physician or the lawyer.

What is more, disagreeable toil does not define labor. To pile stones, then to no purpose repile them, would be toil, to be sure, but we should classify the toiler in another category than that of laborer. Nor is pleasure the central

429

idea in the definition of labor. Because idleness is a disagreeable prick to the conscience, it is but natural to find pleasure in fruitful labor. There is pleasure without labor, however, in amusement and entertainment.

If neither pleasure nor pain can serve, may purpose serve as the central idea in labor? The farmer's purpose is good and the rogue's purpose is bad, and the fool's purpose is misdirected; no one finds fault with the dreamer's purpose, but is he laboring who squanders time and relentless toil in the hopeless task of securing a perpetual motion? Not as we believe.

Is reward a safe criterion by which to judge what is and what is not labor? The tourist climbs the mountain for pleasure and the guide for pay. The two perform the same act, but for different rewards; it is newly found joy for the one and monotonous toil for the other. Certainly the guide labors, but the tourist is a consumer spending money for enjoyment. Should one toil diligently for a dishonest paymaster there would be labor, but no reward. A turn in business may wipe out the fruits of long labor. On the contrary, fortune may favor the idle with unearned rewards. The nature of reward helps little in the definition of labor. These remarks suggest difficulty.

Labor is productive and is classified among productive agencies. Production we have found to be the creation of desirabilities and utilities. I shall define labor as *human effort, mental or physical, directed toward the creation of desirabilities and utilities.* This definition avoids the errors above criticised, and places labor in the category of productive agencies.

2. **Labor, Direct and Indirect.**—In the principles of cost-keeping the labor element of cost is divided into two classes.

All work done directly upon the product and recognizable as pertaining only to the operations upon it is called *direct labor*. But there is much facilitating work not directly applied to any particular product. Thus in factories the fireman, the engineer, the oiler, the crane men, errand boys, office help, etc., are employed in activities that are general and not specific, or the time that they are employed on any one job is so short that intelligent distribution of their labor is uncertain. Such is called *indirect labor*.

3. **The Demand for Labor.**—The total demand for labor, in a broad sense, consists of the available resources which would lie idle apart from human aid. It little matters how rich the mine, how fertile the soil, how luxurious the grass, how invigorating the climate, how abundant the coal, or plentiful the iron, or how manifold the resources of nature, human labor must co-operate before wealth is produced. If resources are more limited in Nevada than in Pennsylvania, the population will be smaller in the former because the demand for labor is larger in the latter. Labor is one of the necessary agents of production and where other such agents abound there labor is in demand.

Men hire labor for what it produces, as they borrow money for what it buys; the motive of the employer is in the product of the labor. If you demand a good, you indirectly employ labor, for the good is the product of labor.

Labor begets labor, because the product of one's labor is the means of employing more labor. When all produce for the market, each buys goods produced by another and pays for them, directly or indirectly, with his own products. A product for sale is a demand for another product, and hence a demand for labor. Every producer finds the most extensive vent for his wares in those places where most wealth is produced.

Could the laborer see that each additional product is equally as effective as is the employer's pocketbook in creating a demand for labor, he would once for all abandon the crude philosophy which teaches that a "limited output increases the demand for labor." The laborer is a merchant bargaining for the sale of his own service. Compare a merchant's opportunities in a rich town with those of the merchant in a community of indolence and apathy. Sales are few and at a small price when the customers have nothing to pay.

4. **Variety of Demand.**—The demand for labor is co-extensive with the demand for goods and services. When the market demand for goods is elastic, so also is the market demand for labor. For the labor that produces staples, whose volume of sale varies little with price movements, the condition of employment is comparatively steady. Labor is uncertain in tenure and wages fluctuate more when the sale of the product depends upon a varying demand. Labor is called upon to readjust itself when fashions change, when bicycles give way to automobiles, when temperance closes the distilleries and breweries, when war gives rise to munition-plants, when men go to fight and women go to work.

Fitting workmen into the industrial system and fitting the industrial system to workmen and these to a changing demand is a grave problem. Crises of unemployment arise, and with these agitators become the mouthpiece of the discontented; industrial strategy fails, thus putting the conservative to their wits' end, while revolutionary socialists take the stump in behalf of "justice and a decent wage."

When in war the enemy makes a surprise attack at one point, the need for additional troops is immediate, but it takes time to supply these from a distant field; the battle is lost because the supply is tardy and the need is quick. So also an abrupt industrial change makes a hasty demand for labor, but much time is required to marshal workers from accustomed employments and school them for the untried task. Some suffer privation and others reap gain; however, the misfortunes of the oppressed would rarely be, were labor adjustments concurrent with demand. The uneven pace of labor and demand gives rise to many problems, and not least among these is the uneven pace of wages and prices. Statistics bear out this reasoning; the tendency of wages is to follow prices, but a curve representing the rise of prices mounts more rapidly and declines more rapidly than does the curve representing the wages of labor.

5. The " Make-Work " Fallacy.—Idleness brings discontent to labor, for to deprive the workman of wages is to deny him the necessities of life, to bring humiliation upon himself and his family, to deaden his self-respect and prepare his mind for acts of crime, rapine, and violence. Rather than idle workmen with the consequent discontent, revolutionary socialism, and crime, the state should provide work at the public expense, even if this work creates no useful thing or renders no valuable service. It would be better artificially to screen the skies to "make work" for the candle-makers than to have these men walking the streets in idleness.

This is not an argument for a make-work policy; the point here is that of the two evils the make-work idea is less than that of idleness. The real fallacy in the "make-work " idea has never been so well expressed as by Frederic Bastiat. He brings out the point in his so-called—

**6. Broken-Pane Philosophy.**[1]—"Have you ever had occasion to witness the fury of the honest burgess, Jacques Bonhomme, when his scapegrace son has broken a pane of glass? If you have, you cannot fail to have observed that all the bystanders, were there thirty of them, lay their heads together to offer the unfortunate proprietor this never-failing consolation, that there is good in every misfortune, and that such accidents give a fillip to trade. Everybody must live. If no windows were broken, what would become of the glaziers? Now, this formula of condolence contains a theory which it is proper to lay hold of in this very simple case, because it is exactly the same theory which unfortunately governs the greater part of our economic institutions.

"Assuming that it becomes necessary to expend six francs in repairing the damage, if you mean to say that the accident brings in six francs to the glazier, and to that extent encourages his trade, I grant it fairly and frankly, and admit that you reason justly.

"The glazier arrives, does his work, pockets his money, rubs his hands, and blesses the scapegrace son. *That is what we see.*

"But if, by way of deduction, you come to conclude, as is too often done, that it is a good thing to break windows—that it makes money circulate—and that encouragement to trade in general is the result, I am obliged to cry, 'Halt!' Your theory stops at what we see, and takes no account of *what we don't see.*

"*We don't see* that since our burgess has been obliged

[1] Quoted by F. A. Walker. Political Economy, pp. 321–322.

to spend his six francs on one thing, he can no longer spend them on another.

"*We don't see* that if he had not this pane to replace he would have replaced, for example, his shoes, which are down at the heels, or have placed a new book on his shelf. In short, he would have employed his six francs in a way in which he cannot now employ them. Let us see, then, how the account stands with trade in general. The pane being broken, the glazier's trade is benefited to the extent of six francs. *That is what we see.*

"If the pane had not been broken, the shoemaker's or some other trade would have been encouraged to the extent of six francs. *That is what we don't see.* And if we take into account what we don't see, which is a negative fact, as well as what we do see, which is a positive fact, we shall discover that trade in general, or the aggregate of national industry, has no interest, one way or other, whether windows are broken or not.

"Let us see, again, how the account stands with Jacques Bonhomme. On the last hypothesis, that of the pane being broken, he spends six francs, and gets neither more nor less than he had before, namely, the use and enjoyment of a pane of glass. On the other hypothesis, namely, that the accident had not happened, he would have expended six francs on shoes, and would have had the enjoyment both of the shoes and of the pane of glass.

"Now as the good burgess, Jacques Bonhomme, constitutes a fraction of society at large, we are forced to conclude that society, taken in the aggregate, and after all accounts of labor and enjoyment have been squared, has lost the value of the pane which has been broken."

7. **"Good for the Trade."**—The make-work idea appears in many forms: "Blessed is that country where the rich are extravagant and the poor are economical. A rich spendthrift is a blessing and a rich miser is a curse; extravagance is a splendid form of charity. Let the rich spend; let them build; let them give work to their fellowmen." (R. G. Ingersoll.)

Miss Giulia Morosini, daughter of the Italian banker, is reported to have spent $250,000 a year on dress. "One thousand dollars," she said, "is a modest price to pay for a gown, and I have many that cost almost five thousand." She was "economical" in shoes, using only forty pairs a year at an average cost of $50 each, and so with gloves and handkerchiefs, which cost only $1,000 each a year. "For lingerie my bill last year amounted to $15,000. Stockings at $10 a pair and corsets at $50 I do not consider extravagant." Upon New York's far-famed speedway she drove her "spiked" team of three horses, which were valued at $30,000, while the superbly appointed "turnout" cost $5,000. How justify this rank extravagance? "It is all good for the trade," said she.[1] Miss Morosini, like Empress Eugénie, wore no pair of gloves more than once, and helped other industries by purchasing many silks and laces.

These extravagances are good for the trades in question. They make not a greater but a less demand for labor as a whole. The labor and capital used to meet these extravagant demands are withdrawn from the production of necessities. When necessities must compete with extravagances for labor and capital there will be fewer improved farms, fewer herds of cattle, fewer railroads, machine-shops, and

[1] *McCall's Magazine*, April, 1909.

factories. When a people turns its means from the building up of the state's productive capacity and to the arts of extravagant consumption, there will be fewer resources and a diminishing demand for labor.

**8. The "Lump-of-Labor" Fallacy.**—The lump-of-labor theory is based upon the assumption that there is a given amount of work to be done; if one group of laborers does this work other groups are unemployed, and if machinery does the work labor goes idle. Consider the girl at the typewriter. She, as the rest of us, desires limited competition and unlimited consumption, but her reasoning leads to gross errors. She argues: a limited number of girls are needed to do the typewriting; if wealthy girls do this work the injury is twofold—the poor are unemployed, and income is turned from those in need only to further add to the coffers of the rich. Thus the idleness of the rich is regarded as a benefit conferred upon the poor.

A professor, who should know better, argued against fellowships for graduate students on the ground that, "we are educating too many for the profession and thereby lowering our own salaries."

We are here taking the social-welfare point of view. It is not overlooked that the employment of additional laborers works individual hardships in numerous cases.

Even the economists of a century ago reasoned upon the assumption that "man's desires are limited by the narrow capacity of the human stomach." They must have been "lump-of-labor" theorists, for we produce only what we desire and if the desire is definitely fixed so also must be the work.

We now know that desires are dynamic, not fixed, that the more we feed them the more rapidly they multiply and grow. The greatest welfare exists where there is most to gratify our desires; then, on the whole, it is to the interest of laboring poor that the rich be productively employed. Were all idle, production would cease and starvation would result. Were half of our laborers to become idle, the result would be depopulation, misery, and returning barbarism. Every idle person, rich or poor, is a contribution to this miserable end. The poor girl should not condemn her rich competitor for her labor, because she in reality creates the means for paying herself. "She adds before she divides, deducts only as she adds, and competes only as she co-operates." The consumer only detracts, while the producer adds to the sum of goods divisible. There cannot be too much produced and our dread is of underproduction rather than overproduction.

If we desire more wealth we are forced to desire the employment of more productive effort. If we object to more labor coming into the field, we are forced to object to a further use of machinery. The poor girl who objects to the competition of the rich girl in typewriting is forced to object to the use of the typewriting-machine she employs.

9. **Questions Raised by the Introduction of Machinery.**— Patent laws are such that the machinery invented in one country may be used throughout the civilized world; Americans, therefore, do not use most machinery because our people are most inventive. Germany makes the most extensive use of many American inventions. Then why is machinery so extensively used in some countries and so little used in others? Differences in the wages of labor is the answer. It is cheaper to use machinery in America,

where wages are high, and cheaper to employ labor in China where wages are low.

If labor-saving machinery is used as a substitute for costly labor, does it not follow that machinery directly competes with and lowers the wages of labor? This has been a standing question since the beginning of the Industrial Revolution; it is a most important and fair question, deserving thoughtful reply. At one time the wage-earners answered this in the negative, and smashed machinery because they thought it robbed them of a living wage.

If we take the consumer's point of view, we at once favor machinery because it augments production, lowers prices, and enables our money to purchase more goods. But we are here taking the laborer's point of view who is interested to know the effect of machinery upon the demand for labor.

*Temporary effect :* The entrepreneur introduces machinery for two reasons—to increase and hasten his volume of output, to lower his cost of production. Within a short period of time the demand for any particular class of goods, say wire nails, will vary little. But a sudden introduction of machinery would enable the number of laborers who have been regularly employed in that business to oversupply the market. The first effect of this machinery will be the displacement of a portion of the labor.

Bearing witness to this fact are the uprisings in Asiatic Turkey since American machinery invaded those ancient lands in 1902. The Bible and ancient history make record of vast supplies of grain from those fertile lands in ages now remote. Through all these centuries grain had been reaped by hand and threshed by oxen driven around in a circle. The first reaper created a sensation, the greatest since Mohammed preached his new religion, and all but produced a state of riot among the Arabs, who declared that it left nothing for them to glean.

Will the entrepreneur turn off all but a sufficient number of working men to maintain the volume of output as it was prior to the installation of machinery? The answer must depend in part upon the nature of the product.

*The nature of the product :* If the product is one for which the demand is inelastic, the chances are that a considerable portion of the labor will not be retained. Should the commodity be one for which the demand is very elastic, the employer will retain the larger portion of his labor. By lowering the price he could dispose of a larger volume of output, and that at a handsome profit until other competitors entered the field.

If the entrepreneur enjoys a monopoly he will continue the employment of such a supply of labor as will fix the volume of output at the point of greatest net return. This, again, will depend upon the elasticity of demand. In competitive industries, where the cost per unit of output diminishes with the increasing size of the business, cutthroat competition is such as, in many cases, to actually increase the demand for labor. Within a century machinery increased the productive power of labor approximately one-hundredfold in the textile trade, yet the number of laborers increased in that industry because of the elasticity of the demand. In this case, as in the case of the monopolist, the volume of production is enlarged and labor retained in anticipation of an increased demand. Generally speaking, the temporary effect of machinery in a particular industry is to displace labor unless the product fills a very elastic demand.

*A misconception of the labor-saving machine :* Some critics attempt to prove that the introduction of machinery does not even temporarily lower the total demand for labor. Consider the manufacture of shoes; they say that while the new machine displaces a number of hand laborers it also takes a number of laborers to build the machine. As labor is reduced in making shoes, it is correspondingly increased in the production of machinery. But, let us ask these critics, in what sense may we speak of labor-saving machinery if machinery saves us no labor? There would certainly be no advantage in producing agricultural implements if the labor required to produce these were the equivalent of the labor they save the farmer.

*Long-time effects :* If we study particular industries rather than the whole field of labor, we find results varying with the nature of the product. It is but natural that over long periods of time the demand will increase for all the different kinds of goods. Even those staples which satisfy the primary needs will meet an increasing demand. Salt fills a most inelastic demand, yet, should the population double, the need for salt would be multiplied by two. Can we say, however, that, despite the development in the use of labor-saving machinery, the demand for labor will keep pace with the growing demand for products? Certainly not; it would be a contradiction in thought to answer this question affirmatively. In no sense, where labor-saving machinery is employed, will the demand for labor increase as rapidly as the increase in the production of and demand for goods.

*How machinery enlarges the demand for labor:* It is in a broader sense that the introduction of labor-saving machinery calls for an increase in the supply of labor. Im-

442 *Introduction to Economics*

proved means of production has a double effect: to illustrate, it makes shoes cheaper, thereby enabling the purchaser to increase his demand for other things, say gloves; it frees a certain amount of labor from the shoe business to go into other lines of business, say the glove business.

If the demand for a good is very elastic, the first effect of labor-saving machinery will be to cheapen the product; this will be followed by an increased demand. If the growth in demand is sufficient, it will actually increase the demand for labor, but never in proportion to the increasing volume of product. The railway-train has supplanted the stage-coach and has set many men to work where the old coach employed one, but the amount of traffic has increased more rapidly than has the number of railway employees. Thus, where the demand is elastic, the amount of labor in a single industry may be increased because of labor-saving improvements in that industry.

The usual effect of cheapening the products of one industry is to create a demand for the products of another industry. If a smaller portion of my wage goes to purchase the common necessities, I have more with which to demand the higher comforts and even the luxuries of life. This new demand gives rise to other industries, thereby making a new demand for labor.

10. **The Laborer's View-Point.**—The owner of large machinery must be a man of means, and when it was introduced into industry a sharp division was made between the capitalists and laborers. This division put an end to the companionship of the employer and his hired man. They no longer worked side by side at the same task, the worker quit living in his employer's home, quit eating at the same table and sharing the same fireside. They be-

came estranged. Their interests, in a narrow sense, grew antagonistic; the employer bought labor with the same merciless interest as he would buy raw materials, and the laborer's interest in his employer's welfare was nil. The one wanted to perform the least labor for the most pay; the other wanted to give the least pay for the most labor.

Readjustments cancel personal skill: The entrepreneur would reduce cost by introducing machinery, and consumers welcome machinery because its effect is to lower prices. It is easy enough for these to admonish the worker to be patient, to preach the ultimate good of machinery as a "long-run" benefit to labor and society in general. We must not be too hasty, however, to pronounce the worker an imbecile who objects to machinery. He lives in a state of merciless competition; he is forced to specialize in a trade; life is too short for the average man to master more than one trade; he lives from hand to mouth and his daily labor means his daily bread. His personal ruin and the poverty of his family result if machinery removes him from work.

Society sees labor as a whole and in the long run it regards the individual's misfortune as a mere incident of progress. The masses of men, among them the laborers, do not act upon the long-run motive. Moreover, what promise has the long run for one who is forced to starve now? If progress takes his job, the same progress should provide his support. The facts are that machinery has displaced many thrifty laborers and reduced them, with their families, to misery. When the burden falls solely upon those who are least prepared to bear it, there is little wonder that they remonstrate. If through patient toil they acquire skill in a trade, machinery cancels this skill; the burden is not less than if the state should cancel their rights of private property in the fruits of their labor.

**11. These Hardships on the Decline.**—At first thought one reasons that if the introduction of labor-saving machinery works hardship, this evil must grow with the expansion of the machine process. But this reasoning is in error. There is a vast difference between going from a hand process to a machine process, and that of going from one kind of machine to another. It was the old-time cobbler who was in serious difficulty when, for the first time, he raised his spectacles from the accustomed awl, peg, and last to behold the new innovation—a revolutionized industrial world replete with competing machinery. Students of the problem go back to the Industrial Revolution for their examples of the extreme hardships which machinery imposes. Certainly we find here and there such hardships in our time, but fortunately they are on the decline.

The majority of laborers now use machinery of some kind, and, since there are only a few principles of machinery, it follows that a thorough acquaintance with one machine makes it easy for the laborer to transfer to another and new type of machine. Consider, for instance, how general has become the use of the gas-engine, how varied the types of machines now run by it: the workman who learns to operate one such engine can with ease adapt himself to any one of a large number of positions. The same is true of the steam-engine, and it is likewise true of electric power.

**12. Machinery and Market Demands.**—The large productive plants of to-day require enormous quantities of fixed capital. The heavy machinery which is installed is built for a specialized type of production. The entrepreneur is anxious to keep this machinery fully employed, and it is to his interest to keep intact a large force of trained workmen. Then the first effect of large machinery is to secure the tenure and stabilize the conditions of workmen. As new transporting facilities develop, the market is extended. Industrial plants expand apace in size with the extension of the market; they come to produce no longer for a local market but for a world market, and no longer for the demand of the immediate future, but for the demand of the distant future. Thus in adjusting productive capacity to demand, large capital is sunk in more or less fixed forms.

Now contemplate the effect of a far-reaching change in demand. This fixed machinery must come to a standstill when the demand turns from its product, and, as for labor, it must either shift to produce for the newly created demand or go idle. A vast change in the market, therefore, finds fixed capital more helpless in making a shift than is the case with labor.

There is another thought which claims serious, if only brief, attention. No principle of demand is better established than this: the demand for comforts and luxuries fluctuates more than the demand for prime necessities. Considering the working population as a whole, investigators find that an effect of machinery is a relative decline in the number of workmen producing necessities, and that the relative proportion of those who produce comforts and luxuries is on the increase. The cumulative effect of machinery, therefore, is to subjugate labor more and more to the vicissitudes of demand.

13. **Machinery Improves the Laborer.**[1]—The handling of the old jack-plane used to cause heart-disease, and made

[1] Read Alfred Marshall's Principles of Economics, sixth edition, Book IV, chap. IX.

carpenters, as a rule, old men by the time they were forty. When Adam Smith wrote (1776), men overworked themselves, ruining their health and constitution in a few years. "A carpenter," said that famous author, "in London, and in some other places, is not supposed to last in his utmost vigor above eight years. Almost every class of artificers is subject to some particular infirmity occasioned by excessive application to their peculiar species of work."[1] Only a few years ago excessive muscular strain was the common lot of the majority of working men in England and elsewhere.

The effect of machinery is to relieve muscular strain and to perform tasks which are beyond human strength. In the making and handling of armor-plates, heavy munitions, and structural steel, man's muscles count for nothing. Machinery makes lighter the work of housekeepers, makes easier all types of manufacturing, and it displaces muscular strain in all the extractive industries.

Machinery also relieves the monotony of life. Mention has been made of the way in which the technical division of labor in modern industry narrows the scope of each person's work. In those trades where there is the most subdivision of work, the individual's task is most narrow; he exercises the same faculties and, without variance of motion, repeats the monotonous routine year in and year out. At first while he learns the simple movements he is required to use judgment in performing them, then he practises these until they become habitual. Thereafter is only the monotony of constant repetition. Such work depletes men both mentally and physically, for development is arrested apart from variety in thought and muscular activity.

[1] Quoted by Marshall, *Idem*, p. 262.

Fortunately, however, these monotonous and routine tasks are most sure to be taken over by inventions. As soon as the motion becomes constant and unvarying, the task of the inventor is simplified. Thus machinery both relieves the strain on human muscles and prevents the monotony of work from involving monotony of life.

**14. Exercises.**—1. A tourist and his guide climb a mountain—the one for pleasure, the other for pay. Is either or are both laboring? The workers on the tower of Babel, which was designed to reach into heaven, got pay. Did they labor? If so, was it productive labor?

2. In a building concern does a bricklayer perform direct or indirect labor? What of the bookkeeper?

3. "The more limited the output of each laborer, the greater will be the demand for additional laborers." Discuss.

4. How may individual and industrial hardships arise from the fact that labor adjustments are slow, whereas changes in the demands for the products of labor may be rapidly made?

5. Define and illustrate the "make-work fallacy." Assume that the 2,000,000 soldiers who return from France will either remain idle for twelve months or will be employed at a good wage in unproductive effort. Which would be better?

6. Would machinery increase or decrease the real wages of labor in a new country, say Australia? in an overcrowded country, say Sicily?

7. Prove this statement: It is to the interest of the laboring poor that the rich be productively employed. Prove this: It is to the interest of the poor that the rich spend their means in productive enterprises rather than for luxurious entertainments.

8. Criticise this: "My automobile is a necessary luxury."

9. What, generally speaking, is the difference between the temporary effects and the long-time effects of the introduction of machinery upon the demand for labor?

10. Would the conditions of labor in a single industry be affected more or less if the demand is very elastic for the products of that industry?

11. How did the introduction of large machinery change the relationship between the laborer and the employer?

12. The hardship which the introduction of machinery imposed upon labor was that of unemployment, but this hardship is on the decline even though more and more machinery is coming into use.   Why is this so?

# CHAPTER XX

## THE PRINCIPLES OF WAGES

1. Wages defined.  2. Problems suggested.  3. Wages differ from profits.
4. Real and money wages.  5. The wage-fund doctrine.  6. The wage
problem is forward-looking.  7. Effect of machinery upon wages.  8. Similarity of wages and rent.  9. The same principles for unlike agents.  10.
How relative rents are determined.  11. How relative wages are determined.  12. Thought and execution.  13. To illustrate.  14. The wage
system in proportionality.  15. The bargain theory.  16. The wage system.  17. Equal wages for equal tasks.  18. Wages equal the marginal
product of labor.  19. The time element.  20. Exercises.

1. **Wages Defined.**—A wage is a price; it is the price
paid by one person to another on account of labor performed.  The employer agrees to pay the workman so
much per piece or unit of output, or agrees to pay him a
sum certain per hour, day, week, or month.  The one payment is called a piece wage; it is payment for the amount
of work performed irrespective of the time expended.  If
the laborer is making bolts at a piece rate of 20 cents he
would receive $1 for an output of five, $6 for an output of
thirty, and so on.  The other method of payment is called
a time wage.  If the employee is paid $3 per day, his pay
would be neither more nor less, whether his output be five
or thirty bolts *per diem*.  All other wage systems, such as
profit-sharing or gain-sharing, are combinations of time
and piece wages.

2. **Problems Suggested.**—Where large numbers of workmen are employed and the personal relations between the
employer and workmen vanish, all laborers in a group
receive the same wage.  The most superior, even should

he exert himself to the utmost, receives the same time wage as the most inferior workman. The first effect is to kill the incentive of the superior workman. Another effect is that the better men, unwilling to accept a wage fixed by the inefficiency of the poorest, organize unions to force from the employer a compensation in keeping with their work.

*The records of day work as a guide in setting piece rates:* The piece wage, when first introduced, must be roughly adjusted to the time wage. For instance, the average worker is paid $3 a day and turns out, say, fifteen bolts in a normal day's work. The day wage would be the equivalent of a piece wage of 20 cents. Upon this basis the piece wage is fixed at 20 cents. Now in contrast with the day wage, which tends to deaden incentive, the piece wage stimulates workmen to the highest pitch. Instead of fifteen bolts the better men produce thirty or even forty, and raise their income from $3 to $6 or $8.

*Tendency to cut rates:* Our first thought turns in praise to the piece wage as better for all; better for the workmen, because it raises their wages and pays them according to their deserts; and better for the employer because it increases his volume of output in a given time, and that, too, with little addition to his overhead expenses. Numerous examples from experience, however, make us less cheerful. The employer sees, with unwilling eye, that his labor is paid an amount excessive as compared with the daily wage of the average workman. Either through cupidity, or because he really believes the worker receives more than his fair share of the product, the employer has "cut" and "recut" the piece wage to lower the earnings of labor. To take an example from the willowing of ostrich feathers: "When the trade started few knew how to willow, and 15 cents was paid for tying one set of knots (one inch). The following season more workers were in the field, and the price went down to 13 cents an inch. Then it dropped to 11 cents, 9 cents, 7 cents, 5 cents, and finally the workers received but 3 cents an inch."

If at the "cut" rate the workman attempts to increase his output to retain his income, the covetous desire of the employer sees a double advantage—less wages paid out, and more work turned in. Is all this to the encouragement of labor? Certainly not, for penalized effort is grudgingly given.

*The reaction of the laborer:* The first reaction of the laborer is to work less strenuously, for if wages are lowered with the increase of output, why not diminish the output and receive a larger wage per piece? His next reaction is to turn to organization as a means of securing by might what should be his by right. There are still other objections to the piece wage.

*Risk:* There is no risk in time wages as to the amount the laborer shall receive; let conditions vary as they will, his income is fixed by contract. The same is not true for those employed at a piece wage. Whatever the conditions, they receive in proportion to product. Unforeseen contingencies arise, machines break down, or raw materials fail to appear; in all such cases the loss falls upon the laborer.

*The disfavor of unions:* The piece wage puts each worker upon his own mettle, appeals to his self-interest or personal ambition, and breaks down the co-operative spirit upon which unions depend. The spirit aroused is that of competition, discord, and suspicion among workmen rather than the fraternal spirit of brotherly benevolence and good-will. It thus breaks the union's grip of the labor-supply and is, in consequence, condemned by the union.

*A cause of overexertion:* "Chips fly faster by job work than by day work." The "driving" or "speeding-up" process seems to characterize the system. Those who are in need, or who are ambitious to get ahead in the world, are anxious to produce to their maximum capacity. They sometimes overdo thus enfeebling their health and strength.

Despite these objections, the piece wage is the only feasible plan in many kinds of factory work. As the defects of the system become better known they are corrected; managers seek to obtain accurate knowledge before adjusting rates of pay and, if right-minded, aim to fix and maintain the pay at a fair and just rate.

3. **Wages Differ from Profits.**—Two men, the one a renter and the other employed, may do precisely the same thing, may hoe side by side in the same potato-patch, may perchance receive incomes exactly equivalent for their services, and yet the one's income is profits and that of the other is wages. Does it follow that wages and profits are essentially the same? They essentially differ.

The first undergoes all the risk; he pays rent for the land and wages for his help, and buys his seed, tools, fertilizer, and gives his own time. Between the plow and the potato-digger there is chance of frost, or devouring bugs, or drought, or excessive rain, and then there are market conditions after the crops to cause apprehension. He takes his chances with the trinity of weather, pests, and prices for such income as he may receive. The second runs no risk, but works for a definitely fixed contractual wage. There are other differences: unlike motives actuate these two men; the one shoulders the responsibility and the other is care-free; the actions of the one are self-willed, and the actions of the other are directed. To call one's own product a wage does not conform to business terminology.

The wage problem, encompassing, as it does, a multitude of troublesome questions, arises from the relationship between the hired man and his employer. He who works for himself never strikes, or boycotts, or pickets the business. He does not go to law for a higher wage or for shorter hours or for improved living conditions. For purposes of sound reasoning we must distinguish between these two types of income. Term them profit and wages, and you have a distinction conforming to business usage and to the theory of the case; you have cleared the ground for a discussion of the practical problems which are, in fact, contract-wage problems.

**4. Real and Money Wages.**—Money wages refer to the content of the pay-envelope, to the number of dollars the wage-earner receives. By real wages is meant not the number of dollars, but the amount of purchasing power received. Money wages may remain the same, while real wages vary because of price movements. Suppose one has received an annual salary of $2,000 for a period of five years, and that meanwhile prices have doubled. His money wage or salary has not changed, but his real wages have been reduced by half. In discussing the wage problem real wages are far more important than are money wages.

**5. The Wage-Fund Doctrine.**—Having defined wages, let us now turn to an examination of the influences which determine the amount of wages. The older British economists, as well as some American writers, have championed the crude and now abandoned Wage-Fund Doctrine. The doctrine is simple and lends itself to brief statement: At any one time there is a certain amount of funds, no more and no less, set aside with which to pay the wages of labor. J. S. Mill says: "This sum is not regarded as unalterable, for it is augmented by saving, and increases with the progress of wealth; but it is reasoned upon as, at any given moment, a predetermined amount." The Englishman, H. Fawcett, says: "The circulating capital of a country is its wage-fund. Hence, if we desire to calculate the average money wages received by each laborer, we have simply to divide the amount of this capital by the number of the laboring population."

Then, at any one time, there is a predetermined amount of funds that is going to be paid to labor. It is impossible for the laborers to receive one penny more or less. This fund is the dividend, and the number of laborers the divisor, and the quotient is the average wage. If the fund be 100,000 and the number of laborers 1,000, the average wage will be 100,000 ÷ 1,000 = 100.

Thus the learned economists of England left the problem. The scholars looked upon this as a simple arithmetical truism, not subject to criticism. It would be difficult to select a simple theory which has done so much to retard thought as this. My reasons for this statement are four: First, it is not a theory at all, for a theory is an explanation of a fact. It is a mere assertion that wages are paid out of accumulated funds, but so is interest, and rent, and the price of bread, cigars, and every other thing for which we pay. The reason we pay for a thing is not because we have money, but because of the services it will render.

Second, this superficial notion took the form of a truism; it glossed over and hid from view the real wage problem, thus removing it from discussion. Third, its effect was to favor capital and do gross injustice to labor. In case a group of laborers wished to strike or otherwise act to improve their income the capitalist, with the address of a moralist, and with the sanction of the economists, would object on the ground that the fund is fixed; therefore, if some get more others must get less. This doctrine made laborers dependent upon capitalists, and made capitalists the benefactors of the race. If laborers asked more, they were met with the admonition to sacrifice instead, for in this way only could the fund be maintained and their wages assured. Fourth, it made the rate of wages depend upon a fund accumulated from the past rather than upon that which labor produces.

**6. The Wage Problem is Forward-Looking.**—Men pay present wages out of accumulated capital, to be sure, but the willingness to hire labor and the amount paid for it depend upon the anticipated product of labor. The plowman's labor will later mature into a crop, the builder's labor into a house, and the manufacturer's labor into a finished good. The present wage is an advance price out of the expected future product.

We shall now see that machinery affects wages as it affects the product of labor.

**7. Effect of Machinery upon Wages.**—The effect of machinery as the effect of legislation, say the minimum wage, upon wages may be approached from two points of view; from the view-point of labor as a whole, or from the view-point of particular classes of labor. Roughly speaking, labor may be divided into two classes—those who are skilled, who use their brain in their work, and those who are unskilled, who use principally brawn in their work.

It goes without saying that the man of brawn cannot effectively compete with the "man of iron"; the machine wins in the contest of strength and speed. But only the unskilled go down, they only are outworked and underbid by the machine. The skilled and thoughtful workman, on the contrary, rises above the machine, takes advantage of its superior strength, and converts its productive capacity into an enlarged wage.

On the whole, whatever increases the productive power of labor will also increase the wages of labor. Wages, I mean real wages, will be increased in the form of a larger money income, as well as in the lowering of prices.

Assume two farms, one fertile and the other poor. The most expert labor can exact no more than a small yield from the latter. This small yield would certainly not justify the proprietor in a large wage expenditure for labor. Poor farm, poor help, and poor wage is the rule. Contrast with this the fertile farm which will respond to skilled labor with a bumper crop. Upon such land the cheapest help is the dearest, for the enhanced yield occasioned by superior labor will leave for the proprietor a larger surplus despite the higher wage. Whether skilled or unskilled, the proprietor of the rich soil can pay more for labor for no other reason than that it yields more.

As soil fertility adds to the productivity and, therefore, to the wages of labor, so also will machinery add to the productivity of labor, and in consequence to wages. Other things equal, wages are high in a rich country where natural resources abound; add machinery to this favorable environment and the labor of man becomes at once both lighter and more remunerative.

**8. Similarity of Wages and Rent.**—The distinguishing difference between rent and wages is this: rent pays for the temporary uses of wealth; wages pay for the temporary services of men. The agencies differ, but the prices (wages and rent) paid for the services of these agencies are determined in virtually the same way. The business man is actuated by precisely the same motive when he buys the services of wealth and the services of labor. These services are alike offered in the market for sale; they are alike priced according to the values attributed to them, and they are valued alike according to their yield. In discussing the rent problem we found rent to be a deduction from₁ the principle of resistance. Because of resistance the output of the rent bearer is limited; this limitation or scarcity gives rise to the value and price of the product. The value attributed to the product makes us willing to pay a rent for the use of it. This reasoning, without modification, applies to the wages paid for the scarce and valuable services of men.

**9. The Same Principles for Unlike Agents.**—All know that human beings differ from rent bearers, but this is not to say that their services differ in the economic sense. Muscular power differs from machine power or from the power of a waterfall only in degree, but the man thinks and the machine does not; men differ from other productive agents in a thousand ways. But differences among productive agencies do not imply that their products are governed by different economic laws.

Many economists have blundered at this point, and so serious was their blunder as to render their system of thought erroneous from one end to the other. For instance, land is unlike the agents produced by labor in a number of respects. Many economists, seeing this differ-

ence, jumped to the conclusion that the products of these unlike agents must therefore obey different economic laws, so
they went to work to patch up a rent theory for the land
agent, and an interest theory for artificial agents.  Do
different economic laws apply to cotton and wool?  Certainly not, yet there is little resemblance between a sheep
and land.  Similar, also, and obeying precisely the same
economic laws are the products of the ditch-digger and the
steam-shovel, yet the one is a man and the other a machine.
*Wages and rent obey the same economic laws despite the
differences in the agents producing them.*

10. **How Relative Rents Are Determined.**—While studying rent we found it to be a physical law that the short
factor limited the output, and that if long factors are
increased the product will not proportionately increase.
The entrepreneur seeks to add to his short factor because
it is most productive.  The important conclusion follows
that because of the higher productivity of the short factor
a higher rent is paid for the use of it.  In other words:
Short factors and high rent, long factors and low rent.

11. **How Relative Wages Are Determined.**—This reasoning applies with equal force in determining the wages
of labor.  A sledge-hammer cannot pound stone, neither
can a man; it takes the two combined in order that each
may liberate the productive powers in the other.  A
mighty man with a tack-hammer would make a puny
showing at crushing stone.  There should be a best physical adjustment between labor and other agents.  The
earnings of labor vary with the adjustment of factors,
wages being high or low as the adjustment is good or poor.

Of the different groups of laborers, some are oversupplied and some are undersupplied.  How the relative

supplies of labor affect the relative wages of labor may be shown by way of illustration. Philip D. Armour, the great packer, once showed a Chicago newspaperman about his office. It transpired that a comparatively young man sitting at a desk in the corner of the big room was drawing a salary of $18,000 a year. "But, Mr. Armour," said the newspaperman, "could you not hire nine men at $2,000 a year who could do more than he does?" "No," said the millionaire packer, "one hundred $2,000 men could not do the work he does." Joseph French Johnson relates this incident and adds "that men are paid, in the long run, in proportion to their power of production. The executive's salary seems exorbitant to the day-laborer, yet the pay of the executive and of the laborer is determined by the same law—executive ability is comparatively scarce, muscle is abundant; hence the one is dear and the other cheap."

12. **Thought and Execution.**—It has been observed many times, but none too many, that some men act before they think, while others think before they act; the invariable conclusion is that only the latter are worthy of their hire. Production is but the wise adjustment of things, and this means a thought or plan executed. The most ingenious plan is in itself of no avail, for it is productive only as it is executed. If it be idle no purpose is served, if it take a wrong course it works destruction, if it goes aright it effects production. The direction of productive agencies is in obedience to a plan, frequently ill devised perchance, none the less a plan. The productivity of an agent depends quite as much upon the plan directing it as upon its own powers, because it works poor or well and to purposes good or bad, depending upon the plan. Much de-

pends upon the plan; the dynamite works good in constructing a road-bed, evil in destroying a newspaper plant, together with the lives of men; poison works well in killing rats and ill in killing people; there is a world of difference whether a razor is used to sever a man's beard or his head.

The wise direction of productive agents is but the carrying through of a good plan with discretion. Entrepreneurs capable of so planning as to turn productive force to its greatest account, and managers with sufficient wisdom to direct forces most effectively in the execution of plans are regretfully scarce, and are the most valuable of men because they are the most productive.

13. **To illustrate:** Let us get at this thought in another way. Assume a situation in which raw materials, machinery, buildings, and other resources, both natural and produced, exist in great abundance, but in a state of poor adjustment. Within this situation there is an army of unskilled laborers. A few inefficient managers, among whom exist petty jealousies, causing them to work at cross-purposes, direct the different operations of production. Long hours and persistent toil enable all concerned to eke out a living.

To put it in figures, let us say that the sum total of all this productive power yields an annual output of $300,000. Assume now that a change comes over the chaotic situation, that an entrepreneur, capable of the most ingenious and far-seeing plans—such as a Carnegie or a Henry Ford —comes into control, and that an executor of plans or director with the rare ability of a Schwab is given the post of manager to make these plans effective in operation. As if by magic a happy change overcomes the situation, for order is brought out of chaos in obedience to the one plan devised by the new master.

In the new order the merits of men are quickly discerned and the most fit are shouldered with responsibility and promoted according to their worth. Weak managers are envious of the capable because they fear them and will deny any promotion that may give talent an opportunity to make itself known. Not only are the men assorted and set to tasks becoming their abilities, but also the machinery and all forms of industrial equipment are readjusted to facilitate one another as do the parts of a powerful engine. Antagonism gives way to co-operation, waste energy to efficiency, and decentralization to unified direction.

In addition to a well-ordered production an effectual agency takes over the distribution of the products. Patterns and quantities are offered upon the market as the seasons warrant and the caprices of the purchasers demand. Pushing now the sale of this, withholding that, determining to whom sales shall be made, at what prices, upon what terms, and a hundred other matters, vital to the life of a business, are under expert direction and control. The costs of doing business go down and incomes go up.

Let us now assume that the income mounts from $300,000 to $1,000,000. The entrepreneur and the manager, what are they worth to the situation? The answer is: $1,000,000—$300,000, or $700,000. In a competitive market ability, as potatoes or anything else, commands a price in keeping with its value, hence the high price for talented labor and the low price for common labor.

14. **The Wage System in Proportionality.**—The problem of determining wages is concerned with the laborer's part in the larger problem of the proportionality of all

productive factors. Different industries bid for these productive factors in the competitive market, and the prices paid, whether wages or rent, are based directly upon the worth of the services such agencies may render. Again the rule presents itself: short factor ►—► large output ►—► high pay; or long factor ►—► small output ►—► low pay.

**15. The Bargain Theory.**—Many are unaware that the productive power of labor is the determining factor in wages; they see merely the surface of the problem and regard human service only in the aspect of a thing salable going to the highest bidder. They take the so-called "bargain theory of wages" at full face value, believing, as they do, that the rate of wages is fixed by bargaining, and that every game of deceit or violence played by the laborer has the effect of enhancing his wage. No one denies the importance of organized bargaining power on the part of labor. Its importance is that the unscrupulous employer cannot take undue advantage of labor in scaling wages below their normal competitive rate. There is, however, an upper limit beyond which no skill at bargaining can raise wages—that is the productive power of labor. For one who produces hats the price of his product is fixed in the open market; he has different costs to meet, and the prices received for his hats less his costs (for machinery, rent, and raw materials) leaves a range more or less definitely bounded in which wages are fixed. The upper limit of this range is the upper limit of the bargaining power of labor.

**16. The wage system** means that the entrepreneurs, either directly or indirectly through their hired managers, buy the labor of other men at a competitive price. So common is this system that the economic organization is sometimes called "the wage system." The term is inapt, however, because it falls so far short of expressing the whole situation. Agriculture is our most important industry and only one-fourth of the work in that field is performed for wages outside the family. So also professional men as well as the proprietors of small shops in the business world devote themselves to their own undertakings.

17. **Equal Wages for Equal Tasks.**—Our study of market prices led to the fact that there cannot be different prices for the same commodity in the same market. This truth holds true respecting the wages of labor. The farmer must pay the same wage, whether his hired men work upon barren soil or in a fertile field.

Jones and Smith each owns a livery-stable, and these are located on opposite corners. The equipment of Jones's stable is a sorry assortment, and, in consequence, his trade is small. In Smith's stable are blooded horses and the best equipment and, in consequence, his trade proves highly remunerative. The work is such, assume it, that each of the owners must employ two men. It goes without saying that the two men in Smith's employ are in position to produce more than the other two. Should they strike for an additional dollar a day, the two from Jones's stable, being on the alert to improve their wage, if but slightly, will underbid and take the job. It is the competition among laborers in the same class which levels their wages to a uniform rate.

18. **Wages Equal the Marginal Product of Labor.**—It is the productivity of that portion of labor which is employed under the most unfavorable circumstances that determines the rate of wages received by a group of laborers.

During the haying-season farmers take full advantage

of promising weather. Suppose that a farmer has ten fields of grass, varying in quality from the most fertile field of timothy and clover to the poorest field of rag-weeds, thistle, and dock. The hay ripens, and upon a cloudless morning the farmer is early afield, with such help as is available, and mows the ten fields. All goes well and by the following afternoon the grass under the hot sunshine has come to perfect cure. Now storm clouds appear, threatening to ruin the crop with rain. He must "make hay while the sun shines," or lose all. Near by is the cross-roads store, the "loafer's joy" for the idle men of the community. In desperation he hastens thither for help. The ragamuffins cease their idle game of quoit to bargain with the farmer. What wage will be paid?

The farmer reasons, let us say, that there will be sufficient time for thirty men, an average of three to a field, to save the hay. But unfortunately he finds only twenty-four men available—enough to save only eight fields.

Suppose that he would be willing to pay $100 to have the hay in field number one saved, and $90 for the saving of number two, $80 for the third, and in order $70, $60, $50, $40, $30, $20, $10. Rather than no help the farmer would, if he had to, pay $100 for the services of the first three, but he is anxious to pay as little as he may. Rather than receive no pay, any three of the laborers, if need be, would work for $10, but they will take as much as may be had. There being but sufficient labor to save the first eight fields, and the eighth being worth $30, it follows that the farmer could not pay more than $30 for the marginal laborers. It was shown in the above paragraph that equal pay for equal tasks governs wages, therefore no three laborers can receive more than $30 or $10 each. The laborers, on their part, can force the employer to pay them as much as $10 each, for their services are worth that sum.

Applying the thought in this example to the whole field of labor or to any non-competing group, we shall find that there is more work to be done than there are workers to do it. Labor everywhere has scarcity and utility and can, therefore, command a wage. The wage, under competitive conditions, will be determined by the marginal productivity of labor.

**19. The Time Element.**—In most cases the product of labor does not mature at the time when the labor is expended and the wage paid. If the marginal product of labor will be worth $10 when it matures, say a year after the labor is expended, the present wage could be no more than the present worth of the product. The customary economic formula reads: *Wages are determined by the discounted marginal product of labor.*

**20. Exercises.**—1. Is there any difference between a wage and a rent, except that one is paid for the productive services of men and the other is paid for the services of productive agents other then men?

2. Would a superior workman prefer to dig coal under a time or piece wage? Should a manufacturer of shoes decide to change from a time to a piece wage, what would be used as a guide for setting the new piece wage? After this change, assume that the workmen increase the output, will the average employer increase the piece wage to further stimulate the output? Do unions favor the time or the piece wage? Why?

3. Is the time or piece wage best adapted for the following kinds of laborers: Farm-hands, stone-cutters, office boys, hat-factory hands, barbers, paper-hangers, railroad-brakemen?

4. "I pay my men a piece wage, so the loss is theirs—not mine—if their output is little." Criticise this statement, which was made by a prominent employer.

5. Distinguish between wages and profits.

6. To be sure, the wage-fund theory is unsound, but what of it? It is inoffensive and harmless. The harangue against it is of no more than mere academic interest. Prove this to be false. Prove that the effect of machinery is in the long run and in most cases to increase wages.

7. Why does skilled labor command higher wages than unskilled labor? Assume a condition under which the unskilled would get the higher wage.

8. Why is there equal pay for equal tasks under free competition?

9. Who is the marginal laborer?

10. Under the conditions set forth in paragraph 18 could the wage of a laborer be other than $10.

11. Prepare a written argument in proof of the last statement in this chapter; namely, "wages are determined by the discounted marginal product of labor."

12. A corporation has decided to vary its wage payments from week to week to conform with the variations of a set of index numbers; if the index numbers show the purchasing power of money to go up wages will be correspondingly cut, and vice versa. Would you predict any labor troubles for this company during a period of rising prices? during a period of declining prices?

# CHAPTER XXI

## CAPITAL

**1. Introduction.**—With the passing of time the economy of self-sufficiency is being more completely displaced by the division of labor and the extensive use of machinery. The newer economy is one of interdependence or an economy of exchange requiring evaluations in terms of money and trading by means of money. The definitions of capital are so numerous as to confuse and bewilder the reader, but the tendency is to regard capital as the present money worth of a person's right to valuable income. Upon one point there is agreement, namely, that interest is a per cent, and that it is the payment for capital. Interest is a per cent of what? You cannot speak of so much shelter as a certain per cent of a house, nor of a quart of milk as a fixed per cent of a cow. Before you may say that a certain return is five per cent of an agent, you must evaluate and reduce to their money equivalents both the return and the agent. Interest is a per cent of a value-sum which is expressed in terms of money.

Capital, then, is a value-sum expressed in terms of money. Capital looks to the future and not to the past; the capital value embodied in a machine is not determined by what the machine cost nor by what its output has been, but by the expected future returns from it.

Suppose that you ask a manufacturer why his product sells high. Would you be satisfied should he reply that it sells high because of high-priced labor, high-priced raw materials, high rents, and so on? This type of reply is well known to business men, and to their customers who encounter it so frequently. It is no explanation, however; it avoids explanation by shifting from the price of one thing back to that of another. The price of a good or the capital value of an agent is not explained by an appeal to the past nor by a shift to the price of something else.

Other considerations: Whether controlled by a monopoly or owned by competitors, whether produced by nature or by the labor of men, whether material as land or immaterial as a franchise—these are matters of no consequence in the definition of capital. Capital is a value concept, and, to give the following discussion a proper setting, I shall restate a portion of the reasoning on value.

2. **Marginal Desirability.**—We have seen that the relative values attributed to goods depend upon their relative marginal desirabilities. Desirability connotes the fitness of a good to gratify a desire, be that desire reasonable, ridiculous, or reprobatory. Take bread, for example, and the question of its desirability must refer to a particular unit of it relative to the desire of some individual. The desirability of bread in general is immeasurable, and the

idea is absurd because it serves no practical purpose. All ambiguities are banished when the thought is limited to the individual desirer and to a unit of the supply.

What is the desirability of shirts in general? No man knows or has need to care. J. F. Johnson asks, what is the desirability of a shirt to the poor man who has only one, and must lie in bed while his wife carefully launders it for him? This question puts the problem aright: it shows desirability to be a personal or individual matter; it enables us to express desirability which, in the case assumed, would be equal to the discomfort he would suffer should the wife ruin the precious garment upon the ironing-board. Assume now that this poor man is prospered through the death of his rich uncle, that he inherits thirty shirts, all of grade A and alike in every particular. What now is the desirability of a shirt? Upon the assumption that no one would care to buy one of these second-hand shirts, he would be little perturbed should a mishap upon the ironing-board ruin one. In other words, the shirts being the same in quality, we may say that his marginal desirability of shirts is negligible.

Marginal desirability as an explanation of value is *inseparable from scarcity*. The desirability of a unit depends upon the intensity of the individual's desire for it, and this intensity itself depends upon the number of units already possessed, for it is a law of physiology as well as of psychology that desires grow less as the amount possessed increases until satiety is reached. This (satiety) is the point zero where desirability ends and there is no value. The economic importance imputed to things (value) is based upon desirability, and desirability upon desire, and desire upon the limitation of supply.

The fitness of a good to minister to well-being is in itself no explanation of value, for if so, air and water would be our most valuable possessions. Nor will scarcity alone explain value, for if so, fortune would attend the catching of house-flies in the winter-time. Desirability combines these two qualities.

Heretofore, we have studied the forces which limit supplies of goods, likewise analysis has been made of the laws of demand. These are the ultimate forces back of the marginal desirabilities of goods. The principle of relative marginal desirabilities, as we have seen, has left in ruins the doctrine that when a trade is made one party gets cheated; it furnishes us the basis for a unified theory of value.

3. **The Labor-Cost Theory of Value.**—Note the contrast between the modern view, just expressed, and the old labor-cost theory of value. This latter theory erroneously teaches that the price or value[1] of a good is proportional to the amount of labor applied in its production or to the wages paid for that labor. If article A cost one day's labor and article B cost two days' labor, then, according to the old idea, the value of B is twice that of A. Value: value :: labor cost : labor cost. Were this theory sound, that is, if the relative values of articles are proportional to labor costs or wage outlays, it is a mere truism that only labor costs can enter into value. If you account for the price of wheat by the labor cost of producing it, you are forced to prove that other outlays, as rents, are in reality

---

[1] Value in the labor-cost theory meant the exchange power of a thing. In this book value is defined as the importance which an individual attributes to a good or service, be that good or service salable or not. Price in the broad sense covers the idea of exchange value.

not costs at all. So much for the theory which teaches that value is proportional to labor cost or to the wages paid for that labor.

**4. Criticisms.**—Certain embarrassing questions confront the advocates of this hackneyed theory: (1) One finds a precious stone worth $500; is its value determined by its labor cost? No, for it has no such cost. (2) A monopoly artificially raises the price of a good; how is labor cost responsible for the rise? The answer is, in no sense. (3) Does the value of money depend upon its labor cost? Even the labor-cost theorists answer in the negative. (4) Wine grows better and sells for a higher price when allowed to age for a number of years. A sprout worth fifty cents grows through time into a tree worth a hundred dollars. What has labor cost to do with the increase of prices caused by growth or improvement through time? Labor-cost advocates regard these as mere exceptions to what they call the "true theory." (5) How account for the value of labor itself? Another exception. (6) And does labor cost determine the value of land, minerals, and other natural products? Again, no. Is it not surprising that thoughtful men should teach a doctrine so monstrous?

**5. Productive Agents Classified.**—The entrepreneur knows that wages do not form his only cost of doing business. He must pay for materials and pay numerous hires, rents, and fees. He asks, if cost determines price, why include only wage costs and omit others of equal importance? In reply, the labor-cost doctrinaire is forced to make this artificial classification of productive agents:

(*a*) Land—so defined as to include all natural agents.

(*b*) Capital—so defined as to include all artificial agents created by labor.

(c) Labor—human effort, be it mental or physical.

**6. Interest as Wages of Past Labor.**—According to the above classification, which is based upon the labor-cost theory, capital consists of productive goods made by human labor. In other words, "capital is canned labor" —past labor having taken the form of present goods. Then, interest or payment for capital is payment for past labor. Both wages and interest are thus labor costs.

To this point capital has been made to consist of productive goods—of tools, instruments, machines, and so forth, created by labor and used to produce more wealth. "We have been told," says F. A. Fetter, "at one moment that rent was not measured by labor or due to it, but was a surplus gained without labor, and in the next we have seen the wealth that was paid over to the landlord as rent used by him as capital and defined as the product of labor." [1]

Just here trouble arises for the untenable theory, requiring a shift in thought. It is necessary to the argument to prove that the returns on capital are uniform, and that no surplus arises from it. To prove that the per cent of return is uniform for all capital, they must quit the idea of capital as tools and shift to the idea of capital as value. We have seen that competition tends to maintain uniformity of returns on capital; if 10 per cent is returned in the shoe business, and only 5 per cent in the hat business, capital will be shifted from the less to the more remunerative employment. Because capital is paid a uniform competitive return, it earns no surplus. No surplus going to capital, the labor-cost theorists tell us that all the interest on capital is a true labor cost.

[1] Proceedings of American Economic Association, December, 1900, p. 240.

**7. Rent in the Labor-Cost Theory.**—The entrepreneur spends money for labor, for agents created by labor, and for natural agents. But the theory tells us that cost determines value, and that the only cost is labor cost, therefore the money paid for the use of natural agents must be eliminated from cost. Call interest the wages of past labor, and wages the payment for present labor, but the payment for the use of natural agents cannot be called wages since labor did not create such agents. The labor-cost theorist defined rent as the payment for the use of land. He believed rent to be no part of cost, thought that it was a surplus over and above cost. If rent is not an element of cost, he tells us that it can have no bearing on value. How they attempt to demonstrate the proposition that rent is not a cost will now be shown.

If the different bushels of a supply of wheat are of uniform grade, they will sell for a uniform price in the market. Like bushels of wheat in a market at a given time will sell at the same price. But the cost of producing the different bushels is not the same. Some may be produced on superior soil and near the markets; some may be grown on inferior soil and distant from the market. Costs vary, but the price is uniform. Which cost is it that determines the price? The greatest cost—that portion of the supply which is produced at the greatest cost determines the price of every portion of the supply. But the greatest cost is upon the marginal land—the land barely worth cultivating. Such land is so inferior that no rent is paid for the use of it. Then if production at the greatest cost determines price, and if this greatest cost takes place where no rent is paid, it must follow that rent does not enter into the cost that determines value. This thought was cogently expressed by Ricardo: "Corn is not high because a rent is paid, but a rent is paid because corn is high."

**8. Bases of Criticism.**—The labor-cost theory of price, requiring, as it does, capital to be defined as "stored-up labor," has been on the defensive from the moment it was first penned. The theory of land rent, the artificial distinction between land and capital, and the false theory of distribution based upon this classification, compose the defense works of the labor-cost theory. The opposing forces, who classify land as capital, attack this doctrine (*a*) by pointing out exceptions to it, (*b*) by showing that all cultivated land pays a rent, thus making rent an element of cost, (*c*) by showing that there is no such marginal land as the theory assumes, (*d*) by showing that valuation as a price appraisal is affected by cost only as cost affects supply, and finally, (*e*) by ranking land, with all other privately owned sources of income, as capital.

**9. Only Valuable Land is Cultivated.**—Having already noted certain exceptions to the labor-cost theory, we shall now see that worthless land is not cultivated. A ton of coal from a worthless mine will sell for the same price as a ton of like quality from the most remunerative mine. But why does capital refuse to operate a mine where the costs of digging a ton are equal to or greater than the price of the ton when marketed? Any schoolboy can give the answer; capital seeks investment only where there is a promise of profit. The scrap-heap engine is valueless, except for junk, not because it could yield no more services, but because the cost of getting such services equals or outweighs their worth. Likewise, land is not cultivated when the cost of getting services from it is equal to or outweighs the worth of such services. Because such land affords no net yield, it is of no value. Only valuable land, land that renders net uses above cost, is cultivated.

The land, tools, seed and labor jointly produce a crop. In our economy it is unthinkable that a farmer would use valueless tools, valueless seed, and valueless land, because the result would be a valueless crop. There is no more judgment in using valueless land than in using valueless seed or tools. It is inconceivable that worthless land could produce a valuable crop, because land is valuable by virtue of its valuable yield.

The value of the crop reverts value to the agents, each and all, which produce it. It would appear a strange decision should the swift runner accredit all his speed to the right leg, denying just due to the left; and not less strange should we accredit all the lifting to two when it requires the combined effort of three men to raise a weight; and not less strange should we accredit the valuable crop to tools and men when it requires tools, men, and land to produce it. Proof of the value of land lies in the valuable product of which it is an essential factor of production. Any land which produces a valuable income must itself be valuable, but the purpose of competitive production is a valuable yield, therefore none other than valuable land is utilized. But the tenant cannot have valuable land gratuitously; he must pay a rent for the use of it. We now see that only valuable land is cultivated, and that such land commands a rent, consequently rent is a part of the cost of producing agricultural products. Because land rent is a part of cost, the pure labor-cost theory fails.

10. **A Productive Agent as a Composite of Different Single Factors.**—We have seen that a single agent is non-productive, and is valueless unless there are other factors

to combine with it. An axe cannot cut wood, neither can a man; it takes the two combined, for the mutual interaction of agents liberates each the productive power in the other. Arid land produces nothing, and is valueless unless water is in prospect. Turn a river into the barren area and the combination, land and water, becomes productive and valuable. Since neither factor alone could produce and because it requires mutual contact for each factor to liberate the productive capacity in the other, it follows that the productive agent is a compound agent made up by uniting a number of single factors. Does land make the water valuable? or does water make the land valuable? Each liberates the productive capacity in the other, but the two in one are valued.

11. **Any Factor Which Is an Integral Part of a Productive Agent is Valuable.**—Consider a rich agricultural State like Minnesota, with its many lakes and rivers. One asks, is not the water there which is used in production a free good? The water in the lakes or rivers is free, because it exists in such abundance as to render the short factor, land, incapable of liberating its productive capacity. Suppose now it were possible for the owner of a bonanza farm in the wheat belt of Minnesota to sell and remove separately the moisture from his farm. The water would not be free, but it would in fact require the total price of the farm to buy it. If one thinks of the air as a separate thing it is free, but, integrated with the chemical qualities of the soil, the farmer would not have it permanently removed, were this possible, for a price less than that of the farm. To harness a free agent and make it an integrated part of a composite productive agent is to make it, as part of the composite agent, valuable. A farm is more

than land; it is the combined productive qualities that grow a crop. Man wastes no effort to harness an agent which is without promise of a valuable return. The conclusion follows that, except for miscalculation and poor judgment, all cultivated land is valuable and, therefore, commands a rent. Let us give this thought a different statement.

**12. Valueless Land and Valueless Composite Agent.**— The writer has in mind an investment of $100,000 made by a Louisiana capitalist, in the fruitless attempt to convert a seemingly bottomless swamp into productive soil. The venture failed and the money was lost because there was no productivity in the situation to exploit. A composite agent is valueless when one of the essential factors is unproductive.

Suppose that this swamp had responded to good treatment, that the composite agent (the land, the capital expended and embodied in its improvement, together with the other essential factors) had produced an annual net yield of $10,000. This capitalized at 5 per cent would give a present worth of $200,000. This yield could not be subdivided, and the different portions of it attributed to the different factors in the composite agent. But why will a man farm except for a yield? And if yield there be, its value is reflected, without exclusion, to the factors which compose the integrated agent of production. The process of capitalization is such as to make all land under cultivation valuable and rent-bearing.

**13. Marginal Land.**—Another way of showing that rent is a part of the cost of production is by showing that there is no one land margin for all purposes. What is marginal land? It is land on the outer edge or fringe of cultivation

—beyond the margin it would be economically unproductive to go. Land may be marginal either because it is physically unproductive or because it is distant from the market. These are instances of the *extensive margin*. There is also an intensive margin. There is a limit beyond which it would not pay to make further expenditure even upon the most fertile acre, for, although more uses might be yielded, the extra cost entailed would outweigh the additional income. This point at which profits cease and loss begins is the *intensive margin*. The margin is, in pure theory, a boundary-line separating the land fit (valuable) for cultivation from the unfit (valueless). It is comparable to the line separating time into past and future. One's last breath is now in the past and his next breath belongs to the future; a mere line separates time past from time future. The above definitions have been given in another connection, but it is well to refresh the memory at this point.

Land suitable for the grazing of cattle may be physically inferior, and far distant from the market. The same cannot be said of land suitable for truck-farming. To express this differently, the extensive margin for truck-farming will be far within the margin for grazing purposes. Likewise marginal land for factory sites will usually be within the margin of land used for growing cotton. In other words, there are numerous land margins corresponding to the numerous uses for land.

Assume that land which is marginal for vegetable-gardening would yield $5 rent per acre if used for the growing of wheat. This $5 must be paid by the vegetable-gardener. It is part of his cost of production, although he is working land which is marginal for his purpose.

Now that land rent is seen to be a part of cost, the labor-cost theory of value will cease to bother us. So long as this theory survived, however, the labor-cost theorists had to classify land (natural agents) as distinct from capital. They could not speak of land as capital and then term interest the wages of past labor.

14. **Other Arguments.**—A classification of any consequence must be true to fact and serve a definite purpose. We have seen that the old classification failed in its purpose as a proof that labor is the only cost and sole source of value. I shall now examine the truth of the claims that land is unlike capital.[1] These claims may be briefly stated and refuted. *First claim:* Land is immovable; capital movable.

Portability is not a basis for distinguishing capital from land; if it is, an office-building must be reckoned as land. The only economic relevancy in the moving of things is this—by moving a thing from where it is less useful to where it is more useful, there is created place utility. Place utility is created by making things more accessible to the market. It is common knowledge that new or improved lines of transportation make land more accessible to the market.

*Second claim:* Land is a gift of nature; capital is a product of labor.

Improved land, as any finished good, is a joint product of man and nature. The question of origins is of interest for some purposes, but not for economic purposes.

*Third claim:* The supply of land is fixed; capital is increasable.

[1] Davenport's Economics of Enterprise, chap. **XI**, deserves careful study on this point.

Land as a productive agent is increased, in the economic sense, by whatever increases its productivity. The extension of transportation, the draining of swamps, irrigation, new methods of cultivation, extensive and intensive utilization—any means of getting more from land increases land as an economic factor. When one thinks of land as a fixed number of square miles, he is thinking in terms of geography—not economics. The economist measures productive agents in terms of their capacity or output, and not in terms of their weight, bulk, or area. There is much difference between the two words "supply" and "amount."

The economists who make the above classification tell us that the capacity of agents is measured in terms of the output of these agents. It is also said by them that all capital goods come from the land. Then, how can they say that a fixed capacity (or supply) turns out an ever-increasing yield? We may ultimately reach the final economic limit to the supply of land forces, but when that is reached we shall also have reached the final limit to the output of capital goods.

*Fourth claim:* Land obeys the law of diminishing returns; capital does not.

This, it should be said, is not now generally accepted by economists. Economists now know that should any productive agent cease to obey the law of diminishing returns, it would lose the element of scarcity and become a free good.

*Fifth claim:* Land yields a differential surplus; income from capital is uniform.

The thought is that the products of labor are reproducible. If a house costing $10,000 yields 10 per cent on the investment, others will build houses in the same vicinity, and will continue building until the return on capital is reduced to normal. On the contrary, it is stated that if one invests $10,000 in a tract of land, a new line of transportation or boom in building may increase the return to a large surplus above normal. Land is, according to the argument, non-reproducible, therefore the landlord may enjoy a durable surplus.

But should the income be increased to $1,000, or 10 per cent on the cost price, would the land still be worth only $10,000? Not so—its capitalization would increase; if the interest rate be 5 per cent, the capitalization would be doubled. There is no difference between the percentual returns on land and other durable sources of income.

Likewise, if one tract of land yields more than another, the difference is not a surplus gain, for the better tract will be capitalized higher than the inferior tract. The incomes on the two tracts will tend to equality of percentual incomes.

All durable agents being capitalized on the basis of anticipated yield, it follows that the present capital value of land or other agents is such as to allow no surplus except in case of a miscalculation.

15. **Land as Capital.**—Whenever a thing is valuable, there is a reason for attributing value to it; land as a productive factor is valuable for the same reason that other factors are valuable, namely, the command it gives the owner over prospective incomes. The estimated worth of its future incomes discounted to their present worth gives the capital value of land. Capital is one's control over incomes expressed in terms of money. The possession of land puts one in control of valuable incomes. Land ex-

pressed in terms of money is capital and it obeys all the laws of capital.

16. **Capital.**—Interest is a payment for the use of capital, and it pays for nothing else. Where interest is there must be a capital sum. But interest is always expressed as a per cent. A per cent of what? Of a certain sum expressed in terms of money. One cannot say that $100 is 5 per cent of a motor-truck, but if the motor-truck be capitalized or priced at $2,000, then $100 becomes 5 per cent of the capital sum. The return on a capitalized sum takes the form of interest.

The word *capital* is derived from the Latin *caput*, a head, a source. The classical Latin at times used the word *caput* for a sum of money put out to interest. We continue to speak of the principal of a money loan as capital. Borrowers in turn regarded capital as funds to invest. The idea was extended to include estimates in terms of capital, not only the sums borrowed and lent, but also the money worth of one's rights in goods.

17. **Capital Contrasted with Wealth.**—During the season of 1918 three gentlemen jointly produced 5,000 bushels of potatoes in Monmouth County, New Jersey. At the end of the season potatoes were selling at $1.50 a bushel, making their total output worth $7,500. The potatoes as such were wealth, and $7,500 the price of that wealth. Each of the three producers had thus a capital of $2,500. Had the price been 50 cents a bushel, the sum of wealth would still have been 5,000 bushels, but the capital of each would have been only $833.33. Had the price been $5 a bushel, due to scarcity of potatoes throughout the country, the sum of wealth controlled by these men would still be 5,000 bushels, but each would have a capital of $8,333.33. Wealth

and capital sometimes move in opposite directions—decreasing wealth may mean increasing capital, and *vice versa*. These men sold the crop to a merchant in London for $7,500, allowing him ninety days' time for payment. The merchant was in this country at the time, and tendered his note for the amount, payable at a New York bank. In transit the potatoes were sunk. The wealth thing (the potatoes) ceased to exist and with it the capital of the purchaser, but the capital of the sellers was not affected. The capital ($2,500) of each of these men ceased to be the money worth of his control over the wealth and became a claim against an individual.

**18. Acquisitive Powers Which Are Not Wealth.**—There is much capital which is not wealth at all.

*Good-will:* The words "Gold Dust" symbolize the good-will enjoyed by the Fairbanks Company for their washing powder of that name. A trade-mark is never more than a symbol for good-will, and it serves two purposes: It safeguards good-will as a source of profit, and enables purchasers on their part to identify the goods they desire. Good-will is established for a good when purchasers learn to like it and call for it in preference to other similar goods. So, also, is good-will established for a firm when, through tactful, prompt, and honest dealings a collective friendliness is created which insures future patronage. Good-will is valuable because, representing, as it does, both trade-getting and trade-holding, it is a cause of income. It is the largest asset of many a successful business man. But good-will does not take the form of lands, buildings, rolling-stock, clothing, food, or any other wealth—it is not wealth at all. It brings no more goods into society; it merely enbles individuals to acquire more income from others. Good-will is acquisitive, not productive in nature. As a source of valuable private income, however, it is capital.

*Franchise:* When a city votes a franchise to a company to operate a bus-line or street-railway, it creates no object of wealth. A franchise is a right of an individual or company to enjoy a privilege which is denied to others. It is capital but not wealth, nor does it, as such, produce wealth. All we can say is that it is a private acquisitive source of valuable income. It is capitalized, as is durable wealth, on the basis of its income, and is capital in the true sense of that word.

*Monopoly rights,* and other sources of mere acquisitive income, cannot be termed wealth. We should be counting twice to term them wealth. But as sources of valuable private income they must be classified as capital.

19. **Extension of the Capital Concept.**—During the Middle Ages land was not an object of purchase and sale; it was no more a marketable thing than are public highways or city parks to-day. The different forms of wealth in cities meanwhile were salable, and they were expressed, as are salable goods to-day, in terms of their money worth. Since land was not priced, or capitalized, the landlord could not speak of his returns as interest, for interest is a per cent of a capital sum. His returns were called rentals.

Due largely to differences in salability, town property came to be thought of in terms of its money worth, and was called capital, but there was no occasion for attaching a money price to land, and it was thought of as different from capital.

The past century has witnessed a vast extension of capitalistic enterprises, every form of natural resource has become readily salable by means of stocks and bonds. All wealth has become liquid and the money economy all-pervasive.

**20. Capital a Right to Income.**—The lender thinks of capital as the principal of a money loan; he parts with the money, however, when he loans it, and his capital is but the money worth of the right he holds against the borrower. The borrower looks upon capital as money invested, or to invest, but when once he has invested it his money is gone and his capital becomes the money worth of his expected incomes. A sale on credit is but another form of lending. The seller's capital takes the form of a right, bearing interest, against the purchaser. If paid at the time of sale the seller is in command of a capital fund to be invested.

Any form of durable wealth is such because of the income it promises. Wealth ownership is but a right to income. If its value is expressed in money this wealth becomes capital and the returns upon it are interest.

Unsalable forms of wealth, such as one's clothing, the food on his table, or his mother's picture, are not capital. Capital is always forward-looking, is a more or less durable source of private income. It may represent the present money worth of real productive agents, or of predatory sources of income. It is a summation of value rather than of welfare, and may reflect scarcity rather than abundance. Capital is the present worth, expressed in money, of a person's right to secure expected valuable incomes.

The next chapter will deal with the interest problem as an outgrowth of the capitalization of expected incomes.

**21. Exercises.**—1. Contrast the two theories of value presented at the beginning of this chapter.

2. Can you think of two exceptions to the labor-cost theory of value which are not mentioned in the fourth paragraph of this chapter?

3. Why was it necessary to classify productive agents as land, labor, and capital, in order to defend the labor-cost theory of value?

4. By what reasoning did the older economists make interest on capital a form of wages?

5. How did they rule rent out of the cost of production?

6. If none but valuable land is cultivated, does it follow that land rent is a cost in the production of agricultural products? Defend your answer.

7. It is argued that land differs from capital upon the grounds of (1) portability, (2) origin, (3) fixation of supply, (4) diminishing returns, (5) surplus returns. Criticise these as to their truth or error and as to their economic relevancy.

8. Contrast wealth and capital. Mention some acquisitive sources of private gain which are capital but not wealth.

9. What changes have brought about an extension of the capital concept? Define capital.

10. Criticise the following quotations from Economic Studies, by Walter Bagehot: (a) "When new capital comes into cotton-spinning, this means not only that new money is applied to paying cotton operatives, but also that new money is applied to buying new spinning-machines." (P. 48.)

Formulate a definition of capital from the use made of the word in this quotation.

(b) "Between a loaf of bread and a steam-engine, between a gimlet and a piece of bacon, there looks as if there were really nothing in common, except that man made both. But, though the contrast of externalities is so great, the two have a most essential common property, which is that which political economy fixes upon; the possible effect of both to augment human wealth. Laborers work because they want bread; their work goes farther if they have good tools, and therefore economists have a common word for both tools and bread. They are both capital and other similar things are, too." (P. 50.)

According to the quotation what is the "essential common property" of capital "which political economy fixes upon?"

Does land have this "common property"?

If "both tools and bread" are capital, can a distinction be made between capital and consumption goods?

From the thought in this quotation could you exclude good health from a definition of capital? What productive agents could you exclude?

(*c*) "Thus, for the present discussion, the acquired skill of a laborer is capital. . . . It is a productive thing made by man, as much as any tool; it is, in fact, an immaterial tool which the laborer uses just as he does a material one. It is co-operative capital as much as anything can be. And then, again, the most unlikely-looking and luxurious articles are capital if they reward and stimulate labor. Artisans like the best of rabbits, the best bits of meat, green peas, and gin; they work to get these; they would stay idle if they were not incited by these, and therefore these are capital." (P. 51.)

If "the acquired skill of a laborer is capital," would his other productive capacities or qualities—his muscle, reasoning faculties, willingness to work—be capital?

If capital be that which stimulates labor, is one's love for his wife and family to be termed capital?

Would this quotation make wages—the reward for labor—capital?

Would you judge from this quotation that capital is stimulus to work? or the reward for working? or the power to work? or a tool with which to work? or the things, as "green peas and gin," which work would create?

(*d*) Other quotations: "The rest is left in money, and this we call the saving, the new capital." (P. 171.) "Capital obtained by abstinence." (P. 169.) "You can say

that the capitalist must be in possession—of certain arti-
les possessing exchangeable value." (P. 185.)

Are the words *saving* and *abstinence* synonyms?

Judging from these quotations, what things are to be
included in capital?

(e) A good definition contains one and only one fundamental idea. Can you formulate a good definition of
capital which embodies all that Bagehot has said?

Would such a definition make capital tangible or intangible? productive or merely acquisitive? external to man
or a quality of man? In so far as money fits into the definition would it be money invested? or money saved? or
money to be acquired?

# CHAPTER XXII

## INTEREST

**1. The Productivity Theory.**—Ask the common man, "What determines the rate of interest?" He will consider this a simple common-sense question and give, with an air of confidence, one or the other of the following replies: "The rate of the productivity of capital determines interest," or "The rate of interest is determined by the supply of loanable money on the market." These replies, however, are false; they represent two of the most persistent fallacies in economics.

One observes that the rate of return on different types of business tends to be about the same. A $50,000 store, or mill, or farm, or mine will return a net yield of $2,500. He reasons from the capital value of the agent to the money worth of the product, and concludes that the rate of interest is proportionate to the productivity of capital.

**2. The Interest Rate Unaffected by Variation in Production.**—Does the capital value of a farm determine the price of the crop, or is it the price of the crop that determines the capital value of the farm? Can you sell your

489

crop for $1,000 because your farm is worth $20,000, or is your farm worth $20,000 because you can sell the annual crop for $1,000? The order of thought must be the reverse of that assumed by the productivity theorist. The farm produces crops, but the capital value of the farm does not determine the price of the crop; it is the price of the crop that determines the capital value of the farm.

Assume now that because of the discovery of a new process the annual crop of the farm is increased from $2,500 to $5,000. Does it follow that the rate of interest is doubled, that it has increased from 5 to 10 per cent? The answer is, the rate of interest has been neither increased nor diminished. The capital value of the farm, however, has been doubled.

It is the capital value of the agent and not the rate of interest which is affected by a change in the productivity of agents.

3. **Unproductive Loans.**—Furthermore, a vast amount of capital is borrowed at interest for purposes of consumption. This capital produces nothing other than immediate gratification for the consumer. Should we assume that all entrepreneurs owned their productive agencies, and that no capital is borrowed for productive enterprise, still we should find that much capital would be borrowed at interest for pure consumptive purposes. Here the borrower's motive for paying interest cannot be the yield of such capital. The productivity theory fails both for loans to be used productively and to be used for the immediate gratification of desires.

4. **The Money Fallacy.**—The other fallacy, above mentioned, is that if money is plentiful interest will be low, and *vice versa*. Interest, it is said, is but the price of money. As the price of potatoes is low when the crop is

abundant, so the price for the use of money will be low when it is plentiful. The faulty notion that the rate of interest is lowered by a large issue of paper notes has a strong hold on the public mind.

Why do men borrow money? They borrow in order that they may purchase goods—tools of production, food, land, clothing, and other. The farmer borrows money with which to stock his farm. The mere issue of money will not increase goods. Double the money and you do not double the construction of railways and machine-shops, nor do you multiply by two the number of horses, swine, and cattle.

Goods remain the same while the money doubles, with the result that, other things equal, it requires two dollars to do the money-work formerly done by one. Prices double, and the borrower must demand $200, whereas he would have borrowed $100 before the increase in the quantity of money.

Because prices, other things being equal, vary with the quantity of money, the demand for money varies with the quantity of it. Other things the same, the demand for money will double when the quantity of it is doubled, and *vice versa*. Interest is the price paid for a money loan, and, like any other price, it marks the point of equilibrium between supply and demand.

Professor Irving Fisher says that "an examination of the figures for per capita circulation of money in the United States for thirty-five years shows that in about half of the cases, when money grows more abundant, interest is higher, and in half of the cases it is lower. In other words, interest changes with absolutely no relation to the quantity of money in circulation." [1]

[1] Elementary Principles of Economics, p. 359.

**5. Variation of Bank Interest.**—The operations of banks lead many to believe that an abundance of money makes interest low; they observe that when the banks have surplus funds they lower the rate in order to attract borrowers. It is true that the banker's prosperity consists in keeping his funds active; it is as much against his interest to have idle money as it is detrimental to the merchant to have an idle stock of goods.

He is compelled by law and custom to maintain certain reserves. When his reserves are far above requirements, he artificially lowers the rate in order to put his idle money to work. When his reserves are low, he must protect them, and the way to do this is to raise the rate high enough to discourage borrowers. Thus the bank rate is artificially varied with respect to reserves, and it is not necessarily in keeping with the true rate of interest prevailing in industry.

When a considerable portion of the money in the community flows into the banks, the banker will lower his rate; but when a relatively larger share goes into the tills and pockets of the people, the bank will raise its rate.

**6. Gross Interest and Net Interest.**—It is advisable to keep in mind the distinction between net or true interest and gross interest. It is well known that the merchant who sells on time has many bad debts and difficulties of collection which are burdensome and costly. His risk is covered in part by charging a higher price; the honest who punctually pay their debts are made to pay a higher price because of the shortcomings of others. In the same manner, when money is loaned to promote an uncertain enterprise or hazardous undertaking, or if the borrower is doubtful, the charge exacted for the loan will be raised to a point at which it will be a compensation for the amount of risk. The ordinary rate of interest on safe securities will not attract capital to an employment known to be uncertain in its returns, or exposed to dangerous accidents. The manufacture of explosives, shipping projects when enemy submarines are threatening, mining operations of uncertain types, are compelled to pay the true interest for their capital and an additional amount to cover risk. Thus gross interest covers both net interest and insurance.

Furthermore, the gross interest is high on petty, short-time loans. If one has $20,000 to loan, he has little difficulty of bookkeeping and labor if he places it out on a safe first mortgage to one person for a number of years. But if he loans to a thousand or more persons, in small sums for varying periods of time, he has much clerical worry and extra cost. To cover this cost he must require a rate higher than that prevailing on safe long-time loans. Gross interest then covers three payments—net interest, insurance for risk, and cost of doing business.

7. **Time-Discount.**—In order to set a number of principles in their true relationship, the example of the evaluation of a farm may be given. The order of thought runs: Farm ➡ crop (usance) ➡ value of crops (value of usance) ➡ rents ➡ time-discount ➡ present capital value of the farm.

The farm and crops form the physical basis for the value problem. Then arises the rent problem, which is concerned with the valuation of usances as they arise, and the payment of rent by one person to another for the temporary uses of the productive agent. Following and closely akin to the rent problem comes the principle of time-discount, which has to do with finding the present worth of a series of future rents or usance values. The present monetary worth of the sum of the future rents of an agent is, of course, the capitalized value of the agent.

It is clear that agents are valuable because they produce a valuable yield, but if the capital value of an agent is determined by its future yields, how shall we account for the limited capital value of a durable agent?

Let us consider an acre of land whose net annual yield is $10. So far as we know, it will continue this yield through time. Why is it not worth ∞, an incalculable sum? Why does it have a limited capital value of $200? Time-discount is the answer. Were there no time-discount, there would be no limit to its capital value. Why will the borrower exchange $106 a year hence for the possession of $100 now? Time-discount. Time-discount is involved in the valuation of every agent which lasts beyond the present.

In the capitalization of any durable agent three ideas must be kept in mind; the value of the usance (yield), the distribution of usances (yields) through time, and time-discount.

**8. Illustration.**

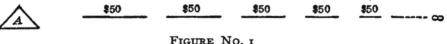

FIGURE No. 1

Let ⟨A⟩ represent a productive agent, and the length the lines to the right will represent the present worth of of succeeding annual incomes. It will be observed that each income when it arises is worth $50, but that the present value of each grows less and less as it is postponed farther and farther through time. The total length of all these lines, representing as they do the present worth of each successive income, is equal to the present worth of the agent.[1]

9. **Time-Discount in Capitalization.**—Capitalization is the process of determining the present money worth of durable sources of valuable incomes. Time-discount neither precedes nor follows this process; it is itself the essence of the process.

High time-discount means a low capitalization, and *vice versa*. This must be so, for the present capital value is but the summation of the present worth of all the anticipated incomes. If one highly discounts a future income, its present worth must be small, and the total present worth of all incomes must be low when all are highly discounted.

Time-discount enables us to compare the value of present consumable goods with that of future goods; it gives the basis for exchanging present ripe goods for the durable agents of production. Exchange or trade is based upon the present worth of goods. The economic world centres in the present. Present ripe goods and services may be compared and exchanged against each other without time-discount, but every valuation and exchange involving durable or future goods would be impossible without time-discount.

In the language of Professor Fetter, "Whenever two

---

[1] To give a formula: Suppose a rent-bearer yield equal annual rentals (*a*) in perpetuity, and the rate of time-discount, *r*, then the value of the agent, or its present worth, P, might be expressed by the geometrical infinite series:

$$P = \frac{a}{1 + r} + \frac{a}{(1 + r)^2} + \frac{a}{(1 + r)^3} + \frac{a}{(1 + r)^4} + \text{etc. to } \infty$$

Taken from Fetter's *Principles of Economics*. 2d. ed., 1910, p. 586. See Tanner's Algebra, pp. 336–339.

non-synchronous gratifications, rents or series of rents, are exchanged, they must be discounted to their present worth to be made comparable." [1]

10. **Capitalization and Interest.**—In keeping with commercial usage interest is here defined as a payment for contract loans made in terms of money. Interest is expressed as a per cent; it expresses the exchange ratio of the present capital value of an agent to that of an annual yield of that agent. If $100 now is exchanged or loaned for $105 to be paid a year hence, we say that the interest is 5/100, or 5 per cent. Thus interest is but a percentual expression of the time-discount on money loans.

Men borrow money in order to invest it in other things. Because money is readily exchangeable for other goods, it follows that the same time-discount involved in the capitalization of goods also prevails in money loans.

11. **Adjustment of Interest to Capitalization.**—We have made clear that the price of durable goods involves some rate of time-discount. Business men borrow and pay interest for money with which to buy these durable goods. The contract interest or price paid for the use of this money will approximate the rate of time-discount which determines the price of durable goods. Were interest on money lower than the rate of time-discount at which goods are priced, all would be borrowers and lenders would disappear. Certainly all would borrow money at a low interest to invest in durable goods yielding a higher rate of return. Lenders would disappear, for would one loan money at 3 per cent which he could invest at 8 per cent?

What, on the contrary, would result were interest on

[1] *American Economic Review*, March, 1914, p. 74.

money higher than the rate of time-discount on the future returns of durable goods? The result would be that none would desire to borrow. What motive would there be for borrowing at 10 per cent to invest at 4 per cent? Men will cease to borrow the moment that interest on money exceeds the rate of time-discount involved in the capitalization of goods. Precisely the same cause that would drive borrowers from the market would multiply lenders in the market. The moment interest on money attains a higher rate than investments will yield, lenders are multiplied and borrowers are absent.

The demand for money and the supply of it reach an equilibrium which conforms in the long run to the rate of time-discount in the capitalization of durable goods. Expressed differently, the interest or price paid for the present use of money conforms to the price of durable agents.

**12. The Present Worth of a Bond.**—The purchase of a government or corporation bond may, with accuracy, be spoken of either as an "investment," or as a "money loan." The price of the bond is the discounted future payments—principal and interest—specified on the face of the bond. Consider a $1,000 "5 per cent" ten-year bond. This bond is an obligation on the part of the issuer to pay $50 a year for ten years, and to return the $1,000 at the end of the loan period. What is the selling price of the bond? The solution consists in finding the total present worth of each $50 payment and that of the principal due ten years hence. Assume that the time-discount as expressed in the rate of interest is 5 per cent. The first $50 payment due one year hence has a present value of $47.62, or $50 ÷ 1.05. The present value of the second payment is $50 ÷ (1.05)$^2$, or \$45.35; the present value of the third is \$50 ÷ (1.05)$^3$, or \$43.19, and so on to the tenth, whose present worth is \$50 ÷ (1.05)$^{10}$, or \$30.69. The present value of the principal is \$1,000 ÷ (1.05)$^{10}$, or \$613.94. Adding these, we find \$47.62 + \$45.35 + \$43.19 + \$41.14 + \$39.17 + \$37.31 + \$35.53 + \$33.84 + \$32.22 + \$30.69 + \$613.94 equals \$1,000.

13. **Money Loans Analogous to Investments.**—As the money paid for a bond may be considered either as a loan or as an investment, so the money paid for shares of stock or for land or buildings may, by analogy, be regarded in the same way. Assuming a discount rate of 5 per cent, a farm from which is expected a net annual yield of \$2,000 will be worth \$40,000. The purchaser makes 5 per cent on his money, as he would by loaning his money or by purchasing a bond. So closely akin is time-discount in the capitalization of goods to the interest on money that many writers call them both interest.

14. **The Interest Rate Reflects Time-Discount.**—While these concepts are closely related, they are not to be confused. The rate of interest is a mere arithmetical expression of the more subtle concept of time-discount, or difference in the value of like goods at different times.

The rate of interest is strictly a monetary concept, and lending money at interest is of comparatively recent origin. Long before men began to puzzle over interest on money they were valuing deferred incomes and durable goods. Men were putting a present worth upon more or less durable sources of income, and carrying on trade in these long before there was a money economy to furnish an arithmetic interest rate. But could they put a present valuation upon durable goods or future incomes apart from time-discount? This is unthinkable, for without discount there would be no limit to the value of durable goods.

Could man place a present capital value on durable sources of income apart from a rate of interest?[1] I answer in the affirmative, and offer as proof the fact that this was done prior to the money economy, and is still done in countless instances.

The rate of interest no more accounts for the value ratio between durable agents and their annual yield than a yardstick accounts for length.

**15. Fallacy of Inversion.**—There are authors who see clearly that interest as a value problem has to do with the discounting of values through time. They clearly distinguish interest as a time-price from rent as a product-price problem. They see that the essence of interest is time, while that of rent is productivity. What they do not see is that both historically and logically the capitalization of productive or acquisitive agents must be given priority above interest.

Noteworthy economists not infrequently fall into this fallacy of inversion. To state the fallacy in the form of a question and answer: How determine the rate of interest yielded by a capital agent? This question, according to the fallacious reply, cannot be answered without a knowledge of the value of the agent; and the value of the agent cannot be obtained without assuming a rate of interest and using it in discounting the income which the agent yields. Note that the answer to the question is assumed, not accounted for. To assume a rate ready-made neither gives a theory nor accounts for anything. There is no more reason for assuming the rate of interest than for

[1] See Davenport's Economics of Enterprise, pp. 231–232.

assuming prices in general. In fact, the above does assume prices, for it is by means of the assumed interest rate that prices are found. To assume the interest rate is to beg the whole question and account for nothing.

16. **Interest Involved in Simple Exchanges.**—The business man notes the doings of Wall Street, or scans his morning paper to find the interest rate ready-made for him. To explain interest or determine why the rate is this or that is not his task. A more difficult task confronts the economist; he can neither assume the rate nor borrow it from the market; he must account for and explain it.

His starting-point is found in the present price of durable goods or deferred incomes. He has the data for determining interest in simple exchanges on the market. Before there can be exchange, goods must be discounted to their present worth in order that their values may be compared. The ratio between the exchange value of a good and a deferred yield of that good shows the rate of time-discount, and this rate governs the interest that will be paid for a money loan. If Crusoe on the lonely island meets in trade a wandering adventurer, some rate of time-discount marks their transactions, and this gives sufficient data for the simple arithmetical calculation of a rate of interest.

17. **Preference for Present Possession.**—Possession, in our exchange economy, gives one control over whatever goods or services he would acquire; it puts at his disposal incomes either present or future. The motive for discounting incomes is not based wholly upon "impatience for present enjoyable goods," for time-discount prevails in the capitalization of goods where there is no thought of consuming incomes by the person who does the discount-

ing. It is the value of incomes which is discounted—what the person who discounts incomes proposes to do with them is another question. He may consume them now or later, may enjoy them himself, or give them to another, may reinvest them or leave them for heirs. Regardless of the disposal he would make of the incomes, he discounts their value through time and this is the significant thing in the interest problem.

Possession or ownership gives one the disposal of incomes for consumption or other purposes. Apart from possession, one would have no value and no occasion for discounting value through time. Possession in some form, either present or future, is a condition which is presupposed in the discount market. Without possession there would be no investments, no capitalization, no exchanging, no borrowing at interest. It is the time aspect in the value of our possessions that causes us to pay more for the present possession of $100 at hand than for the present possession of the right to collect $100 a year hence.

Apart from possession there would be no need for such a word as capital, and without capital no need for such a word as interest. Why is not man himself capital? Capital is a possession and man is not possessed. He never gets capitalized, although he is productive, and this simply because he is not a private possession. Enslave him, however, then possession arises and with it capitalization, capital, and interest.

The motive back of possession is to secure the disposal of valuable incomes; it is a part of human nature to desire this disposal now rather than at a distant future time; this preference for the present over the future disposal of incomes is itself time-discount.

**18. Apparent Exceptions.**—An apparent exception to the desire for present over future possession is found in the use of goods in their proper seasons; coal in winter, straw hats and ice in summer. If it is July, one prefers coal in January rather than at the present. But it is value referred to in time-discount rather than the physical thing. Translate a ton of coal into $10 in money, and you will find that $10 in hand is worth approximately $10.30 six months from now. To the average householder the coal has no value for present purposes; its present value is its future value discounted. Seasonal goods are made comparable and subject to commercial transactions only when translated into value.

Other apparent exceptions arise from the fact that man naturally prefers possession or disposal of present incomes to that of deferred incomes. For instance, people buy life insurance with the full knowledge that no income will accrue until after death. They have the disposal of the income when they choose the beneficiary, otherwise no insurance would be written. But the puzzle is this: How does the present outlay of money for incomes after death show a natural disposition in men to prefer disposal of present over future value incomes? Translate the future income and the present outlay into value, and the premiums now paid will be less than the final income. Time-discount means but one thing—preference for present over future value income.

**19. The Consumption Idea.**—It has been shown that time-discount is not limited to enjoyable income for consumption. Distinction must be made between time-discount and the motives for such discount. Consumption is but one among many such motives; the term possession covers them all. Possession is one's best economic friend, for it gives him power and prestige among his fellows, shields him from personal want, provides him the happy sense of security unknown to those who walk the street in search of a job; finally, it gives him such disposal as he wills over income.

Does impatience for present consumption motivate one to borrow money at interest with which to pay for insurance collectible after death? Do not large capitalists emphasize the building of fortunes rather than consumption? They invest in railroads, works of construction, corporations, and durable sources of income. Old men invest in unimproved lands with little hope of ever enjoying consumable returns from them. Should returns mature while they live, the chances are they will be reinvested in durable goods; in this manner consumption will be postponed.

We must be mindful that the handling of large volumes of capital, together with the bulk of important monetary transactions, appertains to the large corporations and industrial enterprises whose incomes are deferred. Here capital is handled on such a scale as to far exceed all other monetary transactions which affect the interest rate.

In every such transaction there is, and must be, involved a rate of time-discount, otherwise there would be no means of capitalizing as a basis of the necessary exchanges and investments. The things discounted are the future value incomes from these capital agents. Are they discounted for purposes of ready consumption? Is the idea of ready consumption a prerequisite of discount? By no means.

The millionaire who could not consume his possessions

in a lifetime invests for an additional million with as much ardor as he did for his first dollar, and in every such investment he discounts future incomes just as truly as the hungry tramp gives higher appraisal to a present dinner than he does to a distant one.

Present possession tends to guarantee or underwrite one's future as well as his present. Wealth in hand may serve present needs or provide means for future support. Man lives according to a plan, ill devised perhaps, none the less a plan. Possession enables him to look to the future with confidence. At the basis of his plan of life must be disposal of income. This disposal of value incomes he prefers now rather than later, and the extent of this preference is his time-discount.

The theory of interest is an answer to this question: What premium will people pay for the possession of a present income stated in terms of money as compared with an equivalent income in terms of money at a future time? The answer requires an analysis of time-discount, and time-discount is based upon the motive of possession.

**20. Reasons for Differences in Time-Discount among Persons.**—Differences in the psychology of persons as well as differences in incomes explain the various degrees of time-discount among persons.

Differences in the psychology of persons: *Emotions* kindle thought and inspire intellectual action. They burn the objects of our desires indelibly into consciousness, and thus at times vitiate balanced judgment by giving undue weight to some things over others. When it is a matter of present self-interest, emotion turns the magnifying end of the telescope to our intellectual eye, it turns the minimizing end when our future interest is concerned. The emotional medium deflects our thought as water deflects the sunbeam. Emotions are not compelled, not felt because they should be, but felt when there is impressive cause. The more concrete the cause, the more intense is the emotion. One scandalous instance of a brutal drunkard whipping his wife will win votes for prohibition, whereas cool interest attends the writings of the economists on the inefficiency of labor occasioned by the rum habit. Let orators rave and gesticulate wildly on abstract charity, but the effect is not comparable to that of the helpless widow and child dying of hunger in a miserable tenement. Vividly felt examples are to thought what fuel is to fire, and these examples are in the living present rather than in the unfelt future. We wince with a shriek from present contact with a hot stove, and are little moved by the thought of future pain. Such are emotions that present hunger, cold, and need, that present emergencies and pleasures stand as convincing witnesses before the bar of judgment; they make a stronger case than is possible for the absent feelings of the future. The weight of approval favors the disposal of incomes for present rather than for future needs. The nature of our emotions predisposes the mind to time-discount.[1]

*Education* tends to dispel short-sighted emotions. It is forward-looking and constructive, and as such it oftentimes sacrifices the present to the future by using present possession and effort as a source of future income. The boy who patiently strives for higher education is converting present toil into future reward. Thrift and education go hand in hand. Waste and indulgence characterize the

[1] See Halleck's Psychology, chap. X.

ignorant who are devoid of foresight. This is shown in their scanty savings for the future, in their high time-discount and rate of interest.

*Love of posterity* is one of the greatest incentives to thrift. It inspires one both to produce and to save for the welfare of his children. This means, of course, a high estimate on future incomes or a low time-discount. It is thought that the disposition to provide posterity is the greatest single influence in holding down the rate of interest. A severe inheritance tax or other threat to the sure delivery of one's saving to his children would be a most deadening influence on thrift and a direct cause of increasing the rate of discount.

*Self-control* is in part a matter of habit and in part a trait of character. The habitual drunkard loses the habit of thrift when enslaved to a base appetite, and would mortgage his future promise for the temporary gratification of the spree. The sons of foolish rich men are permitted to accustom themselves to expensive luxuries. They are ignorant of the enforced frugality which is imposed upon sons, rich or poor, who are wisely forced to save and to learn the value of income through the toil of earning it. Spending is a habit easy to acquire, and when acquired there is little disposition to save. There can be little provision for future welfare when the mind is disposed to spendthrift habits. High time-discount prevails when appetites and customs are formed contrary to the principle of thrift. Again, traits of character, such as a feeble will or pessimistic turn of mind, affect time-discount. Without will-power one will hardly deny his present emotions to save for the future; in other words, he will have a high time-discount.

The pessimist may regard the future from two points of view; first, in his dyspepsia or cough he may find direful forebodings looking to a termination of life. "What's the use" to save for a future after death? He will consume rather than save. "Soul, thou hast much goods laid up for many years, take thine ease, eat, drink, and be merry"; to-morrow you may die. Expectation of a short life will cause a high time-discount. Secondly, the pessimist may look for the worst in the form of a long life full of want, worry, and woe. In preparation, he will deny his present wants in order to provide for his future needs. The felt necessity of providing for the future means a low time-discount.

*Differences in the incomes of persons:* Incomes differ in their distribution through time; they also differ in size, and they are not equally certain of arriving.

*Regarding the distribution of incomes through time:* (a) For a period there may be no incomes, then they begin and grow larger. If one goes into the dry-goods business in a stable New England city, he will at first undergo the cost of securing a site, building, stock of goods, and mercantile equipment. Then follows a period of building a business, of studying the market, advertising, and courting good-will. Next comes a period of business growth and prosperity. Finally, when the business has grown to the extent of the market, it has reached a stage of returns more or less constant. From first to last the income curve would look somewhat as shown in figure on next page.

This curve represents incomes deferred, and at the beginning of this period one will have ordinarily a high time-discount. Why? Financial burdens are pressing, while incomes years hence are promising. If by **discounting** some of these future incomes he could secure means to meet his present burdens, he would surely discount, and that, too, at a high rate.

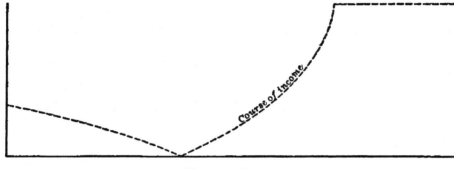

FIGURE NO. 2

(*b*) Some incomes, as the remuneration for professional services, start at a small figure and grow step by step to large returns. For the reason just given, time-discount would be high in the earlier stages of the course of incomes.

(*c*) Certain incomes tend from the beginning to be more or less constant. Incomes of this type are found among those who own improved real estate, stable businesses, and among passive capitalists who loan on long-time contracts. The owner of a constant income, other things being equal, is likely to have a normal time-discount.

(*d*) The mining business typifies a course of income that is large in its early stages, but which diminishes as time advances. Growing costs accompany the driving of entries farther and farther from the mouth of the mine. Some of the best-known mines in this country have been abandoned, not because the coal is exhausted, but because the increasing cost of securing it has come to equal the price of the coal. After the initial cost of opening the mine, a curve representing the course of incomes will appear as follows:

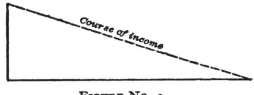

FIGURE NO. 3

(*e*) The size of income has its bearing on time-discount. The poor—those whose incomes are small—tend to have a high time-preference. The sting of poverty arouses the emotions in behalf of present self-interests. Present hunger is more appealing than a sound argument for a good breakfast next year. The poor man knows that he should save, that he cannot have his cake and eat it, too, but his present need makes the stronger appeal, for how could he have a future unless he maintains the present?

(*f*) The uncertainty of income affects time-discount. If one contemplates a short life because of ill-health, or pessimism, or a hazardous occupation, he will have, as we have seen, a high time-discount. If he lives under an unstable government or where outlaws as Villa abound, or if a dangerous military power seeking conquest threatens invasion, the effect will be that of high time-discount. During the Civil War many who were in the territory of Sherman's march to the sea abandoned all idea of saving; they burned their houses and destroyed their property rather than risk its capture by the foe. Time-discount is high where there is risk of securing income. Loans to a questionable character are always at a high rate. On the contrary, if one has a good present income, and if there are chances of his losing it in the future, his time-discount will be low, for he will wish to save a portion of his present means as a provision against a possible "rainy day."

*The following chapter is a continuation of the same subject. The exercises will follow the completion of the discussion.*

# CHAPTER XXIII

## INTEREST, FURTHER CONSIDERED

1. Determining a rate of interest. 2. Borrowers. 3. Adjustments in the market. 4. The supply side of the money market. 5. The order of thought: Production and discount. 6. Questions and answers involving the foregoing principles. 7. Exercises.

**1. Determining a Rate of Interest.**—In a previous chapter we saw how, through the operations of supply and demand, a common market price is established among individuals with different valuations in mind. We find a common rate of interest or market price on money loans in a similar manner. Time-discount is an individual matter varying from person to person, but the market rate of interest, like the market price of corn, is the same for each and all.

I shall not take space to repeat the process of finding the market price, or equating-point between supply and demand, where there are numerous buyers and sellers. A simple illustration will suffice.

Let us imagine the case of a professional man who is fifty-five years of age. He now has abundant savings and a large income, but he looks forward to the not-distant future when his income will diminish below what his needs require. His foresight and mature judgment enable him to paint mentally a vivid picture of his future circumstances, and teach him the necessity of skimping now that he may have larger funds at his future disposal. Will he be a spendthrift now and highly discount his future incomes for his present disposal? Precisely the contrary, for he will wish to take from his present abundance and add to his future funds for the coming need. How may he do this? This may be accomplished by loaning, for the amount now loaned is subtracted from his present possessions and when future payment is made the principal plus interest will then be added to his possessions. Assume that his time-discount is so low that he would be willing, if necessary, to take 1 per cent interest.

On the other hand, let us consider a young man better equipped with imagination than judgment, who is beginning a business career. He has limited means and high expectations for a prosperous future. He may be a new graduate with diploma in hand, looking forward to a home in the millionaire row, with every amusement at his command, and with learning enough to confound the wisest. Youth may indulge in castle-building, for these are the only structures whose final cost do not exceed the original estimate. But after revelling for a time in these imaginative sweets, too often the dry bread of actual toil becomes exceedingly distasteful. The happiest moments of life are those of fond anticipation; or as the Vicar of Wakefield would say: "It has been a thousand times observed, and I must observe it once more, that the hours we pass with happy prospects in view are more pleasing than those crowned with fruition. In the first case we cook the dish to our own appetite; in the latter nature cooks it for us."

At any rate, our young man, now pressed for means and distanced by his competitors, would gladly trade a portion of his anticipated bounty for the present possession of funds. He who would discount the future at a prodigious rate in behalf of his present rate becomes a borrower.

Assume that his time-discount is so high that he would be willing to pay 10 per cent if he had to do so.

These two men—the one a lender who would take 1 per cent, and the other a borrower who would pay 10 per cent —meet and bargain on a loan. While the lender would take 1 per cent, he is anxious to get as much as he can. And while the borrower would pay as much as 10 per cent, he is anxious to pay as little as possible. Perhaps they haggle and chaffer for advantage; the borrower may offer 2 per cent while the lender offers to take 9 per cent; they give and take, finally, adopting the trader's rule: they split the difference and agree on 5 per cent. The interest rate thus determined may not exactly coincide with the time-discount of any borrower and lender, regardless of how many there may be.

**2. Borrowers.**—There are numerous purposes for borrowing money at interest, but these may be divided into three classes: to secure profit from immediate transactions; to invest in durable sources of income; to secure present enjoyable goods and services.

(*a*) *Borrowing to secure present profits* is the cause of a large volume of money loans. An unscrupulous broker found a purchaser who offered $1,000 for a certain lot. Knowing that the real owner would sell it for $400, the broker wished to purchase it at the lower in order to sell it at the higher figure. Finding no accommodation at his bank, he approached a loan shark, who advanced him $400 on condition that he return $500 within fifteen days. The broker made the loan, bought and sold the lot, paid the lender $500, and cleared $500 on the transaction. Was this a loan made at the equivalent of an annual rate of some 600 per cent? Certainly not. From the standpoint of the borrower it was all but a pure case of an ill-gotten profit of $500; it was as if he had surreptitiously traded $500 for $1,000. The $100 gross interest had in it but a small tincture of real interest.

Much money is borrowed for short periods and at call to purchase goods for immediate resale at a profit. Transactions on stock and produce exchanges are financed by such loans. Bank loans for such transactions are not infrequently at rates far in excess of the true market rate. Examples of gross interest in transactions for immediate profit might be multiplied.

Any one, whether his time-discount be high or low, will be a borrower when he can secure immediate profit. In short periods, time-discount plays but a minor part; to secure profits is the motive upon which the borrower acts.

(*b*) *Borrowing for Purposes of Consumption:* Economists who reason that interest is wholly a matter of the discounting of values through time are, in so far, correct, but when economists take the next step and base time-discount upon the impatience for present consumption, they commit gross error. They reason as though borrowers were ruled wholly by their stomachs and love for present ostentation. Economists are correct in basing interest on time-discount, but are erroneous in limiting time-discount to enjoyable goods for ready consumption. High time-discount means a low appraisal upon remote incomes and the sources of such incomes. With little regard for the future, the improvident are willing to pledge recklessly their future income as security for money loans to obtain enjoyable goods. Moreover, what care they to offer an exorbitant interest? For the deferred payment of it will be made with future incomes which at present are lightly appraised.

I shall now give as brief a statement as possible of this, as I believe, false consumption theory. Money loans, of course, will go to the borrowers offering the highest interest, and the highest interest will be offered by those having the highest time-discount; but, according to the theory, time-discount is limited to enjoyable goods for consumption, therefore the highest interest will be offered by those who are at once most greedy for present consumption and least regardful for future incomes.

The reader will note in the statement just given that no mention is made of borrowing for investment in business enterprises. In fact, the theory assumes that borrowers are of a weak-willed, short-sighted, spendthrift type. These same thinkers tell us that the lenders have a low time-discount, that they are the far-sighted, self-controlled men who save.

(*c*) *Borrowing for Investment in Durable Sources of Income.* There are two reasons for not limiting borrowers to those who desire the ready means of gratification: (*a*) The large majority of loans are made for investment in enterprises to bear future returns; (*b*) the spendthrift class who seek to borrow for present enjoyable goods have limited credit, are without sufficient means of securing the repayment of loans to keep up the demand side of the money market.

Turn now to the theory held in this chapter, namely, time-discount, as limited to the discounting of value rather than to the discounting of any particular form of income. It is based upon the desire to have the present possession or disposal of a sum of capital. This disposal may be made for consumption, life-insurance, education, investment, or any other purpose. This is at once in contrast with the consumption theory, for it admits that largest of all borrowing classes—the conservative type with a low time-discount who borrow for durable investments.

It is not true even in a majority of cases that borrowers are those with high time-discount. Some students who read this may feel that they are living examples of the falsity of the claim. The conservative and far-seeing who have a keen appraisal of their economic well-being in the future have low time-discount, yet they are the very type of people who will undergo present hardships and make interest payments at high rates in the present for the means preparatory to their future welfare.

An example, perhaps not strictly economic in all its bearings, yet illustrative of the point, is that of a young man in my class at the time of this writing. To go through college he has, he tells me, relinquished a present salary of $1,500 and is borrowing $600 a year. He does not have an established credit, and must pay 10 per cent annual interest. Is this large present sacrifice of $2,160 a year ($1,500 relinquished + $600 loan + $60 interest) because he so highly estimates the present dollar and so lightly regards the future? On the contrary, his low time-discount—relatively high regard for the future—causes the present sacrifice of high interest, of money and diligent labor. He is not a lender, but a borrower at an extortionate rate, and that because of his low time-discount.

Let us turn now to the conservative type of investors. Our thought goes from the struggling youth, trying to get ahead in the world, and from the ignorant who squander needlessly, and from the spendthrifts who would mortgage their future for present consumption. Instead, we shall have in mind men of means and established credit, the far-sighted generals of industry who are conservative in their time-discount. These are the reliable borrowers on a large scale whom the banks, trust companies, and other loan institutions are pleased to have as customers, and upon whom these institutions chiefly rely.

In former times the borrowers were the poor who, as in cases of famine, must secure means from the more fortunate to provide their necessities of life. Then the obligation for a loan rested against the person of the borrower. At common law, debtors could be imprisoned for debt. But custom has changed; the chief borrowings to-day are for investments in one form or another, and the obligation for the return of the loan rests upon the property of the borrower rather than upon his person. This legal change enables only those of means to make important loans. Whereas the poor were formerly the borrowers, to-day the wealthy are the chief borrowers.

But why would a conservative investor pay for a money loan a rate of interest higher than his time-discount? It is because his present appraisal of future incomes is so high as to justify the present sacrifice. When the market rate of interest is 5 per cent, let us assume that the investor has an opportunity to buy a mill which promises a durable annual net income of $1,000. This will be capitalized at a sale price of $20,000. But if the time-discount of the investor should be two per cent, his personal price appraisal of the mill would be $50,000. He will be glad to trade $20,000 for what to his mind is $50,000. What is more, he will be willing to give a large boot in addition to the $20,000 for the mill. His rate of capitalization is 3 per cent lower than the market rate, and this justifies him in offering his note for a period of time, at any rate up to 3 per cent in excess of the market rate. Investors in remote incomes are willing and anxious to borrow money even at above market interest, note the fact, simply because of their low time-discount.

It is unthinkable that the half-wits, improvident, and short-sighted—those who would deny the future for the present and squander durable wealth for ready consumption—that this impatient and high time-discount class should hold up the demand side of the money market. Imagine our banks and great conservative loan institutions as rendezvous exclusively for the highly impatient. These could not support a loan market because they do not have sufficient security or borrowing power.

Interest eats night and day, and the more it eats the hungrier it grows. The spendthrift borrower soon has his financial foundation gnawed from under him, for debts at interest mount with accelerating speed and hasten the unwary to bankruptcy. Idle avarice and lazy economy cannot, for long, support a money market.

3. **Adjustments in the Market.**—The above illustration of the investor in the mill is not offered as typical, for in our exchange market, where exchanges turn on the slightest margin of advantage, individual appraisals are closely adjusted to the market rate. The advantage of an extreme case is that it tends to objectify how the business man reasons as to the rate of interest he could afford to pay for money. The business man, *first*, makes a study of the productive agent, analyzes the probable costs and receipts in order to anticipate the net incomes; *secondly*, he determines his own price appraisal of the agent; *third*, he finds the sale price at which he could make the purchase; *fourth*, he compares his own price appraisal with the sale

price. If his price appraisal exceeds that of the sale price, he will be anxious to invest and would, if necessary, pay interest exceeding the market rate for money to make the purchase.

Disregarding exceptions, the price appraisal of active business men will closely approximate the market price of established institutions whose incomes are fairly constant. These concerns are capitalized at the rate of discount which prevails in the money market. This market rate of time-discount, or rate of capitalization, is at the equating-point between those with high and low time-discount. The sellers of these investments will be those whose time-discount exceeds the market rate of capitalization, and the buyers, consequently the borrowers, will have a lower discount.

**4. The Supply Side of the Money Market.**—If consumption loans are made by those with high time-discount and investment loans made by those with low time-discount, one may ask who is left to do the loaning? It is answered; the large class of passive capitalists such as retired business men of wealth, those in the investment market who now hold idle funds in anticipation of a more favorable investing period, widows and children to whom funds are left, the idle rich. Also banks, trust companies, life-insurance companies, savings and loan associations—in sum, the institutions which collect surplus and idle funds into reservoirs of loanable funds.

**5. The Order of Thought: Production and Discount.**— Many thinkers still cling to the productivity theory of interest. They make bold the claim that the time-discount theory is strangely dissociated from the production of wealth. I shall refute this false conception by giving a brief review of the order of thought which encompasses both production and discount.

There could be no discounting of values through time unless such values were in prospect. Productive agents yield shoes, hats, food, and other valuable products, not all at once, but distributed through different periods of time. This is true of all agents, as land, tools, or machines.

The production problem studies that group of facts having to do with combining materials into the best composition, giving them proper form, putting them in the right place, and distributing them in their proper season, so that they are suitable for the gratification of desires.

These many ends of production may be combined in the one word *usance*. Back of usance are the productive agents which beget it. These agents obey a number of laws, chief of which is resistance, inaptly called by some diminishing returns. This law deals with the limited productive capacity of agents in a limited period of time. This limiting force gives explanation of the scarcity and, therefore, the value of usance. Because the usance is valuable, men pay a price, called *rent*, for the temporary uses of these usance-producing agents.

The rent problem, then, is a study within the field of production. Were we to stop with the rent problem, we should end with the rise of valuable incomes distributed through time and rent paid for the temporary uses of productive agents. But this is not enough; these agents are capitalized, bought, and sold in the market, and in our money economy funds are borrowed at times to effect these exchanges.

As we further proceed, however, a new and different

problem from production arises; it is the problem of *time-discount*. This begins where the problem of production ends. It assumes these valuable incomes, distributed through different periods of time, as ultimate facts, and concerns itself with discounting the value of these incomes through time to their present worth. But what is their present worth? It is the capitalized value or present price of the right to secure or control such incomes. If you own land, that ownership is your right to the income from it, so with any other agent, whether it be a house, or mill, or franchise, or monopoly right. Control over value-income, not the form of the agent, is the important thing, and this control is capital.

Time-discount, then, as applied to productive agents or mere acquisitive rights to income, is itself the very essence of capitalization.

Now exactly this same time-discount applies to money. Who would give $1,000 now for the return of $1,000 ten years hence? It is the language of custom and business to limit the word interest to payments on money. Much is lost and little gained in the vain attempt to apply the term interest in the general field of capitalization.

6. **Questions and Answers Involving the Foregoing Principles:**

(*a*) *What is the effect of a change in the interest rate upon saving?*

There are persons who would save if the rate of interest dropped to zero, yes, even if they had to pay negative interest to get their money in safe hands. These are exceptions. Others would save more because of a lowering of the rate of interest. Consider a parent whose prevailing motive is to provide for his children. In order to pro-

522 Introduction to Economics

vide them a reasonable income of, say, $5,000 a year, he must save $200,000 if the interest rate is 2½ per cent, $100,000 when interest is 5 per cent, $50,000 when the rate is 10 per cent. But as high wages lead to short hours among the improvident, and longer hours among the thrifty, so a sudden shift to a higher interest rate would make the stronger appeal to save among the thrifty who have most to save.

Time-discounts do not become adjusted to rapid changes in interest rates. If such adjustment took place immediately, modifications of the interest rate would have no effect on saving.

(b) *Would a non-changing high rate of interest cause more saving than a non-changing low rate?*

Contrary to the generally accepted opinion, this question must be answered in the negative. The very form of the question involves an inversion of cause and effect in the explanation of interest. A firm rate of interest, whether high or low, accompanies a stable market with an established rate of discount. If this discount on the future is large, it means certainly a weak disposition to practise present self-denial in order to save. If your time-discount is high, you would sacrifice your provision for the future in behalf of a spendthrift loan. When competition has worked its effect in a stable market such as we assume, a high interest rate will coincide with or reflect the large discount of the future. A high interest rate, therefore, symbolizes the degree of preference for present over future incomes. As interest is high, the disposition to save is low. All know that future incomes are capitalized low when the rate of interest is high. Is not the disposition to sell one's future provisioning at a discounted price to get ready money the antithesis of the disposition that would deny the present to save for the future?

Time-discount that would take from the future in behalf of the present works contrary to saving. Low interest likewise expresses the rate of time-discount and capitalization. Low interest expresses a low discount of the future, consequently a high disposition to save. In a well-adjusted market a large discount or high unwillingness to save is exactly counterbalanced by a high interest or reward for saving. Whatever the rate of discount, it will be equal to the rate of interest that rewards saving. The causal sequence is from the disposition to save, to the rate of interest, and not the reverse. Then, in a community where interest is permanently high, there will be no greater motive for saving than in a community where interest is low.

(*c*) *Is there a tendency to erect lasting structures, to construct durable highways, bridges, and other lasting improvements during periods when the interest rate is high or during the period when it is low?*

Conservative investments, which take durable form, are made at times of firm confidence in the future; they indicate a high appraisal of future incomes. During such periods time-discount is low and the rate of interest likewise low. Because a low interest rate reflects a high appreciation of future incomes, a marked disposition to provide for the future, it follows that durable or lasting structures will be made when the interest rate is low.

(*d*) *What is the motive for paying interest?*

The entrepreneur borrows money with which to buy productive agents which will yield future valuable returns. These deferred incomes are discounted in the price of the agent yielding them. His present value outlay is, therefore, smaller than the anticipated returns. His motive for paying interest is to secure this growth in value through time. If he invests wisely this growth in value will be sufficient, both to pay the interest and to leave him a gain.

(e) *Can there be a zero rate of interest?*

In exceptional cases, money is loaned without interest, but other conditions, such as friendship, fear of thieves, and so forth, enter in to complicate the problem. There are also exceptional cases, as when one is hard put to it for means, when money would not be loaned for many times the market interest. Exceptions aside, one can no more conceive of a zero rate of interest than of a limitless capitalization of durable sources of income. The two amount to one and the same thing. Were interest zero, time-discount would also be zero, the present worth of a dollar fifty years hence would be a dollar. There could be no limit to the present capital value of a permanent agent yielding a penny annually.

(f) *Why is the interest rate high during periods of war?*

During wars there is great social unrest, and timid capital hesitates to venture into durable enterprises. Business ventures are hazardous, because the future is uncertain. Ordinary processes of saving and loaning are in disuse. War materials are destroyed in enormous quantities, men are withdrawn from normal productive pursuits, and production is carried on with meagre equipment. Demand turns from durable enterprises and calls for present consumable goods. This demand for goods to meet temporary needs brings further halt to permanent improvements. Accompanying this enforced neglect of saving and durable investments is a high time-discount. Borrowers are willing to pay back considerably more than a dollar in the future for the present loan of a dollar. The economic pressure of the present, together with the uncertainty of the future, make for high time-discount and its effect—a high rate of interest.

**7. Exercises.**—1. If the net income from a building is $500 a year and the rate of interest is 5 per cent, what would be the price of the building? Show how you make the calculation and point out the different steps in your reasoning.

2. Should a new street-railway make more accessible the building referred to in the above question so that its net yield should increase from $500 to $1,000, how would the price of the building be affected? Would the rate of interest be changed?

3. Can one who adheres to the productivity theory of interest explain why interest is paid for unproductive loans?

4. Criticise the following: Interest is a price and obeys all the laws of price. So a large quantity of money means a low rate of interest.

5. Should the rate of time-discount change from 6 to 4 per cent, what change would take place in the price of a farm whose annual net yield is $4,000?

6. What is the relationship between the price of durative goods, the rate of interest, and time-discount?

7. If it is now August you would prefer a fur coat in January, five months later, rather than at the present. We prefer goods in their season, whether their proper season be now or later. Do these statements form exceptions to the time-discount theory of interest? Does time-discount have reference to physical goods as such or to values?

8. Summarize the reasons for differences in time-discount among persons as given in Chapter XXII, paragraph 20. Can you give other reasons?

9. Explain how differences in time-discount cause some to be lenders and others to be borrowers.

10. How is the rate of interest determined in the market?

11. Point out different motives for borrowing.

12. Could spendthrift borrowers support the money market? Why? What class of borrowers best support the money market? Why?

13. (*a*) Aristotle claimed that, as money does not produce money, nothing more than the return of the principal sum lent can equitably be claimed by the lender. Answer this argument.

(*b*) Now, criticise Franklin's statement to the opposite effect: "Money makes money, and the money that money makes, makes more money."

14. Do laws fixing a rate of interest work well in practice? (See Hadley's Economics, 139–143.)

15. In the World Almanac you may find the legal rate of interest in the different states. What explanation can you offer for these differences?

16. One says: "I can prove that the amount of money determines the rate of interest. Does not the Bank of England raise the rate of discount (interest) when gold is leaving the country? During panics, when it is almost impossible to borrow money, is there not a rise in interest?" How would you answer this?

17. The capital value of an agent goes up as the interest rate goes down. Explain.

# CHAPTER XXIV

## FORMS OF INDUSTRIAL OWNERSHIP: THE CORPORATION

1. **Introduction.**—Ours is an exchange economy whose fundamental characteristic is private property. Some form of ownership, or else the want of it is, therefore, at the basis of our industrial problems. Whether it be a question of the distribution of food products, or of regulating production, or of rate control, or of price maintenance, or of the enforcement of property rights, or of poverty against riches, or of conscription—these and many more are questions of private property. The extent of the relationship of the state to industry must be determined on grounds of private property. So, also, must be determined the rights of private parties in the business dealings of man with man. From earliest times the institution of private property has been subject to modification and change. Public opinion is now in a transitory stage, and this makes the form of ownership not a problem of the next century, but of to-morrow. These problems of ownership—for that

matter all economic problems—must be approached from the standpoint of conditions that are. To this end the student should read broadly and spare no effort in obtaining a clear insight into the problems of ownership. A business may be owned by an individual, partnership, joint-stock association, or corporation.

**2. Individual Ownership.**—Ownership by an individual is the oldest and simplest form of ownership. What may the individual own? He may own tangible forms of wealth, or rights against another, or rights to do something to the exclusion of others. Material wealth, called objects of ownership, falls into two classes: (1) Immovables or land and durable improvements, such as houses; (2) movables or things not attached to the land. In legal terminology the first class (immovables) is known as real property, and the second class (movables) is known as personal property.

One may own rights against another person, as a right to compel him to pay a promissory note or to pay damages in case of a trespass on property (wealth). Under this heading may be considered the right to recover stolen goods and to enforce contracts.

Lastly, a person may own rights to do something to the exclusion of others. Examples of this kind of ownership are patents, copyrights, trade-marks, and franchises. A patent legally guarantees an individual the exclusive privilege of using a new process a given number of years; a copyright likewise excludes competition for a specified time. A trademark is a symbol, name, or other device which one puts upon goods to distinguish them from like goods of other persons. If A adopts a trade-mark, "Royal Pens," to distinguish his product, B cannot use the same words or words so similar in sound, for instance, "Loyal Pens," as might deceive the average purchaser. A franchise is a public grant giving individuals or private groups of individuals privileges which belong to the state. It gives the right of eminent domain, the right to levy tolls and charges for public utilities.

3. **Limits to Private Ownership.**—There are, necessarily, restrictions upon the private ownership of all forms of wealth. Could a real-estate owner prevent a right of way through his land, the public at large would be deprived of common carriers. The public welfare must be protected against a private interest; the state, therefore, reserves the right to compel a landlord to surrender a right of way at a fair market price. This right is termed the right of eminent domain. It is exercised whenever public safety, interest, or expediency so requires. Another restriction on private ownership is that of the right of way. The boundary of an owner's farm extends to the middle of the public road, but he dare not put his fence there; the owner's lot extends to the middle of the street, but he dare not block the street. Close the highway, however, and the owner takes control without further ado, though subject to a definite right of use.

Another consideration, ownership is the right of use in a broad and strictly correct sense. The public right of use is public ownership, but this right extends over all forms of wealth and is exercised when necessity requires. This fact makes the state a joint owner of wealth. A tax on wealth, therefore, is but the share which the state as joint owner receives from the annual income of that wealth. If the annual income from a farm is $100, assuming the rate of interest to be 5 per cent, the price of the farm would be $2,000. If the tax be $25, it follows that the share of the state in the farm is $500, and that of the individual is $1,500. Furthermore, private ownership is restricted from the imposition of a nuisance upon the public. The smell from an ill-kept fish-market, stable, tannery, or fertilizer-plant will not be tolerated in a residential district.

**4. Partnership.**—The proprietor of a large business sees his task grow more and more arduous with the growth of that business. The business comes to be divided into departments. Capital, special skill, and knowledge are required in the development of the business. Need arises for mechanics, efficiency experts, accountants, salesmen, and managers. The pressure of increasing responsibilities may cause the proprietor to invite others with special skill or capital to join with him as partners in the enterprise. A partnership or firm is a group of persons who have united their capital or energies and jointly carry on a business, acting as if one person or entity, and sharing as common owners the profits of the enterprise.

It should be clear that the mere fact of sharing profits is not the test of a partnership. If the landlord lets his farm on shares, agreeing to take one-half of the products of the farm as rent, this would not be a partnership but a lease. If a book-agent receives one-half of the profits on his sales, this again is not a partnership, but an agency. In every partnership there must be a community of interests, a prosecution of business in common with a view to profits. A owns capital, B is an expert manager, and C is a skilful salesman. A furnishes all the capital to start a mail-order house; B and C put in their services in managing the business and selling the goods. They agree to share profits. This is clearly a partnership because it meets the test of a partnership. It is a community of interest, a common prosecution of business with a view to profits.

**5. Limited Partnerships.**—In a general partnership every member is liable legally and morally for the acts of every other member. Each partner is liable for all the debts and obligations of the firm. A and B are partners in a small business. A borrows $50,000 in the firm's name, pockets the money, and leaves the country. The creditor may exhaust the assets of the partnership and, if these are insufficient, go against the private property of B to make up the deficiency. In a limited partnership, however, one or more of the partners, called special partners, are not liable for the partnership debts beyond the sum each has contributed to the capital. The law requires such partnerships to have at least one general partner whose liability is unlimited.

**6. The Disadvantages of a Partnership are Many.**—Each of the partners has a controlling voice in the management of the firm. Conflicting opinions may work to the injury of the policy of the company. The firm is not well adapted to collecting large amounts of capital. It must for the most part depend upon the partners for funds. The fact of unlimited liability of the partners may cause a loss of private property in addition to the original investment. This is to be commended in the sense that it makes the management conservative and careful. The main disadvantage seems to be that the duration of a partnership depends upon the life or the caprice of a partner. The partnership is dissolved with the alienation, or withdrawal, or insanity, or death, or bankruptcy of a partner. Because a partnership may have only a short life, it is unsuited for the formation of large business transactions and contracts which extend over considerable periods of time.

7. **Joint-Stock Association.**—Joint-stock associations are partnerships in which the capital is divided into shares which are owned by the partners. These differ from ordinary partnerships in two respects: (1) They are not dissolved by the same causes. The shares are transferable; for instance, if a shareholder dies, his shares pass to his estate; if he sells his shares, the purchaser succeeds to his rights. Partners may withdraw or new partners may be introduced without a dissolution of the firm. (2) Shareholders do not embarrass the management of the firm; they elect directors and officers who manage the firm. Only the officers have authority to bind the firm in any financial obligation. None the less, each partner stands personally liable for the obligations (debts or contracts) of the firm.

8. **Corporations.**—A corporation is an artificial person created by law for some specific purpose or purposes. The members of a corporation are not the corporation; members may withdraw or die, but the artificial person continues. As a legal person it owns property, may incur debts and form contracts, may sue and be sued, and carry on business as a natural person. The corporation has no conscience, no power to think, but the law regards its officers as agents empowered to carry on all business of the corporation. This form of ownership is found in all nations. At first it applied only to large enterprises, such as steamship companies and railroads, later to smaller enterprises, and to-day all kinds of enterprises, large and small, are at liberty, and find it feasible to adopt this form of organization.

9. **The advantages of corporations** over other forms of ownership are, among others, permanency, limited liability, transferability of shares, concentration of management, and adaptability for securing large funds of capital.

*Permanence:* Stockholders may come and go, may retire, sell their stock or die, but the corporation continues to live. It is adaptable to the undertaking of long-time contracts. There are, to be sure, exceptions to the permanency of a corporation in cases where charters are granted for a limited number of years, as, for example, real-estate companies in Massachusetts, which have a life not exceeding fifty years.

*Limited liability:* A partner in a bankrupt firm may lose his entire investment and, further, he may be forced to sacrifice his personal holdings to satisfy the creditors of his firm. He may be compelled to make good a foolish or fraudulent contract made by his partner. But if the corporation fails the stockholder, generally speaking, will lose no more than his securities in the corporation. Some exceptions will be found to the rule of limited liability in state laws, the one important exception being, that the stockholders of national banks are all subject to a double liability. Limited liability is given by many authorities as the reason why the corporate form of ownership has increased so rapidly in recent years.

Contrary to the popular conception, limited liability was not always an essential feature of the corporation. In England limited liability was not adopted till 1855, and even now English companies must claim this attribute by inserting the word "limited" in connection with their names.

*Transferability of shares:* A share of stock is a unit of

ownership in a corporation. Shares are represented by certificates of stock. If a corporation has issued a thousand shares, the owner of one share owns one thousandth part of the corporation. If the entire stock of a railroad corporation is bought up by a group of persons, they own the railroad. If an owner wishes to sell his stock it is easy to find a buyer. If an owner has one hundred shares for sale, he may sell to a hundred different purchasers, or to fifty, or to one purchaser, depending upon the wishes and purchasing power of the buyer. Sales are made easy because the size of the sale can be adjusted to the means of the buyer. It is difficult for an individual to sell his farm or other private holdings. It is impossible for a partner without the consent of his partners to dispose of his interests in the partnership without destroying the firm. The welfare of a firm depends upon the business ability of the partners, but the case is otherwise in a corporation which is managed by the directors rather than by the owners. Widows, elderly persons, children who have inherited money—any and all classes ˜may buy stock, according to their means, without any change in the policy of the company.

*Concentration of management:* A stockholder may own 99 per cent of the stock in a corporation and still have no authority to transact business for it, since duly appointed officers, and only these, can transact the corporation's business. In this way a heavy responsibility is concentrated upon the few officers in a large corporation, and they have great power either for good or for evil.

The corporation is an excellent institution for a large class of people who have inherited or otherwise acquired means, but who are themselves without the experience or ability to utilize their means effectively. Two conclusions are to be deduced from this fact: (1) It is to the interest of society that the direction of capital be removed from the hands of the weak to the hands of the strong; (2) the incompetent rich, through bad management, may soon squander their means, whereas removing their control by giving the direction of their holdings over to a strong financial director will have the effect of maintaining their fortunes. The corporation, it is argued, tends to maintain large fortunes, but just the opposite may be true, for it puts wealth in salable form.

*Securing large capital :* A century ago the only securities which the investing public could buy were government obligations, as the early stock exchanges knew no other form of securities. The field was closed for investment to those of limited means, since these securities were sold in large amounts, so the small investor welcomed the corporation with its transferable shares sold in any amount to accommodate the purchaser's means. This new form of saving and investment had other advantages. It multiplied the sources from which corporations might draw funds. Corporate securities are purchased by all classes —the humble who work for a pittance, the day-laborer, and the wealthy aristocrat. Some American corporations have upward of 100,000 stockholders. This inflowing of capital from thousands of sources provides the enormous funds necessary to finance our large industrial enterprises.

**10. General Corporation Acts.**—A charter is, so to speak, the soul of a corporation. The first step in forming a corporation is for the interested individuals or incorporators to prepare a charter (articles of incorporation or certificate of incorporation). The charter contains a number of provisions, including the name of the corporation, its objects, amount of capital stock, and like provisions. Application is made to the state to have the charter granted, and when a state does so, it creates a corporation.

Formerly the state legislatures granted charters. When incorporators wished a charter, a bill for that purpose was introduced in the legislature, referred to proper committees, debated through both houses, and signed by the governor of the state, each charter requiring a separate and special act. A century ago the granting of a charter was not an arduous task for our legislatures, because so few of them were requested. As time went on corporations grew more and more popular, and the numerous demands for charters outgrew the capacity of the legislatures to grant them. Were charters granted in this manner to-day, it is doubtful whether legislatures could find time to serve their normal functions. But the time-consuming labor of this system was not its most serious aspect.

In some instances, it proved a cheap and effective means for unscrupulous candidates for the legislature to buy votes. If a group of influential business men desired to form a corporation for a particular purpose, meanwhile wishing to prevent others from incorporating for the same purpose, they could secure their evil aim through their representative in the legislature. A legislator who has power to grant special privileges is tempted to favor the political boss in order to win his support. This system, moreover, leads to political log-rolling. A from Henry County says to B from Clay County: "Vote with me in behalf of my boss, and I will vote with you in behalf of your boss." In this way conspiring groups could control the granting of charters and exclusively serve the favored few. This unfair system of granting charters led to so much favoritism and political corruption that the public called for reform.

This contemptible system was reformed by "enabling acts" or "general corporation laws." An enabling act, in so far as it applies particularly to corporations, is a general corporation act defining the purposes for which corporations may be lawfully formed, the powers which they may possess, the number of incorporators and stockholders, the manner and lawful purpose of issue of capital stock, and so on. Thus the law definitely defines the conditions under which a charter will or will not be given. This enables any group of citizens, regardless of "pull," or politics, or wealth, to secure a charter, if they fulfil the requirements of the act. It is thought that this transfer from special grants to enabling acts was the most important reform in business methods during the nineteenth century. It at once facilitates the granting of charters, stamps out an important means of political corruption, and enables all competitors to share the benefits of the corporate form. The charter of a corporation, formed under general laws, consists of the general law and its one particular certificate of incorporation or articles of association.

11. **Directors.**—As above indicated, the stockholders own the corporation and share its earnings. Ownership implies the power to control, but the stockholders control a corporation only indirectly. They elect the directors and the directors elect the officers who directly manage the corporation. The directors usually comprise a small group of leading stockholders. Their intimate relations with each other and with the workings of the corporation make of them a watchful and effective working unit.

They have power to appoint and to remove officers. The policy and direction of the corporation is really in the hands of the directors. The interests of the stockholders are subject to the directors; unreliable directors have many means of enriching themselves at the expense of small stockholders. The stockholders regard the personnel of the directors as of vital importance.

12. **Election of Directors: Dummy Directors.**—Directors are elected by the majority vote of the stockholders, each stockholder usually having one vote for each share of stock he owns. Should one person own over 50 per cent of the shares, he can elect all the directors. It is not unusual for a small group to maintain a community of interest and dominate the control of corporations. In these cases the large number of small stockholders have no control over the policy and direction of their holdings.

A dummy director does not vote his own will; he serves the interests of his master and votes as he is told. A director, dummy or other, usually must hold at least one share of stock. One who owns over 50 per cent of the shares may go through the legal form of transferring a share to each of a sufficient number of dummies to "pack" the board. After this work of deception, he casts the necessary number of votes to elect his select dummies, thus "packing" the board and assuming imperial rule.

13. **Cumulative Voting.**—This work of iniquity is defeated in some places by cumulative voting. By a power of cumulative voting the minority stockholders may elect representation proportioned in number to the number of shares they hold. The following example will make clear the principle of cumulative voting. If we assume that three directors are to be elected, a stockholder owning 20

shares may cast 20 votes for each of the three directors, or 60 votes for one director. If there are 2,000 shares of stock, and 1,480 shares are owned by the majority holders, while 520 shares are held by the minority, the minority by casting triple votes for one director would give him 1,560 votes. This is a larger vote than the majority could muster for each of three candidates by casting single votes. The minority would elect one director and the majority two.

**14. Inside Information of Stockholders.**—The owner of a share is part-owner of the corporation, and it would seem that any man should be allowed the privilege of examining into his own property. To deny him this privilege would seem contrary to the character and purpose of private property, yet minority stockholders as a rule are not permitted to investigate the books of a corporation. There is a sound reason for this. Large competing corporations make every effort to excel the rival, each competitor working out new inventions, new processes, and trade secrets in the contest for advantage in the market. These secrets and inner workings of a corporation are advantage points which opposing competitors would like to secure. Now, if your business has secret advantages which enable it to excel my business, I would buy a share in your company if that would permit me to examine your books and thereby acquire certain of your advantage points. To reveal or make common knowledge of one's advantage points would deaden one's incentive, retard individual initiative, and introduce a spirit of lethargy in business. It would have a deadening effect like that produced by public ownership. The conclusion to be drawn from this reasoning is that the denying of inside information to the minority holder protects rather than infringes upon private property.

This is not to deny that the stockholder should have some information. This he receives from well-managed companies in regular reports issued annually, and in some cases even quarterly or monthly. In these reports financial information, such as is contained in balance-sheets and income statements, is given as well as information regarding the operations of the company.

15. **Negotiability of Stock-Certificates.**—If one owns a share of stock in a corporation, his ownership is evidenced by a written instrument called a stock-certificate. The stock-certificate is not itself the ownership, any more than a ticket is a ride on a train. The certificate is to the ownership of stock what a deed is to the ownership of land: it is merely a written evidence. If you lose your certificate or a rogue steals it, you still remain a shareholder. A far better evidence of ownership is secured by referring to the books of the company in which are entered the names of stockholders and the number of shares held by each. Should stock-certificates be fully negotiable? Should the real ownership pass from person to person with the transfer of the certificate? This is a debatable question and the arguments pro and con may be stated briefly.

*Affirmative:* (1) Full negotiability would facilitate sales, for there would not be the delay and trouble of transferring names on the books of the company. (2) It would assist stock-exchange brokers who make investigations back of the certificates to determine rightful owners. (3) It would make certificates more acceptable to banks for loans.

*Negative:* (1) If to obtain a certificate would render one secure in ownership, it is argued that there would be a premium upon forgery and theft. Where transfers take place on the books of the corporation, there is thought to be no incentive for iniquitous persons to steal or forge the rightful owner's name to a certificate. Moreover, if certificates were negotiable, as are national bank notes, there would be the danger of losing them, and thereby losing one's ownership in the corporation. (2) The corporation would be unable to keep a record of its stockholders. This would encourage fraud on the part of stockholders and render it very difficult to detect such fraud. (3) Close akin to this last point is the fact that the responsibility of stockholders would be lessened because they would not be known. The corporate form has come into such general use and it embodies tremendous capital, therefore it has tremendous powers either for harm or for good.

Despite these negative arguments, which sound plausible when first encountered, the weight of reason, the sanction of legislation in the important states of the Union, and the tendency of public opinion seem to favor the full negotiability of stock-certificates. Laws making stock fully negotiable have been passed recently in Pennsylvania, Massachusetts, New York, and other states.

16. **Securing Funds.**—The corporation receives its funds from those who purchase its bonds or notes, and those who buy its stock; it is also aided by means of loans at banks, by those who sell it goods on short-time credit, and by the surplus or undivided earnings left in the corporation. One who is a large creditor of a corporation might well lend it assistance in times of trouble. His purpose in maintaining the strength of the company would be to protect the worth of the notes or bonds which he holds against it. But it is very unusual that a small creditor assists a

corporation, because he is almost always protected in that the first claims to be settled are those of the creditors.

Stockholders will at times contribute to a corporation or, what is the same, turn the earnings back into the company rather than take them out in the forms of dividends. Stockholders may largely increase their dividends by contributing funds for the installation of a new improvement or method that will augment earnings. By far the most important way in which stockholders aid corporations is to turn the surplus back into the working assets of the company. To this particular type of aid has been attributed in large part the financial strength of the Carnegie Steel, Baldwin Locomotive Works, the Lehigh Valley Railroad, and others. Shortsighted stockholders insist on immediate dividends, even to the extent of stunting the growth of their company. Farsighted stockholders will not bleed the company, but will enable it to grow upon the strength of its own earnings.

If one takes out $20 in dividends, he isolates it from the benefits of large-scale business. Small isolated sums are largely deprived of earning power, whereas if small sums are allowed to remain in the corporation they co-operate with or become a part of large capital, and take on all the advantages of large scale business. During the growth of a corporation up to the point of largest efficiency, there is an ever-accelerating cumulative strength gained by turning earnings back into the company. If one takes out $20 in annual dividends for five years, he will have received $100, but ordinarily if he leaves the dividends in the company the price of his stock will have increased more than $100.

17. **Funds from Creditors.**—There are three ways of securing funds (or their equivalent) from creditors. First,

a company may so manage its business as to keep itself constantly indebted to trade creditors. If a manufacturing or mercantile company buys, say, on ninety days' time and plans its purchases at such intervals that they may be met in large part by notes receivable, it may carry on a large business relative to its invested capital. Assume that a mercantile company so plans its deferred payments as to keep itself constantly in debt $50,000 to trade creditors; it would thus have the use of that sum of money as truly as if it had made a loan in the open market. It would have continually the use of $50,000 without interest. The Roman law fulfilled the logic of such transactions when it regarded a sale of goods on credit as a sale for cash with a loan of the cash to the buyer from the seller. Funds may be secured from creditors, also, by the issue of notes or the issue of bonds.

18. **Issuing Notes.**—If a corporation wishes to borrow for a comparatively short period of time, it will ordinarily issue notes. A note made to a bank will usually run not over six months, but notes sold to the public are likely to run from two to ten years. The denominations of notes vary with circumstances. If a loan is made from a single large syndicate, a note may be made for $50,000 or $100,000 or more. If, however, notes are offered for sale to the general investing public, they will be issued in small denominations.

Notes, as a rule, are objectionable as a means of securing large sums of money. They move too slowly to satisfy the requirements of a commercial bank. On the other hand, they do not run long enough to satisfy the average individual who desires a steady return from a durable investment. The time limit of notes generally falls between the time limit of banks and of individuals. The issuing company has no means of foretelling whether the public will absorb its entire note issue, nor can it predict the possibilities of renewing its notes if it becomes necessary to do so at the date of their expiration.

With these objections in mind, it becomes a fair question as to why a corporation would ever issue notes. There are, however, occasions which make it advisable and all but imperative for a corporation to issue notes. Financiers becoming expert in reading the signs of the times know the good times and the poor times for making bond issues. If a company is in temporary need of finance at a poor time for a bond issue it will be well to issue short-term notes in order to defer the bond issue. If a company is constructing an improvement which promises immediate returns it may be wise to issue notes.

**19. Issuing Bonds.**—Selling bonds, or selling notes, is borrowing money. The written promise, secured or unsecured, of an individual to pay is called a note. The short-time written obligation of a company is called a note; the written promise to pay issued by a government, or the long-time written obligations to pay issued by a corporation is called a bond. If you hold a government's bond or corporation's bond, that government or corporation is indebted to you.

Is it wise to borrow, or is there any sound reason for remaining heavily indebted to others? The great majority of persons will answer an emphatic "no." This dislike for debt is inherited; in former times businesses were not financed by means of credit. The borrowers were the poor who obligated both their person and their property to the wealthier classes in order to secure necessities in times of need. Debtors have been put in stocks, hanged by the thumbs, suffered long terms of imprisonment, because of inability to pay their debts. Later the obligations for debts came to rest upon the individual's wealth rather than upon his person. To-day wealth is its own guarantee for the borrowings used to improve or to create it. The large debtor class to-day consists of the wealthy who have the means to guarantee and thereby make possible large borrowings. Because large indebtedness yields large returns, the wealthy have become the large debtor class. What reason does a financier have for putting a million in a business rather than loaning it at the market rate of interest? He does it simply because he anticipates a larger return from an investment in business than from an ordinary loan. The excuse of a business for being is that it pays more than the loan market. If one can borrow funds at 6 per cent and make them earn ten per cent in his business, it will be wise to borrow. There is, of course, a limit beyond which a corporation should not extend its borrowings. It is both common practice and sound policy for progressive corporations to maintain debts.

20. **Issuing Stocks and Bonds.**—A corporation may be profitable, enjoying good-will and its securities in demand at the very time when it is approaching decay. A plant may be ruined by a change in demand. For instance, an oil company recently came to naught because the oil deposits became exhausted. A lumber company failed when by an unfavorable decision in court it lost the title to a boundary of timber; and a brick plant was rendered worthless when left to one side by a change in the line of transportation over which its products moved. Examples might be multiplied of failures of corporations due to new inven-

tions, or processes, or fashions, or substitutes, or exhaustion of raw materials, or legal reverses, or manipulations.

In any case where danger threatens the future prosperity of a corporation the management will prefer to sell stocks rather than bonds. Sell your holdings while prices are high; let the price dwindle in another's hands. Again, corporations find it good policy not to declare exceptionally high dividends, for high dividends meet with public disfavor and frequently cause expensive litigation. This may be avoided by issuing more capital stock as a stock dividend, in which no formal payment is received by the corporation for the stock.

On the other hand, one will prefer to maintain his ownership if a business has promise of increasing returns. The case would be different, of course, should the buying public have an exaggerated estimate of the future prosperity of a company. In this case the present price of stock would justify its sale. Buying stock is but buying future incomes, and skilful promoters may deceive the buying public. Buyers pay high prices for stock at times which yields no returns at the time of purchase. The anticipated future incomes discounted to their present worth determine the price of a share of stock or of any other source of income.

Ordinarily the wise promoter studies his proposition intensively and has a truer foresight than the buying public. If his estimate of future returns is higher than that of the public, he will prefer to borrow—issue bonds—rather than sell stock. Bonds bear a fixed return and, therefore, usually sell higher than stock which would yield an equally large return. To own bonds gives the holder no control in the management of a company, therefore stockholders wishing to retain management will sell bonds. A company will sell bonds, also, when the borrowed funds will yield a larger return than the interest paid on the bonds.

**21. Questionable Practices.**—The corporation is the most important and the most efficient form of business organization, and it is at the same time the most efficient business device at the disposal of rascals. At times corporations are so intricately devised that individual responsibility is completely hidden. Among the more common reprehensible acts of corporations are the following:

(1) Majority stockholders sometimes elect themselves to office and vote such large salaries upon themselves as to deprive the minority stockholder of profits. This, where permitted, is legalized robbery: it is a means whereby one confiscates the property of another. It is not less culpable than the act of a state official who would surreptitiously appropriate state funds.

(2) Majority stockholders determine the buying of corporations, and this may enable them to sell their own property to the corporation at such prices as they choose. For instance, let us assume that a prominent corporate director owns a near-by piece of land. He may direct his corporation to buy the land at a figure named by himself. Such exorbitant prices may leave no profits for minority stockholders. This practice, it should be added, is illegal both in common law and under the Clayton Act.

(3) Another means of defrauding minority stockholders is to form a new company to take over the business of the old company. If, for instance, the managers of a store become well known, if through honest dealing they acquire public good-will, they may establish a new store and carry the trade with them.

(4) The officers and directors have the inside information of a corporation and can use it to their own private advantage. If they foresee a decline in stock they can sell while the price is high, and when the price reaches the bottom they can buy treasury stock. If they foresee a rise in stock they may buy the stock of minority stockholders and reap the advantages of a rise, or if they anticipate that the company is approaching receivership they may trade stock for notes held by creditors. These notes will be good because they hold first lien against the assets of the company, whereas the stock may be worthless paper. A partial remedy for such abuses is the law, in New York State and other places, making it illegal for a director to "sell short."

(5) Directors may vote themselves fees for attending meetings. They may be exorbitant, and they represent just so much being subtracted from the stockholders' dividends. Probably the writers on the subject make more of this abuse than is justified; it is not unusual, rather it is a common practice in many corporations, for directors to get a gold piece for attending meetings.

(6) It is not unusual for the directors to juggle accounts. If they wish to boost the price of stock they may have the profits revealed and the losses concealed. Where accounts are subject to audit, a good showing may be made at the date of the balance-sheet by borrowing money which, as is understood by private agreement, is to be returned immediately afterward. Fake sales may give to slow, cheap stock an active, valuable appearance. This is a means of speculation whereby the books record large sales at good prices, but in fact a secret agreement is made at the time of sale to the effect that the stocks are to be taken back within a short time.

(7) Unscrupulous directors may inflict loss or even bankruptcy upon companies for whose management they are responsible. This reduces the price of stocks to a minimum, and the controlling directors buy them up. Such infamy in the past was not an uncommon means of defrauding minority stockholders.

(8) The last form of manipulation which I shall mention is the trick of cheating creditors. The lowest type of merchant is the one who buys on credit, sells, pockets the money and goes into bankruptcy. A similar line of action is the conduct of the most inferior class of corporate directors, who borrow to the full extent of their credit, split a melon, allow the assets of the company to decline, and go into bankruptcy. It must be added that such abuses are very rare.

**22. Remedies.**—Cunning rascality is fast becoming a thing of the past in business life. Lawyers are no longer regarded as a "bunch of banditti"; downright fraud no longer characterizes the activities of banks and stock exchanges; lending is not now a game of usury. Sound moral conduct is the prevailing characteristic of modern business activity, although there are among us scoundrels who would oppress the weak, and certain disgraceful practices are yet to be eradicated. Many persons will commit acts in secret that they would condemn in public. The fact that men will practise the highest order of conduct when held individually responsible for their acts makes it imperative that we go behind the legal person (corporations) and expose the natural persons, the real perpetrators of unfair practices. Inasmuch as men weigh their conduct when under public opinion, publicity is an effective remedy for manipulations. Cumulative voting has much promise for good, because it would give minority stockholders representation in the management, and minority stockholders would do well to attend meetings and take an active interest in their corporation. In the corporate by-laws there should be inserted provisions as to the salaries of officers, the limit to which a corporation may incur debts, the amount of surplus to be set aside each year and other provisions for protection. A most effective guarantee of business honor would be for certified public accountants to make frequent and searching investigations into the conduct of large businesses.

**23. Foresight in Business.**—To-day every part of the world is doing business with every other part. The enormous size of business units, their complex relationships with one another, and their interdependence impose social and moral conditions which were not in the minds of men prior to the Industrial Revolution. Great factories employ thousands of men for officers, clerks, agents, and laborers; they buy and sell on credit the world over. Modern business is based on trust and confidence; these are absolute essentials both in the internal organization of single enterprises and in the business relationships of industries with one another.

Since enterprises are organized for future work, we must have forethought. Business must be conducted by honorable and foresighted individuals, or it must be conducted under governmental restrictions and regulations. In the very nature of things, legislators cannot be expected to take the far-sighted view of the higher type of business men. They feel the urgent pressure of consumers for lower rates and prices; they have the vote-catching and political rather than the industrial point of view. They too often forget that high prices stimulate large crops, and that paying rates make possible the most efficient service. They are capacitated neither by training nor position to conduct industry intelligently. Shipping and commerce under public regulation in England during the war is a striking example of bungling and waste at the hands of the inexperienced.

Reference so far has been made to the higher order of business men, but many business men are short-sighted, are actuated by the nearness of the reward, and are extortionate. Fortunately theirs is a policy of self-destruction. In the Middle Ages the people thought that there must be public regulation of the charges and services of those who produced common necessities. For instance, it was thought that the community was at the mercy of a public baker, and that he could reduce the people to penury through starvation prices. We now reason that extortionate prices would react upon the baker, reducing him to penury. Competition springs up to reduce unfair prices, and an indignant community welcomes the newcomers with all the trade. Able business men are guided by considerations of public policy that compel them to look years and even generations ahead.

**24. An educational transformation** is now in process. A few years ago business was regarded as a game of chance and cunning trickery, and a man's business was looked upon as "his own business." While men were severely trained for engineering and the so-called learned professions, business training was neglected. A man of no aptitude for anything else might go into business, but to-day special institutions are established to train men and women for business. High schools and universities throughout the country are adding departments of business training, the purpose of this training being to give to men and women a knowledge of the scientific principles which underlie and guide business phenomena. One mastering this training becomes possessed of a public point of view; he is enabled to co-operate with the true mission of the state, which would make private acquisition coincide with social production.

We have seen how unprincipled competitors tend to lower the standard of competition. By paying low wages, requiring long hours and by refusing to put in safety appliances, they can produce cheaper, and undersell and drive worthy competitors from the market. In self-defense worthy competitors are forced to the low standard set by the unworthy. We shall now see how the unfittest tend to bring burdensome legislation upon the fittest.

The people must resort to legislation for protection against corporate abuses. It was the short-sighted and extortionate methods of certain railway officials which brought the railroads under the burdensome, but necessary, restrictions of the Interstate Commerce Law and succeeding legislation. If these laws put the railroads to cost and inconvenience, they must be last to complain, for why did they unwittingly force the public to its last resort for self-defense? They were the least fit corporate directors whose unfair methods forced the public to enact and enforce trust legislation. A wise policy rigorously enforced on the part of business men would have been more lucrative in the long run, would have spared the necessity of burdensome legislation, would have avoided much expensive litigation, and, above all, would have given the public trust and confidence rather than distrust and dislike for the corporate industries of the country.

Sound business practice reaches beyond the internal workings of an industry, for industries have a public responsibility and must fit their policies into the general scheme of social well-being. Much, not all, state regulation is a necessary evil and is necessitated by the short-sighted who are ignorant of their own self-interest. The chief means of hastening our educational process is publicity. We must be educated to a clear understanding of directors' responsibility. Under the corporate form their borrowing power is increased and their personal liability is diminished, and they are permitted to speculate with other people's money. This is a patent cause of unintelligent abuse of the corporate form. Increased power and diminished responsibility form a dangerous compound. While the corporate form increases productive power, it also increases acquisitive power; it is a license for the unscrupulous unless the sense of responsibility is made commensurate with the sense of power.

**25. Exercises.—**1. The individual may own *real property, personal property*, and the right to do something to the exclusion of others. Examples of such rights are *patents, copyrights, trade-marks, franchises*. Define each of the terms italicized.

2. What bearing does the safeguarding of the public welfare have upon the limitations of private property?

3. What is the object of forming a partnership? What are its chief characteristics?

4. Jones loans a firm —Smith and Brown—$10,000 to be invested in the business, with the understanding that he is to receive one-third of the profits. Watt sells goods to the firm. Watt sues Jones as a partner along with Smith and Brown. Is Jones liable to Watt?

Would Jones be liable as a partner if it were agreed that

he should receive 6 per cent in any case and 15 per cent of the profits?

5. Two views of partnerships: (*a*) A partnership has no entity apart from the persons who compose it, *i. e.*, a partnership is a band or agency of individuals for convenience of business, and so all income from partnership operation is individual income; (*b*) partnership has an entity as distinct from the individuals who compose it as if it were a corporation.

Would a partnership have to pay an income tax which is administered according to the first view? the second view? (Contrast the act of October 3, 1913, with the act of September 8, 1916, on this point. At this writing a proposed law adheres strictly to the first view above mentioned.)

6. How does a joint-stock association differ from the ordinary partnership? How do they resemble partnerships?

7. Paragraph 8 speaks of a corporation as an *artificial person;* other terms might have been used, as *legal person*, *legal entity*. What is meant?

8. Distinguish a share of stock from a stock certificate. How is stock transferred?

9. Explain how directors are usually chosen, and enumerate their powers. Do you favor cumulative voting? Why or why not?

10. Who is a stockholder? What are his rights? May he have more than one vote? Does he declare dividends? If not, who does? What is a dividend, and who gets it?

11. What are the functions of a receiver? By whom is he employed? What is a receiver's certificate? Is it more or less desirable than a bond? (For answer see any book on corporation finance.)

12. In raising funds under what conditions would you think it advisable to issue notes? bonds? preferred stock? common stock?

13. Summarize the questionable practices of corporations that are outlined in this chapter. How does the in-

creasing foresight in business (paragraph 23) tend to eradi-
cate these practices?

14. A corporation may be *dissolved* by the expiration of
the time for which it was *chartered*, or by the *decree* of a
*court* for various causes such as *insolvency*, non-use of franchise, abuse of charter powers, violation of law, *fraudulent*
and *illegal* acts. The directors or stockholders may apply
for permission to surrender the charter whenever they
deem such a course beneficial to the interests of the stockholders. Upon dissolution, after all debts and *claims* are
paid, the remaining *assets* are divided among the stockholders in proportion to their holdings. (Huffcut.)

(*a*) Define the italicized words.

(*b*) Prepare and answer (in writing) four questions based
upon Huffcut's statement.

# CHAPTER XXV

## LARGE–SCALE PRODUCTION AND MONOPOLY

The student must be on his guard against confusing large production with monopoly. Some purely competitive concerns are far more wealthy and powerful than are some monopolies. Size is not the distinguishing feature between competition and monopoly. But large competitive production and monopoly have many of the same advantages.

1. **Control by Best Talent.**—The large establishment, competitive or monopolistic, comes to be directed by superior talent. Real genius is rare in any kind of activity, as rare in business as in letters or in military leadership. If, in a single line of business, there are fifty individual, one-man concerns, all will not be directed by high-grade talent. The wastes of inefficiency attend the self-seeking activities of the mediocre. If, however, these fifty concerns are united under the control of an able director, the result will be that the labor, raw material, and machinery will be

556

effectively co-ordinated. Large production furnishes the only means whereby the few able generals of industry may control. And the wisest utilization of the agencies of production is the sole guarantee of the largest industrial output.

**2. Selection of Men.**—Methods of precision characterize the large industrial business or combination. A severe system of selection brings the trained intellect to the fore, where, as in large production, fitness is the test for place and ranking. Men in the ranks are watched, timed, and graded for long periods of time. It is to the self-interest of the employer to promote and, therefore, hold the right man. A condition in which labor is congregated and capital combined is in sharp contrast with the condition where one-man concerns are competing. The large and well-managed establishment has a number of departments, and in the course of his development the young man has an opportunity to be tried out in the several fields of labor. One may be a natural salesman and at the same time have little or no ability as a manager. Superior talent has its limitations, and the large corporation furnishes the several opportunities in which the young man may be tested and his natural adaptability discovered. Under the so-called Emerson efficiency method of wage payment, if a laborer is not 80 per cent efficient—mathematically calculated—he is put to another task. Only a large business could afford all the preliminary studies necessary to install such a system.

In early times the father left the control of the business to his children. This succession was not determined by the fitness of the child. Again, it requires but little capital to start a small business. The ease of starting such an enterprise is an open invitation to the unfit, and, in the aggregate, it means a vast waste of productive capacity. It is estimated that 20 per cent of the personnel of the small retail groceries changes each year. These changes represent a want of scientific knowledge, a haphazard or rule-of-thumb procedure which aggregates enormous social waste.

Macrosty's words are well chosen: "Rule of thumb is dead in the workshop; the day is with the engineer and the chemist with their methods of precision; in the counting-house and board-room there is no longer a place for the huckster, or gambler; the future is with the commercial statesman, whether in a large individual business or a combination."[1]

**3. Distribution of Talent.**—"The advantage of management by the best talent is a matter also of the proper distribution of talent. Some man in his independent establishment may have been peculiarly successful on account of his skill as a salesman; another, on account of his organizing ability; a third, on account of his special technical knowledge, and so on. If these various competing establishments all unite into one, to each man can be given the department for which he is peculiarly adapted, and in that way the joint establishment gets the advantage of the peculiar skill of each."[2]

**4. Standardization Aids the Purchaser.**—There are few skilled buyers; one may have bargaining power and yet be a poor judge of quality. The good buyer must be a judge of men as well as of goods; he must be a judge of the market in order to anticipate demand, and to take advantage

---

[1] H. W. Macrosty, The Trust Movement in British Industry, p. 337.
[2] Jenks, The Trust Problem, p. 41.

of the varying conditions of supply. Able buyers command large salaries because there are so few of them. Moreover, the knowledge of expert buyers is limited to one or, at most, to two or three kinds of goods. This being true, how can the average consumer be guaranteed a wise purchase in our modern complex markets? A large number of small producers but adds to his confusion, thus making a purchase little more than a gamble. The large establishment, however, standardizes its output and maintains a uniformly good quality. Its trade-mark gradually becomes a guarantee of quality and thus a protection to the unskilled buyer.

**5. Steady Demand in a Broad Market.**—The large combination can extend its business over a broad territory, whereas, generally speaking, the small establishment is limited to a smaller territory. The local concern is subject to local conditions of prosperity or depression. But the large business covering a vast territory is not necessarily embarrassed by a local depression. The depression in one locality may be offset by the prosperity in another. The local demand, moreover, is altogether seasonal in many cases. This compels the local producer to suffer the inconveniences of an irregular demand. He is confronted with the problems of maintaining his labor supply, of storing goods produced out of season, of making satisfactory agreements with the suppliers of raw material, and of the constant utilization of his plant.

A specific case will reveal some of the chief advantages of a broad market. A dealer in lawn-mowers informs me that his company sells machines in this country, Australia, Central and South America, and in Europe. There is always a mowing-season somewhere within this vast area.

At those times of the year, when large orders are coming in from South America there will be practically no orders from North America. Excepting a period of about six weeks, orders will be coming in from some parts of the world. During these six weeks the plant is run at full speed, and the machines produced during this period are loaded on slow boats, which reach the Pacific Coast in time for the opening of the market there. These slow shipments by boats are less expensive than shipments by rail.

This broad market makes a constant demand; it enables the plant to run the entire year; it avoids the necessity of carrying a large idle stock for considerable portions of time.

**6. The Quantity of Demand.**—The stock of a large selling establishment which sells 100 units of a particular commodity a week may be much less than the aggregate stock of twenty-five concerns whose combined sales are 100 units a week. To make this clear, let us study the variations of demand. *First*, demand varies with times and seasons. Lawn-mowers are demanded in the season when the grass begins to grow, overcoats in the fall, and straw hats in the spring. *Second*, demands are ephemeral. If the fashion leaders appear in russet shoes, the demand for such shoes will begin, grow into a "craze," then decline, and ultimately die. A skilful buyer can fairly predict the demand in such cases.

*Third*, there are chance variations of demand. One day hair-brushes are called for, the next day many tooth-brushes, the third day neither. The merchant kills his business by always being "just out" of the particular good the customer wants. The merchant must carry a stock which in variety and amount will meet these chance variations of demand. Customers will pass by a dozen small shops in order to trade with the big store, because they know that they can usually get what they want in the big store.

The small shop has no basis for figuring these chance variations, and must therefore carry a large idle or reserve stock in order to compete successfully with the large store. On the other hand, the store which is making a large volume of sales can closely approximate these chance variations. The larger the number of individual sales the greater is the tendency to maintain a constant daily mean or average number of sales. It has been calculated that if a large store sells 64 times as many goods as a small store, it will have to carry a stock not 64 times as large, but only 8 times as large. Now, since it sells 64 times as many goods and carries a stock only 8 times as large, the stock charge on a single article will be only one-eighth as much in the large as in the small store. If one merchant supplies a town he will have to carry but one-eighth as many goods as would 64 competing merchants.[1]

**7. Other advantages of large production, with or without monopoly power,** may be expressed in the following summary form:

(*a*) For the *handling of massive materials* the large concern is equipped with the best facilities.

(*b*) The large concern enjoys the full advantages of a

---

[1] It is said in Professor Ely's Monopolies and Trusts that "The mathematical theory of probability teaches that the larger the number of individual variations around an underlying mean, the greater the tendency of these variations to give a steady value of that mean. Those running over tend more and more to balance those running under; and, according to the theory, the mean of a number of variations differs from the true underlying mean by a quantity varying inversely as the square root of the total number of variations." See Merriman, Text-Book of Least Squares, p. 89, or any other work on the subject. The above examples are fonnd in Dr. Ely's book.

*division of labor*, of separate departments, and it can buy the very best machinery.

(*c*) The large factory *saves by-products*. Cottonseed is a by-product of cotton fibre; hide, bone, and fats are by-products of meat. Under the old hand-processes it did not pay to save cottonseed, but under new processes it is accumulated in large quantities and converted into valuable products.

(*d*) The Standard Oil Company *maintains an experiment station* in which there are made chemical investigations of the most elaborate and extensive kind. In fact, a regular investigating department is devoted to the problem of fully utilizing all the elements of crude oil. As a consequence, that company has in the market over three hundred by-products. Many of these valuable products are made from parts of the oil which would have been thrown away by a small plant. A large automobile concern is reported to have set aside $3,000,000 with which to perfect a tractor. No small company could do this. There are numerous social and industrial needs which can be served only by large capital.

(*e*) Small concerns suffer more from *bad debts* than do large concerns, especially those with some monopoly power. Keen competition causes a rather liberal extension of credit. When the American Steel and Wire Company was formed the loss from bad debts for the constituent companies was reduced from $\frac{1}{2}$ of 1 per cent to $\frac{1}{25}$ of 1 per cent.

(*f*) *Cross-freights* often aggregate a large total loss for a number of competing companies. In a large country like this freight rates are significant items in the sale of goods. If an oil-refining company in New Jersey supplies customers in Illinois, while a refinery near Chicago supplies customers in New Jersey, there must be large and unnecessary freight costs. Should these companies combine under one management freights would be saved because customers would be supplied from the nearest refinery. It is estimated that $500,000 was saved annually in cross-freights by the formation of the American Steel and Wire Company.

(*g*) *Cross-deliveries* in cities are no less wasteful than are cross-freights. The following statement may be far from accurate, but it is suggestive. These figures were displayed in 1912 at a national dairy show at Chicago. It represents the actual wastes of the present distribution of milk in an American city.

| *Present System* | *An Efficient System* |
|---|---|
| 173 distributors, requiring the services of: | A simple efficient agency could render superior service with: |
| 356 men and many families. | 90 men. |
| 360 horses. | 50 horses. |
| 305 milk-wagons. | 25 horse-drawn trucks and 6 motor-trucks. |
| 2,509 miles of delivering 62,300 quarts to 45,000 homes. | 300 miles travel. |
| $76,600 invested in milk-room equipment. | $75,000 equipment of one sanitary milk-depot. |
| $108,800 invested in horses and wagons; $282,500 total investment. | $100,000 building and real estate. |
| $2,000 daily cost of distribution. | $600 daily cost of distribution. |
| $720,000 total yearly cost. | $220,000 yearly cost of distribution. |

Resulting economies; better service, purer milk, $500,000 saving a year, or over 66⅔ per cent.[1]

(*h*) *The capacity* of a number of competitors often excels the needs for the output. Prior to the formation of the

[1] This example taken from Materials for the Study of Elementary Economics (p. 911) by Marshal, Wright and Field. Chicago University Press.

Whiskey Trust the distillers had probably 60 per cent more capacity than the market required. When the trust was formed it closed a number of the weaker distilleries and ran the more efficient ones constantly. This tended to make the business more steady, to keep the labor employed, and to enable the idle distilleries to be transferred to other lines of employment.

(*i*) *The formation of agencies to sell* the output of a number of companies may frequently result in large savings. For instance, there are a large number of small competing coal companies in Indiana. "The Indiana coals," says President Van Hise, "are of a kind that deteriorate rapidly when taken out of the mine. Several varieties and sizes of coal are produced; to obtain one size, other sizes must be made. If an order comes to a mine for a certain size, corresponding orders may not come for the other sizes, but such orders may come to an adjacent mine. If a group of mines may co-operate so that the orders will equalize themselves among the different varieties and sizes of coal, it is evident the waste will be greatly reduced."[1]

**8. The Best Size of Establishment.**—All of the above advantages, which have been alleged by different scholars in favor of combination, may be enjoyed by the large competitor as well as by the monopoly. The large competitive establishment may be manned by superior talent, and do business throughout an extended market. The large competitive establishment has a demand, is equipped with the best facilities, enjoys a division of labor, saves by-products, and maintains an investigating department. It can so locate its plants as to save in cross-freights, and it can adjust its capacity to its market.

[1] Concentration and Control, p. 92.

We might enumerate arguments pro and con on the question of the best size of establishments. But the whole argument briefly and accurately summarizes itself in this: there is but one best adjustment of means to the end of the greatest net return. This best adjustment would not contain relatively short or long factors; it would not have too much building for the machinery, or fewer laborers than the machinery demanded. It would have neither a shortage nor an oversupply of raw materials or managerial ability. There would be a proper proportionality of all the factors to one another throughout the establishment. This is but half of the story and the other half is that the establishment must be properly adjusted to the extent of the market.

**9. Some Advantages of Monopoly.**—Apart from the problems of size and proportionality there are certain considerations which seem to favor monopoly. A brief survey of the arguments for and against monopoly will follow. Among the advantages of monopoly now to be considered are: the elimination of cutthroat competition, the saving of invested capital through a proper installation of improvements, the reduction of the costs of advertising and selling.

**10. Cutthroat Competition.**—Assume a number, say ten, of competitors who are producing a commodity the cost per unit of which diminishes as the volume of output increases. It will most certainly be to the advantage of each competitor to broaden his market and increase the number of his sales in order that he may increase his production. By enlarging his production, the cost per unit of output diminishes, and, if fortune favors him, he can undersell and drive his competitors from the market. Obviously each competitor will desire to be the largest producer and will, therefore, lower his price in order to take the market. From the fact that each concern desires to be the largest, it follows that the total productive capacity of the ten concerns above assumed outgrows the total demand of the market for their product. Cutthroat competition between these producers will tend to destroy the gains for each and all. This, moreover, means a large social waste, for when productive capacity overreaches the demand the several plants must be idle a considerable portion of the time. These competitors will sooner or later deem it wise to form a combination to regulate prices and to restrict the output in the interest of all. Thus it is seen how cutthroat competition results in combination and monopoly.

**11. Two Types of Establishments.**—Productive establishments may be divided into two classes with respect to overhead costs. A railroad is typical of one class. It must have large invested capital in the form of rights of way, road-bed, stations, terminals, and the like. It must have these facilities whether the traffic be light or heavy, whether it transports a thousand or a hundred thousand car-loads of goods. Once the equipment is provided, the particular or special cost of transporting an additional passenger or commodity to a certain point is negligible. General costs or overhead charges are very high in comparison with particular costs. There are many industries in which overhead charges are very high in comparison with particular costs. Some of them are: iron and steel blast-furnaces, beet-sugar, cement, paper and wood pulp.

In other industries particular costs are high in comparison with overhead charges. The making of millinery and lace goods is largely a matter of individual skill, and does not require a heavy investment of fixed capital. Clothing, signs, and advertising novelties, some kinds of printing and publishing are exemplary of this class.

Industries in the latter class can adopt new improvements with comparatively little inconvenience or, generally speaking, they may turn to a new and different line of business without material sacrifice. If the opening up of a new car-line eats too heavily into his profits, the owner of a line of jitney-buses can either select a new line or, through trade, convert his property into the form of a grocery-store. But the case is entirely different where the investment is largely in the form of fixed capital which could be used in no other capacity.

12. **Lower Costs from Costlier Tools.**—The rapidity with which mechanical inventions follow one another is amazing. Valuable machinery may become obsolescent over a week's end. At any time important changes are apt to arise, the installation of which would work general revision throughout a factory. Should each producer be ready on a moment's notice to act with fearless vigor in scrapping the old and substituting the latest improvements, even though such change would render the previous investment worthless?

One's self-interest calls for the largest net gain. But the conditions for acquiring net gain vary with the change of circumstances. If land advances in price and wages double, the high cost of these factors will not justify the farmer in maintaining cheap or obsolescent tools. In keeping with the law of proportionality, he should scrap the old and stock up with superior tools, for when his tools are ineffective he must employ more of costly labor and use more of high-priced land to produce a given crop. To retain a tool or machine in use oftentimes proves to be far more costly than the original purchase-price of such agent. The cost of a superior tool may be far more than offset by the saving in wages and land rent.

13. **The Cost of Tools Limited by Saving.**—But the extra cost for tools must not exceed the saving in rent and wages. You lose if the cost for improved tools is $500, while the saving in rent and wages is only $400. Industries with large fixed capital must make sure that additional earnings will be large before the old is scrapped and the new installed.

If your plant represents a fixed capital of $10,000 whose annual earnings amount to $500, the complete installation of improved machinery, costing, say, $10,000, will destroy the old plant, let us assume, as if a fire had levelled it to the ground. No argument is needed to show that your loss in the form of the old plant is $10,000. Would the new installation pay?

The loss in the form of the old plant of $10,000, together with the cost of the new, represents a total of $20,000. It would pay to make the new installation only upon the condition that it would yield a return that, at least, would be capitalized at $20,000.

14. **The Competitor.**—Assume now that a competitor enters the field, and that his plant is stocked with the newest and best. Although his plant represents a fixed capital of, say, only $10,000, yet the improvements are such that he can displace you as effectively as the new machine formerly displaced the old cobbler. Does your ruin mean a social gain? If so, it is well.

Against the notion that your ruin is but an incident in social gain, you would perchance urge two points: (*a*) The first effect of the new investment is to destroy $10,000 in the form of the existing plant; and (*b*) the second effect is that it destroys a potential $10,000 industry in another field of production. ˙You will urge, and rightly so, that the test of social gain is met only when the new plant earns a return sufficient to justify a cost of $20,000.

15. **Factors Should Reproduce Themselves.**—A paying factory reproduces itself. Its parts gradually wear out and are replaced by the newest and best. Such replacements, however, are paid out of the proceeds of the past set aside. We say, for instance, that each item of the merchant's stock must normally sell at a price which will replace that item with one of equal price, together with a surplus sufficient to cover all the costs of selling it, and which will make some contribution to the expense of keeping up the building. Any item failing to do this is carried at a loss; and the merchant who continues to carry items at a loss will see his stock diminish and ultimately disappear. Likewise, a manufacturing plant gradually diminishes in worth unless the items composing it produce a sum sufficiently large to enable the owner to purchase another item of the same character, which in turn will produce enough to install its successor. The factory's equipment of this year, so to speak, is the offspring of last year's equipment, now largely destroyed. Next year's equipment will be the result of present equipment.

Upon applying this reasoning to a manufacturing plant in which heavy fixed capital is involved, it will follow that in many cases sudden changes will involve heavy social losses. The maximum social gain requires that the material changes be slow enough, in most cases, to enable the enterprise to get the chief utilities out of fixed capital.

But a competitor is encouraged to install the new, and, if possible, to drive existing plants out of business. Personal gains are made oftentimes at the expense of existing plants and also at a loss to society.

16. **Monopoly Control.**—The purpose of a monopoly is to secure the largest net gain. Ordinarily, a monopoly would utilize a machine until wear and tear would make it advisable to secure a new one, at which time it would put in the most up-to-date machine. But if the transaction should promise a net gain, the self-interest of the monopolist should at any time cause him to scrap machinery, replacing it by the newest and best. If on Monday morning he installs a machine costing $10,000, his self-interest would make it advisable for him to scrap it on Tuesday morning for an improved machine, if such would yield him a net return on the total cost. In other words, the monopolist would find it fitting and proper to do what society ought to do—introduce improvements upon the principle of net gain. Society is fast coming to recognize the advisability of monopolies, under public control, with respect to railroads. This is true because competition is more wasteful, and all but impossible among railroads, because of the large overhead costs as compared with particular costs. Upon precisely the same grounds we should reason with respect to certain other industries with large fixed capital.

17. **Advertising Waste.**—It is estimated that the annual outlay for advertising amounts to over $1,000,000,000 in the United States. Probably the larger part of this huge sum may be counted as social waste and this is a waste of competition. On the other hand, much advertising is socially productive. Consumers are taught through advertising to know the variety, quality, and relative merits

of goods, to know the most effective uses to which they may be put. It stimulates desire to acquire the best, thus bringing about the introduction of modern improvements. Within recent years advertising has largely eliminated the drudgery of the housewives. It has put the washing-machine in the place of the washboard, has substituted the vacuum cleaner for the scrub-broom, the electric iron for the flat-iron, and the fireless cooker and gas range for the coal and wood stove. Such advertising is educational; it raises the standard of living.

Advertising that is merely acquisitive is social waste. If a $10,000 soap advertisement but supports the extravagant claim of a competitor; if it is designed merely to solicit trade from a competitor, it must be classed as social waste. The individual may thus increase his sales, but at the expense of another. There is a fairly well-defined limit to the amount of soap used; if an alluring advertisement of Pears's causes a larger sale of that brand, it will mean a smaller sale of other brands. Society is a loser when the wealth within it is so utilized as to fatten one's purse at the expense of another's.

The literature on advertising argues that competitive advertising more than pays for itself. Such advertising, it is said, creates a large demand, thus securing to the manufacturer the advantages of large orders and thereby fosters large production, which enables him to lower his price. This claim is groundless in the case of merely acquisitive advertising. Purely acquisitive advertising—advertising that does not educate or enhance the volume of sales of, say, soap—enters into the price of the product and is paid by the final consumer.

There is an elastic limit to the amount which the purchaser can spend for the different classes of goods. And the effect of the competitive appeals is not necessarily to increase the amount of business along a particular line; rather it has the effect of destroying the appeal of other competitors. This writer recently asked an advertising manager his reason for inserting an expensive page advertisement in a prominent journal. His response was: "Did you note that my ad was directly opposite the page ad of our competitor?" When I answered in the affirmative he continued: "Well, I simply put it in there to kill the effect of his." The purpose and effect of much advertising is of this negative wasteful nature.

In most instances large competitive concerns enjoy the same economies as do monopolies, but this is not true in case of competitive advertising. Advertising wastes are most pronounced in the selling campaigns of large competing interests. Monopoly control would have the effect of destroying advertising waste and of maintaining such advertising as would teach the public regarding the merits and uses of goods. Its expensive advertising might be used, as in the case of oil and tobacco, to build up a new foreign market, whereas under competition such expenditures too often partake of the nature of a cutthroat scramble for the local market.

18. **Salesmanship.**—Much that has been said on advertising will apply to salesmanship. Salesmen with the gift of personality and persuasive powers are rare and expensive. Two salesmen may be handling equal lines of goods. They may work equally hard, meet the same number and class of customers, yet the one may take the sales from the other. Competing manufacturers know the advantage of personality in salesmen. Each concern desires

salesmen who can most effectively demonstrate its goods to retail merchants and other distributors, who can please these customers by advising them as to the selection of goods, the amount to be carried, and as to the best method of exhibiting and handling the goods. In short, each competing manufacturer wants salesmen who can take the trade from the other competing firms, and who can tie the customers up with the manufacturer they represent.

These rare and skilful salesmen learn to look out for themselves. The fact is, they tend at times to tie the customers to themselves rather than to the firms they represent. The customers learn to trust such men, are glad to see them come, are pleased to have their advice on what to carry, how to sell it, how to meet new styles and changing conditions. The good salesman never abuses the confidence of his customers, never oversells a small merchant and always has the "you" point of view when in their stores. While all this may seem excellent for the manufacturer represented, it may be, and often is, dangerous for him. Such a salesman will ask an exorbitant salary and his firm is all but compelled to pay it, and cheerfully at that, for his grasp of the market is known to competing manufacturers, who will gladly pay him a high salary. To hire him would be to secure his services, meanwhile buying the market which he controls.

With the formation of a monopoly, however, there is but one source of supply, and the expensive salesman is no longer needed for competitive purposes. "Work is organized," to quote President Van Hise, "so that a travelling salesman or agent does the work in a given community for a large concern instead of several for the different plants of that concern. When the American Steel Hoop and Iron

Company was formed, about two hundred salesmen were discharged."[1]

The remainder of this chapter will consider some evils or disadvantages of monopoly.

**19. Inequality of Classes.**—It is an unfortunate state of affairs where the few opulently rich are standing upon the substratum of general poverty; such is not consistent with democracy. Privately owned monopoly power and the universal franchise are not companionable. The majority vote determines who pays the taxes and finances public works. If I am poor and you are rich, I should vote for a high tax on you and a light tax on myself. If you have a monopoly which oppresses me, charges me a high price and kills my chances for competition, do you expect me to vote to sustain your power?

The house of want becomes jealous and suspicious of the house of have. This jealousy and suspicion grow into envy and ultimately into open conflict. The rule of the czar must ultimately succumb to the rule of the people. Men naturally hope for the destruction of that which they fear, and they fear the giant monopoly.

Professor T. N. Carver uses this homely though most fitting illustration: "I will take the common house cat, whose diminutive size makes her a safe inmate of our household, in spite of her playful disposition and her liking for animal food. If, without the slightest change of character or disposition, she were suddenly enlarged to the dimensions of a tiger, we should at least want her to be muzzled and to have her claws trimmed, whereas if she were to assume the dimensions of a mastodon, I doubt if any of us would want to live in the same house with her.

[1] Concentration and Control, p. 14.

And it would be useless to argue that her nature had not changed, that she was just as amiable as ever, and no more carnivorous than she always had been. Nor would it convince us to be told that her productivity had greatly increased and that she could now catch more mice in a minute than she formerly could in a week. We should be afraid lest, in a playful mood, she might set a paw upon us, to the detriment of our epidermis, or that in her large-scale mouse-catching she might not always discriminate between us and mice." [1]

20. **Elimination of Independent Businesses.**—From earliest times the term *odious* has been applied to monopoly, the reason being that monopoly deadens incentive, destroys independent businesses, and by means of artificial scarcity works personal extortion. Artificial scarcity is as effective in cutting short your rations as is a fire, famine, or pestilence.

In any industry the effect of monopoly is to make a small class of employers and a large class of hired workers. Independent concerns are eliminated. Absolute private monopoly would be industrial despotism. There may be "good trusts" and "bad trusts," as in government there may be good despots and bad despots, but the point is that we don't want the despot. Broad powers are not to be trusted to individual hands. Such is human cupidity that the results are contrary to social welfare when private parties have the opportunity to aggrandize themselves at the expense of others. The temptation is too great when individuals are at liberty to vote the public's money into private pockets. The point is frequently made that monopolies have in many cases actually lowered prices. This

[1] *Essays in Social Justice*, p. 332.

is not denied, nor is it claimed that all such reductions of price are intended to crush competition. The decisive point is that it rests on the discretion of the monopoly to gouge the consumer at will. A well-ordered democracy demands a wide distribution of ownership and responsibility. The problem of ownership is more than a mere matter of efficiency and price. It is a problem of an increased sense of individual responsibility which is best secured by increasing the numbers engaged in independent pursuits. A wide distribution of ownership causes a better distribution of wealth, and thereby reduces pauperism and crime.

It is claimed that monopolies eliminate private concerns by means of bargaining power—the power to exact unfair prices—rather than by superior productive efficiency. There are a few monopolies caused solely by a government grant or a limited natural resource, but in the main the monopoly problem is a question of advantage in trading. Intelligent efforts to equalize bargaining power will take care of the monopoly problem. Recent legislation recognizes that common carriers are monopolies with such bargaining power that they can exact unfair rates. This recognition has led to rate control. Also, it has declared against combinations in restraint of competition.

21. **Monopoly Deadens Initiative.**—To paralyze incentive is to deaden and demoralize industry: It must be admitted that unbridled competition is wasteful, and that it may go to the extreme of industrial anarchy. General Walker's example of the burning theatre[1] furnishes a fitting illustration of this. He says: The destruction of life occasioned by the mad competitive rush for an exit from a

[1] Political Economy (advanced course), p. 267.

burning theatre is a vivid case of the waste of unbridled competition. And the saving of life caused by the exit of the crowd under the regulation of a well-ordered police force is a forceful example of the need for regulation. Discipline can cause no force, but it can save much waste. As between unbridled competition and monopoly, give us the latter. At best, there will be wastes in any human system, but the wastes under regulated competition are not comparable to the losses sustained under the lethargy of monopoly. Competition keeps open the ways of progress by providing a fair and equal chance for all.

*Monopoly kills the incentive for superior workmanship.*— If you are compelled to buy your automobile from me, why should I lie awake at night planning and devising how to cut the cost here or improve the quality there in order to gratify most highly your wishes? But the case would be different and stir me to the highest incentive for superior workmanship if you were at liberty to choose from any one of a dozen producers. I should work for the best in quality, the best in salesmanship, the lowest in price. The truth of this seems to find evidence in the steel business. Prior to the formation of the trust the Carnegie Company was the best-organized steel company in the world, and it was manned by the most efficient steelmakers. It was second to none in its accomplishments and methods. The same, it is thought, cannot be said for the trust. The trust has vast resources and the best management that money can hire. But the best management cannot overcome the lethargy of monopoly.

22. **Summary and Conclusion.**—Many writers fail to differentiate among monopolies. One group begins its treatment of the subject by explaining "the breakdown of

competition" and follows by condemning our "blind faith in competition." They never weary in pointing out the "wastes of competition" and they paint in glowing colors the virtues of all monopoly control as a panacea for all industrial ills. Another group of writers would destroy monopolies without further ado. They think that one principle governs all forms of monopoly, and that unbridled competition may be universal in business affairs.

A one-point-of-view, whether for or against monopolies, is fallacious. We should justly condemn as a quack the practitioner in medicine who would treat acute appendicitis and sore eyes with the same cure-all remedy. We should be no less severe in condemning the one-point-of-view economist. We must diagnose, then prescribe. It will be found in the following chapter that different monopolies obey different principles, that all cases of monopoly are not covered by a common blanket principle.

There are government monopolies organized for government profit and others organized to render service at cost or gratuitously. Here different principles are involved. There are private monopolies, some of which are natural and obey the principle of increasing costs, others are capitalistic and obey the principle of diminishing costs per unit of commodity output. Here again different principles are involved. Some monopolies have large fixed capital, while others with little fixed capital survive through unfair practices and illegal agreements. Again, different principles are involved.

23. **Conclusion of Chapter.**—1. The greatest productive efficiency, on the whole, is to be found in competition rather than in monopoly. The technical advantages of large production may be enjoyed by the large competitor as well as by the monopolist,

2. Regulated monopoly is preferable to unbridled competition of the cutthroat type. A business, such as a railroad, requiring large fixed capital and operating subject to the principle of diminishing costs is in nature a monopoly and should be regulated as such. Antimonopoly moves in such cases are positively destructive. No one will sink large capital in such enterprises unless he may enjoy the protection which the nature of the institution demands.

3. Monopolies which result from artificial combination or unfair practices should not be tolerated. The majority of manufacturing concerns such as steel, oil, tobacco, and sugar, soon reach the magnitude of the single business unit where the point of maximum efficiency is attained. The great corporation increases its size not by enlarging the single individual units, but by increasing the number of such units. The independent producer whose plant has, in all of its parts, attained to the best adjustment enjoys all of the technical advantages of the large concern which controls a number of business units. What is more, he enjoys all the advantages of competition; he has no monopoly to make him secure. Despite opinions to the contrary, · it is the consensus of opinion that one secure in monopoly power tends to become listless, non-inventive, indifferent to new methods and economies.

**24. Exercises.—**1. If fifty small concerns unite it becomes possible for the best talent to direct the business. But does a combination afford the opportunity for the selection of the best men?

2. Were you offered two cakes of soap—Ivory and an unknown brand—you would take the standardized soap, but for all you know the unknown brand is better.

Two important economic principles are involved in the above statement. What are they?

3. In this chapter the paragraphs 1 to 7 inclusive point out fifteen advantages of large-scale production. Show whether each of these advantages may be enjoyed by the large competitor as well as by the monopolist.

4. To quote from C. W. Gerstenberg's Principles of Business (767–768): "To make a pair of 'ladies buck shoes' takes five feet of 'buck' at $.80 a foot. The small pieces left over are used to make children's shoes. What is the material cost of a pair of ladies' shoes? Should we say $4, on the ground that we used up the five feet of leather, and that anything obtained from the small pieces is 'found money'; or shall we say that it is less than $4; that the leather in the children's shoes did cost something? If the latter, what figure should we use? There are two figures which can be used—(1) the cost of similar small pieces of leather if purchased in the open market; or (2) the price which would be realized if the pieces were disposed of." Answer the questions raised.

What is the by-product, the small pieces of leather, or the children's shoes?

5. Base your answer to each of the following questions upon the assumption that an establishment has attained the "best size" and adjustment of factors.

(*a*) Are there any short or long factors?

(*b*) What bearing has the extent of the market for the products of an establishment upon the "best size"?

(*c*) Were the establishment enlarged would it necessarily follow that the cost per unit of output would increase? that the cost would decrease? that the cost would remain constant?

(*d*) Or would the enlargement of the establishment so increase the supply as to lower the price, thus diminishing the profits?

(*e*) Is the "best size" of an establishment fixed at the point where there is the best technical adjustment of physical factors, or at the point which will yield the largest returns in terms of money?

6. What conditions favor cutthroat competition? Does

cutthroat competition lead to the formation of a monopoly? Defend your answer.

7. Why may it sometimes cost more to retain a tool or machine in service than the original purchase price of it?

8. What fixes the maximum that you could afford to pay for a machine which would displace one already in use?

9. Do the same economic principles bear upon competitors and monopolists with respect to scrapping old machinery and installing new?

10. Under what conditions is advertising productive? When is it a social waste? Can you distinguish between acquisitive and productive advertising?

11. Suppose that a number of competing companies are formed into a monopoly, with the result that 200 salesmen are discharged. (*a*) Would this show that the services of these men had been merely acquisitive rather than productive? (*b*) Should you conclude from this that the monopoly proved itself productive by displacing labor?

12. What do you care if monopolies do eliminate the small independent businesses? Is your answer based upon a feeling of sympathy for the person ousted or upon the effect which monopoly control has upon social well-being?

# CHAPTER XXVI

## MONOPOLY AND MONOPOLY PRICE

1. **Motive in Competition and Monopoly.**—Monopoly and competition are antonyms. Complete monopoly means the absence of competition. Conversely, free competition means the absence of monopoly. Monopolies may be local, national, or international. Whether in the country village or in the large city, or in one nation or in many nations, the oneness of an industry's control with respect to price-making is monopoly. But a monopoly price is not free from competition, for although a seller may have undisputed ownership of a complete supply it is the competition on the side of buyers which makes possible a high monopoly price.

Competition means a contest between persons or groups of persons; it is the attempt of contending parties to get the same thing. And this attempt is unrestrained by any outside force. Some writers deny group competition and speak of "each actor . . . separately and individually." But this is an error because group competition is found in all forms of human endeavor. There is social competition such as competition between church organizations, societies, and the like. In athletics, for instance, the Giants are united in team-work, contesting vigorously against the Braves. College teams are contesting against one another in various activities. The competition between social organizations or athletic clubs is the same in spirit as the competition between large corporations, each composed of numerous stockholders. Wherever found, competition implies contest. Contest between persons or groups is altogether different from monopoly which implies oneness of control.

Each individual seeking gain through monopoly is likewise actuated by the selfish motive of maximum returns. "On the scent or in the fight he makes common cause with his pack. But in the division of spoils he is still a solitary eater." [1] The socialist's concept of brotherhood exists no more inside than outside the monopoly or trust. The individual's motive is the same in competition or in monopoly —it is largest self-gain.

**2. The test of monopoly** is the power to suppress competition and to control prices through unified demand or a manipulation of supply. This power may consist of a oneness of demand or of a oneness of supply. When one person or a combination of persons is the sole purchaser of a commodity such oneness of buying power is termed a *buying monopoly*. At an enormous cost a pipe-line has been constructed, connecting Cincinnati with the natural-gas field in southern West Virginia. The great cost of constructing a competing line over this long distance is, considering the market, prohibitive.

[1] Davenport's Economics of Enterprise, p. 476.

This fact gives the controlling corporation a buying monopoly over the owners of the gas-wells. Or one may take example from the distribution of milk in large cities. A large corporation may establish receiving-stations throughout the rural districts, to which the farmers deliver milk. These stations are rather expensive to construct, equip, and maintain. The amount of milk coming in to one station is usually not sufficient to justify a competitor's entering the field, thus leaving the owner of the receiving-station in control of a buying monopoly. In case a local competitor should establish a receiving-station at one point, the large concern, maintaining a chain of such stations covering the principal milk sections of one or more states, would increase the price to the farmers at the competing point until the small competitor is discouraged and quits.

One has a *selling monopoly* if he has bought up the available supply, or if he has control of the power to produce a good.

3. **Temporary Monopoly.**—To buy up the available supply of a reproducible good gives a temporary rather than a permanent monopoly. One's purpose in buying up a supply, generally speaking, is to raise the price in order to secure a profit on his investment. But as soon as the price is materially raised producers increase their output as speedily as possible in order to sell at the higher price, thus giving the monopoly but a temporary existence.

The manufacturer of a commodity may enjoy a temporary monopoly. There are a number of instances in which a single combination produces 75 per cent or more of the output along certain lines. Such a combination must supply, for the time being, a majority of the purchasers. If it makes the price higher the customers must pay the price or do without, since the other sources of supply are insufficient to meet their needs. What is more, the small competitor will hesitate to undersell the corporation possessed of abundant capital, for if it comes to a price war the larger could drive the smaller concern from the market. But if the large concern maintains *exorbitant prices* it cannot long maintain its monopoly power. There is always potential competition in the form of new capital and enterprises seeking investment, or of invested capital seeking more remunerative employment. In case one concern maintains an exorbitant price this potential competition, sooner or later, will become effective.

4. **Capitalistic monopolies** are those which by virtue of a great combination of capital can suppress competition and control the market. In the last paragraph it was pointed out that in case a corporation maintained *exorbitant prices* potential competition will become effective. But a capitalistic monopoly usually takes a more conservative course —holding its price low enough not to tempt competitors to enter the field. The large concern can hold its prices slightly higher than can its small competitor. This is true because the large concern is better known. If wisely managed, its output maintains a high commercial standard and reputation. It gives a large assortment and quality of goods along its line, thus enabling it to fill orders satisfactorily. The average merchant would rather pay a small fraction more to a single large house which can supply his various needs along certain lines than to divide up his orders among a number of small competitors, thus making shipments more irregular and less dependable.

5. **Other forms of monopoly** calling for consideration are skilled labor, legal, natural, quasi-natural or public service. Particular attention has been given to capitalistic monopolies because under existing conditions they illustrate the chief essentials of monopoly power. Their formation illustrates the characteristic trend of modern industry.

6. **Skilled labor,** in the form of closed shops, has a monopoly. It can maintain high prices for its services through restrictive systems, such as apprenticeship, which limits the number who may enter the occupation. This form of monopoly, however, is constantly threatened by the invention of new machinery, by technical colleges which are training men for such work, and by schools and other educational means furnished by the employers.

7. **Legal monopolies** have been organized in some countries for revenue purposes. France has a monopoly of the manufacture of tobacco; Saxony controls the salt supply, and Japan the turpentine supply. Tobacco and salt are particularly good revenue-getters. They are consumed in abundance and the price may be so fixed as to leave a large residue of profit between cost of production and selling price. The United States has a legal monopoly on the post-office, but not for revenue purposes. Governments have such monopolies on minting—converting bullion into coin.

In certain cases the control of copyrights and patents may give important monopoly powers. There are two purposes for the government's granting such monopoly privileges: (*a*) They promote improvements in scholarships and in the arts; (*b*) they protect capital which is employed to manufacture the article patented or to publish the contributions copyrighted. As an instance in keeping with this last point we may cite the experience of Herbert Spencer's invention of a very desirable type of chair. Had it been patented there would have been competing capital for the privilege of manufacturing it. But he took out no patent and could find no manufacturer willing to undertake the risk of producing it.

8. **Natural monopolies** consist in the ownership of certain natural resources, such as the ownership of the anthracite-coal field, the Kimberley diamond-mines in South Africa, and favorable building sites, mineral springs, and the like. In order that a monopoly may be formed of such natural resources there must be a limited amount of these. A natural monopoly controlling a commodity like coal comes to have tremendous if not dangerous powers in the community.

9. **Quasi-natural monopolies** include such public-service corporations as street-railways, railroads, telephones, telegraphs, water and gas plants. One characteristic of these institutions is that their services are consumed in connection with the plant. One cannot have a street-car ride expressed to him as he could a farm-product. If a water company or gas or telephone company has extended its pipes or wires into one's house he must deal with it for the time being, or do without. If a rival enters the field it is at the cost of needless duplication.

This point introduces the second characteristic of public-service corporations: the company on the ground can outcompete a new rival because it can do with little money as much as the new rival can with a large outlay. To illustrate, if the growth of population in a city makes an extra demand for lighting, the gas or electric company can extend its pipes or lines at little cost to supply the demand. But the new rival would be at great cost in constructing a new plant before he could compete. These institutions can increase their output, to a certain point, at a diminishing cost. If it should cost $20,000 to establish a lighting-plant and if only 5,000 lights were demanded, the fixed costs per light would be $4. If the demand calls for 10,000 lights the fixed cost per light would be approximately $2. Then, if we assume that the particular costs per light remain the same, there would be decreasing costs with an increase of output. One company can meet the total demand of a city far more cheaply than can two companies.

Moreover, one company is more desirable because it is more convenient than a number of competing companies. Competition between different telephone systems in the same city causes public inconvenience. Nobody desires more than one car-line in the same streets. We grow impatient at times with one water company for tearing up the streets. What if there were a dozen competing companies?

Competition between public-service corporations cannot be permanently maintained because of the principle of decreasing cost. There is, for instance, an elastic limit to the number of electric lights needed in a city. It costs a company less per light to furnish a large number of lights. If there are a number of competitors, each company will attempt to undersell its rivals in order to increase its sales and volume of output. It can then produce at the lowest cost. All the competitors might increase their output and lower their costs of production, but this would cause the market to be oversupplied. Such would prove a losing venture, because the competitive price of their products would tend to be lower than would their costs of production. In all like cases combination would be wise for the competitors as well as for society.

10. **Voluntary and Enforced Patronage.**—The natural and quasi-natural monopolies are in a position to command enforced patronage. The merchant holds the patronage because of past satisfactory dealings. To make his future more than an accident he must have the collective friendliness of customers. He acquires this collective friendliness or good-will through tactful, fair dealing. He enjoys voluntary patronage; the quasi-natural monopoly enjoys enforced patronage. "The railroad lunch-counter, the exclusive cab or baggage transfer-line, the gas, electric, or telephone company, and the street-car companies expect continued patronage, but this anticipation arises chiefly out of the public's necessity, not from their preference."

11. **Limitation of the Market.**—Monopoly power has been approached by scholars from the point of view of supply. This is due to the fact that monopolies control price by controlling the supply. But a more careful study of supply must be approached through a study of demand. One group of writers teach that monopoly power is derived from the control of some natural advantage in furnishing the supply. Another group teaches that the control of large capital alone may give monopoly power. Now, demand for goods is in reality a demand for the productive power to furnish these goods; the limitation of a demand for a certain class of goods limits in turn the amount of productive power devoted to the output of that class of goods. The natural limitation of the demand for a good.

then, is a protection to a corporation from competition if the corporation occupying the field has sufficient productive capacity to supply the demand. In all forms of monopoly there are natural limitations either in the form of demand or of physical limitations.

If, for instance, the population on an assumed island demand annually $x$ units of sugar, and if within their territory a factory were established with an annual capacity of $x$ units, a new factory would hesitate to enter the field. If a new factory did enter, its purpose would be to force itself into the monopoly rather than to bring about legitimate competition with the established concern. For a short time after the entrance of the new concern there would be overproduction for the island, cutthroat competition, a price war, idle labor and capital in both concerns for a considerable portion of the year. This game would force compromises, agreements, and finally combinations. Numerous examples of a similar nature prove that in a large society the ultimate consequences would be the same as those indicated for a limited society. Why is this so ? Because the market demand is limited.

12. **A Summary of Market Limitations.**[1]—Some of the influences which limit the market demand for goods will now be mentioned. (*a*) The consumer cannot spend more than his income. (*b*) We have seen that his income is divided into numerous lines of expenditure, that if he spends more along certain lines he must spend less along others; thus expenditures limit each other. (*c*) The consumer is ever measuring his present against his desire for future goods, he saves to the extent that he denies his present for his future gratification. It is interesting to

---

[1] Cherington's Advertising as a Business Force, chap. V.

note how the seller of a rather expensive article, say, of the Encyclopædia Britannica, can secure purchasers whose incomes are limited and who are disposed to save. The problem is to make a fair portion of the possible buyers figure that, incomes and savings considered, the price is not prohibitive. This is accomplished by splitting the price into small instalments, so that it looks small; by explaining how delay means waste, because the price is to be increased after a certain time; by treating the price as negligible compared with the worth of the goods. One is likely to change his course if convinced that what he had considered saving is in reality wasting.

(*d*) Price habits tend to become fixed. This fact is becoming more pronounced to the extent that packaged and branded goods take the place of bulk goods in the market. Ties, collars, shoes, gloves, hats, tobacco, matches, and a thousand others, are sold under rather well-established price habits. This fact makes competition largely a matter of service and of skill in selling. It tends to substitute quality and satisfaction for the old haggling method under the "let the buyer beware" principle.

(*e*) Present saving on the part of customers tends to limit the present market, but it has the effect of extending the future market. Savings enter, sooner or later, into the production of more goods. And, as previously stated, in an exchange economy a good is a demand for another good. The richer the community the greater is the demand for the produce which the consumers desire.

(*f*) Numerous appeals to the consumer neutralize one another. Recently an author was wondering how the consumer could save anything. "We expend a billion annually teaching him to spend, and but an insignificant fraction of that sum on teaching him to save." After some deliberation he arrived at the conclusion that, "only the foreign element can save because they cannot read the ads." Because both observation and statistics are against these comments, we conclude that the consumer has a will of his own, and, further, that numerous appeals deaden the effect of one another. If no other advertising existed, the housewife would experience a strong appeal from the page advertisement in her home journal devoted to Pearl La Sage's "Great Parisienne Beauty Marvel," but when she finds that over half her journal is devoted to appeals, the mere fact of their multiplicity deadens the effect one of the other.

(g) The final consumer determines the market limit for all producers. An apparent exception to this is the fact that modern production takes the form of a chain of concerns from the raw material to the finished product; iron-ore mining ➡ smelting into pig iron ➡ steel-making ➡ wire-making.

In such a chain— (A)(B)(C)(D) —B may be the sole purchaser of A's product, and the sole source of C's supply. B thinks of C as his only market, and so in turn C regards D. On further analysis it is clear that D does not limit C, nor does C limit B. They are the consumers supplied by D, who limit in turn the output of D, C, B, A. Supply travels, so to speak, in the direction from A to the consumer:

$$A \twoheadrightarrow B \twoheadrightarrow C \twoheadrightarrow D \twoheadrightarrow \text{Consumer,}$$

whereas demand travels in the opposite direction:

$$\text{Consumer} \twoheadrightarrow D \twoheadrightarrow C \twoheadrightarrow B \twoheadrightarrow A.$$

Demand begins and supply ends with the consumer.

**13. Monopoly price,** we have seen, is fixed at the point where in the judgment of the monopolist the largest net return will ultimately be secured. In most cases, not all, the monopolist will make fewer sales if the price is high and more sales if the price is low. Monopoly prices as well as competitive prices are always at the equating-point of supply and demand. The monopoly, demand present, controls the price only because of its power to control supply.

(*a*) The simplest case in monopoly price-making is found in a few cases *where little or no cost of production is found and where the supply is limited.* Suppose that one has inherited a collection of antiques. Assume that the collection is well known, so that no advertising or other costs are necessary for their marketing. What price will the owner place upon the collection? If the items composing the collection are virtually the same the monopolist could either sell them at a uniform price and all at one time, or he could sell each item separately and at different prices. The latter method would bring a larger total price, because the lowest price received by selling them one at a time would be the same as the uniform price on the items if sold at the same time. Assuming, however, that he sells all at once, he would fix the price at the highest point that would clear the market, that is, at the highest figure at which all the items would be bought. The monopoly price in this instance might be the same as if the collection were sold to a group of competing buyers, by a group of competing sellers.

(*b*) The case would be different if one had a monopoly of an *unlimited commodity where no cost is involved.* Monopoly always implies a property right; so let us say that one owns a natural well, affording all but an exhaustless supply of most highly desired mineral water. Then a price may be fixed so high that "he may only occasionally sell a pint to a king or a millionaire, while if he fixes a very low price he may sell to every peasant and yet get a very low return." The monopolist's problem is to determine the price at which the number of sales multiplied by the price per sale will earn him the largest net return. It is incorrect to think of monopoly prices as always extortionately high, for instead they are frequently lower than competitive prices. Nor is it correct to think of them as always low, for at times they are far above competitive prices. It is correct to think of monopoly price as being fixed at the point where the highest net return will result.

(c) *The elasticity of consumption* enters a new element into our reasoning on monopoly price. There are some commodities, such as the primary necessities, where the volume of sales varies but little with a movement in price. The market demand for such commodities is inelastic. Take milk, for example, which is a common necessity. Without milk the dinner would be spoiled, and yet even though its price is high it forms but a negligible fraction of the cost of the meal. Too much milk also spoils the dinner. In any case, whether the price be high or low, we will buy about the same amount of milk. The monopolist will most assuredly fix the price high.

For other commodities, luxuries, and semiluxuries, the market demand is elastic. Their volume of sales increases with a lowering of price and decreases with a rising of the price. By lowering his price the monopolist does two things: first, lowers the profits on each sale and, secondly, secures a larger number of sales. His purpose will be to strike the point where sales multiplied by profits will yield the largest return. But he meets with other complications; he must determine whether an increase of output will be at constantly decreasing or increasing costs.

(*d*) If the monopolist's cost per unit of output remain constant, 8½ would be the monopoly price in the following table:

| Price | No. Sales | Gross Yield | Cost Per Unit [1] | Total Cost | Profits |
|-------|-----------|-------------|-------------------|------------|---------|
| 10 | 1,000 | 10,000 | 8 | 8,000 | 2,000 |
| 9 | 2,000 | 18,000 | 8 | 16,000 | 2,000 |
| 8½ | 5,000 | 42,500 | 8 | 40,000 | 2,500 |
| 7 | 10,000 | 70,000 | 8 | 80,000 | — 10,000 |

[1] For sake of simplicity costs are taken as uniform, whether the yield be small or large.

**14. Increasing Costs.**—In many cases the *cost per unit of output increases as the volume of output increases.* Other things remaining the same, this will be found true in the mining of coal. The greater the amount mined the greater will be the distance underground at which mining operations will be carried on. The extra cost of moving the coal over the longer distance to the entry of the mine must be subtracted from the profits. Within the Kanawha Valley coal-fields there are mines which formerly returned large profits, but to-day they are abandoned. They are abandoned, not because the coal has been exhausted, but because the mining has been pushed so far from the entrance that the cost of operation leaves no profit. With this thought in mind, how would the anthracite-coal monopoly fix its price? It would, first, consider the quantity of coal sold at various prices; it would consider, secondly, the increasing costs brought about by the different quantities sold at the different prices. If the demand is inelastic the monopolist will sharply restrict output. This would secure a large profit on each ton sold, and would reduce somewhat the volume of sales, thus keeping down costs. Another policy might be to vary the prices upward from time to time in such manner as always to secure the highest net returns for the time being.

15. **Institutions of diminishing costs,** those whose *cost per unit of output diminishes as the volume of output increases,* generally find it advisable to maintain low prices. This is always true with respect to commodities for which there are good substitutes at reasonable prices. It is true when for any other reason the market demand for such goods is elastic. But in case of goods for which the market demand is inelastic the price will be high. The principle of diminishing costs could not operate in case of a monopoly, if the market demand were inelastic. Physically it could operate, but there would be a negligible demand for the increased output.

Public utilities are institutions whose cost per unit of output diminishes up to a certain point. Some years ago the elevated railroads in New York City reduced the fare from ten cents to five cents. The number of fares collected the last year on the ten-cent basis was 115,109,591. The very next year on the five-cent basis the number of fares increased to 158,963,232. These figures indicate that the company suffered an immediate loss. But it is now thought that, political considerations aside, the change has in the long run been profitable. One street-car line in Chicago, some years ago, tried a rate of twelve rides for a quarter, as an experiment. So phenomenal was the increase in traffic that the lower fare proved, it is said, more remunerative than the five-cent rate.

**16. Monopoly Prices Vary.**—Monopoly price, we have seen, is so fixed as to allow the largest net return. In keeping with this principle, a monopolist will vary his prices in different places. There is an English wine which is in ill repute at home, where it sells at a low price; the same wine is highly esteemed in the fashionable circles of Paris, where the monopolist holds it for a high price. Americans are comparatively wealthy and spend rather freely, whereas in comparison the Italians are poor and spend their means more sparingly. An American company is said to sell the same lawn-mower cheaper there than at home. Monopolies charge class prices when practicable. Railroads are exemplary of this, as a few instances will show: They run special trains with extra charge, charge different prices for single tickets and commuter's thirty-trip tickets; charge prices differing entirely out of proportion to the difference of service for first and second class tickets; parlor-cars and drawing-rooms and other special features are provided to appeal to different classes.

**17. Domestic and Export Prices.**—Large corporations and monopolies sometimes sell in a foreign market cheaper than at home. This practice is invariably condemned in the home market. To avoid this public disfavor, the monopolist spares no effort to conceal the fact that he favors the foreign market in price. The public dislikes a monopoly at best, and this dislike is kindled into acute resentment by the idea of discrimination in favor of foreigners. It is not a consistent policy of monopolies to favor the foreign market in price, yet there are probably very few monopolists who do not at times sell at a low price in the foreign market. This practice is technically known as "dumping," and is done in order to protect the home market, to keep the plant going, and to develop a foreign field.

The home demand for a particular product changes from time to time, depending upon the seasons of the year and upon the variations of industrial prosperity. At those periods when the demand in the home market is cut short, as well as in periods of prosperity, the monopoly desires fully to employ its plant. It must keep the capital employed because the interest charge for idle capital is no less than for active capital. A chief problem for the monopoly is to maintain a large and well-organized labor force. This would be all but impossible were a plant forced to run intermittently. To build up and sustain a nicely adjusted organization throughout a large concern requires a rather steady output. Large concerns oftentimes buy practically all of the output of certain raw materials. When the plant is constantly employed it buys these raw materials regularly and in large quantities, thus securing a dependable supply at favorable prices. Thus, in order to keep the plant fully employed, to avoid the wastes of idle capital, to maintain an organized force of laborers and to be guaranteed a steady supply of raw materials, combinations frequently lower the export price in order to dispose of a surplus. This tends to maintain a rather steady price in the domestic market. Such a policy is wise for the monopoly in that it protects the most desirable market. This policy is also advantageous for the domestic market because it eliminates wide price fluctuations. It removes an undesirable speculative or gambling feature from business.

Again, certain concerns, oil and tobacco, for instance,

consistently maintain a low price in certain foreign fields in order to introduce their product and thus develop a foreign market.

18. **Limitations on Monopoly Price.**—There is an elastic market demand for the great majority of commodities. The monopolist would find his price limited even on a necessity such as wheat, for if it is high rye or corn would be substituted. If anthracite coal is priced too high other fuels will be used. A lumber monopoly would find its price limited by other building materials—brick, cement, or stone. If the boat-line asks too much for moving sand and building-stone, the sand and building-stone will not move. The Chesapeake and Ohio Railroad is the chief outlet for the great Kanawha Valley coal-field. Nevertheless, this road must limit its rates, for the coal cannot be mined if the rates absorb the profits. Other coal-fields will supply the market and over other roads. Thus monopoly price is limited by the *principle of substitution* and, in some cases, by the *abandonment of industries*, which depend on the monopoly.

Again, potential competition in case of capitalistic monopolies always threatens to enter the field. Then, too, the monopoly must reckon with legal interference. If the monopoly price be exorbitant, public inspection and litigation are likely to follow. Corporations practise ingenious devices at times to hide large returns so as to give an appearance of normal to swollen incomes.

19. **Exercises.**—1. "The exclusive privilege of making and selling a product is a monopoly in its completest form . . . and it can raise the price of what it sells without having in view any other consideration than its own interest." (J. B. Clark.) What is omitted in this definition?

Monopoly used as a synonym for scarcity: "Landownership is perhaps the greatest single monopoly with which society must grapple. There is no sense of the word in which the private ownership of land is not monopolistic. Were there enough land to go around, and some to spare, landownership would be in no sense a monopoly." (Scott Nearing.) Criticise this statement, mainly from the standpoint of the use of the word "monopoly."

"Monopoly is such a degree of control over the supply of goods in a given market that a net gain will result to the seller if a portion is withheld." (F. A. Fetter.) Would this include a buying monopoly? Will withholding a portion always secure a net gain for the monopoly seller?

"A monopoly, as the derivation of the word implies, is a restriction imposed by a government upon the sale of certain services." (A. L. Perry.) Would this definition hold in the days of Queen Elizabeth? Will it serve now?

2. What is the test of monopoly?

3. Enumerate the kinds of monopoly mentioned in this chapter.

4. In a so-called capitalistic monopoly are there natural limitations which protect the monopoly? (See section 11 above.)

5. What is the practical importance of studying market limitations such as are outlined in paragraph 12 above? What suggestions might such a study give one who is planning an advertising campaign for the Franklin automobile?

6. In what sense can a monopoly "fix the price"?

7. What motive guides the monopoly in the determination of the price of its product?

8. If you had a monopoly of salt which you sell at eight cents a pound, would you raise the price should the government levy a tax of one cent a pound on it? If so how much?

Substitute a good for which there is a very elastic market demand for the word salt in the above, and formulate your reply.

9. "When a commodity is at a monopoly price, it is at the very highest price at which the consumers are willing to purchase it." (David Ricardo.)

What consumers, all or a particular class?

Is the statement true if it means the highest price which the most wealthy would pay?

If he means the highest price that some class would pay, would the same be true in case of any competitive price?

10. Does it make any difference in your reasoning on monopoly price of a good whether the cost of production, with an extension of output, is constant, increasing, or decreasing?

11. Why do corporations sometimes sell cheaper in the export market than in the domestic market? Is this ever justified?

# CHAPTER XXVII

## CONTROL OF TRUSTS

1. **Trust Defined.**—Common parlance applies the word trust to any form of large production or monopoly. This inexact usage renders the term incapable of scientific discussion. More accurately speaking, a trust is not a public utility, nor is it a legal or natural monopoly. It rests upon no special franchise, no right of eminent domain, no single important patent. The following are public utilities, not trusts; railroads, telegraphs, telephones, water-supplies, gas and electric plants.

Trusts apply to industrial combinations, manufacturing corporations in particular, with such technical and financial powers as to dominate in some line of production. They may or may not be monopolies, but they are formed to avoid the wastes of competition. It is fair to assume that the goal of such combinations is at least some monopoly power. So much for trusts in the economic sense. The legal concept of the word should wait for treatment until after a discussion of the pool.

2. **Pools.**—The pool was the usual form of combination prior to the era of trusts. It will not do to say that the pool is an institution belonging only to the past, for while legally dead, there are evidences of its actual survival. This form of combination is held together by an agreement on the part of competitors to accomplish one or more of the following: to limit production, to maintain prices, to divide territory, to divide profits.

Competing manufacturers have formed pools, some of which have accomplished good. There are examples where the association maintained a uniform inspection for the output of the several companies in the pool. Each manufacturer, in consequence, turned out a product of high standard. The output was marketed at a reasonable price, because under the pool there were no cross-freights, better transportation rates, minimum costs of marketing, and few bad debts.

The chief examples of pools, however, have not been among the manufactories but among the railroads. In the early days railroads were looked upon just as any other form of competitive business. Shippers were at liberty to drive the best bargain possible with the railroads, and the railroads were permitted to offer discriminating rates to attract shippers.

The fixed capital of a railroad is large and its particular cost for moving a unit of freight is negligible, so its interest lay in getting a large volume of freight even though the rates were low. Long-distance freights were probably lower in this country than in any other nation. Yet shippers and the public generally objected because the rates were so discriminating as to hinder, in many cases to destroy, competition among shippers. Certain large manufacturing monopolies owe their existence to unfair railroad rates. These effects of unfair rebating upon other kinds of business caused rebating to fall into opprobrium.

In fairness to the railroads, however, it must be said that they did not welcome the rebating which they themselves practised. They wished to get as much as possible, but the nature of their business forced them to practise rate discrimination as a competitive necessity. As a means of relief from this competition, so costly for both the public good and the roads, the railroads sought to form pools. Regarding the wisdom of permitting such pools, I shall quote the opinions of two eminent authorities.

3. **Statements in Point by Taussig and Jenks.**[1]—"The natural step for competitive railways is to put an end to competition by combining to fix rates once for all. Hence railway pools and combinations appeared at an early date, as a means of putting an end to 'ruinous' or 'cutthroat' competition. Such pools are hard to hold together, at least under the English and American law, which make them void and non-enforceable; but, so far as they go, they check the tendency to special rates for favored shippers. They are thus a means of furthering equality of treatment and equality of industrial opportunity. Whether or no it be sound policy to prohibit combinations and price agreements in other industries, almost all careful observers of railways agree that as to them such prohibition is unwise. None the less, our Interstate Commerce Act prohibited combination of any sort; and the prohibition was

[1] Taussig's Principles of Economics (2d ed., 1915), II, pp. 379–380.

made even more drastic by the general anti-monopoly act of 1890, known as the Sherman Law."

In an address before the reconstruction committee of the National Civic Federation (December 2, 1918) Professor J. W. Jenks said;[1] "I suppose you were all very much impressed, as I was, with the fact that when Secretary McAdoo was made director-general of the railways, his very first order was to permit universal pooling of the railroads. That is to say, under the powers that were given him, and in these extraordinary war times, he did exactly what all of the railroad managers, all of the economists, who had studied the subject, and the Interstate Commerce Commission itself from its very first organization on to the present time, had recommended. The bitterest discussions, at the time the Interstate Commerce Act was passed in 1887, were over the anti-pooling section of the Act. The railroads favored pooling under government supervision. But Congress put into the law the anti-pooling clause, and in spite of the fact that the first Interstate Commerce Commission, under the wise leadership of Judge Cooley, and many of the succeeding Interstate Commerce Commissions have recommended that that anti-pooling clause be repealed and pooling under government supervision be permitted, the political feeling of the country has been against it; and it was not until we were under the stress of war that the advantages of centralized action could be secured."

**4. Railroads During the World War.**—Experience as well as the theory of the case attest to the wisdom of railway combinations. Hampering legislation has endeavored to enforce competition among railroads, even though the

[1] *National Civic Federation Review*, December 20, 1918.

laws of economics necessitate combination. In consequence of this legislation the maximum utilization of the
roads has been prevented. When the war came the railroads were forced to assume a gigantic task, they were
strained to the breaking-point under the compulsion of
making vast additions to their normal volume of freight.
One of two things had to be done; either legislative restrictions had to be removed, or the government had to take
over and operate the roads. The latter was chosen, for
the public opinion back of this legislation was unyielding.
That it might correct the results of its own decrees, the
government had to become the operator, so as to ignore
the decrees. Now that the war is over and the government has the roads, all are interested to know what it is
going to do with them.

**5. The Situation at the Close of the War.**—Three measures are advocated for the railroads: absolute private ownership and operation, absolute government ownership and
operation, private ownership and operation under the government's supervision. Absolute private ownership and
operation now seems impossible. Such laws as the Adam-
son bill of August, 1916, fixes the scale of wages the owner
must pay. The owner is not free in the making of contracts which fix his costs of operation. Nor is he at liberty
to make those contracts which determine his income. The
Interstate Commerce Commission fixes the rates, which are
the source of income. One governmental body determines
the outgo and another fixes the income; between these
stands the owner to pay the bills as best he can. They
were not far-seeing statesmen who would fix upon these
means for the promotion of improvements and the growth
of railway systems in keeping with the needs of a rapidly
developing country.

A discussion of the controversial point of public owner-ship and control would not serve our purpose here. The sounder judgment, in my opinion, looks toward such a modification of existing legislation as will give the public the benefits of private ownership and control, but under a governmental supervision that will at once safeguard the public interests and free the railroads from artificial re-straints.

Enough has been said to show that the efforts to do away with pools have conspicuously failed of their object. With respect to manufacturing companies, when they have been forbidden to form contracts for their mutual benefit they have found ways of evading the law. The old way to evade the law was to form a trust.

**6. The Legal Form of Trusts.**—The word trust in its economic sense has been defined, and it is in this sense that the word is now used. In the legal formation of a trust the holders of voting stock in the competing companies would surrender, in most cases, a majority of all their stock to a board of trustees. Thus a central board controlled the vote and directed the policy of the companies. A single voting trust for the competing companies secured harmony in action as to kind of product, volume of output, and price. The holders exchanged their stock for trust certificates, and were paid dividends proportionate to the certificates. The Standard Oil Trust was formed in 1882, but the so-called trust period was from 1888 to 1897.

**7. From Trusts to Holding Companies.**—Under the pres-sure of the law the pool gave way to the trust, then the trust proved to be illegal and was given up in favor of the holding company. In the year 1889 the state of New Jer-sey assumed the responsibility of changing the trust policy of the United States. In that year New Jersey enacted an amendment to its corporation law which read:

> " Any corporation may purchase, hold, sell, assign, transfer, mortgage, pledge, or otherwise dispose of the shares of the capital stock of, or any bonds, securities, or evidences of indebtedness created by, any other corporation or corporations of this or any other state, and while owner of said stock may exercise all the rights, powers, and privileges of ownership, including the right to vote thereon."

Now, a company in any state is at liberty to take out its articles of incorporation in any other state; therefore, any company desiring the privileges of a holding company would turn to the state of New Jersey. Thus, an enactment of this one state legalized holding companies in reality for the whole country. In order to hold their corporations, other states followed in the lead of New Jersey. This is an excellent example of how competition among states leads to loose legislation. Under the governorship of Woodrow Wilson that state again led the way in 1913, when it passed the "Seven Sisters Act" which made illegal holding companies for the purpose of monopolizing or in restraint of trade.

Under the trust form the stock is simply placed in the hands of trustees for management. Whereas the holding company actually owns the stock of the constituent companies. The management and operation in the holding company are virtually the same as under the trust. The difference between the two is a matter of form rather than of reality.

Some leading examples of holding companies are the Standard Oil Company, the United States Steel Corporation, and the American Tobacco Company. In 1911 the first and the last of the above-named companies were dissolved. These were test cases proving the holding company to be illegal when it exists in restraint of trade. Again, under the pressure of law, combinations began to take on a new form of organization. Since 1904 mergers have become important.

8. **From Holding Companies to Mergers.**—The merger is the final stage in the concentration of control. There are no constituent companies in the merger. The master company buys in and cancels the stock of other companies. The only outstanding or remaining stock is that of the master company. To take an example from President Van Hise:[1] "If, for instance, the different companies of the United States Steel Corporation—the Federal Steel, the Carnegie Steel, and others—cease to exist by their stock being cancelled and stock of the Steel Corporation be the only existing issue, we should have the final stage of corporation management for this gigantic company."

This is a brief history of the changing forms of combination. But despite these changes in form the fact of concentrated control persists. "The trust problem" is the problem of obtaining a proper disposition of the centralized control over industries.

9. **The Purpose of Trust Legislation.**—The purpose of trust legislation is to declare a public industrial policy and to provide the means for making that policy effective. Its essence is to prevent artificial monopoly and to maintain competition. Our legislatures and courts have not been indifferent to questions of efficiency in the manufacture of physical commodities, but such questions have been regarded as of little consequence in comparison with

[1] Concentration and Control, p. 71.

such matters as the scope of individual initiative, an equitable distribution of wealth, and a fair field for all producers. Our public policy has in view not so much the technical advantages of monopoly or competition as the economic organization which will give us the kind of society we want. Competitive trade fosters a healthful social stimulus: It bears a social character which monopoly destroys. Competitive prices are governed by forces outside of any one man. They are democratic, not despotic; they are accepted as fair and do not bear the sting of personal extortion. Any contract to control prices or restrain competition is declared void, as against the public policy.

We have seen that public utilities are not competitive in nature. It has been pointed out that artificially to enforce competition among such institutions is harmful. An enlightened public policy must be based upon an analysis of the economic nature of industries. Analysis must precede any attempt to eliminate abuses and to preserve initiative and flexibility. Our policy aims to shield the public against the lethargy of industrial monopoly, which shows itself in poor service, uneconomical production, high and discriminating prices. It would insure a "square deal" to investors and employees.

Our laws are not yet so complete as to remove uncertainty among business men by defining what they may and may not do. As yet, unfortunately, well-meaning capitalists refrain at times from undertaking needed enterprises because our laws are not specific and they are not well adjudicated. Business men with the most commendable motives may find their enterprises subject to costly litigation and possible dissolution. The public policy and the law are not in complete harmony.

**10. The Hazard of the Business Man.**—But our laws must be expressed in general terms, for if we specifically define or enumerate the acts to be considered illegal, unscrupulous competitors will be quick to invent a new means of disobeying the spirit of the law. It has been aptly said that we dare not define the word "fraud," for our definition would be defrauded as soon as we made it. Then, if we cannot protect the honest business man by specifically defining illegal acts, it would be well could we have a board or commission with power to advise on such matters. A capitalist, for instance, wishes to establish a selling agency which would necessitate his making a number of contracts with other business men. Would his agency be legal? Would his contracts be enforcible? If he consults his own attorneys they can render him only unofficial advice. There is no one to whom he may turn for an authoritative reply. He trusts to luck, takes the risk, and hazards his capital. After his business is under way the Attorney-General may institute suit against him: He fights the suit for the existence of his business and it is only upon the outcome of this costly suit that he learns whether his business is legal or illegal.

Why, then, do we not establish a commission to advise the undertakers of business enterprises? The fact is that some members of Congress and perhaps the majority of citizens throughout the country were of the opinion that the Federal Trade Commission would perform this very function. But it is the function of the court to interpret the law. Congress could not constitutionally confer such authority on a commission. Congress is not at liberty to transfer the powers of the judiciary, for authority to take away powers implies the authority to abolish.

In a sense, the frequent change of administrations with the consequent enactment of new trust legislation is unfortunate. Frequent changes in legislation disturb business. It takes time for business to become thoroughly adjusted and for the laws to become reasonably adjudicated. Stable conditions give confidence to capital.

11. **Competition and Attempt to Monopolize.**—To obtain the largest net returns from an establishment is primarily a technical problem of efficiency. It is a problem of adjusting the different parts of an establishment to each other, and of conforming the size of the establishment to the market. The most wisely adjusted plants have competitive advantages; their minimum costs of production enable them to undersell less efficient rivals. This compels the less efficient to bestir themselves, to adopt the newest and best or be left behind.

Deductions from these simple truths have led thoughtful economists to grave errors. Some have advanced the claim that it is illogical to prohibit attempts to monopolize because monopoly is at once the goal and the natural result of competition. Competition weeds out the inefficient and leaves the battle to the strong. This argument has been advanced largely with respect to industrial establishments. That this argument is full of error I shall now proceed to show.

In the first place, it mistakes different things for the same thing. "To compete" and "to attempt to monopolize" are not the same, but antagonistic in principle. The legitimate competitor would not build up his own house by tearing down his competitor's house; his purpose is different—it is to build a better house than that of his neighbor. If one competitor builds a better ferry-boat than another he may take the bulk of the trade: If he sinks his competitor's boat or drives him from the river with a shotgun, again he will take the trade. It will be admitted, however, that these methods of enlarging trade differ. An "attempt to monopolize" is an attempt to eliminate competition. Except in a very few instances of large fixed capital industrial monopolies are artificial and obtained by predatory methods. To use the wording of Professor A. A. Young, "The contention that 'to compete' and 'to attempt to monopolize' are synonymous is clearly unsound. They are definitely antagonistic in principle." [1]

Those who advocate the above view still adhere to the antiquated doctrine that monopoly is the final limit of all so-called institutions of increasing returns. And this in spite of the fact that for fifteen years it has been established that the limit of diminishing costs is the point of best proportionality and not that of monopoly.

12. **Common Law on Restraint of Trade.**—The purpose of restraint of trade is to monopolize or to attempt to monopolize. The common law has held that contracts for this purpose are illegal and non-enforcible. Reasonable restraints, however, have been permissible. English courts have held that where the purpose of a contract is the protection of one's own business, it is legal even though it seriously hampers competition. On the whole, common-law cases have declared illegal contracts which act to the detriment of a third party. Public opinion is and has been antagonistic to combination. The general trend of public opinion and of the courts has been to the doctrine that combination has hurtful powers not possessed by the

[1] *Journal of Political Economy*, vol. 23, p. 215.

individual acting alone. It has been held that certain acts are legal for an individual, but that these same acts would be illegal if done in combination with others. It is significant that in the past particular interest has been attached to the rights of individual litigants rather than to the rights of the general public. To-day emphasis falls upon the point that the community must be protected from unfair practices.

13. **Laissez-Faire and Control.**—The doctrine that the government should keep its hands off business relations was good for its time and place, but changing conditions have rendered it obsolescent. In a community of small business concerns *laissez-faire* vivifies a healthful rivalry in serving the public. But modern methods of industrial warfare under the rule of *laissez-faire* would vitiate the forces of natural economic laws and render monopoly control intolerable. The government must define and enforce the proper limits of industrial enterprise. Laws unenforced are but pious declarations of principle. The doctrine of *laissez-faire* had as its goal the protection of property, the freedom of person, and the stimulation of production. "To let alone" was regarded a fit and proper means of guarding the people's interests.

Conditions differ, for to-day monopoly threatens the people's interests. To protect social interests we must have the regulating power of law. "The official who restrains the plundering monopoly, preserves honest wealth, and keeps open the field for independent enterprise does on a grand scale something that is akin to the work of the watchman who patrols the street to preserve order and arrest burglars."[1] The old doctrine of *laissez-faire* and

[1] John Bates Clark, Essentials of Economic Theory, p. 385.

the new idea of restraint are one and the same in essence and purpose. The former would not have competition destroyed: The latter would have competition preserved. Both adhere to the faith that natural development depends on competition.

14. **The Sherman Anti-Trust Law.**—The common-law proved inadequate to deal with the unfair practices of monopolies and trusts. Restraints of trade were treated as questions of private rights and the broader aspects of public policy were virtually ignored. The public, therefore, was not behind the law, making sure its enforcement. Meanwhile, large combinations were extending their influence and the people felt the pressure of their power. Conflicts of interest as between producers and consumers were difficult of adjustment, due to the complex economic problems in modern industry which neither side understood. Nor were the courts possessed of clear vision. The cases, for the most part, involved complex economic problems, and lawyers rather than economists decided them.

An awakened public opinion first turned against the railroads and the Interstate Commerce Act of 1887 was passed. This was followed by the Sherman Act of 1890. The purpose of this act was to protect the public against the evils of trusts. *The act declared against contracts, combinations, or conspiracies in restraint of trade or commerce.* It provided that persons who monopolize or attempt or conspire to monopolize any part of the trade or commerce between states, or with foreign countries, shall be punished. The punishment for disobeying the law may be by fine (not more than $5,000), or imprisonment (not more than one year), or both, in the discretion of the court.

15. **The Prevention of Trusts.**—In the last several years no little has been said and written on "trust-busting." Many thoughtful persons believe that under our laws existing trusts cannot be destroyed and competition restored. Others believe that the restoration of competition is possible in the fields now dominated by trusts. The fact is that vigorous enforcement of anti-trust laws are too recent to warrant a conclusion on the restoration of competition. The Sherman Law was little more than a dead letter prior to 1911. The methods by which the law was enforced were too gentle to test its power. The punishment of offenders consisted of a light fine rather than imprisonment. It was good business for corporations to break the law. If one is fined $5 for an act which profits him $10, it is good business to perform the act. These fines have been much like the student's matriculation fee—a necessary nuisance, but when paid it is settled once for all. It has rarely happened that a trust has been punished more than once. Other trusts escaped fine, merely being informed that their acts were illegal. Trust activities are little restrained under such enforcement. Not the terminology of the law but the rigor of its enforcement is the significant thing. Trusts fear but little the possibility of a fine, but the lawbreaker does fear the jail.

16. **The Standard Oil Case.**—A few noteworthy cases having to do with holding companies were tried under the Sherman Act. Among these the Standard Oil case of 1911 is typical. The Standard had bought many of the subsidiary companies and had established outright a number of others. The whole company was firmly knit together and the majority stock was controlled by a small group of closely associated individuals. How did the court pro-

ceed to dissolve the combination and restore competition among the several companies?

The court decreed that the stock in the different constituent companies should be divided *pro rata* among the stockholders of the holding company. If, for example, A, B, and C each owned one-third of the stock of the Standard Oil or holding company, they would each come to own one-third of the stock of each subsidiary company. The court permitted the same persons to be elected as officers or directors of two or more of the subsidiary companies. Yet the officers of the different companies were enjoined from making any agreements among themselves to restrain trade. The court prohibited some other formal means for securing unity of control. The court left precisely the same community of interest, the same persons owning jointly the same properties. And thus the holding company was "busted" and the Sherman Law enforced.

**17. Prevention or Destruction.**—The prevention of trusts would be far easier than the destruction of existing trusts. The courts seem to be hindered by precedent and form. Certain trusts have dodged the law and maintained their existence by changing the form of their organization, although in essence they have remained the same. The purpose of the men who conspire under the protection of a legal form remains unchanged. To quote from Durand's excellent little book:[1] "Difficult as it may be to break up trusts already formed and firmly knit together, there seems no serious difficulty in preventing by law the formation of new trusts. Indeed, it is noteworthy that

---

[1] The Trust Problem, pp. 39–40. This writer is particularly indebted to Dr. Durand's book for the treatment of several of the topics here discussed, especially the next topic—"Trust Regulation."

since the government began somewhat actively to bring proceedings under the Sherman Anti-Trust Act, almost no trusts have been organized. If a proper control over the organization of corporations and over their acquisition of corporations and over their acquisition of property and securities were exercised by the states and by the Federal Government, the attempt to organize new trusts would be nipped in the bud."

18. **Trust Regulation.**—A policy of regulation is based upon the existence of trusts and it assumes that they are to continue. We have seen that no blanket principle can apply to all trusts; some few trusts (public utilities and natural monopolies are not trusts) having large fixed capital are in nature possessed of monopoly power and should be regulated accordingly. As for railroads, even the courts have urged that the common-law principle of allowing contracts in "reasonable" restraint of trade is necessary and desirable.[1] A new judicial distinction, doubtless a troublesome and unworkable one, has come to the fore within the last few years. It is that "good trusts" are to be distinguished from "bad trusts." The latter to be restrained and the former to be upheld in its agreements upon "reasonable" prices and other contracts which will not "unduly" restrain trade. Consumers regard all trusts as bad; interested parties pronounce them good. Who is the judge? Right here lies the difficulty. This policy requires the government to act as judge and its judgment must be based upon fact.

Contemplate the enormousness of the task which the government must assume and the matter will appear at once impracticable, if not unworkable. Government regulation upon the basis of "good" will compel the government vir-

[1] 166 W. S. 329; 171 W. S. 567.

tually to prescribe what are to be reasonable prices and profits. The machinery for government regulation must be vast and expensive. Investigation of the facts must be continuous, for a good trust may become bad over a week's end. The government must get frequent data, must keep up with changing costs of raw materials, labor, obsolescence, and new investments. The complex principle of joint costs must not escape attention. The investigation of to-day will be antiquated by the changing demand of to-morrow.

The accounting problem is not least among the difficulties. The Interstate Commerce Commission has had its full quota of difficulty in its attempt to secure a workable accounting system in one line of industry. In this it has not wholly succeeded after painstaking effort, although its problem is simple in comparison with that of securing satisfactory results among a vast number of trusts, differing in nature and necessarily in systems of accounting. Good accountants are scarce and their services costly, yet thorough regulation will require double work in accounting. The trust must have its accountants in order to keep its business straight, and as a basis for its management and price policy. The government must have its corps in order to render judgment on the work of the trust. The complicated machinery and double work required for anything approaching thorough regulation would offset the reason given for allowing the good trust to exist—the reason of efficiency. Furthermore, if "good" be the criterion for a trust's existence, it must follow that any combination which meets the test must be allowed to form itself into a trust and its existence protected for such time as it behaves itself. Prevention is the safer method.

19. **Need of Further Legislation.**—The Sherman Law was worded in terms so general as to permit of a variety of interpretations. The term, "restraint of trade," was a vital part of the law, but it was nowhere defined in the statute. In rendering the opinion in the Standard Oil case Chief-Justice White argued that Congress did not define the term in order "to leave it to be determined by the light of reason." He said that if literally and narrowly interpreted it would deny the right to contract as to subjects embraced in interstate trade. Thus it would tend to restrain rather than promote interstate trade. But in the dissenting opinion Justice Harlan said that ". . . Congress prohibited every contract, combination, or monopoly in restraint of commerce, it prescribed a simple, definite rule that all could understand. . . ."

Also, differences of opinion arose as to whether the law applied to labor-unions and to railway combinations. A narrow interpretation made it a weapon against strikes and boycotts. This was not in keeping with the spirit of the act, and was enough to call for an amendment of the law. Again, in its application to railroads it overlapped the Interstate Commerce Act. Railroads are natural monopolies; rate agreements are inevitable, and therefore call for regulation rather than enforced competition. These facts called for a revision of the law or for further legislation to maintain competition in cases of trusts as such.

20. **Unfair Methods of Competition.**—The purpose of this paragraph is to give an idea of the nature of unfair methods of competition in order that we may appreciate a leading problem which the legislation of 1914 attempted to solve. We shall briefly enumerate some unfair methods which are characteristic of all such practices.

One prominent American corporation[1] is noted for the ingenious methods which it used in overcoming competition. It used "fighting brands" which were sold in competition with the goods of other companies at or below the cost of production. Meanwhile it did not grow poor, because it was securing handsome profits on brands outside of the fighting arena. There were many, among them some labor-unions, who refused to patronize this so-called trust. Thereupon the corporation in question bought up twenty or more concerns and ran them as supposedly independents. These concerns went through the outward forms of competition with their owner and were for a time well supported by the opponents of the trust. Other methods employed by this concern were those of forming exclusive contracts with dealers who sold its products, whereby such sellers were not to receive supplies from competing companies. It furthermore placed the business of its competitors under secret espionage.

Such practices are destructive, never constructive. Their purpose and effect is to destroy the business of others. Oftentimes a smaller corporation, threatened with ruin because of the unscrupulous procedure of a successful rival, will wish to sell its holdings if only at a nominal sum. But at least one successful rival boasts thus: "We are receiving overtures to buy out opposition. We will not buy them out; we knock out." In a criminal indictment[2] brought against the company that made the above boast the following charges, among others, were enumerated: (*a*) Inducing, hiring, and bribing employees of competitors to reveal the secrets of their business; (*b*) bribing common carriers, telegraph and telephone com-

[1] Meyer Jacobstein's The Tobacco Industry in the United States. Columbia University Studies, 1907.
[2] Indictment presented February 22, 1912. *Federal Reporter*, vol. 201, pp. 699–705.

panies, to reveal secrets relative to the carriage of competitors' goods; (c) falsifying to banks to the injury of competitors in order to prevent their securing needed funds; (d) also falsifying to prospective purchasers regarding the merits of the competitors' goods; (e) instructing its agents how to remove essential parts and thus cause a speedy breakdown of the competitors' product; (f) cutting prices to a prospective buyer of a competitor, or taking a competitor's product in exchange and advertising it as "junk" "For Sale at Thirty Cents on the Dollar"; (g) offering "knockers" or a defective product, which it constructed in imitation of the competitor's product, and using the same to demonstrate the inferiority of the rival's goods; (h) bringing harassing lawsuits against competitors, buying off their agents, and so forth.

21. **The anti-trust legislation of 1914** consists of two statutes, the Federal Trade Commission Act and the Clayton Act ("an Act to supplement existing laws against unlawful restraints and monopolies and for other purposes"). The President signed the first September 26, 1914, and the last twenty days later. In the preceding national election the Progressive party, led by Mr. Roosevelt, stood for the policy of "monopoly-accepted-and-regulated"; the Republican party, led by Mr. Taft, stood for the policy of "monopoly-prosecuted"; the Democratic party, led by Mr. Wilson, stood for the policy of "competition-maintained-and-regulated."

These acts are but two parts of the same legislation and are to be considered together. The Trade Commission Act embodies the provisions against unfair methods of competition (which logically belongs in the Clayton Act), otherwise it provides the machinery and methods to make the Clayton Act effective.

Unfair methods of competition, whether on the part of

firms or individuals, are declared unlawful. As in the Sherman Act, "unfair methods" are not defined. This term is so vague that business men must be left in doubt at times as to the legality of their acts. Yet, as above pointed out, to specifically define what are illegal acts would provide the unscrupulous a means of disobeying the spirit of the law while obeying the letter. However, a wise provision is inserted which protects the well-meaning law-breaker. It is that no penalty shall be given for the initial offense. The Trade Commission and the courts are, in the light of reason, to interpret as to the fairness or unfairness of methods as cases arise.

22. The Federal Trade Commission.—A function of the commission is to be "smelling around all the time for rats." And when unfair practices are found it is significant that the proceedings against such practices begin with the commission. The commission is not obliged to take action, and neither the court nor a prosecuting attorney can take the initiative, therefore the unscrupulous trust, in matters of unfair competition, is at the mercy of the commission. It is compelled to proceed only "if it shall appear to the commission that a proceeding by it in respect thereof would be to the interest of the public." Many argue that the law is weakened by virtue of leaving its enforcement to a body who are not compelled to act. None the less, the provision seems wise in light of the endless toil which would be occasioned if proceedings were brought in all cases—the trivial as well as the important. The commission nips in the bud needless litigation by issuing orders to offenders to discontinue unfair practices. In case its orders are disobeyed, application is made direct to the circuit court of appeals for enforcement. In this

particular the Federal Trade Commission is less powerful in its field than is the Interstate Commerce Commission in the field of transportation, for since 1906 a penalty has been provided for disobeying its orders.

But it is a problem of deep significance as to whether or not a commission is strengthened by giving it power to enforce its commands. Though used in a different connection I shall use the wording of President Hadley to make clear this point: "In the days of its (the Massachusetts Railroad Commission)[1] most successful operation it had practically no power except the power to report; but its reports showed such a clear understanding of the points at issue that they were accepted as authority by impartial men on both sides. The Interstate Commerce Commission was in some respects modelled upon the Massachusetts commission, and such success as it has enjoyed (President Hadley wrote this in 1896) has been based on its power of applying sound economic principles to difficult cases. It is true, though it sounds paradoxical, that the power of these commissions is lessened by increasing their powers. They are engaged in building up new laws, new traditions, and new methods of business, where it is absolutely essential that their reasoning should command the assent of clear-headed men on both sides. When they cease to rely on their reason and fall back on authority, they lose the educational power which is the source of their dominant influence."[2]

The commission, as a body of expert investigators into the facts of unfair practices injurious to the public interest, is easily the important feature of the new legislation, for indeed the law as such embodied little not found in

[1] Parenthesis mine.  [2] Hadley's Economics, p. 177.

the Sherman Act. The findings of the commission, with an unimportant exception, are treated by the court as conclusive. Its powers for investigation (except in cases of banks and common carriers) are unlimited. It can demand and examine the books and papers of corporations; it can command witnesses to appear and testify. It is significant that the law makes witnesses immune from prosecution on their testimony. It can require annual reports ·or special reports on any subject-matter it desires from all companies engaged in interstate or foreign commerce. These reports will reveal a vast amount of information, previously unobtainable, and of inestimable importance in dealing with the trust problem.

The law forbids the commission's making known "trade secrets" and names of customers; otherwise it is at liberty to give its findings publicity. A chief characteristic of Professor Jenks's The Trust Problem, first published in 1900, was his insistence upon publicity as the primary force in the control of trusts. Public sentiment, however, was not then ripe for such a measure, and trust officials preferred to hold council behind closed doors. But the wisdom of a policy of publicity was apparent, and it has grown gradually into public favor. The corporations themselves are coming more and more to adopt the policy. Many of them upon their own initiative are making full reports to the public. Public and business sentiment is ripe for a full measure of publicity and the policy has taken the form of law.[1] It is fortunate that the Federal Trade Com-

[1] The Bureau of Corporations (established in 1903) was a body of expert investigators, but could not determine what information it might make public. Probably valuable findings have not been published. In its field the Interstate Commerce Commission, through publicity, has rendered invaluable aid.

# 626 *Introduction to Economics*

mission, with its unlimited opportunity to observe and investigate the trusts, should have this power. Constant touch with these problems will eminently fit the commission to advise with respect to needed trust legislation.

Returning to other features of the law, it is noteworthy that labor-unions and "agricultural or horticultural" associations are not covered by these statutes.

**23. Holding Companies and Interlocking Directorates.**—The Clayton Act declares it illegal for one company to buy the stock of another when it would lessen competition or tend to monopoly. This is but a repetition of previous law against the holding company. A famous decision (the Northern Securities decision) as early as 1904 made it clear that such cases fall definitely within the scope of the Sherman Act.

The law forbids interlocking directorates (the same persons acting as directors of different corporations) in large banks and in other corporations whose capital, surplus, and undivided profits aggregate over $1,000,000. This portion of the act has met with public approval. May it not be, however, that we give too much emphasis to the monopoly power of interlocking directorates, and too little emphasis to the common ownership of corporations? A safer provision, though one for which public sentiment is not ripe, would be to deny to private ownership the privilege to form monopoly. None the less, this phase of the law has much promise of good.

**24. The Webb-Pomerene Act.**—Both the Sherman Act of 1890 and the Clayton Act of 1914 forbid combination in restraint of trade, but in so doing they not infrequently forbid combination in promotion of trade. Suppose that Jones, Smith, and Brown are competitors in the oil business; the first two combine and institute certain so-called unfair methods for mutual advantage in promoting the trade. The combination effects economies, and Brown is outdistanced in the output, the service, and the price. Two results follow: The trade of the combination is promoted, while that of Brown is restrained. The Sherman and the Clayton laws play their part by coming to the aid of Brown, but in so doing they hamper the promotion by Smith and Jones. If to restrain one interest is to promote another, it follows that to remove the cause of the one is to eliminate the cause of the other.

The Webb-Pomerene Act of 1918 appears to stand in striking contrast with the two acts above named. The purpose of the law is to promote export trade by permitting combinations among competitors for the sale of goods in foreign markets. The law limits itself to foreign trade; it would permit no league of competitors whose power would affect trade in the United States. This law stands for combination, while the Sherman and Clayton Acts stand for competition; it is in this sense that the law of 1918 appears in contrast with the other two. Considering, however, that the Webb-Pomerene law is applicable only in the foreign field, may it not be that the three laws are conducive to the same ends?

No satisfying answer can be given this important question within the space at my disposal. Suffice it to say that exporting combinations can amass the large capital which is necessary to enable the small as well as the large producers to participate in foreign trade. Competition must be had in the home market if the small producer share his due portion of trade; exporting combinations must be had if the small producer share his due portion of foreign trade. The American policy favors a fair field for producers large and small. There is a fighting chance for all producers in domestic trade only when competition is maintained. The difficulties of establishing trade in foreign markets are so great as to deny the privilege to all excepting those who possess large capital.

The primary advantage of export combinations will be found in the power of great capital. This advantage is primary because of the large capital that is required to establish trade in a foreign market. In some cases we shall be forced practically to create a new demand for our goods. American tobacco, for instance, was introduced into certain markets only after an extensive educational campaign that had to break down religious scruples and to create the taste for tobacco. J. W. Jenks says:[1] "One may question the value to those peoples of this 'educated taste': one cannot question the skill and power needed to accomplish the result." Strong competition will be met in the foreign market; we must establish connections, maintain selling agencies, employ the ablest salesmen, and advertise extensively. These necessary outlays cannot be met without the possession of very large capital.

The three laws in question declare for domestic competition and for combination in the foreign market. Shielded from restraint at home and aided by combination in the export market, the individual producer is enabled to share the benefits of both markets. Seeing that two of these laws declare for competition while the third favors combination, the superficial will jump to the conclusion that these laws stand forth in bold contrast. They are, however, not antagonistic in principle. They jointly declare

[1] The Trust Problem, p. 75.

the public policy—that of maintaining at home the kind of industrial society we want, a competing chance in a fair field. Meanwhile provision is made for the most effective marshalling of our forces, so that each and all may share the trade in foreign markets.

The question may arise as to the reaction this law may cause among foreigners. Will they welcome the fact that America, while refusing to tolerate combinations in trade at home, will advocate combinations for the capture of foreign trade? To the degree that the foreigner will study this law at all, he will view it from the point of view of his own personal interest. The foreign consumer will be the ultimate purchaser of our exported products, and he will probably not be offended at our arrangement to give him the best in service, the first in quality, and the lowest in price. Combination will enable us to do these things. Combination in restraint of trade at home tends to monopolize the domestic market. Combinations on our part to enter the foreign market will, on the contrary, but accentuate competition. For the other nations of the world will compete with America for the same trade, will marshal their forces and exert every effort in the attempt to underbid us and capture the foreign market.

The Webb-Pomerene Act is new and patience will be required that it may have a fair test. Doubtless imperfections will be exposed in this law and amendments made, but it marks the beginning of a new policy toward export trade. Time alone will test the wisdom of this policy; meanwhile its results will be watched with deepest interest.

**25. Exercises.**—1. Define the following: trust, pool, holding company, merger. State the characteristic features of each.

2. Should a fusion be made of Company A and Company B into a new Company C, should you term this an amalgamation or a merger?

If a fusion is made of Company A into Company B, would this be an amalgamation or a merger?

3. Should you think it wise for railroads to form pools? Defend your answer. Will the same arguments you make in case of railroads hold true in case of farmers? retail merchants? salt manufacturers?

4. State some reasons why the ownership of less than 50 per cent of the stock in a holding company may give control. (For brief summary see Gerstenberg's Syllabus of Corporation Finance, II, chapter XIII.)

5. Summarize the advantages and disadvantages of holding companies. (See Lough's Corporation Finance.)

6. Make a brief of this case—The Northern Securities Company vs. U. S. (193 U. S. 197).

Ask no aid from teacher or librarian in finding the case.

7. How may lax legislation respecting holding companies in one state force other states to pass lenient laws?

8. Why are not the laws more specific, defining exactly what is and what is not legal, so that business men will be freed from all hazards in their investments?

9. "To compete" and "to attempt to monopolize" are not the same, but antagonistic in principle. Explain.

10. Which one of the following views do you think to be nearest the truth, and why? (*a*) The trust is a natural and inevitable outcome of modern conditions and is a distinct economic gain. (*b*) The trust is a result of special privileges and corporate abuses. (*c*) The trust is the greatest invention of this or any other age. (Fetter.)

11. What relation has combination to large fortunes? to small fortunes?

12. What is the public policy with respect to combinations with monopoly power? Is the public policy adverse to large-scale production as such?

13. What was the purpose of the Sherman Anti-Trust Law?

14. Is it better to prevent the formation of combinations in restraint of trade or to destroy them after they are formed? Reasons?

15. Point out the chief difficulties that might be encountered in the administration of a policy of trust regulation.

16. What do you consider the most important feature of the Federal Trade Commission Act?

17. Do you consider the Webb-Pomerene Act antagonistic in principle to the Clayton Act?

If you were doing a small independent business and hoped to reach both the domestic and the export markets, should you wish the repeal of either of these acts?

# INDEX

Printed in the United States
by Baker & Taylor Publisher Services